Part I

Introduction

The AP® Government and Politics: United States Examination

This section provides an overview of the advanced placement program, introduces the types of questions you will encounter on the exam, offers helpful test-taking strategies, and explains the grading procedure used by the College Board. In addition, a correlation chart is provided that shows where key information commonly tested on the exam is covered within *Government in America, AP Edition, 16e.* Review this section carefully before trying the sample items in the following parts.

The Advanced Placement Program

This book will help prepare you to take the Advanced Placement® (AP) Government and Politics: United States Exam at the end of the year. To succeed on the exam, you need to follow a plan of curriculum review and practice. This book offers both of these. First, you will review each content area of government and politics that appears on the AP® Government and Politics: United States Exam. Then, for each section, you will complete some practice drills that replicate actual AP Exam questions. You will not only receive extra, guided study for your coursework, but you will also have the opportunity to apply what you have learned in class to a testing situation. You will become familiar with the types of questions on the AP® Government and Politics: United States Exam and how to approach them. Go through each review section thoroughly and complete all of the accompanying drills. If you have difficulty with particular sections, that is your cue to refer to your textbook for a more detailed review.

For even more practice, this book includes two full-length sample AP® Government and Politics: United States Exams. These will help you practice taking the exam under real-life testing conditions. The more familiar you are with the AP® Government and Politics: United States Exam ahead of time, the more comfortable you will be on testing day. The more comfortable you are, the better your chances of achieving a high score.

The AP Program is sponsored by the College Board, a nonprofit organization that oversees college admissions tests. The AP Program offers high school students the opportunity to take advanced college-level courses. According to the College Board, AP courses are intended to offer a curriculum equivalent to that of an introductory college class. If you receive a score of 3 or higher (5 is the highest possible grade), you may be eligible for college credit. Thousands of colleges and universities grant credit to students who score well on AP Exams. If you are taking several AP courses and score well on multiple AP Exams, you may even be eligible to enter college as a sophomore. Some institutions grant sophomore status to incoming first-year students who have demonstrated mastery of many AP subjects. In addition, the College Board confers a number of AP Scholar Awards on students who score 3 or higher on three or more AP Exams. Additional awards are available to students who receive very high grades on four or five AP Exams.

The curriculum for each of the 34 AP courses is designed by a development committee, consisting of college professors and high school teachers. Every AP course is different, and your textbook, *Government in America: People, Politics, and Policy*, AP Edition, 16e is widely and successfully used in AP classes across the nation. The committee develops guidelines for a test that represents equally and accurately the skill levels of over 100,000 AP® Government and Politics: United States students across the country. Your score on the AP® Government and Politics: United States Exam reflects your abilities in comparison to other high school students enrolled in the course. Colleges use this information not only to award credit for introductory college classes but also to choose the most suitable applicants.

Why Take an AP Course?

You may be taking one or more AP courses simply because you are thirsty for knowledge. Of course, the fact that selective colleges look favorably on applicants who have AP courses on their transcripts is another powerful incentive. Because AP classes should involve rigorous lessons, they signal to college admissions officers that AP students are willing to challenge themselves to get the most from their education. Because AP course work is more difficult than average high school work, many admissions officers evaluate AP grades on a kind of curve—if you receive a *B* in an AP class, for example, it might carry the same weight as an *A* in a regular high school class. Furthermore, the score you achieve on the AP Exam places you in the context of your peers across the nation and across years.

Your AP® Government and Politics: United States course teaches you many of the skills you will need in college. For example, your teacher will make writing assignments and encourage you to use resources beyond your textbook. Some of these resources may be primary sources that permit you to analyze events, issues, and data as a political scientist does. The Government and Politics: United States course will challenge you to gather and consider information in new—and sometimes unfamiliar—ways. Your ability to use these methods and skills will give you an advantage as you enter college.

Taking an AP Examination

You should challenge yourself further by taking the AP® Government and Politics: United States Exam at the end of your high school course. A wealth of information—which colleges grant credit for AP Exam scores (and the scores that they require), the exam schedule, when you need to sign up, the cost, the availability of fee reductions—is available either from your AP teacher or school guidance counselor or at www.collegeboard.com or apcentral.collegeboard.com/apc/Controller.jpf. At the College Board's websites you will have to establish an account to get access to all of the information, but there is a wealth of information, and it is free. Even if you use the website as a primary source of information, you should also communicate with your AP teacher or school guidance counselor. There are many state and local programs that help you defray the costs of taking the exam.

When you register for the AP Exam, you can arrange to have your score sent automatically to a number of colleges for free. In fact, your score can be received at colleges and universities only if it has been sent there directly by the College Board. If you would like your score to be sent to other schools, you must pay an additional fee. You can also cancel your score (you must do so before you find out your score), but either of these requests must be made directly to the College Board. Your exam grade will be sent to you by mail, usually in early or mid-July. If you simply cannot wait to find out your score, Educational Testing Service (the organization that develops and scores tests for the College Board) will release your score to you over the phone around July 1 for an additional fee.

AP® Government and Politics: United States: Course Goals

The goal of the AP® Government and Politics: United States course is to provide students with an understanding of the operation of American national government. Specifically, you will develop

- an understanding of the principal themes in U.S. government and politics

- the ability to analyze historical, quantitative, and graphical evidence

- skills to express your knowledge in writing

AP® Government and Politics: United States courses vary somewhat from teacher to teacher and from school to school. Yet the focus of your course should reflect these goals, and the instruction you receive will grow out of these basic principles.

Understanding the AP® Government and Politics: United States Examination

The AP® Government and Politics: United States Exam takes two hours and 25 minutes. It consists of a multiple-choice section and a free-response section. You can expect to see graphs, charts, and quotations in both sections of the test. You are expected to know the foundations of

U.S. government and how and why it has evolved, but this is not an exam on history. The AP®️ Government and Politics: United States course is a course in political science.

The AP®️ Government and Politics: United States Exam incorporates graphical, cartographic, and quantitative materials. This cross-disciplinary approach reflects the methods used today in colleges and universities to present subject matter.

Exam Content

The Government and Politics: United States Development Committee has created a list of major topics and has divided them into the six groups below. These topics are the focus of your AP course, and will be revisited in questions on the AP®️ Government and Politics: United States Exam. Those topics are listed in the table on the next page. You may want to use this table throughout the course to review what you have learned. It is also an excellent place to begin your pre-exam review of subjects.

Grading Procedures

Your score on each section of the exam will account for 50 percent of your total score. The raw scores of the exam are converted into the following 5-point scale:

5—Extremely Well Qualified

4—Well Qualified

3—Qualified

2—Possibly Qualified

1—No Recommendation

The Chief Reader, the person in charge of scoring all of the exams, in consultation with statisticians from the Educational Testing Service and personnel from the College Board, determines what total scores will be required for an AP score of 5, of 4, etc. Great care goes into assuring that your score accurately reflects where you stand in relation to the other students who took the exam you did and in relation to the students who took the exam in prior years. Colleges want to know that your score of 5 means the same as the 5 presented last year from a school across the country from where you are.

AP® Government and Politics: United States Exam Topics	
Constitutional Underpinnings of United States Government	Historical development and adoption of the Constitution
	Separation of Powers
	Checks and balances
	Federalism
	Theories of modern government
Political Beliefs and Behaviors	Theories of modern government, including elitist, pluralist, and hyperpluralist
	Views that people have about government and their elected officials
	Characteristics and impact of public opinion
	Voting patterns of citizens
	Characteristics of political beliefs and the differences between liberals and conservatives
Political Parties, Interest Groups, and Mass Media	Characteristics, organization, and history of political parties
	Impact of key elections
	Voting patterns and the effect on the political process
	Laws that affect elections
	Interest groups and political action committees
	Legislation affecting the political process
	The mass media and its effect on politics
Institutions of National Government	Characteristics and power of each institution
	Relationships among each institution
	Linkage between these institutions and the political process, political parties, interest groups, the media, and public opinion
	How public policy is formulated and implemented
Public Policy	The nature of public policy
	The creation of public policy
	The impact of the three branches of government on public policy
	The impact of the bureaucracy on public policy
	The relationship between public policy and linkage institutions
Civil Rights and Civil Liberties	The Bill of Rights and how it evolved
	The incorporation of the Fourteenth Amendment
	Judicial review and key Supreme Court cases
	The fight for minority rights

How these scores are used in admission, credit, or placement decisions varies from college to college, with credit and placement decisions often being made at the departmental level. Some colleges give undergraduate course credit to students who achieve scores of 3 or better on AP Exams. Other colleges require students to achieve scores of 4 or 5. If you are considering using your AP Exam score for college credit, check with individual colleges or at www.collegeboard.com to find out their specific requirements for credit. Below is a breakdown of how the grading of the AP® Government and Politics: United States Exam works.

Section I: Multiple-Choice Questions

You will have 45 minutes to complete the 60 questions in the multiple-choice section of the test. This section accounts for 50 percent of your overall score. Each question has five answer choices, and only one choice is correct. Most of the questions in this section will be fairly straightforward. Some may require interpretation, such as determining cause and effect or drawing a comparison. Others will ask you to analyze data in charts or graphs, or to evaluate a political cartoon or other illustration. The questions vary in degree of difficulty.

Types of Multiple-Choice Questions

Not all multiple-choice questions are the same. The AP® Government and Politics: United States Exam will contain the following types of questions:

Definition or Identification Questions

These questions ask you to recognize something and know what it is. Here is an example.

1. Class action suits

    (A)   permit a small number of people to sue on behalf of all other people similarly situated.

    (B)   are filed by students seeking to force a school district to offer additional sections of perpetually overenrolled courses.

    (C)   have to do with constitutional issues, thus broadening the standing to sue.

    (D)   are routinely filed by teachers' groups to prepare the way or strikes.

    (E)   may be filed only if all of those with standing to sue agree to participate.

The correct answer is *A*. A small group of people who believe, for example, that they have been harmed by a product can sue the manufacturer on behalf of all the people who believe they were harmed. This is the definition of class action.

Cause-and-Effect Questions

This type of question asks which event caused another, or what is the result of something. Here is an example:

2. The increasing speed of technological advance

    (A)   has significantly reduced the scope of American government.

    (B)   helps reduce and accelerate government policymaking.

    (C)   has helped reduce the cost of health care in the United States.

    (D)   has dramatically affected health policy, but has had no effect on environmental and energy policy.

    (E)   has created many new practical and moral problems of the political system.

The answer is *E*. You can use the process of elimination. The scope of government has not gotten smaller; policymaking has not become faster; health care costs have risen; if technology has affected health policy, it is unlikely that it has not also affected environmental and energy policies. Answers *A–D* are obviously wrong, leaving *E*.

"Roman Numeral" Questions

Here you are given a question, then several statements, phrases, or words relating to the question. You must decide which of the statements, phrases, or words are correct. It may be one or more than one.

3. Registered voters directly elect which of the following?

    I.   the president and vice president

    II.   Supreme Court justices

    III.   senators

    IV.   the Electoral College

    (A)   I only

    (B)   IV only

    (C)   I and II only

    (D)   III and IV only

    (E)   II, III, and IV only

The answer is *D*. Registered voters vote for electors who then vote for the president and vice president. This is not *direct* election. So any choice that includes *I* is wrong (*A, C*). Justices of the

Supreme Court are appointed by the president and approved by the Senate, so you can also eliminate choice *E*. Voters vote directly for both senators and, as noted above, the Electoral College.

EXCEPT/NOT Questions

In this type of question, four of the answer choices are correct, and you must find the answer that is *wrong*. Be sure to read the question carefully. Here is an example of this type of question.

4. Which of the following is NOT specifically mentioned in the Constitution, including its amendments?

   (A)   Protection against double jeopardy

   (B)   Right to bear arms

   (C)   Freedom of speech

   (D)   Right to privacy

   (E)   Right to trial by jury

The answer is *D*. Double jeopardy is addressed in the Fifth Amendment. The right to bear arms is mentioned in the Second Amendment. Freedom of speech is protected by the First Amendment. Article III provides for trial by jury. Only the right to privacy is not specifically mentioned in the Constitution.

Supreme Court Decisions

You will be asked to identify, interpret, or compare one or more well-known Supreme Court decisions. Here is an example:

5. *New York Times* v. *Sullivan* addressed

   (A)   equal opportunity in the workplace.

   (B)   libel.

   (C)   prior restraint.

   (D)   business monopolies.

   (E)   obscenity.

The answer is *B*. The Court held that statements about public figures are libelous only if made with "reckless disregard for the truth." There is no way to guess here. All the choices are topics the Supreme Court has ruled on, and all might involve a newspaper. You need to remember significant cases and the issues they address.

Graphic Questions

You can expect to see questions based on graphs, tables, and maps.

DISTRIBUTION OF INCOME AMONG FAMILIES

(percentage share by economic level)

	1970	1980	1990	2000
Lowest fifth	5.5	5.1	4.6	3.6
Second fifth	12.0	11.6	10.8	8.9
Third fifth	17.4	17.5	16.6	14.9
Fourth fifth	23.5	24.3	23.8	23.0
Highest fifth	41.6	41.6	44.3	49.6

6. Which of the following conclusions about income distribution is supported by the table?

    (A)   The share of income received by the lowest fifth increased, and the share received by the fourth fifth decreased.

    (B)   The share of income received by the second fifth increased, and the share received by the fourth fifth decreased.

    (C)   The share of income received by the highest fifth increased, and the share received by the lowest fifth decreased.

    (D)   The number of people earning high incomes increased.

    (E)   The middle class disappeared.

The numbers clearly show that *C* is the answer. Choice *D* might be attractive, but note that the table gives percents. Although the *percent* of families in the highest fifth increased, you know nothing about the actual number of people. Always read the questions and answer choices carefully.

Grading Multiple-Choice Questions

The multiple-choice section of the exam is worth 50 percent of your total grade. The raw score of Section I is determined by crediting one point for each correct answer and by deducting one-fourth of one point for each incorrect answer. No points are gained or lost for unanswered questions. If you don't know what the correct answer is and can only eliminate one or two of the five choices, do not make a wild guess—leave the answer blank. But if you can eliminate three of the five choices, you should make an educated guess.

Strategies for Multiple-Choice Questions

Having a firm grasp of U.S. government and politics is, of course, the key to your doing well on the AP® Government and Politics: United States Examination. In addition, being well-informed about the exam itself increases your chances of achieving a high score. Below is a list of strategies that you can use to increase your comfort, your confidence, and your chances of excelling on the multiple-choice section of the exam.

- Make yourself completely familiar with the instructions for the multiple-choice questions *before* you take the exam. You will find the instructions in this book. By knowing the instructions cold, you will save yourself the time of reading them carefully on the day of the test.

- Pace yourself and keep track of the remaining time as you complete the multiple-choice section. Remember, you have 45 minutes to answer all 60 questions. It is important that you do not get stuck on one question for too long.

- Always read the entire question carefully and underline and define key words or ideas. You might want to circle words such as *NOT* or *EXCEPT* in that type of multiple-choice question.

- Read *every* answer choice carefully before you make your final selection.

- Use the process of elimination to help you choose the correct answer. Even if you are sure of an answer, cross out the letters of incorrect choices in your test booklet as you eliminate them. This cuts down on distraction and allows you to narrow the remaining choices even further.

- If you are able to eliminate three answer choices, it is better to make an educated guess at the correct answer than to leave the answer blank. If you can only eliminate one or two answers, leave the answer blank: you are more likely to lose a point by guessing among more than two answers.

- Make a mark in your test booklet next to any questions you cannot answer. Return to them after you reach the end of Section I. Sometimes questions that appear later in the test will refresh your memory of a particular topic, and you will be able to answer one of those earlier questions.

Section II: Free-Response Questions

The second portion of the AP® Government and Politics: United States Exam is an hour-and-40-minute free-response section consisting of four questions. You must answer all four—none of them is optional. You may, however, have some choice within a question. All four questions count equally, and together they account for 50 percent of your overall score.

Because the free-response questions are open-ended, this is your opportunity to demonstrate your understanding of U.S. government and politics. You will see directives like *define, identify, describe,* and *explain.* Knowing facts or terms may earn you points if the task is to *define* or to *identify,* but to *describe* or to *explain* requires using your knowledge to construct an argument. You should use your knowledge to construct a thorough and intelligent response.

- Scan all four questions quickly to form initial impressions of the topics about which you are being asked to write. You do not have to answer the questions in the order in which they are presented. Begin with the question you think you can respond to best. (If you are to run short on time, you would rather run short on a question about which you think you know the least, than the one about which you know the most.)

- Read and reread the question to be sure you understand exactly what is being asked. Underline directives such as *define, identify, describe,* and *explain.* These are the tasks that must be accomplished for you to earn credit for a response. You can jot notes in the margins of the exam booklet.

- There is often a question that requires interpreting a graph or table. Be sure to answer specifically what is asked about the chart. For example, you may be asked to describe a trend in the data. A trend is a change in the value of a variable over time. Comparing two data points for the same time (for example, 1994 House reelection rate versus 1994 Senate reelection rate) is not a identifying a trend.

- Take a couple of minutes to brainstorm about the topic. Write down the things that come to your mind. Then look them over to see which ideas will go well together to serve as examples for your response to the question and to determine the order in which you will present them. This, in essence, is the outline for your response. Remember, you have, on average, 25 minutes for each response. Five minutes invested in brainstorming and outlining up front can produce a much better response with less expenditure of time overall. But do keep track of time.

- You may use any organizational approach that makes sense to you as long as you respond to the question and all of its parts. But keep in mind that Readers will review hundreds of thousands of AP® Government and Politics: United States Exams in one week, so strong organization is to your advantage. Using the question structure as your guide is often a very good approach, because it ensures that you address every aspect of the question. Think carefully before doing something more creative, as it makes it more difficult for you (and for the Reader!) to see that you have answered the entire question.

- Now you are ready to begin writing. What you write is the only evidence that the Reader has about what you know regarding the question that has been posed. You will not get any benefit of the doubt about your knowledge. Flesh out the ideas you used to construct your outline, using precise language and examples to bolster you points. Correctly used, appropriate examples give the Reader confidence that you have an understanding of the question that merits awarding the points allocated to that part of the question.

Your answer will be judged based on whether or not you have accomplished your task—to define, identify, describe, or explain—as laid out in the question. You earn points for accomplishing the assigned tasks. There is no need to venture beyond the scope of the question.

You will not earn extra points, and, because each question is scored independently, you will not be able to make up for a question you feel you did not answer well enough by overcompensating on another question.

Many free-response questions on the AP® Government and Politics: United States Exam will ask you to address a single topic in a straightforward way. Here is an example of such a question:

1. The system of checks and balances ensures that no branch of government has unfettered power. Describe—using examples—how each branch has exercised this power over another branch.

In your response to this question, you need to furnish *examples* that help you *describe* how each of the three governmental branches has used the system of checks and balances to wield power.

Some free-response questions are divided into several parts, or subquestions. You might be presented with a list of items, such as specific court cases or interest groups, which you are asked to address in your response. These partitioned questions often contain directives like *identify, describe,* and *explain.* Here is an example:

2. Choose two of the following Supreme Court cases.

   - *California Board of Regents* v. *Bakke*
   - *Roe* v. *Wade*
   - *Gideon* v. *Wainwright*
   - *Rust* v. *Sullivan*
   - *Miranda* v. *Arizona*
   - *Korematsu* v. *United States*

For each case you selected, do each of the following.

   a. Describe the position of each side.

   b. Describe the Supreme Court's ruling.

   c. Explain whether the ruling increased or decreased the rights of individuals.

First, you need to recognize (at least two of) the cases and choose the two you want to use in the remainder of your response. Do not be intimidated by a list of six cases. You could know absolutely nothing about four of the cases and still earn all of the points for the question. Second, you would need to describe the positions of the opposing sides in each of the two cases chosen (four descriptions). Third, you must describe the Court's ruling, i.e., present a simple statement of the Court's holding in the cases chosen. Finally, you must take a position on whether the rights of individuals were increased or decreased in each of the chosen cases and support your position.

A simple statement of your conclusion about the increase or decrease of individual rights by the court in your chosen cases would not be sufficient to earn credit for the *explain* part of the question. The Reader must finish your response knowing how you think rights were expanded or contracted or why you have taken the position you have for each of the chosen cases. It is often the *explain* part of a question that separates the best-prepared students from the rest.

It cannot be overemphasized: Pay close attention to exactly what the question asks you to do, and do it—nothing more, nothing less! For example, in the question posed above, asking you to describe the positions of the parties in two cases, the Supreme Court's ruling, and to explain the cases' impact on the expansion or contraction of individual rights, you might know the full story of Clarence Gideon and how his case made it to the Supreme Court, but even a brilliant explanation of this saga would earn you no points because that is not requested in the question. To earn points, answer the question that is asked—not the one you wish had been asked.

You will not be asked about your personal political opinions, so do not include them in your answer. You do not get extra credit for going beyond the scope of a question, and that just wastes your valuable time. Similarly, students sometimes will write a response that is completely off-topic when they don't know the answer. You are better off re-reading your other answers and adding to them if you can't write on one of the questions. But even writing a little on a topic might earn a few points that a description of your prom night (and yes, some essays do exactly that!) won't. The AP Exam is a political science exam. Make sure that your answer is a political science answer.

Grading Free-Response Questions

The free-response section of the exam is worth 50 percent of your total grade. It is graded by a group of AP® Government and Politics: United States instructors and professors known as "faculty consultants." Each essay may be read by anywhere from one to 20 Readers. The Readers do not know whose essay they are reading, nor from which school the essay originates. Each faculty consultant generally will only read responses to one of the free-response questions during the reading and will not know what you scored on the multiple-choice part of the exam. You begin with a 0 score on each free-response question, and earn points as you correctly address each aspect of the question. The scale for scoring each free-response question is specifically adapted to the question. For example, one question may be scored using a 5-point rubric while another is scored using a 9-point rubric. Then, your score on each free-response question is weighted so that it counts the same as each of the other three free-response questions. These weighted scores are then summed, and this total counts the same as your total multiple-choice score in your final score.

Strategies for Free-Response Questions

Here is a list of strategies that you can use to increase your chance of excelling on the free-response section of the exam.

- You have one hour and 40 minutes to outline and write four essays. This is plenty of time to accomplish your task, but not so much that you have any to waste. You must manage your time carefully.

- Be careful not to stray from the focus of the question asked. As you read a question, underline any key words and directives that indicate how you should address the material in your response.

- As you formulate your answer, always consider whether or not it answers the question directly.

According to many Chief Readers, students more often lose points for not doing what the question requires them to do than for not knowing what the question requires them to know. Some frequently used directives are listed below, along with descriptions of what you need to do in writing your answer.

- *identify:* simply name what the question asks. For example, if the question asks you to identify an example of a Supreme Court case dealing with civil rights, the point is earned simply by writing, "*Brown* v. *Board of Education* is a Supreme Court case dealing with civil rights."

- *describe:* give a detailed account. Readers often think of *describing* as identifying and adding a few basic facts. If the question asks you to describe a Supreme Court case dealing with civil rights, the point might be earned by writing, "*Brown* v. *Board of Education* held that segregation in schools was unconstitutional. The case overturned the 'separate but equal' doctrine."

- *explain:* communicate how or why. An important part of explaining is what AP® Government and Politics: United States Readers call "closing the loop": making sure that your explanation takes the Reader back to that which is to be explained. If the question asks you to explain why *Brown* v. *Board of Education* was implemented so slowly, it would not be enough to write, "*Brown I* required that schools be desegregated with all deliberate speed"; this would be at best a description. You must show why it explains the speed of implementation: "*Brown I* required that schools be desegregated with all deliberate speed. This allowed opponents of the decision to drag their heels while claiming that they were merely being deliberate in their compliance, slowing the integration of schools." Notice how this comes all the way back to what the question asks you to explain.

- *compare:* address similarities and differences between two or more things. You must address BOTH parts of the difference to receive any credit. For example, if the question asks about the difference between *Brown* v. *Board of Education I* and *Brown* v. *Board of Education II*, you would earn the point if you wrote, "*Brown I* required integration with all deliberate speed, but *Brown II* demanded faster action." You would not earn the point simply by writing, "*Brown I* required integration with all deliberate speed," since that doesn't compare *Brown I* to anything. This is also true if you are asked to explain a difference; your explanation needs to show why both aspects of the difference are as they are.

Preparation Strategies for the AP® Government and Politics: United States Examination

To become comfortable with both the content and the format of the AP® Government and Politics: United States Exam, begin preparing for the test in advance. You want to have plenty of time to devote to each of the six main subject areas on the test while practicing your free response skills at the same time. The more relaxed study time you allow yourself, the more prepared you will be and the better you will do on the exam.

Aim to finish the review sections about a week and a half before the exam. Then take the first practice test at the back of this book. Treat the practice test exactly like the real exam. Find a quiet place where you can work without interruption and give yourself only two hours and 25 minutes. This allows you to become familiar with the actual testing conditions so that you will be less nervous on testing day.

After you have scored your practice test, take a day just to review your answers. Look at the types of questions you got wrong. Do they fall under the same content area or areas? If so, you should focus further study on those particular areas for the next two days or so. Count the number of questions you skipped. Did they fall near the end of the section? This could mean that you were running out of time. Did you feel rushed? It might be wise, then, to plan ahead of time which kinds of questions you should skip over. For example, if you got every data question right and a lot of questions about Supreme Court cases wrong, plan to skip a few of those case questions so that you can answer all of the data questions in the section. You need to make sure that you answer the questions you are more likely to know and that you skip the ones that might slow you down.

Now that you know what adjustments to make to your test-taking strategy, give yourself a few days of extra practice with your problem areas and then take the second practice test at least three days before the real exam (do not overwhelm yourself before the real thing!). Again, analyze your performance. Did your adjustments pay off? Is there anything you should do differently? Use your last few days to do any fine-tuning and to relax before the exam.

Below is a brief list of basic tips and strategies to think about *before* you arrive at the exam site.

- Try to plan your schedule so that you get *two* very good nights of sleep before exam day. On the day of the exam, make sure that you eat good, nutritious meals. These tips may sound corny or obvious, but your body must be in peak form for your brain to perform well.

- Arrive at the exam site 30 minutes before the start time. This saves you additional worry about arriving late.

- It is a good idea to have a photo I.D. with you when you arrive at the exam site. (It is essential if you are taking the exam at a school other than your own.) Carrying a driver's license or a student I.D. card will allow you to prove your identity if the exam site requires such proof.

- Bring at least two pencils for the multiple-choice section. Make sure that your pencils are labeled #2 and that they have good erasers. The machine that scores Section I of the exam cannot recognize marks made by other types of pencils. Also, it cannot read a correct answer if a previous answer has not been erased completely. For the free-response section of the exam, bring two black pens; pencil will make your essays hard to read, which is not to your advantage.

- It is helpful to have a watch with you at the exam. Most testing rooms will have clocks, and most test administrators will give you periodic reminders of how much time you have remaining. Still, having your own watch makes it easy to keep close track of your own pace. The watch cannot have a calculator or an alarm, however, as these are not permitted in the exam room.

- Do not bring books of any kind, laptop computers, wireless instant-messaging devices, cameras, or portable radios. If you must bring a cellular phone with you, turn it off and give it to the test proctor until you are finished with your exam.

The test administrators are very clear and very serious about what is *not* allowed during the examination. Below is a list of actions to avoid at all costs, since each is grounds for your immediate dismissal from the exam room.

- Do not consult any outside materials during the exam period. Remember, the break is technically part of the exam—you are not free to review any materials at that time either.

- Do not speak during the exam, unless you have a question for the test proctor. Raise your hand to get the proctor's attention.

- When you are told to stop working on a section of the exam, you must stop *immediately*.

- Do not open your exam booklet before the test begins.

- Never tear a page out of your test booklet or try to remove the exam from the test room.

- Do not behave disruptively—even if you are distressed about a difficult test question or because you have run out of time. Stay calm and make no unnecessary noise. Remember, too, the worst-case scenario is not a poor score that will follow you for your entire college career. If you are displeased with your performance on test day, you can cancel your exam scores.

Using class lectures, assignments, and activities, you can immerse yourself in all six themes of AP® Government and Politics: United States and prepare yourself for every type of question that you will be asked. Extensive classroom preparation and your own regular practice and study will be the foundation for your success on the AP® Government and Politics: United States Exam.

Part

II

Topical Review with Sample Questions, Answers, and Explanations

1

Introducing Government in America: Government, Politics, and the Policymaking System

☐ Chapter Overview

Politics and government matter. By emphasizing the role of public policy, Edwards' text helps students understand how government and politics affect their everyday lives. To that end, Chapter 1 establishes the foundation for the balance of the text by introducing questions fundamental to the study of politics, government, and public policy. We begin by exploring the key functions of government. We then turn to consider the nature of American democracy, focusing on three specific questions: What is the nature of a democratic politics? How can citizens affect policy? And conversely, how does policy affect citizens? We conclude by exploring contemporary debates over the limits of democracy and the proper role of government in the United States today.

☐ Study Outline

 1.1 Learning Objective 1.1: Identify the key functions of government and explain why they matter. (p. 9)

Government

- The institutions through which public policy is made are collectively known as government. The key functions of government are:
  - **Maintain a national defense:** A government typically maintains armed forces to protect its sovereignty.
  - **Provide public goods and services:** The government provides **collective goods**, those goods and services which cannot be denied to anyone, as well as other goods and services which may be provided by both the government and the private sector, such as college and medical care.
  - **Preserve order:** The government is responsible for maintaining public order, sometimes using extreme measures, if needed.
  - **Socialize the young:** The government pays for public education as a means of instilling knowledge and pride in the nation in the young.
  - **Collect taxes:** The government uses tax money to fund the public goods and services it provides.

1.2 Learning Objective 1.2: Define politics in the context of democratic government. (p. 11)

- **Politics** is the process by which government leaders and policies are selected.
- The activities in which citizens engage in order to influence that selection are known as **political participation**, which may take the form of voting, running for office, or by getting involved in political action groups.
- **Single issue groups** include members who are uncompromisingly committed to a particular issue.

Learning Objective 1.3: Assess how citizens can have an impact on public policy and how policies can impact people. (p. 12)

- The **policymaking system** is the process by which the people shape public policy.

- The political processes and channels through which the concerns of the people are translated into public policy are **linkage institutions**, such as political parties, elections, interest groups and the media.

- Through these linkage institutions, concerns reach the **policy agenda** from which the policymaking institutions select issues to be addressed.

Learning Objective 1.4: Identify the key principles of democracy and outline theories regarding how it works in practice and the challenges democracy faces today. (p. 15)

Democracy in America: Traditional Democratic Theory

- Traditional democratic theory suggests that five characteristics are needed in order to make a political system democratic:
  - **Equal right to vote:** The public has the right to **vote** for government representatives, and the principle of one person, one vote is generally respected.
  - **Opportunities for effective political participation:** Citizens must have equal opportunities to express their **political views** by such means as voting or joining political groups such as **political parties**.
  - **Enlightened understanding:** The public should be informed about various political and social issues to formulate judgments and make **informed decisions**.
  - **Citizen control of the political agenda:** The issues taken up by the government should reflect those issues that are of concern to the people.
  - **Social inclusion:** All people subject to the laws of a nation must have the opportunity to become citizens and to possess all the **rights of citizenship**.
- In addition, democratic political systems must balance two principles that often conflict:

- □ **Majority rule:** Decisions are made by a vote of the **majority** to reflect the will of the largest percentage of citizens.
- □ **Minority rights:** The American political system protects some rights of the **minority** against the majority.
- □ Freedom of speech and of petition, for example, allows the minority to express its opinions despite **majority rule**.

Three Contemporary Theories of American Democracy

- Traditionally, two main competing theories describe contemporary American politics: pluralist theory and elite theory. A third, hyperpluralist theory, has been developed more recently.

Pluralist Theory

- The political system is composed of groups representing **competing interests**.
- The existence of such groups indicates that the government allows sufficient access to policymaking.
- The interests of the public may be more widely represented in government.
- Power is **decentralized** so that no one body or group has too much influence over policymaking.

Elite and Class Theory

- Government favors only a narrow percentage of the public, primarily the **wealthy**. Wealth is the main cause of political influence.
- Many political groups may exist, but the distribution of government resources among them is not necessarily equal. The more wealth and influence a group has, the more it benefits from the government.
- Groups do not have equal access to policymaking or equal power; **big business** plays a prominent role in politics because corporations that have money also have power.
- Businesses have tremendous advantages in their ability to organize, both through the concentration of their interests and through the interlocking relationships among the

people who run business and the government, and therefore out-compete other groups.

Hyperpluralism

- The proliferation of political groups has weakened the government.
- Policies are often made by "subgovernments" or "iron triangles" composed of interest groups, the bureaucracies that regulate these groups, and the congressional committees that oversee these bureaucracies.
- With so many interests vying for political influence and so many points of access in government, power is decentralized, and, ultimately, policies become muddled and therefore less effective.

Challenges to Democracy

- Modern democracies face numerous challenges from a variety of sources:
  - **Increased complexity of issues:** An increase in the knowledge base makes it difficult for average citizens to make informed decisions.
  - **Limited participation in government:** Citizens do not take full advantage of participation opportunities, as demonstrated by poor voter turnout.
  - **Escalating campaign costs:** An increase in the costs of running for office makes candidates increasingly dependent on PACs and further removed from democratic theory.
  - **Diverse political interests:** Diversity of population can lead to weak coalitions, which may result in policy gridlock.

American Political Culture and Democracy

- American democracy is held together by a unifying political culture, a common set of political values that are widely shared in the nation, which includes liberty, egalitarianism, individualism, belief in a free market, laissez faire economics, and populism.
- In recent years, some scholars have worried that a polarization has taken place within the nation—a so-called culture war—threatening a division that might jeopardize the

nation's health. Other scholars disagree, saying there is little evidence of irreconcilable differences among groups, especially outside of political elites.

 Learning Objective 1.5: Outline the central arguments of the debate in America over the proper scope of government. (p. 25)

The Scope of Government in America

- The scope of responsibilities of the United States' government includes economic, military, and domestic activities. However, **individualism** in America makes the scope of the United States government comparatively small in relation to other democracies.

For Additional Review

To understand more fully the important ideas of the government in America, review the relevant vocabulary terms in the chapter. To aid in your review, create flash cards or make sentences using the vocabulary terms. Review these vocabulary study aids in preparation for the test.

To understand more fully the important ideas of the government in America, develop and use effective strategies for taking notes on readings. Create a system of note-taking which allows you to write quickly and get down the basic concepts. Use the structure of the textbook as the structure of your notes. Review these notes in preparation for the test.

❑ Review Questions

Multiple-Choice Questions

1.	Which of the following best illustrates elite theory?
	a.	The idea that large interest groups such as AARP (American Association of Retired Persons) dominate government decision-making.
	b.	The idea that a small group of wealthy individuals dominate government policy-making.
	c.	The idea that contending interests are so strong within the United States that government is often weakened.
	d.	The fact that more than 20,000 special interest groups lobby Congress each year.
	e.	The idea that because of technologies such as the Internet and television, Americans are increasingly isolated from their government, jeopardizing the strength of traditional groups in society.

2. All of the following are characteristic beliefs associated with American political culture EXCEPT
   a. liberty.
   b. equality of opportunity.
   c. individualism.
   d. government regulation of the economy.
   e. political equality.

3. According to pluralist theorists, which of the following statements describe the American political system?

   I. The public interest is normally served in the United States through a process of bargaining and compromise.
   II. Organized interest groups fairly shape the public agenda by broadly representing the interests of Americans.
   III. Multiple small groups among the wealthiest one percent of the public are in some way responsible for most policymaking.
   IV. Policymaking reflects the desires of those who control many of the largest corporations in the United States.

   a. I and II
   b. II and III
   c. I and III
   d. II and IV
   e. III and IV

4. All of the following are examples of public policy EXCEPT
   a. The president issues an executive order requiring corporations doing business with the government to have affirmative action hiring plans.
   b. Congress writes a law requiring lobbyists to disclose which interest groups employ them.
   c. The Supreme Court upholds the death penalty for a murder conviction.
   d. The Federal Trade Commission writes a rule that corporate claims in television ads be true.
   e. The American Association of Retired Persons passes a rule giving access to their insurance policies only to dues-paying members.

5. Democratic theory includes which of the following?
   a. "one person, one vote"
   b. freedom of religion
   c. majority rule
   d. a bicameral Congress
   e. a republican form of government

6. Basic functions common to all national governments include all of the following EXCEPT
   a. collecting taxes.
   b. maintaining a national defense.
   c. providing universal health care.
   d. preserving order.
   e. socializing young citizens.

7. Members of single interest groups
   a. work to limit the bias in national laws favoring married couples.
   b. lobby the government to enact laws limiting the percentages that credit card companies can charge to finance monthly balances.
   c. regulate the discount rate that the government charges to banks for the loans that they choose to make.
   d. are reluctant, usually, to compromise on the issue that defines their narrowly defined goal.
   e. have bound together in recent years to "bundle" soft money contributions to presidential candidates.

8. All of the following can create public policies EXCEPT
   a. Congress.
   b. the president.
   c. an interest group.
   d. the courts.
   e. the bureaucracy.

9. Which characteristic of American politics is concerned with the rights of the minority?
   a. the election process
   b. the congressional policymaking process
   c. interest group bargaining and compromising on political issues
   d. the president altering his policy proposals in response to public opinion
   e. the Bill of Rights guarantee of civil liberties

10. Government has grown to be big and active because

    I. the public expects government to solve problems.
    II. it is hard to cut programs such as Social Security and national defense.
    III. Democrats, the "party of big government," have been in power in recent years.
    IV. the government is committed to reducing income inequality.

    a. I and II
    b. II and III
    c. III and IV
    d. I, II and III
    e. II and IV

11. All of the following are core political ideas in the United States EXCEPT
    a. liberty.
    b. individualism.
    c. socialism.
    d. self-government.
    e. equality.

12. One effect of the American political system's use of checks and balances is
    a. the fact that the three branches operate independently of one another.
    b. that policy mistakes are completely avoided.
    c. the absolute guarantee that governmental power will not be abused.
    d. an unusually expedient decision making process.
    e. severe fragmentation of the governing authority.

13. Which of the following is an output of the American political system?
    a. the judiciary appointment process
    b. a general election
    c. law passed by Congress and presidential decision in foreign policy
    d. a primary election
    e. executive bureaucracy

14. All of the following statements concerning African Americans today are correct EXCEPT
    a. African Americans are twice as likely as whites to graduate from college.
    b. African Americans are twice as likely as whites to live in poverty.
    c. African Americans are twice as likely as whites to be unable to find a job.
    d. African Americans are twice as likely as whites to die in infancy.
    e. African Americans have equal rights under the law.

15. Which of the following statements provides the most accurate description of democracy as practiced in the United States?
    a. The will of the majority always prevails.
    b. The will of the people is checked by nothing.
    c. The people govern through elected officials.
    d. The people govern through mandates.
    e. The people directly govern themselves.

16. The characteristics and beliefs of a particular people about government and politics is known as
    a. scientific socialism.
    b. political culture.
    c. elitism.
    d. pluralism.
    e. capitalism.

17.   This natural rights' philosopher stated in a 17th century political document that all individuals have certain natural rights, including those of life, liberty, and property.
    a. Thomas Paine
    b. Thomas Jefferson
    c. Jean Jacques Rousseau
    d. John Locke
    e. James Madison

18.   All of the following statements about majoritarianism in the United States are true EXCEPT
    a. Policy makers often ignore the opinion of the majority when making policy decisions.
    b. The majority of the public supports general statements about civil liberties but are less likely to support specific applications.
    c. Public policy tends to change with the changes in majority opinion on major issues.
    d. The public is interested in and well-informed on all policy issues.
    e. Majorities do sometimes rule in the American political arena.

19.   In which famous document did James Madison argue that government is most dangerous when a single group gains complete political control?
    a. *Common Sense*
    b. *Federalist* No. 10
    c. the Constitution
    d. the preamble to the Declaration of Independence
    e. *The Wealth of Nations*

20.   All of the following are considered inputs into the American political system EXCEPT
    a. the activities of interests groups.
    b. the activities of political parties.
    c. laws passed by Congress.
    d. voting in elections.
    e. letters to representatives.

Free-Response Questions

1.   There is a common set of values generally espoused by United States citizens—a political culture.

    a. Identify three elements of American political culture.

    b. Describe two of these elements.

    c. Explain why citizens might espouse these values but object to specific applications.

2.   Government is a set of institutions by which people make collective decisions.

    a. Identify three functions government serves.

    b. Provide two explanations why people might choose to use government to pursue these functions.

☐ Answers and Explanations

Multiple-Choice Questions

1. Which of the following best illustrates elite theory?

    (a) is incorrect because the AARP is an interest group and therefore does not fit the description of elite theory.

    (b) is correct because the elite theory holds that a small group of wealthy and well-placed individuals dominate government decision making.

    (c) is incorrect because contending interest groups do not fit the description of the elite theory.

    (d) is incorrect because interest groups do not fit the description of the elite theory.

    (e) is incorrect because Americans are not isolated from government by technology.

    Page reference: 17, AP Topic: Theories of democratic government

2. All of the following are characteristic beliefs associated with American political culture EXCEPT

    (a) is incorrect because liberty is one of the basic tenets of American political culture.

    (b) is incorrect because equality of opportunity is one of the basic tenets of American political culture.

    (c) is incorrect because individualism is one of the basic tenets of American political culture.

    (d) is correct because Americans generally believe that a largely unregulated economy, similar to a laissez faire system, would be in the national interest.

    (e) is incorrect because political equality is one of the basic tenets of American political culture.

    Page reference: 20–23, AP Topic: Theories of democratic government

3. According to pluralist theorists, which of the following statements describe the American political system?

    (a) is correct because elite theorists believe that the government is mainly controlled by an elite and wealthy minority, most of whom are involved in big business, while pluralists think political power is more generally distributed.

    (b) is incorrect because statement III is reflective of the elite theory.

(c) is incorrect because statement III is reflective of the elite theory.

(d) is incorrect because statement IV is reflective of the elite theory.

(e) is incorrect because statements III and IV are reflective of the elite theory.

Page reference: 16–18, AP Topic: Theories of democratic government

4. All of the following are examples of public policy EXCEPT

(a) is incorrect because the president can issue an executive order relating to public policy.

(b) is incorrect because Congress can write a law relating to public policy.

(c) is incorrect because the Supreme Court can make rulings that affect public policy.

(d) is incorrect because the Federal Trade Commission can write rules relating to public policy.

(e) is correct because the AARP is an interest group and therefore cannot make policies that would be binding on all citizens, but rather are limited to making rules that apply only to members of their organization on issues over which they have control.

Page reference: 20–23, AP Topics: Theories of a democratic government and public policy

5. Democratic theory includes which of the following?

(a) is incorrect because "one-person, one-vote" is not necessarily a part of a democracy.

(b) is incorrect because freedom of religion is not necessarily a part of a democracy.

(c) is correct because a democracy is founded on the needs and wants of the people and the closest representation of the whole populace is the majority; therefore, in a theoretical democracy, decisions are made by majority rule.

(d) is incorrect because a bicameral Congress is not necessarily a part of a democracy.

(e) is incorrect because a republican form of government is not necessarily a part of a democracy.

Page reference: 15–23, AP Topic: Theories of a democratic government

6. Basic functions common to all national governments include all of the following EXCEPT

(a) is incorrect because collecting taxes is a basic function of government.

(b) is incorrect because maintaining a national defense is a basic function of government.

(c) is correct because while universal medical care might be desirable, and while all governments provide some social services, not all governments can afford universal coverage.

(d) is incorrect because preserving order is a basic function of government.

(e) is incorrect because socializing young citizens is a basic function of government.

Page reference: 9–23, AP Topic: Theories of a democratic government

7.   Members of single interest groups

(a) is incorrect because single interests are not related to marriage characteristics.

(b) is incorrect because single interests are not related to interest rates charged by credit cards.

(c) is incorrect because single interests are not related to discount rates of banks.

(d) is correct because single interest groups tend to be associated with hyperpluralism and because they are formed around one narrowly defined issue, they rarely engage in the compromises characteristic of pluralistic bargaining.

(e) is incorrect because single interests are not related to soft money.

Page reference: 18, AP Topics: Theories of a democratic government and interest groups

8.   All of the following can create public policies EXCEPT

(a) is incorrect because Congress has the authority to produce public policies.

(b) is incorrect because the president has the authority to produce public policies.

(c) is correct because interest groups can affect public policies, but do not have the power or authority to create public policies.

(d) is incorrect because the courts have the authority to produce public policies.

(e) is incorrect because the bureaucracy has the authority to produce public policies.

Page reference: 9–23, AP Topics: Theories of a democratic government and public policy

9.   Which characteristic of American politics is concerned with the rights of the minority?

(a) is incorrect because the election process is based on majority rule.

(b) is incorrect because the congressional policymaking process is based on majority rule.

(c) is incorrect because interest group bargaining and compromising is not guaranteed to protect minority rights.

(d) is incorrect because the president responding to public opinion is based on majority rule.

(e) is correct because the Bill of Rights was added to the Constitution to protect the expression of unpopular ideas, among other things, and these rights are not dependent on majoritarian concerns, but are designed to protect the rights of the minority.

Page reference: 15–23, AP Topic: Theories of democratic government

10. Government has grown to be big and active because

    (a) is correct; government is big and active because people expect government to take action, and once programs are enacted it is hard to scale them back.

    (b) is incorrect because statement III is factually inaccurate.

    (c) is incorrect because statements III and IV are factually inaccurate.

    (d) is incorrect because statement III is factually inaccurate.

    (e) is incorrect because statement IV is factually inaccurate.

    Page reference: 25–26, AP Topic: Theories of democratic government and public policy

11. All of the following are core political ideas in the United States EXCEPT

    (a) is incorrect because liberty is a core political idea in the United States.

    (b) is incorrect because individualism is a core political idea in the United States.

    (c) is correct because socialism is an economic system where there is government ownership and management of the economy and that is not a core political idea of the United States.

    (d) is incorrect because self-government is a core political idea in the United States.

    (e) is incorrect because equality is a core political idea in the United States.

    Page reference: 15–23, AP Topic: Theories of democratic government

12. One effect of the American political system's use of checks and balances is

    (a) is incorrect because the separation of the powers of the branches does not lead to fragmentation.

    (b) is incorrect because separation of powers does not eliminate mistakes.

    (c) is incorrect because separation of powers does not prevent abuse.

    (d) is incorrect because separation of powers does not expedite decision making.

(e) is correct because even though checks and balances limit government's power by requiring each branch to obtain the consent of the others for its actions, it also results in severe fragmentation in the American political system.

Page reference: 15–23, AP Topic: Theories of democratic government

13.   Which of the following is an output of the American political system?

(a) is incorrect because the judiciary appointment process is an input.

(b) is incorrect because a general election is an input.

(c) is correct because laws passed by Congress and decisions made by the President are products of the United States government and therefore fit the definition of an output.

(d) is incorrect because a primary election is an input.

(e) is incorrect because the executive bureaucracy is an input.

Page reference: 15–23, AP Topic: Theories of democratic government

14.   All of the following statements concerning African Americans today are correct EXCEPT

(a) is correct because African Americans are not twice as likely to graduate from college as whites, but instead still lag behind whites in college graduation rates.

(b) is incorrect because African Americans are twice as likely as whites to live in poverty.

(c) is incorrect because African Americans are twice as likely as whites to be unable to find a job.

(d) is incorrect because African Americans are twice as likely as whites die in infancy.

(e) is incorrect because African Americans do have equal rights under the law.

Page reference: 23–24, AP Topic: Theories of democratic government

15.   Which of the following statements provides the most accurate description of democracy as practiced in the United States?

(a) is incorrect because majority will does not always prevail.

(b) is incorrect because the will of the people is checked by law and the rights of the minority.

(c) is correct because democracy in the United States is a system of electing policymakers and of organizing government so that policy represents and responds to the public's preferences.

(d) is incorrect because the people do not govern by mandate.

(e) is incorrect because the people do not govern directly.

Page reference: 20–23, AP Topic: Theories of democratic government

16. The characteristics and beliefs of a particular people about government and politics is known as

(a) is incorrect because scientific socialism does not fit the definition provided.

(b) is correct because political culture is an overall set of values and beliefs widely shared within a society.

(c) is incorrect because elitism does not fit the definition provided.

(d) is incorrect because pluralism does not fit the definition provided.

(e) is incorrect because capitalism does not fit the definition provided.

Page reference: 20–23, AP Topic: Theories of democratic government

17. This natural rights' philosopher stated in a 17th century political document that all individuals have certain natural rights, including those of life, liberty, and property.

(a) is incorrect because Thomas Paine wrote *Common Sense*.

(b) is incorrect because Thomas Jefferson wrote the Declaration of Independence.

(c) is incorrect because Rousseau wrote *The Social Contract*.

(d) is correct because John Locke, in his *Second Treatise on Civil Government*, stated that all individuals had the natural rights of life, liberty, and property.

(e) is incorrect because James Madison wrote the Constitution.

Page reference: 15, AP Topic: Theories of democratic government

18. All of the following statements about majoritarianism in the United States are true EXCEPT

(a) is incorrect because it is a correct statement relating to majoritarianism.

(b) is incorrect because it is a correct statement relating to majoritarianism.

(c) is incorrect because it is a correct statement relating to majoritarianism.

(d) is correct because majoritarianism is the traditional political philosophy which asserts that the majority has the right to make the decisions in the government.

(e) is incorrect because it is a correct statement relating to majoritarianism.

Page reference: 15–26, AP Topic: Theories of democratic government

19.   In which famous document did James Madison argue that government is most dangerous when a single group gains complete political control?

(a) is incorrect because Thomas Paine wrote *Common Sense.*

(b) is correct because James Madison, in *Federalist* No. 10, wrote his warning against factions and their influence in government.

(c) is incorrect because, even though James Madison contributed heavily to the Constitution, he did not include his warning against factions in that document.

(d) is incorrect because the Preamble to the Declaration of Independence was written by Thomas Jefferson.

(e) is incorrect because *The Wealth of Nations* was written by Adam Smith.

Page reference: 16–18, AP Topic: Theories of democratic government

20.   All of the following are considered inputs into the American political system EXCEPT

(a) is incorrect because the activities of interest groups are inputs.

(b) is incorrect because the activities of political parties are inputs.

(c) is correct because laws passed by Congress constitute an output, not an input.

(d) is incorrect because voting in elections is an input.

(e) is incorrect because letters to representatives are inputs.

Page reference: 15–23, AP Topic: Theories of democratic government

Free-Response Questions

This rubric provides examples of many, but not all, of the possible correct responses to the free-response questions. Occasionally, there will be weaknesses pointed out in the suggested answer, providing students with examples of what to avoid.

1.   There is a common set of values generally espoused by United States citizens—a political culture.

a.   Identify three elements of American political culture.

   ▪   Identification of any three of the following would earn credit.

      ▫   Liberty

- Political equality
- Popular rule/populism
- Individualism
- Laissez-faire economics

b. Describe two of these elements.

- Liberty generally implies freedom, either from government or to engage in chosen activities or to abstain from certain activities.

- Political equality implies an equal chance to participate in politics if one chooses to do so.

- Popular rule/populism is an expression of popular sovereignty/majority rule/government "by the people."

- Individualism is the general idea that persons should take responsibility for their own advancement and that rights inhere in persons, not groups.

- Laissez-faire economics espouses limited government in market activities.

c. Explain why citizens might espouse these values but object to specific applications.

- There is a well-known difference between diffuse and specific support for principles. Thus, individuals voice support for liberty but are quite willing to support regulation of behavior of which they disapprove. Likewise, they voice support for political participation—as long as the participation supports positions they support. The same caveat applies to popular rule. And, individuals often ignore the extent to which they benefit from collective actions. Similarly, advocates of "getting the government out of the marketplace" generally find it useful to have a stable monetary system, to have contracts enforced, to have law and order, to have their fellow citizens educated, to have their food free of adulteration, to have roads on which to drive, etc.—much of which is provided by government.

2. Government is a set of institutions by which people make collective decisions.

a. Identify three functions government serves.

- Identification of any three of the following would earn credit.
  - Dispensing justice

- Ensuring "domestic tranquility"/order
- Providing for national defense
- Promoting general welfare
- Providing "public goods"
- Political socialization
- Collecting taxes

b. Provide two explanations why people might choose to use government to pursue these functions.

- Having government perform any of these functions divides labor and allows the development of expertise. For example, instead of each person having to provide for personal safety or to dispense justice for crimes committed against them, we can call police, have prosecutors act, and have governments incarcerate. Thus, people may choose government because it allows them to simplify their lives.

- Second, engaging in collective action allows for the achievement of economies of scale. Thus, people might choose to have government build roads, for example, because it is cheaper for all concerned to do this collectively rather than individually.

2

The Constitution

□ Chapter Overview

A country's constitution is its basic law; it establishes political institutions, allocates power between them, and often provides basic guarantees of the rights of its citizens. Constitutions thus usually establish how political power is distributed and exercised in a given country. In this chapter, we begin by exploring the historical development and foundational philosophies of the U.S. Constitution. We consider the specific compromises reached at the Constitutional Convention. Next, we examine the debates over ratification. We conclude by considering the basic tenets of the government established by the new constitution, and consider the mechanisms whereby it might be changed. By the end of the chapter, students should have a good understanding of how the U.S. Constitution sets the stage for how politics in the United States works today.

□ Study Outline

Learning Objective 2.1: Describe the ideas behind the American Revolution and their role in shaping the Constitution. (p. 35)

The Origins of the Constitution

Declaration of Independence (1776)

- The document lists grievances against the king of England.
- The document justifies revolution.
- The document is based on the idea of **natural rights**.

Philosophy of John Locke

- Rights that are derived from people's basic moral sense supersede the authority of a government.
- **Consent of the governed:** A government is legitimate only if the people approve of it (social contract).
- **Limited government:** Because natural rights are superior to a government, governments should have limited power.
- Government should protect people's property.

The American Revolution ends in 1783.

 Learning Objective 2.2: Analyze how the weaknesses of the Articles of Confederation led to its failure. (p. 40)

The Government That Failed: 1776–1787

The Articles of Confederation

- The Articles established the first government of the United States (enacted in 1781).
- The Articles was designed to preserve the independence of the states.
- The Articles created a national government without any centralized power; proves to be ineffectual.

Key Provisions of the Articles of Confederation

- **Unicameral** national legislature
- No executive or judicial institutions
- Most power rests with state legislatures
- No power to tax
- No regulation of foreign or interstate trade
- No national currency
- No national defense

Weaknesses of the Articles

- Without the power to **collect taxes**, the national government had few financial resources with which to repay its war debts.

- The development of a national economy was inhibited also by the government's inability to establish and **regulate trade**.

- The Articles **prevented the formation of a unified nation** out of a collection of states with different political, economic, and social concerns.

- States retained full sovereignty.

Consequences of the Weaknesses of the Articles

- **Shays' Rebellion** was not easily quelled, because the government had no power to raise a militia. The incident provided the final proof that the Articles were not a sufficient plan of government.

- **Annapolis Convention** in 1786 attempted to suggest reforms of the Articles, but it was determined instead to ask Congress to schedule a convention for 1787.

 Learning Objective 2.3: Describe the delegates to the Constitutional Convention and the core ideas they shared. (p. 44)

Making a Constitution: The Philadelphia Convention

- Many issues were hotly debated during the writing of the **Constitution**. In effect, the framers faced the momentous task of defining the nature of government. They did, however, agree on some basic principles:

  - The government should check the self-interest of the people yet protect their individual liberties and advance natural rights such as equality.

  - Factions should not be allowed to create political conflict and thereby undermine the government.

  - No one faction should have the opportunity to prevail upon the others.

Gentlemen in Philadelphia

- Although the 55 founders at the Constitutional Convention were almost all wealthy and well-educated, they had divergent views about major issues, including:
    - Human nature
    - Political conflict and the nature of **factions**
    - Purposes of government
    - Nature of government

 Learning Objective 2.4: Categorize the issues at the Constitutional Convention and outline the resolutions reached on each type of issue. (p. 45)

Critical Issues at the Convention

The Equality Issues

- Two plans were proposed to ensure **equal representation** of the people in the legislature: the Virginia Plan (representation in the national Congress should be determined by the **population** of each state) and the New Jersey Plan (each state should be allowed the same number of representatives in the national Congress).
- The **Connecticut Compromise**, or Great Compromise, established a **bicameral legislature**. The **Senate** would include two representatives from each state as per the New Jersey Plan, and representation in the **House** would be determined by the population of each state.
- The **Three-Fifths Compromise** mandated that only three-fifths of slaves be counted in determining state representation (this was repealed by the **Fourteenth Amendment** in 1868).

The Economic Issues

- The authors identified interstate tariffs, worthless paper money, and economic recession as serious problems of the American economy.
- These concerns led the Philadelphia delegates to strengthen the economic powers of the new national government to address these problems.

The Individual Rights Issues

- The **writ of habeas corpus** cannot be suspended.

- **Bills of attainder**, which punish people without a trial, cannot be passed.

- **Ex post facto laws**, which are retroactive criminal laws, are prohibited.

- **Religious qualifications** cannot be used as a prerequisite for public office.

- All citizens are entitled to a **trial by jury** in a criminal case.

Learning Objective 2.5: Analyze how the components of the Madisonian system addressed the dilemma of reconciling majority rule with the protection of minority interests. (p. 50)

The Madisonian System

- James Madison warned that both the majority (poorer and less-educated Americans) and minority (the wealthy elite) factions could pose a threat to the stability of a government.

- To protect government from the will of the majority, the president would be chosen by the **Electoral College** and, until the Seventeenth Amendment in 1913, senators would be chosen by states' legislatures, not directly by the people.

- Madison proposed that the national government be divided into three branches: the **executive**, **legislative**, and **judicial**. Each branch would have its own powers and responsibilities.

- A system of **checks and balances** would ensure that no branch could become more powerful than the others. The majority or the minority might be able to take control of any one branch but not necessarily the whole political system.

- Establishing a **federal** system of government allowed power to be shared between the national and state levels of government.

Checks and Balances

Legislative Branch

- The House and the Senate can veto a bill of the other house.

- The Senate approves presidential nominations for judges and other officials.

- The legislative branch can impeach the president (House impeaches, Senate removes).
- The legislative branch controls the budget.
- The legislative branch can pass laws over a president's veto with a two-thirds majority.

Executive Branch

- The president can veto bills passed by Congress.
- The president can nominate judges and other government officials.

Judicial Branch

- The judicial branch can declare laws passed by Congress to be unconstitutional.
- The judicial branch can declare acts of the president to be unconstitutional.
- The Constitution did not grant to the courts the power to check the other branches.
- The Supreme Court did not assert its authority to declare laws **unconstitutional** until the case of *Marbury v. Madison* in 1803.

The Constitutional Republic

- The Constitution established that the government would be one of elected representatives.

 Learning Objective 2.6: Compare and contrast the Federalists and Anti-Federalists in terms of their background and their positions regarding government. (p. 54)

Ratifying the Constitution

- The approval of at least nine states was needed to ratify the Constitution, and it did not come easily.

Anti-Federalists

- Anti-Federalists feared that the Constitution favored an elite minority.

- Anti-Federalists believed that the Constitution failed to protect too many individual freedoms.

- Anti-Federalists believed that a strong central government would limit the power of the states.

- Anti-Federalists published scathing articles and political cartoons denouncing the Constitution as a tool of the aristocracy.

Federalists

- Federalists published a series of articles called the *Federalist Papers* to defend the Constitution.

- Federalists asserted that the Constitution would benefit the growing middle class of tradesmen as well as the wealthy plantation owners.

- Federalists promised to add a **bill of rights** to guarantee individual liberties.

- The Constitution was ratified in 1787, largely because the authors promised to add a bill of rights.

- The Constitution established the United States as a **federal republic** in which power would be divided among levels of government.

- The Constitution is considered a "**living document**" because it can be amended as the United States grows and changes.

 Learning Objective 2.7: Explain how the Constitution can be formally amended and how it changes informally. (p. 57)

Changing the Constitution

Formal Amendment Process

- Amendments can be proposed by Congress with a 2/3 vote in each House or by National Convention called by 2/3 of states.

- Amendments can be ratified by 3/4 of state legislatures or by Conventions in 3/4 of the states.

Informal Amendment Process

- **The Constitution can be informally amended through judicial interpretation** (established in *Marbury v. Madison*).

- **The Constitution can be informally amended by changing political practice, technology, and increased demands on policymakers.**

- Over the years, the Constitution has become **more democratic** than the authors intended.

Learning Objective 2.8: Assess whether the Constitution establishes a majoritarian democracy and how it limits the scope of government. (p. 64)

Understanding the Constitution

- The Constitution did not establish a majoritarian democracy because majorities do not always rule in America.

- There has, however, been a gradual democratization of the Constitution.

- The Constitution limits the scope of government by protecting individual rights and by dispersing power among institutions.

For Additional Review

Create a "story board" to trace the events leading up to the establishment of the Constitution through the ratification process. List all events/ideas from the Declaration of Independence through the ratification of the Bill of Rights. For each event, write a brief statement describing the importance of the event/idea. Use this story board when reviewing and studying for the unit test.

Make a chart comparing and contrasting the Articles of Confederation and the Constitution. How did they organize government differently? In what ways did the Constitution amend the failures of the Articles? Use this chart when reviewing and studying for the unit test.

☐ Review Questions

Multiple-Choice Questions

1. Under America's first constitution, the Articles of Confederation,
   a. the national government dominated state governments.
   b. the executive branch had more power than Congress.
   c. Congress was a unicameral body.
   d. states were represented in Congress proportionally according to population.
   e. reflected the Founding Fathers' belief that a national standing army was necessary.

2. Which of the following founders was the "principal architect" of the Constitution?
   a. Edmund Randolph
   b. George Washington
   c. Thomas Jefferson
   d. Alexander Hamilton
   e. James Madison

3. The Three-Fifths Compromise at the Constitutional Convention
   a. allowed cloture to be invoked, ending a filibuster in the Senate, with the support of 60 senators.
   b. prescribed the proportion of states required to ratify a constitutional amendment.
   c. provided a formula by which slaves would be counted for apportioning the House of Representatives.
   d. established the percentage of votes necessary for electors to be chosen under the original provisions of the Electoral College system.
   e. established the percentage of members of the House required to pass a bill raising revenue.

4. Any law passed by a legislature that punishes an individual without a trial, under the Constitution, violates the constitutional concept of
   a. a bill of attainder.
   b. an ex post facto law.
   c. double jeopardy.
   d. eminent domain.
   e. habeas corpus.

5. The idea of limiting the role of government to protecting "life, liberty, and property" is generally attributed to
   a. Karl Marx.
   b. Thomas Jefferson.
   c. Thomas Hobbes.
   d. John Locke.
   e. Alexander Hamilton.

6. Granting supremacy to the national government was done in part to
   a. protect the rights of minorities.
   b. promote the economic interests of those at the Constitutional Convention.
   c. prevent the people from instituting the ideas of John Locke.
   d. protect debtors from abusive creditors.
   e. ensure that the United States would remain a nation of small farmers.

7. The Founding Fathers designed a system of checks and balances for the national government. Which of the following best illustrates that concept?

   I. Congress overrides a president's veto.
   II. The Supreme Court declares a law unconstitutional.
   III. The president issues an executive order reducing the size of the bureaucracy.
   IV. The House and Senate cannot agree on a Conference Committee report.

   a. I and II
   b. II and III
   c. III and IV
   d. II and IV
   e. I and IV

8. A law goes into effect declaring that a business practice that has been legal in the past will be illegal in the future, and the law is made retroactive. Why would the Supreme Court likely rule the new law unconstitutional?
   a. It would constitute a bill of attainder.
   b. It would violate double jeopardy.
   c. It would bypass grand jury indictment.
   d. It would violate the concept of eminent domain.
   e. It would be an ex post facto law.

9. Which plan proposed at the Constitutional Convention called for a bicameral legislature with one chamber having members from states calculated proportionally based upon population and the other having two members per state?
   a. Connecticut Compromise
   b. Virginia Plan
   c. Annapolis Convention Plan
   d. Philadelphia Plan
   e. New Jersey Plan

10. The case of *Marbury v. Madison* (1803) established which principle?
    a. the supremacy clause
    b. judicial review
    c. natural rights of citizens
    d. the writ of habeas corpus rule
    e. the separation of powers

11. A state must honor the public acts and records of any other state under the
    a. full faith and credit clause.
    b. supremacy clause.
    c. elastic clause.
    d. commerce clause.
    e. extradition clause.

12. Which of the following is an informal way of amending the Constitution?
    a. passage of an amendment by a simple majority vote in two consecutive sessions of Congress
    b. a vote of two-thirds of the state legislatures specifically requesting Congress to call a national convention to propose amendments
    c. passage of an amendment by a vote of two-thirds of the state legislatures without congressional approval
    d. changes in social and cultural attitudes that lead to substantive changes in how people interpret the Constitution
    e. passage of an amendment by a vote of two-thirds of Congress

13. The outcome of a conflict between the Constitution and the states is determined by
    a. the Great Compromise.
    b. the supremacy clause.
    c. *Federalist* No. 10.
    d. judicial review.
    e. ex post facto laws.

14. The Articles of Confederation failed for all of the following reasons EXCEPT
    a. The national government lacked the power to tax.
    b. The national government lacked the ability to regulate trade.
    c. There was no national judiciary.
    d. The central government was too weak.
    e. There was no provision to amend the Articles.

15. Which of the following was stipulated in Article III of the Constitution?
    a. creation of the Supreme Court
    b. executive powers
    c. powers of Congress
    d. full faith and credit clause
    e. the separation of powers

16. The significance of Shays' Rebellion was:
    a. It demonstrated that the Articles of Confederation was weak and unable to adequately respond to a crisis.
    b. It exposed the flaws in the Constitution.
    c. It demonstrated the superiority of the national standing army.
    d. It demonstrated the effectiveness of the national court system.
    e. It increased the power of the president.

17. The original Constitution provided that U.S. senators were to be elected by
    a. the Supreme Court.
    b. direct vote of the people.
    c. the House of Representatives.
    d. the President.
    e. state legislatures.

18. The issue of representation in Congress was dealt with by
    a. the Slave Trade Compromise.
    b. the Voter Registration Compromise.
    c. the Commerce Compromise.
    d. the Great or Connecticut Compromise.
    e. the Executive Compromise.

19. Individuals who supported the new Constitution were known as
    a. Anti-Federalists.
    b. States' Righters.
    c. Federalists.
    d. Philosophes.
    e. Confederates.

20. The series of essays which encouraged the ratification of the Constitution was known as
    a. *Common Sense.*
    b. *The Spirit of the Laws.*
    c. *The Social Contract.*
    d. *The Federalist.*
    e. *The Second Treatise of Civil Government.*

Free-Response Questions

1. The Constitution has had 17 formal amendments since the adoption of the Bill of Rights, yet there are basic elements that have changed because of informal processes as well.

    a. Describe the most common process of formally amending the Constitution.

    b. Identify one formal amendment and describe how it has changed the meaning of the Constitution.

    c. Identify one informal change in the Constitution, and describe how it has changed the meaning of the Constitution even without formal amendment.

2. When James Madison proposed a new constitution, he tried to balance the need for "proper energy" in government with a clear limitation on government power as well.

    a. Identify two features Madison proposed for keeping any branch of government from becoming too powerful.

b. Explain how each feature identified in (a) balances the need for strong government with a need for limited government.

c. Identify one feature Madison proposed for dividing powers between national and state governments.

d. Explain how this feature balanced the need for a strong central government while assuring the states of adequate power.

☐ Answers and Explanations

Multiple-Choice Questions

1. Under America's first constitution, the Articles of Confederation,

   (a) is incorrect because the state governments retained virtually all the power under the Articles of Confederation.

   (b) is incorrect because there was no executive branch under the Articles of Confederation.

   (c) is correct because the Articles of Confederation had a unicameral legislature.

   (d) is incorrect because the states were equally represented under the Articles of Confederation.

   (e) is incorrect because there was no standing army under the Articles of Confederation.

   Page reference: 40–43, AP Topic: The Constitutional underpinnings of the United States government

2. Which of the following founders was the "principal architect" of the Constitution?

   (a) is incorrect because Edmund Randolph's role was far more limited than James Madison's.

   (b) is incorrect because George Washington's impact on the document was far more limited than James Madison's.

   (c) is incorrect because Thomas Jefferson was not at the Constitutional Convention.

   (d) is incorrect because Alexander Hamilton's role was far more limited than James Madison's.

   (e) is correct because James Madison provided the intellectual impetus for the Constitution, arriving at the convention with the Virginia Plan and as a result, in terms of his impact on the Constitution, Madison was known as "the Father of the Constitution."

3. The Three-Fifths Compromise at the Constitutional Convention

    (a) is incorrect because a 3/5 ratio may be correct in the case of invoking cloture, but it does not stem from the Constitution.

    (b) is incorrect because it does not relate to the treatment of slaves.

    (c) is correct because although all of the options could provide for a 3/5 ratio, only the treatment of the slaves was specified in the Constitution.

    (d) is incorrect because it does not relate to the treatment of slaves.

    (e) is incorrect because it does not relate to the treatment of slaves.

    Page reference: 45–47, AP Topic: Considerations that influenced the formulation and adoption of the Constitution

4. Any law passed by a legislature that punishes an individual without a trial, under the Constitution, violates the constitutional concept of

    (a) is correct because one of the civil liberties issues addressed in the original Constitution attempted to limit the practice of passing laws that singled out individuals and therefore, the idea in the United States was that such bills of attainder were unfair, and that laws should apply to all citizens equally.

    (b) is incorrect because an ex post facto law is a retroactive criminal law.

    (c) is incorrect because double jeopardy is a protection against being tried twice for the same offense.

    (d) is incorrect because eminent domain is taking private property for public use.

    (e) is incorrect because habeas corpus requires a person under arrest to be brought before a judge.

    Page reference: 50–53, AP Topic: Considerations that influenced the formulation and adoption of the Constitution

5. The idea of limiting the role of government to protecting "life, liberty, and property" is generally attributed to

    (a) is incorrect because Karl Marx's theories are the basis for communism.

    (b) is incorrect because Thomas Jefferson loosely borrowed Locke's ideas for the Declaration of Independence.

    (c) is incorrect because Thomas Hobbes' theories did not include those particular ideas.

(d) is correct because Locke believed in a representative democracy with limited powers, concepts that underscore the Constitution.

(e) is incorrect because Alexander Hamilton's ideas created the basis of the economic system.

Page reference: 44–45, AP Topics: Considerations that influenced the formulation and adoption of the Constitution and Theories of democratic government

6. Granting supremacy to the national government was done in part to

    (a) is incorrect because minority rights were generally limited by both the states and national government prior to the Civil War.

    (b) is correct because those at the Constitutional Convention were primarily merchant and manufacturing elites, and the Constitution gives the national government powers to further the development of a national economy of merchants and manufacturing at the expense of the states and agrarians.

    (c) is incorrect because the Constitution employs the ideas of John Locke.

    (d) is incorrect because the Constitution protected the rights of creditors against debtors.

    (e) is incorrect because it did not address the issue of agrarianism.

    Page reference: 44–50, AP Topic: Considerations that influenced the formulation and adoption of the Constitution

7. The Founding Fathers designed a system of checks and balances for the national government. Which of the following best illustrates that concept?

    (a) is correct because checks and balances require the interaction between two branches of government, therefore, the overriding of a president's veto by Congress or the invalidation of a congressional law by the Supreme Court would be examples of checks and balances.

    (b) is incorrect because issuing an executive order is not an example of checks and balances.

    (c) is incorrect because III and IV are not examples of checks and balances.

    (d) is incorrect because IV is not an example of checks and balances.

    (e) is incorrect because IV is not an example of checks and balances.

    Page reference: 52, AP Topic: Checks and balances

8. A law goes into effect declaring that a business practice that has been legal in the past will be illegal in the future, and the law is made retroactive. Why would the Supreme Court likely rule the new law unconstitutional?

(a) is incorrect because a bill of attainder does not fit the definition provided.

(b) is incorrect because double jeopardy does not fit the definition provided.

(c) is incorrect because bypassing a jury indictment does not fit the definition provided.

(d) is incorrect because eminent domain does not fit the definition provided.

(e) is correct because the definition in the frame of the question is that of an ex post facto law, something banned in the original Constitution.

Page reference: 44–53, AP Topic: Constitutional underpinnings

9. Which plan proposed at the Constitutional Convention called for a bicameral legislature with one chamber having members from states calculated proportionally based upon population and the other having two members per state?

(a) is correct because the "great compromise" that led to a Senate based upon equal state representation and a House allocated proportionally based upon population was the Connecticut Compromise.

(b) is incorrect because the Virginia Plan called for representation to be based on population.

(c) is incorrect because Annapolis was the location of a failed convention in 1786.

(d) is incorrect because Philadelphia was the location of the Constitutional Convention.

(e) is incorrect because the New Jersey Plan called for equal representation.

Page reference: 44–53, AP Topic: Considerations that influenced the formulation and adoption of the Constitution

10. The case of *Marbury v. Madison* (1803) established which principle?

(a) is incorrect because the *Marbury* case did not establish the supremacy clause.

(b) is correct because the case of *Marbury v. Madison* was the landmark decision of the Supreme Court declaring that it was an inherent duty of the judicial branch to "determine what the law is," thus establishing judicial review.

(c) is incorrect because the *Marbury* case did not relate to the natural rights of citizens.

(d) is incorrect because the *Marbury* case did not relate to the natural rights of citizens.

(e) is incorrect because the *Marbury* case did not relate to the separation of powers.

Page reference: 61, AP Topics: Constitutional underpinnings and the Federal judiciary

11.   A state must honor the public acts and records of any other state under the

(a) is correct because the full faith and credit clause, found in Article IV of the Constitution, guarantees that the legal records, laws, and judicial proceedings of one state will be honored by another state.

(b) is incorrect because the supremacy clause deals with the relationship between the national government and state governments.

(c) is incorrect because the elastic clause deals with implied powers.

(d) is incorrect because the commerce clause deals with a delegated power of Congress.

(e) is incorrect because the extradition clause deals with returning criminals to the state where the crime was committed.

Page reference: 51, AP Topic: Constitutional underpinnings

12.   Which of the following is an informal way of amending the Constitution?

(a) is incorrect because an amendment is a formal method.

(b) is incorrect because a 2/3 vote to propose an amendment is a formal method.

(c) is incorrect because an amendment is a formal method.

(d) is correct because an informal method of amending the Constitution would be a practice or development that led to a change in how the Constitution was applied, even with no direct changes to the document through the formal amendment process.

(e) is incorrect because an amendment is a formal method.

Page reference: 57–61, AP Topics: Constitutional underpinnings and Federalism

13.   The outcome of a conflict between the Constitution and the states is determined by

(a) is incorrect because the Great Compromise settled the issue of representation.

(b) is correct because the supremacy clause requires all states to adopt laws that conform to the limits of the U.S. Constitution.

(c) is incorrect because *Federalist* No. 10 is an explanation of the Constitution.

(d) is incorrect because judicial review is the power of the Supreme Court to declare laws unconstitutional.

(e) is incorrect because ex post facto laws are forbidden.

Page reference: 78–83, AP Topic: Constitutional underpinnings

14. The Articles of Confederation failed for all of the following reasons EXCEPT

(a) is incorrect because the national government did not have the power to tax.

(b) is incorrect because the national government did not have the power to regulate trade.

(c) is incorrect because there was no national judiciary.

(d) is incorrect because there was no central government.

(e) is correct because the Articles of Confederation could be amended with unanimous consent of all of the states.

Page reference: 40–43, AP Topics: Constitutional underpinnings

15. Which of the following was stipulated in Article III of the Constitution?

(a) is correct because Article III of the Constitution established the judicial branch of the new federal government.

(b) is incorrect because executive powers are established in Article II.

(c) is incorrect because congressional powers are established in Article I.

(d) is incorrect because full faith and credit is in Article IV.

(e) is incorrect because separation of powers divides the powers of the national government.

Page reference: 50, AP Topics: Separation of powers and Checks and balances

16. The significance of Shays' Rebellion was

(a) is correct because the government under the Articles did not have the power to raise a military and therefore could not deal with the crisis.

(b) is incorrect because it occurred before the Constitution.

(c) is incorrect because the government under the Articles could not raise an army.

(d) is incorrect because the government under the Articles did not have a court system.

(e) is incorrect because the government under the Articles did not have a president.

Page reference: 40–43, AP Topic: Constitutional underpinnings

17. The original Constitution provided that U.S. senators were to be elected by

(a) is incorrect because the Supreme Court did not elect senators.

(b) is incorrect because Senators were not directly elected by the people until the 17th Amendment.

(c) is incorrect because the House did not elect senators.

(d) is incorrect because the President did not elect senators.

(e) is correct because the original Constitution limited the participation of the people by having state legislatures elect senators.

Page reference: 44–53, AP Topic: Constitutional underpinnings

18. The issue of representation in Congress was dealt with by

(a) is incorrect because the Slave Trade compromise settled the dispute over the slave trade between the northern and southern states.

(b) is incorrect because the Voter Registration compromise settled the issue of voter qualifications.

(c) is incorrect because the Commerce compromise settled the conflict between the national and state governments concerning trade.

(d) is correct because the Great Compromise, also known as the Connecticut Compromise, settled the dispute over representation between the Virginia and New Jersey plans.

(e) is incorrect because the Executive compromise settled the conflicts concerning the national executive.

Page reference: 46, AP Topics: Constitutional underpinnings and Federalism

19. Individuals who supported the new Constitution were known as

(a) is incorrect because the Anti-Federalists were opposed to the Constitution and worked against ratification.

(b) is incorrect because States' Righters were in favor of the majority of the governmental powers remaining in the states.

(c) is correct because the supporters of the Constitution who worked for ratification were known as Federalists.

(d) is incorrect because the Philosophes were the supporters of the Natural Rights philosophy.

(e) is incorrect because Confederates were opposed to a strong central government.

Page reference: 54, AP Topic: Constitutional underpinnings

20. The series of essays which encouraged the ratification of the Constitution was known as

(a) is incorrect because *Common Sense* was written in support of the Declaration of Independence.

(b) is incorrect because *The Spirit of the Laws* was written to outline a government based on separation of powers.

(c) is incorrect because *The Social Contract* opposed divine right of kings and support a government based on a social contract.

(d) is correct because the collection of essays written in support of the Constitution is known as *The Federalist*.

(e) is incorrect because *The Second Treatise of Civil Government* was used as the basis for the Declaration of Independence.

Page reference: 54, AP Topic: Considerations that influenced the formulation and adoption of the Constitution

Free-Response Questions

This rubric provides examples of many, but not all of the possible correct responses to the free-response questions. Occasionally, there will be weaknesses pointed out in the suggested answer, providing students with examples of what to avoid.

1. The Constitution has had 17 formal amendments since the adoption of the Bill of Rights, yet there are basic elements that have changed because of informal processes as well.

   a. Describe the most common process of formally amending the Constitution.

   - The Constitution is the cornerstone of American democracy. It was written by the Founding Fathers to guarantee that American democracy would survive for all times. The Constitution can be amended either formally or informally.

   - The process for formal amendments begins with the proposal of an amendment. This comes either by a two-thirds vote of each house of Congress or by the vote of two-thirds of the states in a national convention. The proposed amendment must be ratified by three-fourths of the states in either votes of the state legislatures or a ratifying convention in each state.

   b. Identify one formal amendment and describe how it has changed the meaning of the Constitution.

- The Fourteenth Amendment to the Constitution followed the Civil War. Before that, the Bill of Rights only applied to acts of the federal government. But the Fourteenth Amendment specifies that no state shall deprive anyone of life, liberty, or property without due process. This gave the federal government power over many areas that had been left to the states in 1787, such as state court procedures.

c. Identify one informal change in the Constitution, and describe how it has changed the meaning of the Constitution even without formal amendment.

- The constitution can be amended informally in a number of ways. That means that the Constitution might have changed meaning without having a formal amendment added. Often, this involves custom and usage. For example, a president can issue an executive order or negotiate an executive agreement with other nations. These are not part of the Constitution, but presidents have learned to use them anyway, and as a result have gained powers that the founders originally gave to Congress. As a result, they are, in a way, the same as formal amendments to the Constitution.

2. When James Madison proposed a new constitution, he tried to balance the need for "proper energy" in government with a clear limitation on government power as well.

a. Identify two features Madison proposed for keeping any branch of government from becoming too powerful.

b. Explain how each feature identified in (a) balances the need for strong government with a need for limited government.

- In order for any branch to be kept from being too powerful, Madison designed a government that included the twin concepts of separation of powers and checks and balances. In a system such as that, power is divided among three branches of government—the legislative, the executive, and the judicial. Each branch has a specific grant of power and each one is given "checks over the other. For example, Congress must approve presidential treaties and can override a president's veto. Congress can even impeach and remove a president from power. The president can veto a bill of Congress. And the Supreme Court can declare acts of the president or laws of Congress unconstitutional. In other words, this is a Madisonian design that is intended to limit the powers of each of the branches of government, preventing any one branch from becoming too powerful by allowing other branches to stop them.

c. Identify one feature Madison proposed for dividing powers between national and state governments.

d. Explain how this feature balanced the need for a strong central government while assuring the states of adequate power.

- In order to keep the federal government from gaining too much power, the Constitution created a system of federalism, that is, a system that divided power between the national government and the state governments. The powers of the national government are listed in Article I of the Constitution and the Tenth Amendment makes it clear that powers not listed in Article I are reserved for the states. As a result, the concept of federalism was designed to keep the national government from becoming too strong.

- In recent years, many observers have argued that the national government has become too strong. As a result, the federal design has been seen as under siege. But President Reagan designed a "new federalism," consisting of changing categorical grants to block grants that devolved power from the national government to the states. Also, Congress passed a law that outlawed "unfunded mandates." So, the powers of the national government and the states have come more into balance.

3

Federalism

☐ Chapter Overview

"Federalism" refers to the division of power between the national government and the states. Under our federal system, significant government powers are divided between the central government and small governmental units; neither completely controls the other, and each has some room for independent action. We begin by defining federalism and differentiating it from other forms of political organization, chiefly unitary and confederal systems. We then examine the basic principles of American federalism, including the division of power between the national and state governments and the principles of national supremacy and state obligations. Next, we consider how American federalism has changed over time, evolving from a system of dual federalism to a system of cooperative federalism, to the contemporary system of new federalism as it exists today. We conclude by evaluating the impact of federalism on public policy and politics in the United States.

☐ Study Outline

 Learning Objective 3.1: Define federalism and contrast it with alternative ways of organizing a nation. (p. 75)

Defining Federalism

- **Federal government:** Government is **divided into more than one level.** Different bodies share power over the same group of people.

- **Unitary government:** Only one **central government** has authority over a nation. There are no levels of government that share power.

- **Confederation:** An association of states with some authority delegated to a national government. The states in such a system retain most of the power.
- Intergovernmental relations **become especially important in a federal system because of the elaborate communication necessary to share power**.

 Learning Objective 3.2: Outline the constitutional basis for the division of power between national and state governments, the establishment of national supremacy, and states' obligations to each other. (p. 77)

The Constitutional Basis of Federalism

Supremacy Clause

- The Supremacy Clause is located in Article VI.
- The Supremacy Clause asserts the authority of the national government over the states.
- In cases of discrepancy, federal laws usually supersede state laws.

Tenth Amendment

- The tenth amendment is located in the Bill of Rights.
- The tenth amendment grants all powers not specifically reserved for the national government to the states.
- The tenth amendment is often cited in arguments in favor of states' rights.

Enumerated Powers

- Enumerated powers are located in Article I, Section 8 of the Constitution.
- Enumerated powers are granted to the national government, and specifically to Congress.

Implied Powers

- Implied powers were established in *McCulloch v. Maryland*, an 1819 Supreme Court case in which the states battled the formation of a national bank.

- The Supreme Court, under Chief Justice John Marshall, ruled against the states, thereby reinforcing the supremacy of the national government.
- The constitutional basis for implied powers is Article I, Section 8. This is known as the elastic clause, also called the necessary and proper clause.
- Implied powers give Congress the authority to pass any laws necessary to carry out its duties as enumerated in the Constitution.
- The elastic clause, as interpreted in *McCulloch v. Maryland*, allows Congress to act on implied powers that are not specifically defined in the Constitution.
- The case of *Gibbons v. Ogden* in 1824 expanded congressional power to regulate commerce.

Full Faith and Credit Clause

- The full faith and credit clause is located in Article IV, Section 1.
- Full faith and credit requires each state to formally recognize the documents and judgments handed down by courts in other states.
- Full faith and credit helps coalesce the state laws under a national umbrella.

Extradition

- Extradition is located in Article IV, Section 2.
- Requires the return (**extradition**) of fugitive criminals arrested in one state to the state in which the crime was committed for prosecution.

Privileges and Immunities Clause

- The privileges and immunities clause is located in Article IV, Section 2.
- The privileges and immunities clause helps unify the states by assuring that all citizens are treated equally when they travel from state to state.

Learning Objective 3.3: Characterize the shift from dual to cooperative federalism and the role of fiscal federalism in intergovernmental relations today. (p. 84)

Intergovernmental Relations Today

- **Dual federalism:** Each level of government has distinct responsibilities that do not overlap.

- **Cooperative federalism:** Levels of government share responsibilities.

- Shared costs: To receive federal aid, states must pay for part of a program.

- Federal guidelines: To receive funding, state programs must follow federal rules and regulations.

- Shared administration: Though programs must adhere to basic federal guidelines, they are administered according to the state's directives.

- **Fiscal federalism:** The system of distributing federal money to state governments.

- About a quarter of states' fiscal spending is derived from federal aid.

- Money is distributed through relatively restrictive **categorical grants** and **block grants**, which allow states more spending discretion.

- **Mandates**, however, can create economic hardships for states when Congress creates financial obligations for the states without providing funding for those obligations.

Learning Objective 3.4: Explain the consequences of federalism for diversity in public policies among the states. (p. 94)

- States have certain powers which allow them to adopt policies different from other states.

Learning Objective 3.5: Assess the impact of federalism on democratic government and the scope of government. (p. 95)

Federalism and Democracy

- Federalism contributes to democracy by increasing access to the government at all levels, but it also creates disadvantages due to differences in the resources of individual states.

- These differences can lead to inequities among the states in areas such as education.

For Additional Review

To understand more fully the idea of federalism, create a "Taking Stock" table for federalism. The table should have three columns:

1. What do I know about federalism? (fill in this column at the beginning of the unit)
2. What do I not know about federalism? (fill in this column at the beginning of the unit)
3. What have I learned about federalism? (fill this in upon completion of each section of the chapter)

Use this table to guide your reading and note-taking as well as a study tool for the topic of federalism.

To understand more fully the idea of federalism, create a chart or Venn diagram identifying the major powers of the federal, state, and current powers. Use this diagram to serve as a useful study tool for the topic of federalism.

☐ Review Questions

Multiple-Choice Questions

1. Which of the following forms of fiscal federalism allow the states the broadest financial discretion?
    a. categorical grants
    b. block grants
    c. mandates
    d. foreign assistance
    e. U.S. military funding

2. The Constitution grants Congress the power to establish post offices and post roads. This is an example of
   a. enumerated powers.
   b. implied powers.
   c. reserved powers.
   d. concurrent powers.
   e. executive powers.

3. In a confederation,
   a. power is divided between a central government and regional governments.
   b. the sovereignty within a nation is held entirely by the central government.
   c. sovereignty is shared at the national, state, and local levels.
   d. power is held at the regional level, with the central government exercising only such influence as the regional governments give it.
   e. regional governments hold sovereignty regarding domestic policy while the national government holds sovereignty in national security policy.

4. The fiscal relationship between the national and state governments involves complex relationships. Which would *least* likely be favored by state governments?
   a. unfunded mandates
   b. categorical grants
   c. block grants
   d. revenue sharing
   e. formula grants

5. "Enumerated" powers are those given to
   a. the Supreme Court.
   b. the federal bureaucracy.
   c. state governments.
   d. the military.
   e. the national government.

6. The system of federalism that allowed states to do most of the fundamental governing from 1789 to 1937 was
   a. home rule.
   b. regulated or "marble cake" federalism.
   c. dual federalism.
   d. shared powers.
   e. cooperative federalism.

7.   The case of *McCulloch v. Maryland* (1809) ruled that

I.   The federal government could exercise only the enumerated powers of the Constitution.
II.   The implied powers in Article I of the Constitution allowed Congress to create a nationally chartered bank.
III. The state governments could levy taxes on national government institutions.
IV.   Neither states nor the federal government could tax one another.
V.   The state courts had sole jurisdiction over regulatory affairs within their boundaries.

a.   I, III, and V
b.   I and IV
c.   II and III
d.   II and IV
e.   IV and V

8.   "Dual federalism" refers to the fact that
a.   the Constitution provides two layers of government in the nation—the national and the state.
b.   there are two major forms of aid from the national government to the states—categorical and block grants.
c.   both the national and state governments can levy taxes on citizens.
d.   there are two distinct eras in American history—the era before cooperative federalism and the era since the development of cooperative federalism.
e.   there is a distinct line between policies surrounding public education and private education in the states.

9.   The power of the national government to regulate interstate commerce was expanded in the landmark case of
a.   *Marbury v. Madison.*
b.   *Plessy v. Ferguson.*
c.   *McCulloch v. Maryland.*
d.   *Miranda v. Arizona.*
e.   *Gibbons v. Ogden.*

10. The notion that when state and federal laws conflict, the national laws will prevail, is the
a.   necessary and proper clause.
b.   supremacy clause.
c.   extradition clause.
d.   full faith and credit clause.
e.   privileges and immunities clause.

11. The Founding Fathers had successfully rebelled against a unitary form of government. They had tried a confederation which was not working. Thus, they developed a _____ form of government.
    a. Constitutional Monarchy
    b. Federal
    c. Socialist
    d. Fascist
    e. Popular Democratic

12. The levels of government recognized specifically in the Constitution are
    a. counties and regional governments.
    b. states and the people.
    c. states and cities.
    d. national and state.
    e. national, state, and local.

13. Federalism as a form of government helps accommodate
    a. differences across states.
    b. governments in small geographic areas.
    c. citizens who want a strong government.
    d. citizens who want uniform policies across their political system.
    e. citizens who do not want policies to change over time.

14. National policies override state policies when there is a conflict and the Constitution gives the national government power in that policy area. This is a statement of
    a. the due process clause.
    b. the equal protection clause.
    c. the privileges and immunity clause.
    d. the supremacy clause.
    e. the full faith and credit clause.

15. A major basis for Congressional power is the implied powers it holds. The basis for these implied powers is
    a. federalism.
    b. the Supreme Court's decision in *Marbury v. Madison*.
    c. the Equal Protection Clause.
    d. the fact that Congress was the first branch of government created.
    e. the "Necessary and Proper" Clause.

16. The constitutional provision that makes same-sex marriage controversial is
    a. judicial review.
    b. full faith and credit clause.
    c. privileges and immunities clause.
    d. due process clause.
    e. unfunded mandates.

17. Both the national and states' governments can establish court systems. This is an example of
    a. reserved powers.
    b. a mandate.
    c. concurrent powers.
    d. full faith and credit clause.
    e. fiscal federalism.

18. The Constitution provides for the power of extradition. Extradition is an example of
    a. states' taxing powers.
    b. grants-in-aid.
    c. formula grants.
    d. interstate relations.
    e. categorical grants.

19. A power delegated to the national government is the power to
    a. regulate foreign and interstate commerce.
    b. police citizens.
    c. establish educational systems.
    d. establish the drinking age.
    e. regulate marriage and divorce.

20. An example of a concurrent power is
    a. declare war.
    b. establish educational systems.
    c. establish the drinking age.
    d. tax.
    e. regulate marriage and divorce.

Free-Response Questions

1. The Constitution designed a system in which various types of powers were assigned to different levels of government. Those types of powers are variously described as:

    - enumerated powers

    - reserved powers

    - concurrent powers, and

    - implied powers

    Select three of the types of powers listed above.

    a. Define each of the chosen types of powers.

    b. Explain how each of the chosen types of powers affects the distribution of powers between national and state governments.

2.   Cooperative federalism is a term often used to describe the complex fiscal relationship between the national and state governments. In your essay, do the following:

   a.   Define categorical grants and block grants, and describe the differences between them.

   b.   Identify an advantage and a disadvantage of categorical grants.

   c.   Identify an advantage and a disadvantage of block grants.

☐ Answers and Explanations

Multiple-Choice Questions

1.   Which of the following forms of fiscal federalism allow the states the broadest financial discretion?

   (a) is incorrect because categorical grants are given to the states with very limited discretion in spending.

   (b) is correct because block grants are given to the states with only general spending guidelines.

   (c) is incorrect because mandates leave the states with no discretion in spending.

   (d) is incorrect because it is solely the province of the national government.

   (e) is incorrect because it is solely the province of the national government.

   Page reference: 80, AP Topic: Federalism

2.   The Constitution grants Congress the power to establish post offices and post roads. This is an example of

   (a) is correct because enumerated powers are listed in Article I, Sec. 8 and one example is the establishment of post offices and roads.

   (b) is incorrect because implied powers are not specifically listed in the Constitution.

   (c) is incorrect because reserved powers belong only to the states.

   (d) is incorrect because the example listed in the question is an enumerated power not shared with the states, therefore, it is not an example of a concurrent power.

   (e) is incorrect because executive powers are not found in Article I.

   Page reference: 81, AP Topics: Separation of powers, Federalism, Beliefs that citizens hold about their government and its leaders

3. In a confederation,

(a) is incorrect because it describes a federal government, not a confederation.

(b) is incorrect because it describes a unitary government, not a confederation.

(c) is incorrect because it describes a federal government, not a confederation.

(d) is correct because it is the only correct definition of a confederation provided.

(e) is incorrect because it describes a federal government, not a confederation.

Page reference: 75, AP Topics: Considerations that influenced the formulation and adoption of the Constitution, Federalism

4. The fiscal relationship between the national and state governments involves complex relationships. Which would *least* likely be favored by state governments?

(a) is correct because mandates allow the states no discretion in spending money. From the state's position, the least liked of mandates are "unfunded mandates" that require states to spend money without any financial assistance from the national government.

(b) is incorrect because categorical grants allow the states some modicum of control over the supervision of spending and therefore would be preferred over mandates.

(c) is incorrect because block grants allow the states some modicum of control over the supervision of spending and therefore would be preferred over mandates.

(d) is incorrect because revenue sharing allows the states some modicum of control over the supervision of spending and therefore would be preferred over mandates.

(e) is incorrect because formula grants allow the states some modicum of control over the supervision of spending and therefore would be preferred over mandates.

Page reference: 91, AP Topic: Federalism

5. "Enumerated" powers are those given to

(a) is incorrect because enumerated powers are not given to the Supreme Court.

(b) is incorrect because enumerated powers are not given to the federal bureaucracy.

(c) is incorrect because enumerated powers are not given to state governments.

(d) is incorrect because enumerated powers are not given to the military.

(e) is correct because it is the definition of enumerated powers which are the powers given to the national government.

Page reference: 81, AP Topics: Separation of powers, Federalism, Beliefs that citizens hold about their government and its leaders

6. The system of federalism that allowed states to do most of the fundamental governing from 1789 to 1937 was

    (a) is incorrect because it not a form of federalism.

    (b) is incorrect because regulated or "marble cake" federalism is a form of cooperative federalism.

    (c) is correct because before the creation of cooperative federalism with the passing of "New Deal" programs in the mid-1930s, federalism generally conformed to the dual federalism model allowing the states to do most of the fundamental governing.

    (d) is incorrect because shared powers refer to cooperative federalism.

    (e) is incorrect because cooperative federalism is different from dual federalism.

    Page reference: 85, AP Topic: Federalism

7. The case of *McCulloch v. Maryland* (1809) ruled that

    (a) is incorrect because it contradicts the correct answer.

    (b) is incorrect because it contradicts the correct answer.

    (c) is incorrect because III contradicts the correct answer.

    (d) is correct because the *McCulloch* case is a landmark decision that had two major findings, that state and national governments could not destroy one another by taxing and that the implied powers allowed the establishment of a national bank even though that was not explicitly mentioned in Article I, Section 8.

    (e) is incorrect because IV contradicts the correct answer and V is not related to the question in any way.

    Page reference: 80, AP Topics: Federalism, Linkages between institutions

8. "Dual federalism" refers to the fact that

    (a) is correct because dual federalism is used to describe the original view of the relationship between the levels of government as clearly separated, or layered.

    (b) is incorrect because categorical and block grants relate to cooperative federalism, not dual federalism.

    (c) is incorrect because it describes concurrent powers, not dual federalism.

    (d) is incorrect because it is not a correct description of dual federalism.

(e) is incorrect because it is not a correct description of dual federalism.

Page reference: 85, AP Topic: Federalism

9.   The power of the national government to regulate interstate commerce was expanded in the landmark case of

(a) is incorrect because *Marbury v. Madison* established judicial review and did not deal with the power to regulate interstate commerce.

(b) is incorrect because *Plessy v. Ferguson* segregated public accommodations and did not deal with the power to regulate interstate commerce.

(c) is incorrect because *McCulloch v. Maryland* addressed whether the federal government could exercise powers not explicitly stated in the Constitution and did not deal with the power to regulate interstate commerce.

(d) is incorrect because *Miranda v. Arizona* dealt with rights of the accused and did not deal with the power to regulate interstate commerce.

(e) is correct because *Gibbons v. Ogden* had to do with expanding the national government's power to regulate interstate commerce.

Page reference: 82, AP Topic: Federalism

10.   The notion that when state and federal laws conflict, the national laws will prevail is the

(a) is incorrect because the necessary and proper clause does not deal with the supremacy of national law.

(b) is correct because the supremacy clause assures that states comply with guiding provisions of the national government. Where the Constitution is silent, states have a great deal of discretion in their decision making. But where there is a constitutional requirement, states cannot have laws that are at variance with the national requirement.

(c) is incorrect because the extradition clause does not deal with the supremacy of national law.

(d) is incorrect because the full faith and credit clause does not deal with the supremacy of national law.

(e) is incorrect because the privileges and immunities clause does not deal with the supremacy of national law.

Page reference: 78, AP Topics: Considerations that influenced the formulation and adoption of the Constitution, Federalism

11. The Founding Fathers had successfully rebelled against a unitary form of government. They had tried a confederation which was not working. Thus, they developed a _____ form of government.

(a) is incorrect because the Founding Fathers did not create a Constitutional Monarchy.

(b) is correct because the Founding Fathers created a Federal system of government in the Constitution.

(c) is incorrect because the Founding Fathers did not create a Socialist form of government.

(d) is incorrect because the Founding Fathers did not create a Fascist form of government.

(e) is incorrect because the question refers to the geographic division of government, not to the location of the sovereignty.

Page Reference: 75, AP Topics: Considerations that influenced the formulation and adoption of the Constitution, Federalism

12. The levels of government recognized specifically in the Constitution are

(a) is incorrect because the Constitution does not mention counties and regional governments.

(b) is incorrect because people are not a level of government.

(c) is incorrect because the Constitution does not mention cities.

(d) is correct because the Constitution creates a federal system of government which includes a national government and state governments.

(e) is incorrect because the Constitution does not mention local government.

Page Reference: 77, AP Topic: Federalism

13. Federalism as a form of government helps accommodate

(a) is correct because federalism, by providing for state governments, makes allowances for differences that occur across states.

(b) is incorrect because federalism best serves large geographic areas, not small.

(c) is incorrect because federalism does not guarantee a strong government.

(d) is incorrect because federalism does not guarantee uniform policies.

(e) is incorrect because federalism does not guarantee policies which do not change over time.

Page reference: 78, AP Topic: Federalism

14. National policies override states' policies when there is a conflict and the Constitution gives the national government power in that policy area. This is a statement of

(a) is incorrect because the due process clause does not deal with the supremacy of national power.

(b) is incorrect because the equal protection clause does not deal with the supremacy of national power.

(c) is incorrect because the privileges and immunity clause does not deal with the supremacy of national power.

(d) is correct because the supremacy clause is the correct term for the description provided in the question.

(e) is incorrect because the full faith and credit clause does not deal with the supremacy of national power.

Page reference: 78, AP Topics: Considerations that influenced the formulation and adoption of the Constitution, Federalism

15. A major basis for Congressional power is the implied powers it holds. The basis for these implied powers is

(a) is incorrect because federalism is a geographic arrangement, not the basis for the implied powers of Congress.

(b) is incorrect because the *Marbury v. Madison* case established judicial review, not implied powers.

(c) is incorrect because the Equal Protection Clause does not relate to the topic of implied powers.

(d) is incorrect because the fact that Congress was created first is not relevant to the topic of implied powers.

(e) is correct because the "Necessary and Proper" clause found in Article I, Section 8 of the Constitution provides the basis for the implied powers of Congress.

Page reference: 80, AP Topic: Federalism

16. The constitutional provision that makes same-sex marriage controversial is

(a) is incorrect because judicial review does not relate to relations between the states.

(b) is correct because full faith and credit is the provision of the Constitution which requires each state to recognize the public acts, records, and judicial proceedings of all other states, which includes marriages.

(c) is incorrect because privileges and immunities do not relate to the relations between the states.

(d) is incorrect because the due process clause does not relate to the relations between the states.

(e) is incorrect because unfunded mandates do not relate to the relations between the states.

Page reference: 83, AP Topic: Federalism

17.   Both the national and state governments can establish court systems. This is an example of

(a) is incorrect because reserved powers belong only to the states.

(b) is incorrect because mandates do not relate to spheres of powers of the national and state governments.

(c) is correct because concurrent powers are those powers which can be exercised by both the national government and the states, such as the power to establish court systems.

(d) is incorrect because full faith and credit does not relate to spheres of power of the national and state governments.

(e) is incorrect because fiscal federalism does not relate to spheres of powers of the national and state governments.

Page reference: 78, AP Topic: Federalism

18.   The Constitution provides for the power of extradition. Extradition is an example of

(a) is incorrect because the states' taxing power is a concurrent power and does not deal with relations between the states.

(b) is incorrect because grants-in-aid are an example of cooperative federalism and do not deal with relations between the states.

(c) is incorrect because formula grants are an example of cooperative federalism and do not deal with relations between the states.

(d) is correct because extradition is an example of a Constitutional power which deals with relations between the states.

(e) is incorrect because categorical grants are an example of cooperative federalism and do not deal with relations between the states.

Page reference: 83, AP Topics: Federalism, Linkages between policy procedures

19.   A power delegated to the national government is the power to

(a) is correct because delegated powers are those given to the national government by the Constitution, and regulating foreign and interstate commerce is an example of a delegated power.

(b) is incorrect because the power to police citizens is a concurrent power, exercised largely by the states.

(c) is incorrect because the power to establish educational systems is a reserved power of the states.

(d) is incorrect because the power to establish the drinking age is a reserved power of the states.

(e) is incorrect because the power to regulate marriage and divorce is a reserved power of the states.

Page reference: 82, AP Topic: Federalism

20.   An example of a concurrent power is

(a) is incorrect because declaring war is a delegated power of the national government.

(b) is incorrect because establishing educational systems is a reserved power of the states.

(c) is incorrect because establishing the drinking age is a reserved power of the states.

(d) is correct because concurrent powers are those which belong to both the national and state governments, and the power to tax is an example of a concurrent power.

(e) is incorrect because regulating marriage and divorce is a reserved power of the states.

Page reference: 78, AP Topic: Federalism

Free-Response Questions

This rubric provides examples of many, but not all of the possible correct responses to the free-response questions. Occasionally, there will be weaknesses pointed out in the suggested answer, providing students with examples of what to avoid.

1.   The Constitution designed a system in which various types of powers were assigned to different levels of government. Those types of powers are variously described as:

- enumerated powers
- reserved powers
- concurrent powers, and

- implied powers

Select three of the types of powers listed above.

a. Define each of the chosen types of powers.

b. Explain how each of the chosen types of powers affects the distribution of powers between national and state governments.

- The Constitution provides for several types of powers that are given to the federal government or kept away from it, including enumerated powers, reserved powers, concurrent powers, and implied powers. In this essay, I will discuss enumerated powers, concurrent powers, and implied powers. These are all powers that governments have.

- The enumerated powers are specific powers listed in the Constitution as given to the federal government. The reserved powers are powers reserved to the state governments. Implied powers are powers that are implied but not expressly discussed in the Constitution. The implied powers were given to the national government by the Supreme Court case of *McCulloch v. Maryland*. In this case, the state of Maryland tried to tell the Supreme Court that the national government couldn't do anything unless the Constitution specifically said that they could do it. But the Supreme Court took a loose interpretation of the Constitution and said that if the powers were "necessary and proper," the national government could use them. This allowed the national government to establish a national bank.

- The reason that these powers are important in politics these days is that Republicans think that state governments should have more powers while Democrats think that the national government should have more power. A narrow vision of implied powers will limit the federal government to only its enumerated powers and give states much more authority than just the reserved powers.

2. Cooperative federalism is a term often used to describe the complex fiscal relationship between the national and state governments. In your essay, do the following:

a. Define categorical grants and block grants, and describe the differences between them.

b. Identify an advantage and a disadvantage of categorical grants.

c. Identify an advantage and a disadvantage of block grants.

- In American politics, the priorities of government are set by the ways government spend money. A further issue concerns which level of government has the power to set those priorities by making decisions about how to spend money. These issues, where money is spent and which level of government makes decisions about where money is spent, form the basis for understanding the issues surrounding categorical and block grants.

- Categorical grants are grants from the national government to the state government for specific purposes and they have strings attached. In contrast, block grants are moneys given by the national government to the states for more general purposes. Usually, categorical grants give money to states to spend with almost no discretion— if the states agree to receive categorical grants they agree to spend the money in specific ways. With block grants, states will often have choices to make on how to spend money.

- One advantage of a categorical grant is that it allows the national government to have greater fiscal responsibility for the money that it collects. Members of Congress may feel that since they are ultimately responsible for the money collected from their constituents, they should exercise specific control over how that money is spent. For example, the Interstate Highway Act is a categorical grant. As a result, if states accept money under that act, Congress knows that it will be spent for building and maintaining the interstate highways. However, a disadvantage of categorical grants is that the states can be blackmailed by the national government. The Interstate Highway Act illustrates that as well. In order to receive that money, states must comply with all of the provisions of the grant. So, as a result, when the national government stipulated that in order to receive this grant, states would have to raise their drinking age to 21, all 50 states complied. So, although the national government does not have authority to raise the drinking age, it can make the states do that with categorical grant money.

- One advantage of block grants is that it allows the states, which are closer to the people, the ability to channel the use of that money to the specific needs of the state. Northern states might have needs that are different from Southern states, and urban states might have needs that are different than rural states. For example, if the national government wants to improve science and math education, needs might be different in a state like Texas, where many students speak Spanish, than in a state like Minnesota, where language barriers are not as big an issue. The disadvantage of block grants is that the national government does not have as much control over the money and states might "waste" the free money that the federal government gave them. That would mean that the national government was not a good steward of its money.

- In all, the politics of intergovernmental relations is fascinating and reflects partisan differences as well as policy preferences. Categorical and block grants illustrate those differences very well.

4

Civil Liberties and Public Policy

☐ Chapter Overview

This chapter explores the nature of civil liberties—those individual legal and constitutional protections against the government—afforded in the United States. We begin by exploring the specific protections afforded the people and trace the process by which these protections increasingly came to limit the powers of both the national and state governments. Next, we turn to examine the scope of specific rights, including freedoms of speech and religion, freedom of the press, the right to privacy, the protection of private property, the right to bear arms, and the rights of criminal defendants. We conclude by considering the way in which the civil liberties guaranteed under our Constitution and the Bill of Rights affect our democratic government in the United States. By the end of the chapter, students should understand the scope and nature of their rights under the U.S. Constitution and how these rights have evolved over time.

☐ Study Outline

 Learning Objective 4.1: Trace the process by which the Bill of Rights has been applied to the states. (p. 107)

The Bill of Rights

- The Bill of Rights protects freedoms at a national level, but these freedoms were not necessarily guaranteed in some state constitutions.

- The **First Amendment** established the four great liberties of freedom of the press, of speech, of religion, and assembly.

- In the case of *Barron v. Baltimore* (1833), the Supreme Court ruled that the Bill of Rights did not protect individuals against state governments.

- In *Gitlow v. New York* (1925), the Court reversed its earlier decision, citing the due process clause of the **Fourteenth Amendment** as reason to protect individuals' free speech and free press rights, found in the **First Amendment**, against state government incursions.

- *Gitlow* began a tradition called the selective **incorporation doctrine**, by which the Supreme Court has gradually, on a case-by-case basis, ensured the protection of most freedoms listed in the Bill of Rights from state infringement by means of the due process clause of the Fourteenth Amendment.

 Learning Objective 4.2: Distinguish the two types of religious rights protected by the First Amendment and determine the boundaries of those rights. (p. 109)

Freedom of Religion

- **Establishment Clause:** In the First Amendment, prohibiting Congress from making laws establishing any religion in conjunction with the government.
  - Some critics interpret the clause loosely: The government should not favor one religion over another in its policies. Others, including Thomas Jefferson, argue that the establishment clause endorses the **separation of church and state**.
  - The establishment clause is at the center of the debate over prayer in school and over federal funding to private religious schools.
  - *Lemon v. Kurtzman* (1971): The Supreme Court allowed federal funding of parochial schools, provided that the money neither advances nor inhibits religious teaching, but instead is used for administrative purposes. In 2002, the Supreme Court also permitted state vouchers to be used for parochial schools in *Zelman v. Simmons-Harris*.
  - *Engel v. Vitale* (1962) and *School District of Abington Township, Pennsylvania v. Schempp* (1963): Forbade the practice of prayer in school as a

violation of the establishment clause and a breaching of the separation of church and state.

- ❑ Federal funds may be used to construct school buildings and to provide administrative and academic supplies, but not to endorse religious teaching.

- ❑ Student religious groups cannot be denied access to school buildings for the purpose of meeting or worship if other groups are also allowed access.

- **Free Exercise Clause:** A First Amendment right that guarantees the freedom to practice or not practice any religion.

  - ❑ The Court has upheld that the government cannot infringe on people's beliefs, but it can regulate religious behavior to some degree.

  - ❑ State laws can ban religious practices that conflict with other laws, but they cannot forbid religious worship itself.

 Learning Objective 4.3: Differentiate the rights of free expression protected by the First Amendment and determine the boundaries of those rights. (p. 116)

Freedom of Expression

Speech

- Courts grapple with the definition of "speech." Political protests and picketing are protected by the First Amendment, but **libel**, **slander**, and **obscenity** are not.

- Fraud and incitement to violence are considered action, not speech, and are not protected.

- The Constitution forbids **prior restraint**, or government censorship of the press. This policy was strengthened by the case of *Near v. Minnesota* (1931), in which the Court ruled in favor of the press.

- Prior restraint is granted in situations where **national security** might be compromised.

- As decided in *Schenck v. United States* (1919), freedom of speech may be curtailed when it threatens **public order**.

- Acts of symbolic speech, such as protesting and flag burning (*Texas v. Johnson*, 1989), are protected under the First Amendment.

- **Commercial speech**, such as advertising, is more closely regulated by the **Federal Trade Commission**.

- Commercial speech on radio and television is regulated by the **Federal Communications Commission**.

- The broadcast media have significantly less freedom than do print media (*Red Lion Broadcasting Company v. Federal Communications Commission*, 1969), though they are not required to print replies from candidates they have criticized (*Miami Herald Publishing Company v. Tornillo*, 1974).

The Press

- Freedom of the press can conflict with the **right to a fair trial**, but the press does have a right to report on any criminal proceeding, and all trials must be open to the public.

- However, in *Branzburg v. Hayes* (1972), the Supreme Court ruled in favor of fair trial over a reporter's right to protect sources, and in *Zucher v. Stanford* (1978) the Court sided with the police over the press.

- *Roth v. United States* (1957): The Court asserted that obscenity is not protected under the First Amendment. However, the definition of "obscenity" continues to be a point of controversy.

- *Miller v. California* (1973): Allowed community standards, varying in different parts of the country, to be used in determining if material is obscene.

- Cases of libel are usually difficult to win because public figures must prove that the insults were intentionally malicious, as mandated in *New York Times v. Sullivan* (1964).

Learning Objective 4.4: Describe the rights to assemble and associate protected by the First Amendment and their limitations. (p. 126)

Freedom of Assembly

- **Freedom of assembly** includes, first, the right to protest, picket, or hold a demonstration within reasonable limits called "time, place, and manner restrictions" and with virtually no limitations on the content of a group's message.

- In *NAACP v. Alabama* (1958), the Supreme Court held that the right to establish groups of people with similar political interests, from political parties to the Ku Klux Klan, was also protected under as freedom of assembly.

 ## Learning Objective 4.5: Describe the right to bear arms protected by the Second Amendment and its limitations. (p. 128)

Right to Bear Arms

- The right to keep and bear arms is protected by the Second Amendment, but it has rarely been the subject of Supreme Court review.
- States have generally had wide latitude in restricting firearms as the Second Amendment has not been incorporated.
- In *District of Columbia v. Heller* (2008), however, the Supreme Court ruled that the Second Amendment did protect an individual's right to possess a firearm unconnected with service in a militia, and to use that firearm for traditionally lawful purposes, such as self-defense within the home.
- This was extended to state and local laws (Washington, D.C. is governed by Congress and is not a state) in *McDonald v. Chicago* (2010).

 ## Learning Objective 4.6: Characterize defendants' rights and identify issues that arise in their implementation. (p. 130)

Defendants' Rights

- As with free speech, the courts must continually interpret the vague language of the Constitution to apply it to today's issues and events.
- **Searches and seizures:** The **Fourth Amendment** protects citizens from **unreasonable searches and seizures**.
  - Police investigators cannot search private property without a **search warrant** issued by a court unless there is reason to believe that the evidence will disappear or be destroyed or removed in the meantime.

- The police cannot arrest someone unless there is **probable cause** to believe that he or she is guilty.

- The **exclusionary rule** prevents prosecutors from using evidence acquired through unreasonable search and seizure. *Mapp v. Ohio* (1961) extended the exclusionary rule to state as well as federal cases.

- In recent years, the Supreme Court has made exceptions to the exclusionary rule; for example, when police are thought to have acted in "good faith," even if their actions technically violate the rule, the Court has allowed use of the evidence seized.

- The **U.S.A. Patriot Act** (2001) and the 2008 revisions to the **Foreign Intelligence Surveillance Act** that followed revelations about warrantless eavesdropping by federal agencies expanded the government's right to investigate terrorism suspects without warrants.

- **Self-incrimination:** The **Fifth Amendment** protects people from being forced to supply evidence against themselves.

  - Because a person is innocent until proven guilty, the prosecution is responsible for proving a defendant's guilt.

  - *Miranda v. Arizona* (1966): Established that suspects must be informed of their constitutional rights before they are questioned by the police.

- **Right to counsel:** The **Sixth Amendment** guarantees that all accused persons tried in a federal court have the right to be represented by an attorney.

  - *Gideon v. Wainwright* (1963): Extends this privilege to cases tried in state courts as well.

  - Most cases are settled by **plea bargaining** between lawyers instead of by a trial.

  - The Sixth Amendment requires a trial by a jury of 12 people in federal cases; in state cases this number may be fewer, and a conviction does not require a unanimous vote.

- **Cruel and unusual punishment** is prohibited by the **Eighth Amendment**, though the term is not clearly defined in the Bill of Rights.

  - In *Gregg v. Georgia* (1976) and *McCleskey v. Kemp* (1987), the Supreme Court confirmed that the death penalty does not violate the Bill of Rights—that is, it is not considered "cruel and unusual."

- The Supreme Court has, however, placed an increasing number of restrictions on who can be executed, such as the mentally ill (*Ford v. Wainwright*, 1986), mentally retarded persons (*Atkins v. Virginia*, 2002), those under the age of 18 when they committed their crimes (*Roper v. Simmons*, 2005), and those who committed individual crimes where the victim's life was not taken (*Kennedy v. Louisiana*, 2008).

- The Court has also required that a jury, not just a judge, find an aggravating circumstance necessary for imposition of the death penalty (*Ring v. Arizona*, 2002) and that lawyers for defendants in death penalty cases make reasonable efforts to fight for their clients at a trial's sentencing phase (*Rompilla v. Beard*, 2005).

- Debate over the death penalty continues. DNA tests sometimes prove the innocence of inmates on death row, leading some states to declare moratoria on executions. The number of executions has generally been declining.

 Learning Objective 4.7: Outline the evolution of a right to privacy and its application to the issue of abortion. (p. 143)

Right to Privacy

- The right to privacy is not specifically guaranteed by the Bill of Rights, but the Supreme Court has interpreted the first ten amendments to imply this right.

  - *Griswold v. Connecticut* (1965) asserted the right to privacy, which became more controversial when the principle was applied, in *Roe v. Wade* (1973), to forbid states from controlling abortions during the first trimester of pregnancy.

  - *Webster v. Reproductive Health Services* (1989): The Supreme Court upheld a Missouri law that prevented the use of state funds for abortion clinics and that prohibited state employees from performing abortions.

  - The Supreme Court, while allowing abortions, has increasingly permitted regulation of them (*Planned Parenthood v. Casey*, 1992).

  - Medical technology also causes debate over the right to privacy in cases of surrogate parenthood and physician-assisted suicide.

4.8 Learning Objective 4.8: Assess how civil liberties affect democratic government and how they both limit and expand the scope of government. (p. 145)

Understanding Civil Liberties

- When any of the Bill of Rights, including defendants' rights, conflicts with majority rule, rights prevail.

- Civil liberties limit the scope of government action, yet substantial government effort may be necessary to protect the exercise of those rights.

For Additional Review

Make a three-column table. In the first column, write all of the civil liberties discussed in this chapter. In the second column, list all Supreme Court cases that have addressed each liberty, including the date, the chief justice, and brief synopsis of the case. In the third column, list the corresponding amendment or any previous court cases on which the Supreme Court based its decisions about each civil liberty. Use this chart when studying and reviewing the information for the unit test.

Make a chart describing the paradox about civil liberties and the scope of government. In one column, list the ways that civil liberties expand the scope of government. In the other column, list the ways that civil liberties limit the scope of government. Be sure to include specific examples of both. Use this chart when studying and reviewing the information for the unit test.

☐ Review Questions

Multiple-Choice Questions

1.   *Roe v. Wade* (1973) ruled that a woman's right to an abortion came from the
      a.   right of symbolic speech.
      b.   right of the people to "be secure in their persons, houses, papers, and effects."
      c.   "right to remain silent."
      d.   due process of law.
      e.   right to privacy.

2. In *Engel v. Vitale* (1962), the Supreme Court ruled that
   a. the reciting of a state-required prayer in public school constituted an impermissible establishment of religion under the First Amendment.
   b. the Gideon Society could distribute Bibles in public schools under the free exercise clause of the First Amendment.
   c. the eminent domain clause of the Fifth Amendment prevents government from taking religious property for public purposes.
   d. public school children may wear crosses as necklaces as a permissible mode of symbolic speech under the First Amendment.
   e. the Second Amendment "right to bear arms" does not apply in religious facilities.

3. The "exclusionary rule" means
   a. the Senate has removed a member from voting membership because of a violation of ethics rules.
   b. the House Rules Committee has refused to schedule a debate on a bill.
   c. the bureaucracy has failed to enforce unpopular legislation.
   d. the president has decided to "impound" some programmatic money appropriated by Congress.
   e. evidence gathered in violation of the Fourth Amendment has not been allowed to be introduced during a trial.

4. Which of the following cases made decisions regarding the establishment of religion?

   I. *Mapp v. Ohio* (1965)
   II. *Texas v. Johnson* (1989)
   III. *School District of Abington Township, Pennsylvania v. Schempp* (1963)
   IV. *Lemon v. Kurtzman* (1973)

   a. I and II
   b. II and III
   c. III and IV
   d. I and III
   e. II and IV

5. Which of the following forms of expression is protected by the First Amendment?
   a. obscenity
   b. libel
   c. fighting words
   d. symbolic speech
   e. slander

6. Which of the following rights is protected by the Fifth Amendment?
   a. the right of privacy
   b. protection against self-incrimination
   c. the right to bear arms
   d. the right to counsel
   e. the right to a speedy and public trial

7. The Bill of Rights begins with the words "Congress shall make no law. . ." telling the reader that the Bill of Rights is intended to protect citizens only from the national government. Yet, most of the provisions of the Bill of Rights now limit the states as well. Which of the following provisions is most relevant in explaining that change?
   a. equal protection clause of the Fourteenth Amendment
   b. double jeopardy clause of the Fifth Amendment
   c. rights "retained by the people" in the Ninth Amendment
   d. grand jury indictment provision in the Fifth Amendment
   e. due process clause of the Fourteenth Amendment

8. The right of citizens to be made aware of their constitutional guarantees against self-incrimination and to be represented by counsel was established in
   a. *Gitlow v. New York* (1925).
   b. *Mapp v. Ohio* (1965).
   c. *Miranda v. Arizona* (1966).
   d. *Gideon v. Wainwright* (1963).
   e. *Lemon v. Kurtzman* (1971).

9. All of the following concepts are guaranteed to a citizen accused of a crime EXCEPT
   a. a speedy and public trial by an impartial jury.
   b. security against unreasonable search and seizures.
   c. protection from capital punishment.
   d. a citizen will not be put in jeopardy of life or limb twice for the same offense.
   e. having the assistance of counsel.

10. The right of government to keep a newspaper from publishing information that would be harmful to the reputation of politicians who led a military conflict
    a. would be denied as "prior restraint."
    b. would be allowed under the "no quartering of soldiers" provision of the 3rd Amendment.
    c. would be denied as entailing a "clear and present danger."
    d. would be allowed as denying "seditious speech."
    e. would be allowed under the U.S.A. Patriot Act.

11. Which of the following provisions is most relevant in explaining the incorporation of the Bill of Rights against the states?
    a. the equal protection clause of the Fourteenth Amendment
    b. the double jeopardy clause of the Fifth Amendment
    c. the rights "retained by the people" in the Ninth Amendment
    d. the grand jury indictment provision in the Fifth Amendment
    e. the due process clause of the Fourteenth Amendment

12. The Supreme Court, in 1925, ruled that the First Amendment applied to the states in
    a. *New York Times Co. v. Sullivan.*
    b. *Miranda v. Arizona.*
    c. *Benton v. Maryland.*
    d. *Roth v. United States.*
    e. *Gitlow v. New York.*

13. The Supreme Court case that dealt with the publication of the "Pentagon Papers" was
    a. *Gitlow v. New York.*
    b. *New York Times v. The United States.*
    c. *Schenck v. U.S.*
    d. *Miranda v. Arizona.*
    e. *Gideon v. Wainwright.*

14. Select the following statement that is true.
    a. It is very difficult to identify opinions about abortion in polls.
    b. Since *Roe v. Wade*, public opinion on abortion has not changed dramatically.
    c. A much higher percentage of Americans oppose the decision in *Roe v. Wade* now than when it was rendered.
    d. Since the decision, public opinion has changed dramatically; a much higher percentage of Americans now support the decision.
    e. Since *Roe v. Wade*, public opinion on abortion has changed dramatically.

15. Cruel and unusual punishment and excessive bail and fine are forbidden by which Amendment?
    a. First Amendment
    b. Eighth Amendment
    c. Sixth Amendment
    d. Eleventh Amendment
    e. Fourth Amendment

16. Which Supreme Court case, in 1973, in an attempt to redefine obscenity, ruled that local standards might affect the assessment of obscenity?
    a. *Roe v. Wade*
    b. *Miller v. California*
    c. *Lemon v. Kurtzman*
    d. *Roth v. United States*
    e. *Barron v. Baltimore*

17. Civil liberties, the personal guarantees and freedoms that the government cannot abridge by law
    a. are not absolute and must be balanced against other considerations.
    b. are all guaranteed by state constitutions.
    c. are also known as civil rights.
    d. are in the core of the original Constitution.
    e. are absolute.

18. A false written statement that defames the character and reputation of an individual is known as
    a. symbolic speech.
    b. libel.
    c. hate speech.
    d. obscenity.
    e. Both libel and slander are written attacks on a person's character and reputation.

19. The "Right to Privacy" is
    a. in Amendment I of the Constitution.
    b. in Article I of the Constitution.
    c. in Amendment V of the Constitution.
    d. not specifically mentioned in the Constitution.
    e. left to the states to define.

20. The individual right considered to be the most fundamental of all of the rights in the Bill of Rights is
    a. freedom of religion.
    b. right to an attorney.
    c. right to bear arms.
    d. freedom of expression.
    e. freedom from cruel and unusual punishment.

Free-Response Questions

1. The U.S.A. Patriot Act was passed after the terrorist attacks of September 11, 2001.

   a. Describe the U.S.A. Patriot Act.

   b. Identify and describe a provision in the Bill of Rights affected by the U.S.A. Patriot Act.

   c. Describe how the U.S.A. Patriot Act might limit the application of the provision in the Bill of Rights identified in b.

2. Under the Constitution, the Supreme Court has the right of judicial review.

   a. Define judicial review.

   b. Describe the application of judicial review to the decisions in two of the following cases:

      - *Brown v. Board of Education* (1954)

      - *Engel v. Vitale* (1962)

      - *Texas v. Johnson* (1989)

      - *Roe v. Wade* (1973)

   c. Explain how each selected decision could be seen as an "activist" decision.

◻ Answers and Explanations

Multiple-Choice Questions

1. *Roe v. Wade* (1973) ruled that a woman's right to an abortion came from the

    (a) is incorrect because symbolic speech was not addressed in *Roe*.

    (b) is incorrect because the right to security of persons, houses, papers and effects was not addressed in *Roe*.

    (c) is incorrect because the right to remain silent was not addressed in *Roe*.

    (d) is incorrect because due process was not addressed in *Roe*.

    (e) is correct because in *Roe v. Wade*, the Supreme Court extended the right to privacy to include a right to abortion.

    Page reference: 143, AP Topic: The development of civil liberties and civil rights by judicial interpretation

2. In *Engel v. Vitale* (1962), the Supreme Court ruled that

    (a) is correct because the *Engel* decision was based on the establishment clause of the Constitution.

    (b) is incorrect because the *Engel* case does not relate to Gideon Bibles.

    (c) is incorrect because the *Engel* case does not relate to eminent domain.

    (d) is incorrect because the *Engel* case does not relate to symbolic speech.

    (e) is incorrect because the *Engel* case does not relate to the right to bear arms.

    Page reference: 112, AP Topic: The development of civil liberties and civil rights by judicial interpretation

3. The "exclusionary rule" means

    (a) is incorrect because the exclusionary rule does not relate to procedures of the Senate.

    (b) is incorrect because the exclusionary rule does not relate to procedures of the House.

    (c) is incorrect because the exclusionary rule does not relate to procedures of the bureaucracy.

    (d) is incorrect because the exclusionary rule does not relate to the procedures of the executive branch.

(e) is correct because the exclusionary rule prohibits police from using illegally seized evidence at trial.

Page reference: 132, AP Topic: Knowledge of substantive rights and liberties

4.   Which of the following cases made decisions regarding the establishment of religion?

(a) is incorrect because I has nothing to do with religious liberty.

(b) is incorrect because II and III have nothing to do with religious liberty.

(c) is correct because the *Lemon* decision dealt with defining the boundaries of excessive entanglement between church and state.

(d) is incorrect because I and III have nothing to do with religious liberty.

(e) is incorrect because II has nothing to do with religious liberty.

Page reference: 111, AP Topic: The development of civil liberties and civil rights by judicial interpretation

5.   Which of the following forms of expression is protected by the First Amendment?

(a) is incorrect because obscenity has been ruled not to be protected under the First Amendment.

(b) is incorrect because libel has been ruled not to be protected under the First Amendment.

(c) is incorrect because fighting words have been ruled not to be protected under the First Amendment.

(d) is correct because freedom of speech is subject to almost no limits regarding symbolic acts like flag burning.

(e) is incorrect because slander has been ruled not to be protected under the First Amendment.

Page reference: 116–117, AP Topic: Knowledge of substantive rights and liberties

6.   Which of the following rights is protected by the Fifth Amendment?

(a) is incorrect because the right to privacy is covered by other amendments.

(b) is correct because the most famous provision of the Fifth Amendment is that no one is required to provide testimony against himself or herself in court.

(c) is incorrect because the right to bear arms is protected by the 2nd Amendment.

(d) is incorrect because the right to counsel is protected by the 6th Amendment.

(e) is incorrect because the right to a speedy and public trial is protected by the 6th Amendment.

Page reference: 134–135, AP Topic: Knowledge of substantive rights

7. The Bill of Rights begins with the words "Congress shall make no law. . ." telling the reader that the Bill of Rights is intended to protect citizens only from the national government. Yet, most of the provisions of the Bill of Rights now limit the states as well. Which of the following provisions is most relevant in explaining that change?

(a) is incorrect because the equal protection clause does not apply.

(b) is incorrect because the double jeopardy clause does not apply.

(c) is incorrect because the 9th Amendment does not apply.

(d) is incorrect because the 5th Amendment does not apply.

(e) is correct because the Bill of Rights has largely been incorporated by the states through the due process clause of the Fourteenth Amendment; that amendment, adopted after the Civil War, has been ruled to make states comply with provisions of the national constitution.

Page reference: 107, AP Topic: The impact of the Fourteenth Amendment on the constitutional development of right and liberties

8. The right of citizens to be made aware of their constitutional guarantees against self-incrimination and to be represented by counsel was established in

(a) is incorrect because the *Gitlow* case does not relate to this topic.

(b) is incorrect because the *Mapp* case does not relate to this topic.

(c) is correct because *Miranda v. Arizona* extended the rights of the accused to those who did not know the Constitution. In that case, the Supreme Court said that knowing that the rights existed was as fundamental as having the rights.

(d) is incorrect because the *Gideon* case does not relate to this topic.

(e) is incorrect because the *Lemon* case does not relate to this topic.

Page reference: 130–139, AP Topic: Knowledge of substantive rights and liberties

9. All of the following concepts are guaranteed to a citizen accused of a crime EXCEPT

(a) is incorrect because a speedy and public trial is protected by the Bill of Rights.

(b) is incorrect because protection from unreasonable search and seizure is forbidden by the Bill of Rights.

(c) is correct because capital punishment has never been ruled to violate the cruel and unusual provision of the Eighth Amendment.

(d) is incorrect because double jeopardy is forbidden by the Bill of Rights.

(e) is incorrect because right to counsel is protected by the Bill of Rights.

Page reference: 139, AP Topic: Knowledge of substantive rights and liberties

10.　　The right of government to keep a newspaper from publishing information that would be harmful to the reputation of politicians who led a military conflict

(a) is correct because under the First Amendment, banning of prior restraint of publication is a very strong rule.

(b) is incorrect because the topic does not relate to the 3rd Amendment.

(c) is incorrect because the topic does not relate to "clear and present danger."

(d) is incorrect because the topic does not relate to "seditious speech."

(e) is incorrect because the topic does not relate to the Patriot Act.

Page reference: 117, AP Topic: Knowledge of substantive rights and liberties

11.　　Which of the following provisions is most relevant in explaining the incorporation of the Bill of Rights against the states?

(a) is incorrect because 1781 is when the Articles of Confederation were enacted.

(b) is incorrect because 1776 is when the Declaration of Independence was written.

(c) is correct because the Bill of Rights was ratified and added to the Constitution in 1789.

(d) is incorrect because 1789 is when the Constitution was enacted.

(e) is incorrect because 1787 is when the Constitution was written.

Page reference: 108, AP Topic: Knowledge of substantive rights and liberties

12.　　The Supreme Court, in 1925, ruled that the First Amendment applied to the states in

(a) is incorrect because the *New York Times* case is a 1963 case involving the 1st Amendment.

(b) is incorrect because the *Miranda* case relates to the rights of the accused.

(c) is incorrect because the *Benton* case relates to double jeopardy.

(d) is incorrect because the *Roth* case relates to obscenity.

(e) is correct because the *Gitlow* case incorporated the speech provision of the 1st Amendment in 1925.

Page reference: 109, AP Topic: The development of civil liberties and civil rights by judicial interpretation

13.   The Supreme Court case that dealt with the publication of the "Pentagon Papers" was

(a) is incorrect because *Gitlow* did not relate to the Pentagon Papers.

(b) is correct because *New York Times v. The United States* ruled that the "no prior restraint" rule prohibited prosecution before the papers were published.

(c) is incorrect because *Schenck* did not relate to the Pentagon Papers.

(d) is incorrect because *Miranda* did not relate to the Pentagon Papers.

(e) is incorrect because *Gideon* did not relate to the Pentagon Papers.

Page reference: 118–119, AP Topic: The development of civil liberties and civil rights by judicial interpretation

14.   Select the following statement that is true.

(a) is incorrect because it is an inaccurate description of the opinions concerning abortion.

(b) is correct because the *Roe* decision, even though making abortion legal, did not significantly change attitudes toward abortion.

(c) is incorrect because it is an inaccurate description of the opinions concerning abortion.

(d) is incorrect because it is an inaccurate description of the opinions concerning abortion.

(e) is incorrect because it is an inaccurate description of the opinions concerning abortion.

Page reference: 143, AP Topic: The development of civil liberties and civil rights by judicial interpretation

15.   Cruel and unusual punishment and excessive bail and fine are forbidden by which Amendment?

(a) is incorrect because the 1st Amendment protects religion, speech, press, and assembly.

(b) is correct because the 8th Amendment prohibits cruel and unusual punishment and excessive bail and fine.

(c) is incorrect because the 6th Amendment protects rights of the accused.

(d) is incorrect because the 11th Amendment deals with each state's sovereign immunity.

(e) is incorrect because the 4th Amendment deals with search and seizure.

Page reference: 139, AP Topic: Knowledge of substantive rights and liberties

16. Which Supreme Court case, in 1973, in an attempt to redefine obscenity, ruled that local standards might affect the assessment of obscenity?

(a) is incorrect because *Roe* deals with the right to an abortion.

(b) is correct because the *Miller* case stated that obscenity must be defined by "contemporary community standards."

(c) is incorrect because the *Lemon* case deals with freedom of religion.

(d) is incorrect because the *Roth* case deals with obscenity but was in 1957.

(e) is incorrect because the *Barron* case deals with application of the Bill of Rights to the national government.

Page reference: 119, AP Topic: The development of civil liberties and civil rights by judicial interpretation

17. Civil liberties, the personal guarantees and freedoms that the government cannot abridge by law

(a) is correct because even though civil liberties are personal freedoms that cannot be abridged by the government, they are subject to boundaries.

(b) is incorrect because civil liberties are not guaranteed by state constitutions.

(c) is incorrect because civil liberties and civil rights are different.

(d) is incorrect because civil liberties are found in the Bill of Rights.

(e) is incorrect because the rights are subject to boundaries.

Page reference: 145–146, AP Topic: Knowledge of substantive rights and liberties

18. A false written statement that defames the character and reputation of an individual is known as

(a) is incorrect because symbolic speech is not defamatory and is protected by the Constitution.

(b) is correct because libel is speech that defames a person's character and reputation which is put in writing and is not protected by the Constitution.

(c) is incorrect because hate speech is speech that belittles a person or group on the basis of characteristics.

(d) is incorrect because obscenity offends the prevalent morality of the time, but does not defame character or reputation.

(e) is incorrect because slander is a spoken defamation of character.

Page reference: 118–126, AP Topic: Knowledge of substantive rights and liberties

19. The "Right to Privacy" is

(a) is incorrect because Amendment I does not specifically address privacy.

(b) is incorrect because Article I does not address privacy.

(c) is incorrect because Amendment V does not specifically address privacy.

(d) is correct because the "right to privacy" is not specifically mentioned in the Constitution but was established through judicial interpretation of the Constitution.

(e) is incorrect because definition of the right to privacy is determined by the Supreme Court, not the states.

Page reference: 143, AP Topic: The development of civil liberties and civil rights by judicial interpretation

20. The individual right considered to be the most fundamental of all of the rights in the Bill of Rights is

(a) is incorrect because the freedom of religion, though important, is not considered as important as expression.

(b) is incorrect because the right to an attorney, though important, is not considered as important as expression.

(c) is incorrect because the right to bear arms, though important, is not considered as important as expression.

(d) is correct because the freedom of expression, which includes press and speech, was considered by the founders to be absolutely necessary for the establishment of a democracy.

(e) is incorrect because the freedom from cruel and unusual punishment, though important, is not considered as important as expression.

Page reference: 116–124, AP Topic: Knowledge of substantive rights and liberties

Free-Response Questions

This rubric provides examples of many, but not all of the possible correct responses to the free-response questions. Occasionally, weaknesses will be pointed out in the suggested answer, providing students with examples of what to avoid.

1. The U.S.A. Patriot Act was passed after the terrorist attacks of September 11, 2001.

    a. Describe the U.S.A. Patriot Act.

        ▪ In the aftermath of the terrorist attacks on the World Trade Center on September 11, 2001, Congress passed a law called the U.S.A. Patriot Act that was designed to give law enforcement agencies more power to investigate and arrest terrorists. Congress thought that under the crisis circumstances that existed, it was reasonable to give those expanded investigation powers even if it meant that some of the protections of the Fourth Amendment would be compromised. The significance of the Patriot Act was that civil libertarians thought that it provided a dangerous compromise for average citizens who might be investigated.

    b. Identify and describe a provision in the Bill of Rights affected by the U.S.A. Patriot Act.

        ▪ The Fourth Amendment requires that if people are to be investigated, it must be with a valid search warrant signed by a judge and based upon probable cause. This amendment was meant to keep people safe from investigations and is based on the idea that people are innocent until proven guilty.

    c. Describe how the U.S.A. Patriot Act might limit the application of the provision in the Bill of Rights identified in b.

        ▪ Some people believe that the Patriot Act compromises the Fourth Amendment too much. Critics of the act fear that it will infringe upon some of citizens' basic rights of privacy. It is easier for the government to gather information about what a person is doing without a warrant as is most often required under the Fourth Amendment.

2. Under the Constitution, the Supreme Court has the right of judicial review.

    a. Define judicial review.

        ▪ Judicial review was established in the Supreme Court case of *Marbury v. Madison* early in our nation's history. In that case, the Court ruled that the Supreme Court should have the power to make sure that laws and executive actions conformed to the Constitution.

b. Describe the application of judicial review to the decisions in two of the following cases:

- *Brown v. Board of Education* (1954)
- *Engel v. Vitale* (1962)
- *Texas v. Johnson* (1989)
- *Roe v. Wade* (1973)

- In the case of *Engel v. Vitale*, the state of New York had written a law that required school children to recite a prayer at the beginning of each school day. The Supreme Court used the Engel decision to declare that law unconstitutional, as a violation of the establishment clause of the First Amendment.

- In *Texas v. Johnson*, the court ruled that as an act of political speech, burning an American flag is an allowable form of symbolic speech. This overturned a Texas state law prohibiting flag burning, making it an example of judicial review.

c. Explain how each selected decision could be seen as an "activist" decision.

- These decisions were seen as activist decisions because the Court didn't just stick to the words of the Bill of Rights. It found that there was a right that was not mentioned in so many words. This was seen as an activist decision.

5

Civil Rights and Public Policy

☐ Chapter Overview

Civil rights refer to the central rights necessary to ensure full participation in the political and civil life of a society. In this chapter, we explore the development of civil rights in the United States. We begin by considering the uneven development of civil rights in the nineteenth century, focusing in particular on the initial expansion of civil rights under the Civil War Amendments, and their gradual erosion in practice through discriminatory state laws and Supreme Court decisions. We then examine developments in the twentieth century that led to an expansion of civil rights protections afforded to a diverse array of groups in the United States. We conclude by considering the ways in which civil rights policy affects democracy and increases the scope of government. By the end of the chapter, students should have a solid understanding of the historical development and current status of civil rights as a public policy issue in the United States.

☐ Study Outline

 Learning Objective 5.1: Differentiate the Supreme Court's three standards of review for classifying people under the equal protection clause. (p. 155)

The Constitution and Inequality

- The original Constitution did not mention equality, and under most state constitutions only white males were allowed privileges such as voting rights. The Fourteenth Amendment first clarified the concept of equality by ensuring that all citizens must receive "equal protection of the laws."

- The Supreme Court's modern interpretation of equality has brought civil rights to the forefront of the political agenda.

- The courts have identified three **standards of review** for determining whether an inequality in public policy is impermissible.

- Race and ethnic classifications are inherently suspect and therefore subject to "strict scrutiny": They are presumed unconstitutional unless they serve a compelling public interest and are the least restrictive means of accomplishing that interest.

- Gender classifications are subject to "intermediate scrutiny," meaning that they must bear a substantial relationship to an important governmental purpose.

- In all other cases, a classification must simply bear a rational relationship to some legitimate governmental purpose (called the "reasonableness" or "rational basis" standard) and are presumed constitutional until proven otherwise.

 Learning Objective 5.2: Trace the evolution of protections of the rights of African Americans and explain the application of nondiscrimination principles of issues of race. (p. 158)

African Americans' Civil Rights

Slavery and Segregation

- *Dred Scott v. Sanford* (1857) upheld the constitutionality of slavery and forbade Congress from banning it in new states.

- The **Thirteenth Amendment** (1865) outlawed slavery after the Civil War.
- The **Fourteenth Amendment** (1868) extended rights of citizenship to former slaves.
- With the **Fifteenth Amendment** (1870) guaranteeing the ability to vote, many African Americans were elected to government posts.
- In the 1876 election, a deadlock in the Electoral College led to a deal that allowed the Republican candidate, Rutherford B. Hayes, to be selected by a commission created by the House of Representatives, in exchange for the promise to withdraw federal troops from the southern states.
- Civil rights advances came to a halt and Jim Crow laws took effect segregating blacks from whites in the South, and preventing blacks from voting and running for public office.
- The Supreme Court officially recognized a policy of "separate but equal" facilities, thereby allowing the practice of segregation, in *Plessy v. Ferguson* (1896).

Equal Education and the Civil Rights Movement

- *Brown v. Board of Education* (1954) overturned the *Plessy* decision—asserting that segregation is unconstitutional—and ordered the desegregation of public schools.
- Brown was the beginning of a string of Supreme Court decisions holding various forms of discrimination unconstitutional.
- Brown and these other cases gave the civil rights movement momentum that would grow in the years that followed.
- Congress also passed the **Civil Rights Act** (1964) which
    - outlawed racial discrimination in public places,
    - prohibited discrimination in employment,
    - withheld government funding from any school or institution that practiced discrimination,
    - established the Equal Employment Opportunity Commission to monitor job discrimination, and granted the Justice Department power to enforce civil rights laws by suing institutions still practicing segregation.

- *Swann v. Charlotte-Mecklenberg County Schools* (1971): The Supreme Court allowed busing to be used as a means to balance racial percentages in schools, which became a matter of great national controversy.

Voting Rights

- The **Fifteenth Amendment** (1870) formally granted African Americans **suffrage**—the right to vote—but had little effect in practice.
- Southern states circumvented the law by instituting **literacy tests** that most former slaves could not pass.
- **Poll taxes** were implemented and most former slaves could not afford to pay.
- **Grandfather clauses** were implemented to exempt from literacy tests illiterate whites whose grandfathers had been allowed to vote before 1860.
- **White primaries** were implemented that restricted voting in Democratic Party elections (the only ones that mattered given Democratic dominance in the South) to whites.
- Most of these were struck down in the early 20th century.
- Grandfather clauses were found unconstitutional in *Guinn v. United States* (1915).
- The Supreme Court outlawed the use of **white primaries** to exclude African Americans from the election process in *Smith v. Allwright* (1944).
- The **Twenty-Fourth Amendment** (1964) outlawed the use of poll taxes.
- Congress passed the **Voting Rights Act** in 1965 to prevent states from using any methods to disenfranchise voters.
- The law provided for enforcement by allowing federal registrars to oversee elections and voter registration; therefore only with the Voting Rights Act did the Fifteenth Amendment's guarantee of suffrage without regard to race become meaningful in practice.

Other Minority Groups

- Other minority groups, including Native Americans, Hispanic Americans, and Asian Americans, have all suffered discrimination and benefited from advances made in the civil rights movement. The Civil Rights Act applies to all races and has encouraged many minority groups to speak out for their rights.

- **Native Americans** were isolated on "reservations" until the **Dawes Act of 1887** and they were given the right to vote only in 1924.

- Beginning in 1970, they have used courts to pursue equal rights, largely through the Native Americans Rights Fund (NARF).

- **Hispanic Americans** (or "Latinos" as some prefer to be called) are now the largest minority group, with heritage from many Caribbean, Central American, and South American nations.

- They have pursued equal rights in court through the **Mexican American Legal Defense Fund (MALDEF)**, as well as through labor organizations such as the **United Farm Workers**, led by César Chavez from the 1960s through the 1980s.

- **Asian Americans** are the most rapidly growing group, and while often hailed as the most successful, they have suffered significant discrimination, most notably the internment of Japanese Americans in isolated camps during World War II, which the Supreme Court upheld in *Korematsu v. U.S* (1944).

- Though smaller in numbers than most minority groups, the **Arab and Islamic** population has faced significant challenges since the 9/11 attacks.

 Learning Objective 5.3: Trace the evolution of women's rights and explain how civil rights principles apply to gender issues. (p. 170)

The Rights of Women

- Women were also excluded from the rights of equality implied in the Constitution.

- The women's rights movement grew out of abolitionism in the 1840s, when female activists encountered discrimination among male activists.

- The efforts of the first generation of feminists culminated in the **Nineteenth Amendment** (1920), which granted women the right to vote.

- Progress bogged down after the Nineteenth Amendment was ratified and the **Equal Rights Amendment (ERA,** 1923) was intended to enforce full equality for women, who still were discriminated against in such areas as employment.

- It was passed by Congress in 1972 but was never ratified by the necessary three-fourths of state legislatures.

- The Second Wave of feminists relied heavily on the courts for progress. In *Reed v. Reed* (1971), the Supreme Court for the first time found a law unconstitutional based on arbitrary gender bias, and in 1976, *Craig v. Boren* established an "intermediate scrutiny" standard for determining gender discrimination.

- Since then, it has struck down laws that discriminate against both women and men.

- Recent efforts to promote gender equality have focused on the workplace.

- Civil rights legislation barring discrimination in the workplace applies to women as well as to other minority groups, and it includes employment opportunities, equal pay, and pregnancy leave.

- In 1986, the Supreme Court established a woman's right to sue employers for sexual harassment under the Civil Rights Act.

- The Supreme Court has not yet ruled on the issue of **comparable worth**, which insists that women be paid the same as men for jobs that require the same skills.

- Title IX of the Education Act of 1972 has helped to end employment discrimination because it forbids gender discrimination in federally subsidized education programs (which include almost all colleges and universities), including athletics.

- The Supreme Court extended this to prohibiting all-male schools in 1996 in a case involving the Virginia Military Academy.

- Women are allowed to serve in all branches of the military but cannot serve in ground combat units of the Army and Marine Corps.

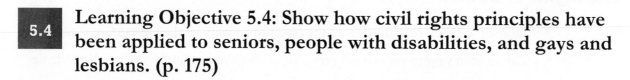 **Learning Objective 5.4: Show how civil rights principles have been applied to seniors, people with disabilities, and gays and lesbians. (p. 175)**

Other Groups Active under the Civil Rights Umbrella

- Discrimination laws prevent employers and universities from rejecting applicants because of their age.

- Congress also revoked the policy of mandatory retirement, unless a compelling reason can be provided based on age.

- The **Americans with Disabilities Act of 1990** protects disabled Americans against job discrimination and requires employers to provide "reasonable accommodations," but controversy has arisen over who is considered disabled.

- **Gay rights** are protected by some laws but are frequently challenged by courts, legislatures, and voters.

- The **"don't ask, don't tell"** military policy introduced by President Clinton in 1993 bypasses restrictions on homosexuality by preventing labeling; even this restriction was struck down by a federal court in 2010 as the President and the Secretary of Defense asked Congress to repeal the law barring service by homosexuals.

- The right to privacy also factors into debates over gay rights; *Lawrence v. Texas* (2003) overturned state antisodomy laws as well as the Court's own decision in *Bowers v. Hardwick* (1986).

- Massachusetts, Hawaii, and Vermont have each legalized some form of **civil union** between same-sex couples, but the Defense of Marriage Act (1996) allowed other states to disregard these unions.

Learning Objective 5.5: Trace the evolution of affirmative action policy and assess the arguments for and against it. (p. 180)

Affirmative Action

- **Affirmative action** is a policy that attempts to go beyond preventing discrimination and provide members of groups who have suffered discrimination some compensatory treatment.

- While originally tolerant of affirmative action programs, courts have become less so in the past decade.

- The Supreme Court ruled against set-aside government contracts for minority-owned businesses in *Adarand Constructors v. Pena* (1995), stating that even if the intent is to advance the opportunities of minorities, it still classifies people by race and is therefore unconstitutional unless it meets the strict scrutiny test: it must be narrowly tailored to achieve a compelling state interest.

- Courts have permitted affirmative action in education, but with tight restrictions.

- In *Regents of the University of California v. Bakke* (1978), the Court ruled that race could be used as one factor in choosing between applicants, but that enrollment quotas were unconstitutional.

- In *Grutter v. Bollinger* (2003), the court ruled that there was a compelling state interest in promoting diversity on campuses, and allowed a narrowly tailored program to continue.

- In *Gratz v. Bollinger* (2006), however, the court ruled that a blanket bonus system was in effect a quota and was therefore unconstitutional.

- In *Parents Involved in Community Schools v. Seattle School District No. 1* (2007), the court ruled that racial balancing (rather than remedying past discrimination) was not in itself a compelling state interest.

For Additional Review

Use the following system to take notes on your reading:

1. Use a notetaking column to record the information from the sections of the chapter.
2. Read your notes and create a column and formulate questions on the specific topics. This sets up a perfect stage for exam-studying later.
3. Cover the notetaking column with a sheet of paper and look at the questions you have written and recite your answers.
4. Reflect on the material: What is the significance of these facts? What principles are the facts based on?
5. Review the material in preparation of the unit test.

Debate continues over the policy of affirmative action. Make a chart listing arguments on each side of the issue and use this chart when reviewing and studying for the unit test.

☐ Review Questions

Multiple-Choice Questions

1. Affirmative action laws are designed to remedy which kind of discrimination?
   a. de facto
   b. ex post facto
   c. de solis
   d. habeas corpus
   e. de jure

2. The landmark case of *Brown v. Board of Education* ruled that segregated schools were not acceptable because of the
   a. constitutional provision against Bills of Attainder.
   b. due process of law clause of the Fifth Amendment.
   c. "involuntary servitude" clause of the Thirteenth Amendment.
   d. "equal protection" clause of the Fourteenth Amendment.
   e. command not to "deny or disparage" rights "retained by the people" under the Ninth Amendment.

3. The Thirteenth Amendment effectively invalidated which Supreme Court decision?
   a. *Dred Scott v. Sandford*
   b. *Plessy v. Ferguson*
   c. *Korematsu v. U.S.*
   d. *Smith v. Allwright*
   e. *Guinn v. U.S.*

4. Which of the following are incorrectly paired?

   I. Thirteenth Amendment—Right of women to vote
   II. Fifteenth Amendment—Right of African American males to vote
   III. Twenty-First Amendment—Banning of poll tax
   IV. Twenty-Sixth Amendment—Right of 18-year-olds to vote

   a. I and II
   b. II and III
   c. III and IV
   d. I and III
   e. II and IV

5. In the case of *California v. Bakke*, the Supreme Court ruled that
   a. Japanese Americans could be placed in camps during World War II.
   b. migrant workers were entitled to compensation in case of injury through unemployment insurance.
   c. affirmative action admissions to a medical school could cause "reverse discrimination."
   d. women were entitled to equal pay for equal work.
   e. the "white primary" was unconstitutional.

6. Racial discrimination in public accommodations such as restaurants and hotels was banned in
   a. the Civil Rights Act of 1964.
   b. the Open Housing Act of 1968.
   c. the Twenty-Fourth Amendment.
   d. the Equal Rights Amendment.
   e. *Reed v. Reed.*

7. Affirmative action refers to
   a. the U.S. Senate approving a presidential appointment to the cabinet under its "advice and consent" function.
   b. the president "faithfully executing" the appropriations of money under laws created by Congress.
   c. the Supreme Court upholding a lower court decision.
   d. interest group lobbying efforts in pursuit of the common goals of group members.
   e. a policy giving special consideration to groups that have been disadvantaged historically.

8. The proposed Equal Rights Amendment (ERA) was proposed by Congress but fell three states short of the 38 needed for ratification. If adopted, the ERA would have banned discrimination based upon
   a. race.
   b. religious faith.
   c. gender.
   d. sexual orientation.
   e. physical disabilities.

9. The biggest difference between civil rights and civil liberties is that
   a. civil liberties protect the majority while civil rights protect minorities.
   b. civil liberties have to do with individual protections while civil rights are protections on the basis of group attributes.
   c. civil liberties have to do with the freedoms of expression and religion while civil rights have to do with rights of people accused of crimes.
   d. civil liberties allow interest groups to organize into interest groups and make demands on government while civil rights allow for groups seek redress of grievances through mass protests.
   e. civil liberties protect individual political beliefs while civil rights protect individual political actions.

10. Which Supreme Court case upheld the placing of Japanese citizens in internment camps during World War II?
    a. *Craig v. Boren*
    b. *Smith v. Allwright*
    c. *Korematsu v. United States*
    d. *Santa Clara Pueblo v. Martinez*
    e. *Yamamoto v. Roosevelt*

11. Which of the following bars educational institutions that receive federal funds from discriminating against female students?
    a. Title IX of the Education Amendments of 1972
    b. The Equal Rights Amendment
    c. The Civil Rights Act of 1964
    d. Jim Crow Laws
    e. Black Codes

12. One area in which African Americans have made substantial progress since the 1960s
    a. is elective office.
    b. is federalism.
    c. is in the penal system.
    d. is in the penal and judicial systems.
    e. is in the parochial system.

13. All of the following statements are true EXCEPT
    a. Women are more supportive than men of government programs for children.
    b. Women are more supportive than men of government programs for the poor.
    c. Women and men differ in their opinions and their votes.
    d. Women tend to have a greater tendency to vote for Democratic candidates than men.
    e. Women tend to have a greater tendency to vote for Republican candidates than men.

14. The strict scrutiny test applies to
    a. race and ethnicity.
    b. age.
    c. gender.
    d. ethnicity.
    e. race.

15. What happened when federal troops withdrew from the South in 1877?
    a. Jim Crow laws were passed which segregated the races and, through the *Plessy v. Ferguson* decision, the Supreme Court established the separate but equal doctrine.
    b. Laws were enacted that integrated the races.
    c. In *Plessy v. Ferguson*, the Supreme Court justices ended separate and unequal treatment of African Americans.
    d. Laws were enacted that desegregated the races.
    e. Racism came to an end in the South.

16. The Supreme Court overturned the constitutionality of separate but equal facilities in
    a. *Reed v. Reed.*
    b. *Plessy v. Ferguson.*
    c. *Craig v. Boren.*
    d. *United States v. Virginia.*
    e. *Brown v. Board of Education.*

17. The Equal Rights Amendment states "Equality of rights under the law shall not be denied or abridged by the United States or any state on account of sex." Which of the following is true about the Equal Rights Amendment (ERA)?
    a. Congress never approved the ERA.
    b. The ERA fell three states short of the three-fourths majority it needed to be ratified.
    c. Congress required special ratifying conventions in the states.
    d. The ERA was not ratified by a single state.
    e. Congress forced the ratification of ERA.

18. At the end of the Civil War, as a result of the northern victory, what Amendments became part of the Constitution?
    a. Ninth, Tenth, and Eleventh
    b. Thirteenth and Fourteenth
    c. Thirteenth, Fourteenth, and Fifteenth
    d. Tenth and Eleventh
    e. Fourteenth, Fifteenth, and Sixteenth

19. A clause of the Fourteenth Amendment guarantees all citizens receive "equal protection under the law." The restraints of equal protection apply to
    a. private individuals.
    b. actions of governments, not private individuals.
    c. commercial activities of large corporations.
    d. actions of the federal government only.
    e. actions of the states only.

20. Rational basis is a
    a. test applied by the court when a classification is based on race requiring the government to show that there is a compelling reason for the law and no other less restrictive way to meet the interest.
    b. clause in the Fifth Amendment prohibiting state governments from depriving any person of life, liberty, or property without due process of law.
    c. clause in the Fourteenth Amendment that forbids any state to deny to any person within its jurisdiction the equal protection of the laws.
    d. test that has been applied when a law classifies based on sex, requiring the government to show that there is a compelling reason for the law and no other less restrictive way to meet the interest.
    e. standard developed by the courts to test the constitutionality of a law; when applied, a law is constitutional as long as it meets a reasonable government interest.

Free-Response Questions

1. One of the key issues in civil rights had to do with gaining the right to vote for groups of citizens. African Americans and women fought for and eventually earned the right to vote through constitutional amendments, Supreme Court decisions, and congressional laws. Among the issues related to voting rights are:

   - the poll tax

   - the white primary

   - the grandfather clause

   - literacy tests

   - state laws prohibiting women OR blacks OR those younger than 21 from voting

   - discriminatory governmental practices that made it difficult to register and vote

a. Identify and describe one Supreme Court case that declared one of these practices unconstitutional.

b. Identify and describe one law passed by Congress that made one of these practices illegal.

c. Identify and describe one constitutional amendment that addressed one of these practices.

2. Women have been participants in and beneficiaries of a civil rights movement during the past 50 years.

a. Describe the impact of the battle for the Equal Rights Amendment on the debate over women's equality.

b. Define "comparable worth" and explain the impact it has had on the debate over workplace equality.

c. Describe current policy regarding women serving in the military, and identify one argument in favor of the policy and one against it.

☐ Answers and Explanations

Multiple-Choice Questions

1. Affirmative action laws are designed to remedy which kind of discrimination?

(a) is correct because the idea of affirmative action is that preventing discrimination by law (de jure) can accomplish only so much, therefore in order to remedy patterns of discrimination that have developed over time in fact (de facto), affirmative action is needed.

(b) is incorrect because ex post facto laws do not relate to affirmative action.

(c) is incorrect because de solis does not relate to affirmative action.

(d) is incorrect because habeas corpus does not relate to affirmative action.

(e) is incorrect because de jure is not addressed by affirmative action.

Page reference: 180–183, AP Topic: The development of civil liberties and civil rights by judicial interpretation

2. The landmark case of *Brown v. Board of Education* ruled that segregated schools were not acceptable because of the

(a) is incorrect because the due process clause of the 5th Amendment does not relate to the "separate but equal doctrine."

(b) is incorrect because the 13th Amendment deals with slavery and not segregation.

(c) is incorrect because the Brown decision is based on the 14th Amendment, but it was the Supreme Court case which made the ruling.

(d) is correct because *Brown v. Board of Education* decided that the equal protection clause required desegregation of schools because "separate educational facilities are inherently unequal."

(e) is incorrect because the Ninth Amendment does not relate to segregation.

Page reference: 160, AP Topic: The development of civil liberties and civil rights by judicial interpretation

3.   The Thirteenth Amendment effectively invalidated which Supreme Court decision?

(a) is correct because the Supreme Court, in the *Dred Scott* case, ruled that African Americans were chattel (owned property); however, the Thirteenth Amendment banned slavery, thus effectively overturning the *Dred Scott* decision.

(b) is incorrect because the *Plessy* case established the "separate but equal" doctrine.

(c) is incorrect because the *Korematsu* case upheld Japanese internment camps.

(d) is incorrect because the *Smith* case dealt with voting rights.

(e) is incorrect because the *Guinn* case dealt with grandfather clauses.

Page reference: 155–164, AP Topic: The development of civil liberties and civil rights by judicial interpretation

4.   Which of the following are incorrectly paired?

(a) is incorrect because the 15th Amendment did give African American males the right to vote.

(b) is incorrect because II is correct.

(c) is incorrect because the poll tax was banned in the Twenty-Fourth Amendment and the Twenty-Sixth Amendment did give 18 year olds the right to vote.

(d) is correct because the Thirteenth Amendment was one of the three Civil War amendments and banned slavery and women received the right to vote in the Nineteenth Amendment

(e) is incorrect because both II and IV are.

Page reference: 158, AP Topic: Knowledge of substantive rights and liberties

5. In the case of *California v. Bakke*, the Supreme Court ruled that

    (a) is incorrect because the *Bakke* case does not deal with Japanese Americans in WWII.

    (b) is incorrect because the *Bakke* case does not deal with migrant workers.

    (c) is correct because in the case of *Regents of the University of California v. Bakke*, the Supreme Court found the university's quotas for enrolling minorities unconstitutional, therefore, Allan Bakke was denied enrollment in favor of a minority applicant to fulfill the university's quota, an unconstitutional "reverse discrimination."

    (d) is incorrect because the *Bakke* case does not deal with equal pay for women.

    (e) is incorrect because the *Bakke* case does not deal with white primaries.

    Page reference: 181, AP Topic: The development of civil liberties and civil rights by judicial interpretation

6. Racial discrimination in public accommodations such as restaurants and hotels was banned in

    (a) is correct because the 1964 Civil Rights Act was a broad sweeping law that had many characteristics; among its provisions was one banning discrimination in public accommodations.

    (b) is incorrect because open housing was not addressed in the 1964 Civil Rights Act.

    (c) is incorrect because the Twenty-Fourth Amendment abolished poll taxes.

    (d) is incorrect because the Equal Rights Amendment dealt with gender equality.

    (e) is incorrect because *Reed* dealt with sex discrimination.

    Page reference: 162, AP Topic: The development of civil liberties and civil rights by judicial interpretation

7. Affirmative action refers to

    (a) is incorrect because "advice and consent" does not relate to affirmative action.

    (b) is incorrect because "faithfully executing" does not relate to affirmative action.

    (c) is incorrect because the Supreme Court upholding a decision does not relate to affirmative action.

    (d) is incorrect because interest group lobbying does not relate to affirmative action.

    (e) is correct because the purpose of affirmative action is to correct for past discrimination.

    Page reference: 180–181, AP Topic: Knowledge of substantive rights and liberties

8. The proposed Equal Rights Amendment (ERA) was proposed by Congress but fell three states short of the 38 needed for ratification. If adopted, the ERA would have banned discrimination based upon

    (a) is incorrect because race was not a component of the ERA.

    (b) is incorrect because religious faith was not a component of the ERA.

    (c) is correct because all of the options have to do with different aspects of "equality," but only the rights of women were addressed in the ERA.

    (d) is incorrect because sexual orientation was not a component of the ERA.

    (e) is incorrect because physical disabilities was not a component of the ERA.

    Page reference: 171–175, AP Topic: Knowledge of substantive rights and liberties

9. The biggest difference between civil rights and civil liberties is that

    (a) is incorrect because it is an incorrect description of the difference between civil liberties and civil rights.

    (b) is correct because this question asks students to differentiate between two basic issues, and while the answers all provide contrasts, only answer (b) is correct—civil liberties are individual rights, while civil rights ban discrimination against groups.

    (c) is incorrect because it is an incorrect description of the difference between civil liberties and civil rights.

    (d) is incorrect because it is an incorrect description of the difference between civil liberties and civil rights.

    (e) is incorrect because it is an incorrect description of the difference between civil liberties and civil rights.

    Page reference: 145, AP Topic: Knowledge of substantive rights and liberties

10. Which Supreme Court case upheld the placing of Japanese citizens in internment camps during World War II?

    (a) is incorrect because the *Craig* case dealt with gender classifications.

    (b) is incorrect because the *Smith* case dealt with voting rights.

    (c) is correct because the Japanese internment camps were upheld in the *Korematsu* decision.

    (d) is incorrect because the *Santa Clara Pueblo* case dealt with gender issues of tribal membership.

(e) is incorrect because the *Yamamoto* case dealt with an assassination attempt.

Page reference: 168–169, AP Topic: The development of civil liberties and civil rights by judicial interpretation

11.   Which of the following bars educational institutions that receive federal funds from discriminating against female students?

(a) is incorrect because the Equal Rights Amendment was not ratified.

(b) is correct because Title IX is the only legislation that specifically barred educational institutions receiving federal funds from discriminating against female students.

(c) is incorrect because the Civil Rights Act of 1964 did not specifically deal with educational institutions.

(d) is incorrect because Jim Crow Laws related to race.

(e) is incorrect because Black Codes related to race.

Page reference: 170–175, AP Topic: The development of civil liberties and civil rights by judicial interpretation

12.   One area in which African Americans have made substantial progress since the 1960s

(a) is correct because African Americans have gained significant ground in getting elected to office at all levels of government.

(b) is incorrect because federalism does not relate to the issue of African American progress.

(c) is incorrect because African Americans have not made substantial progress in the penal system.

(d) is incorrect because African Americans have not made substantial progress in the penal system.

(e) is incorrect because parochial issues do not relate to African American progress.

Page reference: 158–165, AP Topic: Knowledge of substantive rights and liberties

13.   All of the following statements are true EXCEPT

(a) is incorrect because women are more supportive than men of government programs for children.

(b) is incorrect because women are more supportive than men of government programs for the poor.

(c) is incorrect because women and men do differ in their opinions and their votes.

(d) is incorrect because women do tend to have a greater tendency to vote for Democratic candidates than men.

(e) is correct because women do not tend to vote for Republican candidates more than men, making this the only incorrect choice.

Page reference: 170–175, AP Topic: AP Topic: Knowledge of substantive rights and liberties

14. The strict scrutiny test applies to

(a) is correct because the strict scrutiny test is applied by the court when a classification is based on race or ethnicity, requiring the government to show that there is a compelling reason for the law.

(b) is incorrect because the strict scrutiny test does not relate to age.

(c) is incorrect because the strict scrutiny test does not relate to gender.

(d) is incorrect because the strict scrutiny test does not relate to ethnicity alone.

(e) is incorrect because the strict scrutiny test does not relate to race alone.

Page reference: 157, AP Topic: Knowledge of substantive rights and liberties

15. What happened when federal troops withdrew from the South in 1877?

(a) is correct because when Reconstruction ended in 1877, the states attempted to return former slaves to as close to the condition of slavery as possible by passing Jim Crow laws which, in *Plessy*, the Court upheld by asserting the separate but equal doctrine.

(b) is incorrect because Jim Crow laws segregated the races.

(c) is incorrect because *Plessy* established separate but equal.

(d) is incorrect because laws were enacted that segregated the races.

(e) is incorrect because racism did not end.

Page reference: 158–159, AP Topic: The development of civil liberties and civil rights by judicial interpretation

16. The Supreme Court overturned the constitutionality of separate but equal facilities in

(a) is incorrect because the *Reed* decision dealt with sex discrimination.

(b) is incorrect because the *Plessy* decision established the "separate but equal" doctrine.

(c) is incorrect because the *Craig* decision dealt with gender classifications.

(d) is incorrect because the *U.S. v. Virginia* dealt with VMI's male-only policy.

(e) is correct because the Supreme Court, in the *Brown v. Board of Education* decision, struck down the "separate but equal" doctrine that had justified segregated schools, but school districts responded slowly.

Page reference: 160, AP Topic: The development of civil liberties and civil rights by judicial interpretation

17. The Equal Rights Amendment states "Equality of rights under the law shall not be denied or abridged by the United States or any state on account of sex." Which of the following is true about the Equal Rights Amendment (ERA)?

(a) is incorrect because Congress did approve the ERA.

(b) is correct because the ERA was approved by Congress in the 1970s, but it fell short of the three-fourths majority it needed for ratification.

(c) is incorrect because the Constitution establishes the process for ratification.

(d) is incorrect because the ERA was ratified by many states.

(e) is incorrect because the ERA was not ratified.

Page reference: 171, AP Topic: Knowledge of substantive rights and liberties

18. At the end of the Civil War, as a result of the northern victory, what Amendments became part of the Constitution?

(a) is incorrect because the Ninth, Tenth, and Eleventh Amendments were not added as a result of the northern victory in the Civil War.

(b) is incorrect because the Fifteenth Amendment was also added as a result of the northern victory in the Civil War.

(c) is correct because the "Civil War Amendments" which were added to the Constitution after the northern victory in the Civil War are the Thirteenth, Fourteenth, and Fifteenth Amendments.

(d) is incorrect because the Tenth and Eleventh Amendments were not added as a result of the northern victory in the Civil War.

(e) is incorrect because the Sixteenth Amendment was not added as a result of the northern victory in the Civil War.

Page reference: 158–163, AP Topic: Knowledge of substantive rights and liberties

19. A clause of the Fourteenth Amendment guarantees all citizens receive "equal protection under the law." The restraints of equal protection apply to

(a) is incorrect because the equal protection clause does not restrict the actions of individuals.

(b) is correct because 14th Amendment, adopted after the Civil War, contains an equal protection clause which restricts the actions of governments but not those of private individuals.

(c) is incorrect because the equal protection clause does not restrict the actions of corporations.

(d) is incorrect because the equal protection clause does not restrict the actions of the federal government only.

(e) is incorrect because the equal protection clause does not restrict the actions of the states only.

Page reference: 161–162, AP Topic: The development of civil liberties and civil rights by judicial interpretation

20. Rational basis is a

(a) is incorrect because the test does not relate only to race.

(b) is incorrect because the clause of the 5th Amendment is the due process clause.

(c) is incorrect because the clause of the 14th Amendment is the equal protection clause.

(d) is incorrect because the test does not relate only to sex.

(e) is correct because the rational basis test is a standard developed by the courts to test the constitutionality of a law and when it is applied, a law is considered constitutional as long as it meets a reasonable government interest.

Page reference: 157, AP Topic: The development of civil liberties and civil rights by judicial interpretation

Free-Response Questions

This rubric provides examples of many, but not all of the possible correct responses to the free-response questions. Occasionally, weaknesses will be pointed out in the suggested answer, providing students with examples of what to avoid.

1. One of the key issues in civil rights had to do with gaining the right to vote for groups of citizens. African Americans and women fought for and eventually earned the right to vote through constitutional amendments, Supreme Court decisions, and congressional laws. Among the issues related to voting rights are:

   - the poll tax
   - the white primary

- the grandfather clause

- literacy tests

- state laws prohibiting women OR blacks OR those younger than 21 from voting

- discriminatory governmental practices that made it difficult to register and vote

- A basic right of American citizens is the right to vote. In civil rights, the first step toward making progress regarding equality is the right to participate in the elections of members of congress and other representatives. Until all groups attain the right to vote, they can never truly be equal with other groups. To attain the right to vote, a number of barriers had to be overcome, including the poll tax, the white primary, the grandfather clause, and the literacy test. Both constitutional guarantees and laws addressing governmental practices had to be written. In short, it took concerted action of all areas of government to attain the right to vote.

a. Identify and describe one Supreme Court case that declared one of these practices unconstitutional.

- One Supreme Court case that addressed this issue was the one that banned the white primary. In *Smith v. Allwright*, the court ruled that primary elections were a basic part of the election process, so people couldn't be kept from voting in primaries because of their race.

b. Identify and describe one law passed by Congress that made one of these practices illegal.

- The big law passed to help African American vote was the Voting Right Act of 1965. It ruled that states could not use literacy tests to make it hard for some people to vote and that the federal government could use voter registrars to try to get more black people to be able to vote.

c. Identify and describe one constitutional amendment that addressed one of these practices.

- There were several Amendments to the Constitution that affected voting. The Twenty-Fourth Amendment banned the poll tax, which helped disproportionately poor African Americans gain access to the polls.

2. Women have been participants in and beneficiaries of a civil rights movement during the past 50 years.

- Even though women actually outnumber men in the United States, they are considered a minority group because they were denied equal rights under the law until only recently. After more than a century of political activism, women are by degrees achieving the privileges afforded them by their civil rights.

a. Describe the impact of the battle for the Equal Rights Amendment on the debate over women's equality.

- One of their big fights was a fight that women didn't win. The Equal Rights Amendment proposed by Congress went to the states for ratification, but not enough states ratified it for it to become law. However, it did have the impact of raising the conscience of the United States and helped women make progress.

b. Define "comparable worth" and explain the impact it has had on the debate over workplace equality.

- A major difference in the United States is the difference between the salaries of men and women in the work place. Although women work very hard, they often are not paid as much as men. Some believe that this is because of discrimination, often because jobs that are more frequently held by women are paid less than similar jobs commonly held by men. For example, schoolteachers are paid much less than corporate trainers. The idea of comparable worth is that people who do jobs with similar requirements should be paid similar salaries. This idea has led to calls for new laws that will let women be paid as well as men.

c. Describe current policy regarding women serving in the military, and identify one argument in favor of the policy and one against it.

- Women's rights to serve in the military are important. In today's military, women are allowed to serve in many roles, including as combat pilots and on warships. There are no official limits on what ranks a woman can hold. However, they are still not allowed to serve in ground combat units of the army or marine corps. The military believes that conditions in the field don't allow sufficient privacy for men and women, so the policy is good. But others believe that this policy is based on the stereotype of women as weaker than men.

6

Public Opinion and Political Action

☐ Chapter Overview

Public opinion is defined as the collective political beliefs and attitudes of the public and groups within the public. Public opinion can be measured to provide insight into what the electorate is thinking about politics. In this chapter, we examine the nature of public opinion and political participation in the United States. We being by considering the ways in which public opinion is formed, and how that opinion shapes public policy. Next, we explore the process and agents of political socialization. We then turn to consider the question of measuring public opinion. Then we explore the influence of political ideology on political behavior. We conclude by exploring the various ways citizens can influence the political process, through voting, protest, and other avenues of political participation. By the end of the chapter, students should have a thorough understanding of the role and limits of public opinion and political participation in American politics.

☐ Study Outline

 Learning Objective 6.1: Identify demographic trends and their likely impact on American politics. (p. 193)

The American People

- The Constitution requires that a **census** be taken every 10 years and the census collects demographic data about the population of the United States.

- This information is used to distribute money to federal and state programs, **reapportion** seats in the House to each state, determine each state's number of electors in the Electoral College, redraw state and federal congressional districts, and allocate funds for public services such as schools, roads, and public transportation.

- Census reports confirm the United States is a nation of immigrants, a **melting pot** of cultures, ideas, and people.

- According to recent census data, the percentage of minorities is increasing while the percentage of Caucasians is decreasing, and this could lead to a **minority majority** in the next few decades.

- In 2008, for the first time, Hispanic Americans were the largest minority group, outnumbering African Americans.

- **Reapportionment** in the last two decades has given more seats to the increasingly populated states of **California**, **Florida**, and **Texas**, whereas states in the Northeast have lost seats.

- **Senior citizens** make up the largest population group by age, and this gives them significant political influence but it will also put a serious strain on the Social Security system in the next few decades.

- Despite ethnic, age, and geographic diversity, the United States has a common **political culture**, with a set of political values that is widely shared.

 Learning Objective 6.2: Outline how various forms of socialization shape political opinions. (p. 200)

How Americans Learn About Politics: Political Socialization

- People learn about politics and form their political beliefs through the process of **political socialization**.

- There are several different means through which people informally acquire political information.

- **The family:** Families have a significant degree of influence, especially over younger members. Most people identify with the same party that their parents do.

- **The mass media:** Most Americans, especially children and teenagers, watch a significant amount of **television**.

- Political information is often disseminated through TV.

- Younger people are much less likely to watch the news than are adults, however, and as a result, young people's political knowledge is significantly lower today than that of young people a few decades ago.

- **School:** Schools educate children in American values such as democracy and capitalism, both through academics and through practices such as reciting the Pledge of Allegiance.

- A good education also tends to produce more politically active and aware citizens.

- In addition to the influence of the educational system, young people are also influenced by members of their peer group when formulating their political attitudes and beliefs.

- **Religious** groups and associations also influence political attitudes; for example, during the last decade, fundamentalist Christians have played an ever-increasing role in the politics of the United States.

- Socialization is a dynamic process, with learning taking place over one's entire lifetime. Socialization is part of the very important nurturing process.

 Learning Objective 6.3: Explain how polls are conducted and what can be learned from them about American public opinion. (p. 202)

Measuring Public Opinion and Political Information

- **Polls** are the most common means of assessing public opinion.

- A **random sample**, or group that statistically represents the whole population of the United States, is asked to fill out a questionnaire or answer some questions over the phone.

- Commonly, modern polls rely on **random digit dialing** to draw telephone samples.

- A famous nonrandom sample, *The Literary Digest* poll of 1936, wrongly predicted that Republican Alf Landon would defeat Franklin Roosevelt in that year's election.

- The wording of a question is critical, and ambiguously worded questions can affect the accuracy of a poll.

- The size of the sample can also affect the accuracy of a poll and thus the level of confidence in the poll (**sampling error**).

- **Exit polls** are conducted by media as voters leave the voting booth in order to predict the outcomes of elections.

- Some critics argue that polls allow politicians to be influenced easily by shifts in public opinion and that polls receive more media attention than do candidates' political platforms during elections.

- Others assert that, by advancing the public's political agenda to poll-sensitive politicians, polls advance the principles of democracy.

- Recent polls indicate that Americans have little political knowledge and little faith that the government is acting on their behalf.

- Public opinion polls have shown a trend indicating that Americans trust government less than they used to.

 Learning Objective 6.4: Assess the influence of political ideology on Americans' political thinking and behavior. (p. 210)

What Americans Value: Political Ideologies

- In recent years, more Americans have considered themselves conservative than moderate or liberal.

- **Conservatism** favors limited government and freedom of the private sector is more likely to support military spending, free markets, prayer in school, and reduced taxes, and opposes abortion, affirmative action, and government spending on social programs.

- **Liberalism** favors an active central government with social and economic responsibilities, a more equal distribution of wealth, more government regulation of big business, more government spending on social programs, and abortion and opposes increases in defense spending and military actions, prayer in school, and tax breaks for the wealthy.

- Some groups are more likely to hold one ideology than the other.

- Women and minorities tend to be more liberal.

- The **gender gap** is the pattern that predicts that women are more likely to vote for a Democratic candidate; however, this was less prevalent in the 2004 elections.

- Traditionally, people of higher socioeconomic classes tend to be conservative; this trend is declining, however.

- Ideology is not an important concept to most Americans.

- Today only about 20 percent of Americans are ideologues—people who think consistently in ideological terms.

- Most people think in terms of how policies affect groups they like or dislike.

 Learning Objective 6.5: Classify forms of political participation into two broad types. (p. 214)

How Americans Participate in Politics

- Americans express their political views and try to influence policy by voting, petitioning, participating in protests, or corresponding with their representatives.

- Patterns of conventional participation are changing.

- **Voter turnout** has been declining over the last few decades, though it is still the most common way people participate in politics.

- Young people are the group least likely to vote.

- **Campaign contributions** to candidates as a form of political participation are on the rise.

- **Protest** and **civil disobedience** have a long tradition in American history.

- Protests against globalization and war continue to be a means of political expression today.

- People of high socioeconomic status are much more likely to participate in politics, although African Americans and Hispanic Americans are becoming more active.

For Additional Review

Use the following questions to guide your note-taking on political socialization:

1. What is political socialization?
2. Why do we need to socialize?

3. What are agents of political socialization?
4. What is political participation?
5. What forms can political participation take?
6. What is the relationship between political socialization and participation?

Use these notes when studying and reviewing for the unit test and the AP Government and Politics exam.

Create a chart of the methods for conducting different types of public opinion polls. For each method listed, describe the method and list the advantages and disadvantages of the method. Use this chart when studying and reviewing for the unit test and the AP Government and Politics exam.

❑ Review Questions

Multiple-Choice Questions

1. The nurturing process through which people learn their knowledge, feelings, and evaluations about the political world is called
   a. political socialization.
   b. political efficacy.
   c. propaganda acquisition.
   d. political ideology.
   e. public opinion.

2. Sampling error refers to
   a. the pollster making mistakes in selecting a sample.
   b. the sample not being representative of the population.
   c. coding mistakes that mean that responses are not accurately reported.
   d. the level of confidence in the findings of a public opinion poll.
   e. using a nonrandom procedure for drawing a sample of the population.

3. Which type of poll is most likely to be used by the media to predict the outcome of an election?
   a. a benchmark poll
   b. an exit poll
   c. a matchup poll
   d. a focus group poll
   e. a purposive poll

4. Liberals are likely to support all of the following EXCEPT
   a. freedom of choice in abortions.
   b. government regulation.
   c. increased taxes on the rich.
   d. social welfare programs.
   e. prayer in schools.

5. The "gender gap" refers to the idea that women
   a. are denied equal protection of the law in economic matters in the United States.
   b. cannot take combat roles in the military.
   c. are more likely to vote for Democrats than are men.
   d. are proportionally underrepresented among members of Congress.
   e. live on average longer than men, affecting their Social Security costs.

6. Which of the following would older Americans be more likely to support than younger Americans?
   a. protection of Social Security
   b. decreased military spending
   c. gays serving in the military
   d. increased spending on education
   e. increased spending on environmental protection

7. Which of the following is the most common form of political participation in the United States?
   a. expressing one's ideas in a public opinion poll
   b. participating in a mass demonstration
   c. voting in a presidential election
   d. contacting a public official regarding a public issue
   e. joining an interest group for the purpose of influencing legislation

8. Which of the following is a random sample?
   a. interviewing people in a nonsystematic fashion
   b. a selection mechanism that gives each person an equal chance of being selected
   c. going up to people on the street and asking for their opinions
   d. asking every student in the Introduction to Psychology course to fill out a survey
   e. putting your survey on the web and asking readers to fill it out

9. Which of the following is true?

   I. Children tend to support the same party as their parents.
   II. Americans who are not very knowledgeable about politics tend to not vote.
   III. Younger Americans today are more informed about politics than those of 50 years ago.
   IV. Women hold more liberal attitudes than men.

   a. I, IV
   b. I, II, III
   c. II, III, IV
   d. II, IV
   e. I, II, IV

10. Which of the following are true?

    I.   Older Americans are more likely to vote than younger Americans.
    II. Men are more likely to vote than women.
    III. Those with higher education are more likely to vote than those with less education.
    IV. Democrats are more likely to vote than Republicans.
    V.   Hispanic voters are more likely to vote than non-Hispanic voters.

    a. I and III
    b. II and IV
    c. III and V
    d. I, II, and IV
    e. II, III, and V

11. Which of the following is a major weakness of public opinion polls?

    a. Polls can only measure the opinions of political elites.
    b. It is difficult to measure the intensity of feelings about issues.
    c. Polls are so fraught with error that their results are nearly meaningless.
    d. The opinions of the poor and homeless are overrepresented.
    e. All of the above.

12. Which of the following polls is most likely to help a candidate evaluate the short-term effect of a certain campaign event?
    a. an exit poll
    b. a tracking poll
    c. a push poll
    d. a stratified sample
    e. a cross-sectional poll

13. A conservative friend of yours avoids watching MSNBC because she believes it is a liberal news network. Your friend is engaging in
    a. prejudice questioning.
    b. selective exposure.
    c. infotainment.
    d. stereotype challenging.
    e. narrowcasting.

14. A system adopted by the states that requires voters to establish their eligibility to vote in order to reduce or eliminate voter fraud is
    a. voter registration.
    b. voter verification.
    c. voter certification.
    d. voter qualification.
    e. voter suppression.

15. The best description of public opinion is
    a. the distribution of the public expression of the will of the people.
    b. the distribution of the population's beliefs about politics and policy issues.
    c. the distribution of media reflection of public attitudes.
    d. the distribution of the public expression of voter attitudes.
    e. the distribution of random samples of attitudes.

16. In general, public opinion
    a. has no relation to government action at all.
    b. has an impact on government action only during elections.
    c. constrains only the actions of incumbents in government.
    d. constrains the actions of government.
    e. has very little impact on government action.

17. Political participation in the government is an essential component of
    a. freedom.
    b. independence.
    c. free enterprise
    d. self-expression.
    e. self-government.

18. Voters who characterize themselves as Independents can best be characterized by which of the following descriptions?
    a. They typically have greater party loyalty to the Independent Party than Democrats and Republicans have to their parties.
    b. They will never cast a vote for a Democrat or a Republican.
    c. They typically have lower voter turnout than Democrats and Republicans.
    d. They typically have higher voter turnout than Democrats and Republicans.
    e. They are not permitted by most states to vote in general elections.

19. The degree to which the sample estimates might differ from what the population actually thinks is called the
    a. standard deviation error.
    b. questioning error.
    c. probability error.
    d. sampling error.
    e. population error.

20. Most political scientists and political observers assess public opinion primarily through
    a. polls.
    b. social media blogs.
    c. letters to the editor.
    d. voter registration rolls.
    e. reports from interest groups.

Free-Response Questions

1. In the United States, people can participate in politics in many different ways.

   a. Describe how each of the following conventional forms of political participation might impact public policy in the United States.

      - Voting in a presidential election

      - Joining an interest group

      - Running for political office

   b. Describe how participating in a mass demonstration of protest might impact public policy in the United States.

   c. Describe the relationship between social class and participation in the United States.

   d. Explain how the relationship between social class and participation impacts Americans' perceptions regarding equality.

2. One of the most consistent ways that Americans learn about public opinion is through polling.

   a. Describe the advantage of a random sample for public opinion polling over a nonrandom sample.

   b. Describe one advantage and one disadvantage of telephone surveys compared to person-to-person interviewing.

   c. Describe what public opinion polls tell us about Americans' levels of political information.

   d. Describe what public opinion polls tell us about Americans' political attitudes.

☐ Answers and Explanations

Multiple-Choice Questions

1. The nurturing process through which people learn their knowledge, feelings, and evaluations about the political world is called

   (a) is correct because political socialization is defined in the root of the question.

   (b) is incorrect because political efficacy refers to a different concept.

   (c) is incorrect because propaganda acquisition refers to a different concept.

(d) is incorrect because political ideology refers to a different concept.

(e) is incorrect because public opinion refers to a different concept.

Page reference: 200, AP Topic: Public opinion and voters

2. Sampling error refers to

(a) is incorrect because this can cause an error, but it is not a sampling error.

(b) is correct because in all sampling, there is a potential that the sample drawn is not perfectly reflective of the population as a whole.

(c) is incorrect because this can cause an error, but it is not a sampling error.

(d) is incorrect because this can cause an error, but it is not a sampling error.

(e) is incorrect because this can be accounted for mathematically.

Page reference: 203, AP Topic: Public opinion and voters

3. Which type of poll is most likely to be used by the media to predict the outcome of an election?

(a) is incorrect because a benchmark poll can be used during an election, but for different purposes.

(b) is correct because exit polls are used by media on election days to predict the outcome of an election.

(c) is incorrect because a matchup poll can be used during an election, but for different purposes.

(d) is incorrect because a focus group poll can be used during an election, but for different purposes.

(e) is incorrect because a purposive poll can be used during an election, but for different purposes.

Page reference: 205, AP Topic: Public opinion and voters

4. Liberals are likely to support all of the following EXCEPT

(a) is incorrect because liberals do favor freedom of choice in abortions.

(b) is incorrect because liberals do favor government regulation.

(c) is incorrect because liberals do favor increased taxes on the rich.

(d) is incorrect because liberals do favor social welfare programs.

(e) is correct because liberals would not favor prayer in government-sponsored schools.

Page reference: 210–214, AP Topic: Public opinion and voters

5. The "gender gap" refers to the idea that women

    (a) is incorrect because the gender gap does not deal with equal protection of the law.

    (b) is incorrect because the gender gap does not deal with combat roles in the military.

    (c) is correct because gender gap refers to the fact that since 1980, women have tended to be more supportive of Democrats than have men, and this trend is especially strong among unmarried women.

    (d) is incorrect because the gender gap does not deal with underrepresentation in Congress.

    (e) is incorrect because the gender gap does not deal with life expectancy.

    Page reference: 212, AP Topic: Public opinion and voters

6. Which of the following would older Americans be more likely to support than younger Americans?

    (a) is correct because younger voters tend to be more supportive of expanded welfare and environmental programs while older voters tend to support more spending on defense issues and to protect their Social Security benefits.

    (b) is incorrect because it is an inaccurate response to the question.

    (c) is incorrect because it is an inaccurate response to the question.

    (d) is incorrect because it is an inaccurate response to the question.

    (e) is incorrect because it is an inaccurate response to the question.

    Page reference: 199, AP Topic: Public opinion and voters

7. Which of the following is the most common form of political participation in the United States?

    (a) is incorrect because even though this is a form of political participation, it is not the most common form.

    (b) is incorrect because even though this is a form of political participation, it is not the most common form.

    (c) is correct because, even though there are many ways of participating in politics, voting is the only way in which more than half of Americans participate in politics.

(d) is incorrect because even though this is a form of political participation, it is not the most common form.

(e) is incorrect because even though this is a form of political participation, it is not the most common form.

Page reference: 214–219, AP Topic: Public opinion and voters

8.   Which of the following is a random sample?

(a) is incorrect because it is an inaccurate description of a random sample.

(b) is correct because a random sample is one in which each person in the population being sampled has an equal chance of being selected.

(c) is incorrect because it is an inaccurate description of a random sample.

(d) is incorrect because it is an inaccurate description of a random sample.

(e) is incorrect because it is an inaccurate description of a random sample.

Page reference: 203, AP Topic: Public opinion and voters

9.   Which of the following is true?

(a) is correct because typically children tend to support the same party as their parents, and women generally hold more liberal attitudes than men.

(b) is incorrect because Americans who are not very knowledgeable about politics do still vote.

(c) is incorrect because younger Americans today tend to be less informed about politics than 50 years ago.

(d) is incorrect because selection II is inaccurate.

(e) is incorrect because selection II is inaccurate.

Page reference: 210–214, AP Topic: Public opinion and voters

10.   Which of the following are true?

(a) is correct because of the statements, the two that are accurate are that older and better educated people are more likely to vote than are younger and less educated people.

(b) is incorrect because statements II and IV are inaccurate.

(c) is incorrect because statements III and V are inaccurate.

(d) is incorrect because statements II and IV are inaccurate.

(e) is incorrect because statements II and V are inaccurate.

Page reference: 214–219, AP Topic: Public opinion and voters

11. Which of the following is a major weakness of public opinion polls?

(a) is incorrect because polls can measure opinions of political elites.

(b) is correct because while a respondent might answer affirmatively to any question, it is likely that his or her feelings about issues such as abortion, or the death penalty are much more intense than their feelings about the Electoral College or types of voting machines. However, polls rarely have mechanisms to differentiate degree of passion on an issue.

(c) is incorrect because polls are not fraught with errors.

(d) is incorrect because polls do not over-represent the opinions of the poor and homeless.

(e) is incorrect because all of the choices are not accurate.

Page reference: 203–206, AP Topic: Public opinion and voters

12. Which of the following polls is most likely to help a candidate evaluate the short-term effect of a certain campaign event?

(a) is incorrect because an exit poll is an inaccurate choice for the description provided.

(b) is correct because tracking polls enable a campaign to chart its daily rise or fall in support.

(c) is incorrect because a push poll is an inaccurate choice for the description provided.

(d) is incorrect because a stratified sample is an inaccurate choice for the description provided.

(e) is incorrect because a cross-sectional poll is an inaccurate choice for the description provided.

Page reference: 202–207, AP Topic: Public opinion and voters

13. A conservative friend of yours avoids watching MSNBC because she believes it is a liberal news network. Your friend is engaging in

(a) is incorrect because prejudice questioning is an inaccurate choice for the example given.

(b) is correct because selective exposure is the process by which people consciously choose to get the news from information sources that have viewpoints compatible with their own.

(c) is incorrect because infotainment is an inaccurate choice for the example given.

(d) is incorrect because stereotype challenging is an inaccurate choice for the example given.

(e) is incorrect because narrowcasting is an inaccurate choice for the example given.

Page reference: 237, AP Topic: Public opinion and voters

14. A system adopted by the states that requires voters to establish their eligibility to vote in order to reduce or eliminate voter fraud.

(a) is correct because voter registration is a system designed to reduce voter fraud by limiting voting to those who have established eligibility to vote by submitting the proper documents, including proof of residency.

(b) is incorrect because voter verification is an inaccurate choice for the description provided.

(c) is incorrect because voter certification is an inaccurate choice for the description provided.

(d) is incorrect because voter qualification is an inaccurate choice for the description provided.

(e) is incorrect because voter suppression is an inaccurate choice for the description provided.

Page reference: 210, AP Topic: Public opinion and voters

15. The best description of public opinion is

(a) is incorrect because it is an inaccurate description of public opinion.

(b) is correct because public opinion is the distribution of individual preferences for or evaluations of a given issue, candidate, or institution within a specific population.

(c) is incorrect because it is an inaccurate description of public opinion.

(d) is incorrect because it is an inaccurate description of public opinion.

(e) is incorrect because it is an inaccurate description of public opinion.

Page reference: 220, AP Topic: Public opinion and voters

16. In general, public opinion

(a) is incorrect because public opinion does impact government.

(b) is incorrect because public opinion has a continuous impact on government.

(c) is incorrect because public opinion impacts people running for office, as well.

(d) is correct because it is the public's task in a democracy to decide who will lead; therefore, the voices will be heard, holding public officials accountable.

(e) is incorrect because public opinion does have a significant impact on government.

Page reference: 220, AP Topic: Public opinion and voters

17. Political participation in the government is an essential component of

(a) is incorrect because political participation only indirectly relates to the concept of freedom.

(b) is incorrect because political participation only indirectly relates to the concept of independence.

(c) is incorrect because political participation only indirectly relates to the concept of free enterprise.

(d) is incorrect because political participation only indirectly relates to the concept of self-expression.

(e) is correct because political participation—all the activities used by citizens to influence the selection of political leaders or the policies they pursue—is absolutely necessary to the existence of self-government.

Page reference: 214–218, AP Topic: Public opinion and voters

18. Voters who characterize themselves as Independents can best be characterized by which of the following descriptions?

(a) is incorrect because it is an inaccurate description of Independents.

(b) is incorrect because it is an inaccurate description of Independents.

(c) is correct because the genuine Independents do not vote consistently and appear to have very little interest in politics.

(d) is incorrect because it is an inaccurate description of Independents.

(e) is incorrect because it is an inaccurate description of Independents.

Page reference: 213, AP Topic: Public opinion and voters

19. The degree to which the sample estimates might differ from what the population actually thinks is called the

(a) is incorrect because the standard deviation error is an inaccurate choice for the description provided.

(b) is incorrect because the questioning error is an inaccurate choice for the description provided.

(c) is incorrect because the probability error is an inaccurate choice for the description provided.

(d) is correct because a sampling error measures the degree to which the sample's opinions might differ from what the population actually thinks. This is the level of confidence in the findings of a public opinion poll and the more people interviewed, the more confident one can be in the results.

(e) is incorrect because the population error is an inaccurate choice for the description provided.

Page reference: 203, AP Topic: Public opinion and voters

20. Most political scientists and political observers assess public opinion primarily through

(a) is correct because polls are surveys of public opinion and they are the tool most political scientists and political observers use to assess public opinion.

(b) is incorrect because, even though social media blogs may express political opinion, they are not the method most used by political scientists and political observers.

(c) is incorrect because, even though letters to the editor may express political opinion, they are not the method most used by political scientists and political observers.

(d) is incorrect because, even though voter registration rolls may express political opinion, they are not the method most used by political scientists and political observers.

(e) is incorrect because, even though reports from interest groups may express political opinion, they are not the method most used by political scientists and political observers.

Page reference: 202–208, AP Topic: Public opinion and voters

Free-Response Questions

This rubric provides examples of many, but not all of the possible correct responses to the free-response questions. Occasionally, there will be weaknesses pointed out in the suggested answer, providing students with examples of what to avoid.

1. In the United States, people can participate in politics in many different ways.

    a. Describe how each of the following conventional forms of political participation might impact public policy in the United States.

    - Voting in a presidential election
    - Joining an interest group

- Running for political office

- Political participation is a fundamental indicator of the health of a democracy. Since in a democracy, the government should respond to the people, the people should participate at high rates. Yet, in the United States, only about half of the people vote. If voting were the only mechanism for participation, that would, perhaps, indicate a problem with democracy.

- Voting in a presidential election is the most common form of political participation. People can vote very easily in the United States since there is no fee for registering to vote, since the racial and gender barriers to voting have been reduced in recent years, and since we now have a motor-voter law that allows people to register even when they renew their driver's licenses. Voting is fundamental in a democracy because it allows people to elect the person who best reflects their ideas about how government should operate. By electing officials, the people have representatives in government. That is the nature of a republican government, and it is therefore a way to influence public policy. In other words, elections are the way that people can staff government with people who will do the people's business.

- There are many less common forms of participation. Many people join interest groups. By joining an interest group, people make their views known, and give interest groups resources that they can use to press for policy changes. Very few people actually run for office, but doing so allows them to change policy directly if they win, and to contribute to debates about policy even if they don't win.

b. Describe how participating in a mass demonstration of protest might impact public policy in the United States.

- Conventional participation, such as voting or joining interest groups, is not the only way that people can affect public policy. Through nonconventional methods such as engaging in nonviolent civil disobedience, people can also get their ideas to be noticed by government. Martin Luther King, Jr. led much of the civil rights movement by using civil disobedience. Although he and other African Americans could not win elections in the South at that time, he could use civil disobedience to gain attention for the civil rights struggle. Eventually, that attention led to national outrage and the civil rights laws were passed. So, as one can see, civil disobedience, though a nonconventional form of participation, can have influence just as a conventional method might.

c. Describe the relationship between social class and participation in the United States.

- Interestingly, the two forms of participation discussed above might be seen as being tactics of people with different social status. People in higher income categories are far more likely to vote than are poor people.

d. Explain how the relationship between social class and participation impacts Americans' perceptions regarding equality.

- The gap in voting between those in different income categories would seem to indicate that equality cannot be realized in U.S. society. However, even poor people can engage in civil disobedience. As a result, equality might be realized.

2. One of the most consistent ways that Americans learn about public opinion is through polling.

a. Describe the advantage of a random sample for public opinion polling over a nonrandom sample.

- A random sample is better than a nonrandom sample because a random sample gives everyone an equal chance of being selected and therefore is more likely to be representative of the population as a whole. With a nonrandom sample, we cannot estimate how likely the sample is to represent the people.

b. Describe one advantage and one disadvantage of telephone surveys compared to person-to-person interviewing.

- Telephone surveys are both great and bad. They are great because everyone with a phone can be surveyed, and most people have phones. They are bad because people without telephones cannot be surveyed (for example, people who only have cell phones), and because people are less likely to respond to a phone survey than an in-person survey.

c. Describe what public opinion polls tell us about Americans' levels of political information.

- Surveys tell us that Americans don't know much about politics. They can't answer even simple questions well. Surveys show that Americans know very little about political issues and even less abut geography.

d. Describe what public opinion polls tell us about Americans' political attitudes.

- Public opinion polls do show that Americans most often see themselves as moderates and are less supportive of liberalism than they used to be.

7

The Mass Media and the Political Agenda

☐ Chapter Overview

The power of the mass media has expanded dramatically since the beginning of the twentieth century. In this chapter, we examine how the mass media function as part of the American political process. We begin by examining the way in which political campaigns and political leaders use the media to communicate their messages. Then, we explore the historical evolution of the media in the United States. Next, we consider the major factors that influence media coverage and attention, and analyze how media coverage affects politics and public policy. Along the way, we also examine how policy entrepreneurs try to use the media to influence the public agenda. We conclude by assessing the effect of the media on the scope of government and democracy in America. By the end of the chapter, students should have a good understanding of how the media function as a political institution, and how they interact with other political actors and institutions to affect politics in the United States.

☐ Study Outline

 Learning Objective 7.1: Describe how American politicians choreograph their messages through the mass media. (p. 227)

The Mass Media Today

- Political leaders have learned to use the media to set their agendas.

- A **media event** is an event that is staged by a political leader with the purpose of getting it covered in the media to shape an image or draw attention to a chosen issue.
- In addition, they can more deliberately use the media to run advertisements.
- Such advertisements are often 30 seconds in length and make up the majority of spending on political campaigns.
- Presidents also use the media to make direct appeals to the public.

7.2 Learning Objective 7.2: Outline the key developments in the history of mass media and American politics. (p. 229)

The Development of Media Politics

- Politics and the mass media go hand in hand.
- However, whereas they once worked together to communicate with the public, today they often oppose each other.
- The mass media came into existence in the 19th century with the birth of the daily newspaper, and blossomed with radio and the television in the middle of the 20th century.
- Franklin Roosevelt (FDR) built a close relationship between the office of the president and the press.
- **Press conferences**, now a common means by which presidents convey their goals and opinions to the public, began with FDR in the 1930s.
- He was also the first president to address the electorate directly through radio broadcasts.
- The Watergate scandal and the Vietnam War changed the government's relationship with the press, as the press became more suspicious about political motives.
- Today the media engage in **investigative journalism**, often with the intent of revealing political **scandals**.

The Print Media

- Only a few corporations own most of the newspapers in the United States, as well as radio and television stations.

- These major corporations have significant control over information conveyed in the media.
- Newspaper readers tend to be politically informed, active citizens, but newspaper circulation has been declining since the advent of television and the Internet.
- Most daily city newspapers are struggling financially.

The Emergence of Radio and Television

- Now, most Americans, especially young people, get their information from the **broadcast media**.
- Television shifts the public's focus from a politician's achievements and political views to his or her **appearance** and performance in front of the cameras.
- Cable television encourages **narrowcasting**, which allows viewers to select what information they do and do not want to see.
- Critics fear that this will lead to an even less informed electorate that can selectively avoid politics.
- Media in America is free and independent because it is privately owned, but that also means it is totally dependent upon advertising.
- Over four-fifths of the newspapers in America are owned by large corporations (**chains**), as is much of the broadcast media, as well.
- The Federal Communications Commission (FCC) is a regulatory agency that monitors the use of the airwaves.
- While it is independent, the FCC is subject to many political pressures.
- Congress controls the funding of the agency and presidential appointments to the agency are made with political considerations in mind.
- The FCC prevents monopolies, conducts periodic examinations of stations as part of its licensing authority, and issues fair treatment rules concerning access to the airwaves for political candidates and officeholders.
- If a person is attacked on the air, they have the right to respond on the same station; however, the fairness doctrine that was once in place (which required equal time to differing views) was abolished.

From Broadcasting to Narrowcasting: The Rise of Cable News Channels

- The first major news networks were described as "broadcasting" because messages were sent to a broad audience.

- With the development of cable TV, narrowcasting (media programming on cable TV or Internet that is focused on one topic and aimed at a narrow audience) is a more appropriate term.

- While there is now a wide variety of news programs available, the quality of content has not necessarily improved. The profit motive is still the driving force behind most news programs.

The Impact of the Internet

- The Internet has made political information easily accessible.

- Citizens can use it to easily retrieve voting records and text of legislation, for example.

- However, researchers have discovered that few Americans are taking advantage of the technology to be better-informed citizens.

- The Internet has also changed reporting.

- Being faced with competition from everyone who has an opinion on a topic, the rise of blogs and Twitter has made it more difficult for traditional reporters to file well-researched, objective, and in-depth stories.

- The most popular blogs, though, are written by people who are well-informed and educated, with strong analytical and writing skills.

Private Control of the Media

- In the United States, control of virtually all media outlets is in private hands. Media in America today tend to be part of large conglomerates, such as Disney or General Electric.

- In the newspaper business, chains control newspapers that together represent over 80 percent of the nation's daily circulation.

- Because of private ownership of the media and the First Amendment right to free speech, American journalists have long had an unfettered capacity to criticize government leaders and policies.

- But the American media are totally dependent on advertising revenues to keep their businesses going, which means that getting the biggest possible audience is the primary objective.

7.3 Learning Objective 7.3: List the major criteria that determine which news stories receive the most media attention. (p. 242)

Reporting the News

- Newscasting is a business geared toward achieving high ratings.
- This can have detrimental consequences for both the political agenda addressed in the news and for the political knowledge of Americans.
- Profits largely determine what is considered news, and sensational, unusual, or negative events usually receive more attention than more positive or everyday policymaking does.
- This leads the public to believe that most of politics is scandalous and to distrust political leaders.
- Journalists usually have regular **beats**, such as the White House, the Senate, or the Pentagon.
- Most of their information comes directly from press secretaries at these institutions.
- This has significant advantages for politicians, who can control how much information is reported to the public, including intentional leaks (**trial balloons**), which can gauge political reaction.
- News reporting, especially through the broadcast media, has very little depth of content.
- Information is reported in **sound bites**, which gloss over the complexity of issues and focus the public's attention on politicians rather than on their policies.
- Sound bites allow politicians to craft political personas without having to directly address an issue.
- They do not have to say much when a typical sound bite is only seven seconds long and this contributes further to Americans' lack of political knowledge.
- **Bias** is not apparent so much in the way news is presented, but it is a factor in determining what news is reported and what news is not.

- There is little evidence of bias toward an ideological position or political party, but dramatic or sensational stories are more likely to draw an audience, so they are more likely to be featured in the news.

 Learning Objective 7.4: Analyze the impact the media has on what policy issues Americans think about. (p. 248)

The News and Public Opinion

- The mass media have an enormous influence over the **public agenda**.

- When they select what issues to focus on, news organizations define which are the most pressing political topics and thereby determine the political priorities of the public.

- By selectively assigning importance to certain issues, the media essentially tell Americans what to think about.

- The media have shifted attention to individual politicians and away from government as a whole.

- The biggest consequence of this is the increasing amount of attention paid to the president, which as a result enhances his power.

- The media perform a watchdog function by forcing the government to be answerable to the public.

- However, they strongly discourage Americans from thinking critically about politics.

- At the same time, because the news is based on ratings, its content reflects what citizens want to see and read—and they seem to express little interest in politics.

Learning Objective 7.5: Explain how policy entrepreneurs employ media strategies to influence the public agenda. (p. 249)

Policy Entrepreneurs and Agenda Setting

- Policy entrepreneurs seek to influence the policy agenda by getting the media to pay attention to the issues that they are particularly concerned with.

- They employ a variety of strategies to obtain media coverage, including press releases, press conferences, and letter writing.
- Sometimes they will resort to staging dramatic events that are so interesting and unusual that reporters can hardly resist covering them.

 Learning Objective 7.6: Assess the impact of the mass media on the scope of government and democracy in America. (p. 250)

Understanding the Mass Media

- The media acts as a key linkage institution between the people and government.
- The media's watchdog function also helps to restrict politicians.
- The watchdog orientation of the press can be characterized as liberal or conservative.

For Additional Review

As you are reading, take notes on how the media and its role in American society have changed over the last century. Your notes should indicate a "change over time" not only in the types of media, but in the financing, ownership, control and influence of the media. Use these notes to prepare for the unit test and for the AP Government and Politics exam.

Create a chart in order to compare and contrast the impact of the media on public opinion. List the sources of information along the side of the chart (internet, television, blogs, radio, etc.) and across the top of your chart, create two columns where you will discuss the "pros" and "cons" of each type of media as a source of information. Be sure to address narrowcasting and selective exposure when rating the use of the media. Use this chart when studying for the unit test and when preparing for the AP Government and Politics exam.

☐ Review Questions

Multiple-Choice Questions

1. Which of the following is most likely to be able to effectively use the national media to set the policy agenda?
   a. Supreme Court
   b. Congress
   c. president
   d. state legislators
   e. governors

2. Which of the following is the best example of a media event?
   a. the State of the Union Address
   b. news report of a presidential candidate reading to elementary school students
   c. assassination attempt
   d. signing bipartisan legislation
   e. private meeting with lawmakers to discuss an issue

3. The Federal Communications Commission (FCC) is which of the following?
   a. an arm of the U.S. Congress devoted to communications issues
   b. a special interest group
   c. the federal judiciary
   d. an independent regulatory agency
   e. a White House agency

4. Which of the following is the best example of a trial balloon?
   a. A presidential nominee leaks the name of one of his choices for vice president to gauge public opinion.
   b. A president interviews a nominee for a federal judicial appointment.
   c. Special interest groups testify in order to block a confirmation.
   d. A citizen launches a fake story on a website to criticize a politician.
   e. A leading newspaper endorses a candidate early in the process to gauge public opinion.

5. All of the following can be accurately stated about sound bites EXCEPT
   a. Presidential candidates use them to state a theme of their campaign.
   b. They are 15 seconds or shorter.
   c. They are the way many citizens learn about their candidates.
   d. They provide detailed policy information.
   e. They are used by advertisers as well as politicians.

6. What is the main focus of the media during a presidential campaign?
   a. issues that the candidates support
   b. background and qualification of the candidates
   c. personality of candidates
   d. platform of the party
   e. accomplishments of the candidate

7. Which of the following best describes the impact of the Internet on politics?
   a. citizens are more informed
   b. citizens have more access to information
   c. citizens are more likely to be liberal
   d. citizens have more trust in government
   e. citizens have less freedom of expression

8. Which of the following have been decreasing over the years?
   a. news outlets
   b. press conferences
   c. State of the Union Addresses
   d. media events
   e. trial balloons

9. Which of the following best describes newspaper coverage under yellow journalism?
   a. dull
   b. thorough
   c. comprehensive
   d. sensationalized
   e. government propaganda

10. Which of the following best describes the correlation between the media and trust in government?
    a. As the availability of news has increased, trust in government has decreased.
    b. There is no relationship between the two.
    c. News stories are supportive of political leaders and lead to increased trust.
    d. The media has caused trust in government to rise.
    e. The media has caused trust of local government to decrease more than trust of national government.

11. What is narrowcasting?
    a. the tendency of the media to frame political events using well-established stereotypes
    b. the tendency of the media to focus on domestic events rather than international events
    c. the increasing reliance of the media on political pundits
    d. targeting media programs at specific segments of the population
    e. political coverage that is superficial

12. Why do the media typically have little influence on public opinion?
    a. The media are required to present both sides of a story, leaving little room to influence public opinion.
    b. The media are owned by the same corporations that conduct public opinion polls.
    c. People tend to ignore all political information from the media due to its well-known biases.
    d. Public opinion is static and seldom changes.
    e. Typically, people only pay attention to media coverage that is consistent with their own political preferences.

13. What is agenda setting?
    a. the ability of the media to influence public opinion about which issues the government should address
    b. the tendency to remember only those news stories that are consistent with one's predispositions
    c. the ability of the media to influence the public's opinions on issues
    d. the media's focus on scandal and corruption
    e. the public's ability to determine which issues the media covers

14. The deepest bias among political journalists is
    a. the desire to produce content that will gain the highest ratings or readership.
    b. to promote a liberal agenda.
    c. to provide accurate—even if boring—information to the public.
    d. to promote a conservative agenda.
    e. to create fame and celebrity for the journalist.

15. All of the following are considered "mass media" EXCEPT
    a. radio.
    b. television.
    c. newspapers.
    d. peer-reviewed periodical.
    e. the Internet.

16. With the development of cable television came
    a. fewer news choices.
    b. fewer well-trained reporters.
    c. a loss of news coverage on local stations.
    d. a loss of objectivity in news coverage.
    e. around the clock news coverage.

17. Since the creation of broadcast media, the government has
    a. undertaken the funding of the industry.
    b. strictly censored publishing.
    c. taken a "hands off" approach to the industry.
    d. engaged in regulation of the industry.
    e. strictly censored programming.

18. This has grown into an unprecedented source of public information for the world.
    a. CNN
    b. MSNBC
    c. PBS
    d. BBC
    e. Internet

19. The relatively high cost of advertising using this medium accounts, in part, for the high cost of political campaigns.
    a. newspapers
    b. Internet
    c. television
    d. radio
    e. blogs

20. The mass media targets
    a. the wealthy.
    b. the largest audience possible.
    c. elected officials.
    d. registered voters.
    e. specialized markets.

Free-Response Questions

1. The independent media in American politics can both hurt candidates' chances for getting elected to office as well as help candidates' chances at getting elected to office.

    a. Identify and describe two ways the media may hurt the chances of a candidate for office.

    b. Identify and describe two ways candidates can use the media to help their campaigns.

2. The mass media greatly impacts the course of a president's administration. Defend this statement by doing all of the following:

    a. Define three of the terms below.

        - press conferences

        - fireside chat

        - sound bites

        - media event

    b. For each term you defined, explain its impact on the course of a presidential administration.

☐ Answers and Explanations

Multiple-Choice Questions

1. Which of the following is most likely to be able to effectively use the national media to set the policy agenda?

    (a) is incorrect because the Supreme Court does not use the media to set policy agenda.

    (b) is incorrect because Congress does not use the media to set policy agenda as effectively as the president.

    (c) is correct because most modern presidents have successfully used television to make direct appeals to the public. President Reagan, for example, used prime time television to make direct appeals to citizens to take grassroots action on a political issue. Other organizations such as Congress are more decentralized and therefore have a more difficult time collectively using the media.

    (d) is incorrect because state legislators do not use the media to set policy agenda as effectively as the president.

    (e) is incorrect because governors do not use the media to set policy agenda as effectively as the president.

    Page reference: 229–239, AP Topic: Linkages between institutions and the media

2. Which of the following is the best example of a media event?

    (a) is incorrect because the State of the Union Address is not the best choice for the question.

    (b) is correct because media events are deliberately staged events by political figures to get attention. While the State of the Union gets broad media coverage, it is an event required by the U.S. Constitution and therefore is not the best example of a media event. Events that are not in a politician's control would not be good examples of media events, nor would events that do not get much media attention.

    (c) is incorrect because an assassination attempt is not the best choice for the question.

    (d) is incorrect because signing bipartisan legislation is not the best choice for the question.

    (e) is incorrect because a private meeting with lawmakers to discuss an issue is not the best choice for the question.

    Page reference: 228, AP Topic: Linkages between institutions and the media

3. The Federal Communications Commission (FCC) is which of the following?

(a) is an inaccurate description of the FCC.

(b) is an inaccurate description of the FCC.

(c) is an inaccurate description of the FCC.

(d) is correct because the Federal Communications Commission is an independent regulatory agency.

(e) is an inaccurate description of the FCC.

Page reference: 234, AP Topic: Linkages between institutions and the media

4. Which of the following is the best example of a trial balloon?

(a) is correct because a trial balloon occurs when a political figure leaks information to the public to try to decide what the public would think if an event were to occur. Al Gore leaked his choice of Joe Lieberman as a running mate in order to see if the public approved of his choice—this type of event is referred to as a trial balloon.

(b) is incorrect because this is not an example of a trial balloon.

(c) is incorrect because this is not an example of a trial balloon.

(d) is incorrect because this is not an example of a trial balloon.

(e) is incorrect because this is not an example of a trial balloon.

Page reference: 242, AP Topic: Linkages between institutions and the media

5. All of the following can be accurately stated about sound bites EXCEPT

(a) is incorrect because the selection is an accurate description of a sound bite.

(b) is incorrect because the selection is an accurate description of a sound bite.

(c) is incorrect because the selection is an accurate description of a sound bite.

(d) is correct because it is the exception to sound bites (sound bites do not provide much information to citizens about candidates).

(e) is incorrect because the selection is an accurate description of a sound bite.

Page reference: 244, AP Topic: Linkages between institutions and the media

6.   What is the main focus of the media during a presidential campaign?

(a) is incorrect because issues are not the main focus of the media during a presidential campaign.

(b) is incorrect because background and qualifications are not the main focus of the media during a presidential campaign.

(c) is correct because political races today are called candidate-centered because of the focus on candidate personality, rather than issues, background or qualifications.

(d) is incorrect because the platform of the party is not the main focus of the media during a presidential campaign.

(e) is incorrect because accomplishments of the candidates are not the main focus of the media during a presidential campaign.

Page reference: 229–241, AP Topic: Linkages between institutions and the media

7.   Which of the following best describes the impact of the Internet on politics?

(a) is incorrect because the Internet has not made citizens more informed.

(b) is correct because the Internet has not made citizens more informed or changed their opinion, but has made information more widely available.

(c) is incorrect because the Internet has not made citizens more liberal.

(d) is incorrect because the Internet has not made citizens more trusting of government.

(e) is incorrect because the Internet has not lessened freedom of expression.

Page reference: 238–239, AP Topic: Linkages between institutions and the media

8.   Which of the following have been decreasing over the years?

(a) is incorrect because news outlets are not decreasing.

(b) is correct because presidents are holding fewer regularly scheduled press conferences.

(c) is incorrect because State of the Union Addresses are not decreasing.

(d) is incorrect because media events are not decreasing.

(e) is incorrect because trial balloons are not decreasing.

Page reference: 227–247, AP Topic: Linkages between institutions and the media

9. Which of the following best describes newspaper coverage under yellow journalism?

(a) is incorrect because it is an inaccurate description of yellow journalism.

(b) is incorrect because it is an inaccurate description of yellow journalism.

(c) is incorrect because it is an inaccurate description of yellow journalism.

(d) is correct because yellow journalism involved increasing newspaper sales by writing stories with sensationalized coverage and dubious accuracy.

(e) is incorrect because it is an inaccurate description of yellow journalism.

Page reference: 246–249, AP Topic: Linkages between institutions and the media

10. Which of the following best describes the correlation between the media and trust in government?

(a) is correct because trust in government has declined as the availability of information about government has increased.

(b) is incorrect because it is an inaccurate selection for the description of the relationship between media and trust in government.

(c) is incorrect because it is an inaccurate selection for the description of the relationship between media and trust in government.

(d) is incorrect because it is an inaccurate selection for the description of the relationship between media and trust in government.

(e) is incorrect because it is an inaccurate selection for the description of the relationship between media and trust in government.

Page reference: 246–252, AP Topic: Linkages between institutions and the media

11. What is narrowcasting?

(a) is incorrect because the selection is an inaccurate definition of narrowcasting.

(b) is incorrect because the selection is an inaccurate definition of narrowcasting.

(c) is incorrect because the selection is an inaccurate definition of narrowcasting.

(d) is correct because narrowcasting is media programming on cable TV or the Internet that is focused on a particular interest and aimed at a particular audience, in contrast to broadcasting.

(e) is incorrect because the selection is an inaccurate definition of narrowcasting.

Page reference: 234, AP Topic: Linkages between institutions and the media

12. Why do the media typically have little influence on public opinion?

(a) is incorrect because media do not have to present both sides of an issue.

(b) is incorrect because the media are not necessarily owned by the same corporations that conduct public opinion polls.

(c) is incorrect because people do not ignore the media due to bias.

(d) is incorrect because public opinion is not static and unchanging.

(e) is correct because studies show that people tend to ignore media information that is inconsistent with their existing beliefs or personal experiences.

Page reference: 248–249, AP Topic: Linkages between institutions and the media

13. What is agenda setting?

(a) is correct because agenda setting is the process of forming the list of issues to be addressed by the government.

(b) is incorrect because it is an inaccurate definition of agenda setting.

(c) is incorrect because it is an inaccurate definition of agenda setting.

(d) is incorrect because it is an inaccurate definition of agenda setting.

(e) is incorrect because it is an inaccurate definition of agenda setting.

Page reference: 248–249, AP Topic: Linkages between institutions and the media

14. The deepest bias among political journalists is

(a) is correct because the media depend on an audience for success, and even survival. This compels them to seek out stories that will attract viewers or readers. While the dynamics of narrowcasting sometimes results in slanting a story ideologically to capture higher ratings, the primary driver is the audience.

(b) is incorrect because it is an inaccurate selection for the prompt.

(c) is incorrect because it is an inaccurate selection for the prompt.

(d) is incorrect because it is an inaccurate selection for the prompt.

(e) is incorrect because it is an inaccurate selection for the prompt.

Page reference: 246–247, AP Topic: Linkages between institutions and the media

15. All of the following are considered "mass media" EXCEPT

(a) is incorrect because radio is an example of mass media.

(b) is incorrect because television is an example of mass media.

(c) is incorrect because newspapers are an example of mass media.

(d) is correct because a peer-reviewed journal is an academic journal specific to a particular discipline and does not receive mass circulation.

(e) is incorrect because the Internet is an example of mass media.

Page reference: 229–241, AP Topic: Linkages between institutions and the media

16. With the development of cable television came

(a) is incorrect because it is an inaccurate response to the prompt.

(b) is incorrect because it is an inaccurate response to the prompt.

(c) is incorrect because it is an inaccurate response to the prompt.

(d) is incorrect because it is an inaccurate response to the prompt.

(e) is correct because the advent of cable television provided the opportunity for 24 hour a day news channels and programs.

Page reference: 233–234, AP Topic: Linkages between institutions and the media

17. Since the creation of broadcast media, the government has

(a) is incorrect because the government does not fund media.

(b) is incorrect because the government does not strictly censor publishing.

(c) is incorrect because the government has not taken a "hands off" approach to media.

(d) is correct because, since its inception, the government has regulated broadcast media using the Federal Communications Commission.

(e) is incorrect because the government does not strictly censor programming.

Page reference: 234, AP Topic: Linkages between institutions and the media

18. This has grown into an unprecedented source of public information for the world.

(a) is incorrect because CNN is an inaccurate answer to the question.

(b) is incorrect because MSNBC is an inaccurate answer to the question.

(c) is incorrect because PBS is an inaccurate answer to the question.

(d) is incorrect because BBC is an inaccurate answer to the question.

(e) is correct because the Internet, since its creation, has become a massive source of public information around the world.

Page reference: 238–239, AP Topic: Linkages between institutions and the media

19. The relatively high cost of advertising using this medium accounts, in part, for the high cost.

    (a) is incorrect because newspaper advertising is not as expensive as television.

    (b) is incorrect because Internet advertising is not used to the same degree as television.

    (c) is correct because television advertising is an important part of political campaigns, and due to the expense of television advertising, the use of this medium has contributed to the high cost of campaigning.

    (d) is incorrect because radio advertising is not as expensive as television, nor is it used as extensively.

    (e) is incorrect because blogs are not used extensively for campaigning.

    Page reference: 232–249, AP Topic: Linkages between institutions and the media

20. The mass media targets

    (a) is incorrect because it is an inaccurate selection for the prompt.

    (b) is correct because the mass media, driven by ratings, selects programming in order to reach the largest audience possible.

    (c) is incorrect because it is an inaccurate selection for the prompt.

    (d) is incorrect because it is an inaccurate selection for the prompt.

    (e) is incorrect because it is an inaccurate selection for the prompt.

    Page reference: 231–252, AP Topic: Linkages between institutions and the media

Free-Response Questions

This rubric provides examples of many, but not all of the possible correct responses to the free-response questions.

1. The independent media in American politics can both hurt candidates' chances for getting elected to office as well as help candidates' chances at getting elected to office.

    a. Identify and describe two ways the media may hurt the chances of a candidate for office.

    - The media may hurt candidates running for office through investigative journalism or allowing negative advertising to be run unopposed. Through investigative journalism, reporters will search for scandals and negative information about a candidate in order to receive higher ratings for their news programs. Such reporting can tarnish the reputation of a candidate and hurt his chances at being elected. Additionally, with the rise of the Internet, many scandals involving political figures have originated on websites only to later be picked up by the mainstream media. Negative advertisements may also be run against a candidate. Media outlets may choose to run such advertisements. Even though there is an expectation that the candidates have the right to respond, such negative advertisements often either drive down voter turnout or have a negative impact on the candidate.

    b. Identify and describe two ways candidates can use the media to help their campaigns.

    - On the other hand, having access to the media greatly helps candidates. Candidates can stage media events, leak trial balloons, make direct appearances on television, go on debates, or use sound bites to promote their campaigns. Media events occur when a candidate for office stages an event to draw positive attention to him or herself, such as appearing at a school or charity event. This event is covered in the media as a news story and provides attention to the candidate without the candidate having to spend any money on the campaign. An example of a trial balloon would be when a candidate leaks information to a reporter hoping that the story will get into the mainstream media in order to gauge public opinion of a campaign event. For example, a presidential candidate may leak information about his choice for vice president and then take polls to see if this choice helps the campaign or not.

2. The mass media greatly impacts the course of a president's administration. Defend this statement by doing all of the following:

a. Define three of the terms below.

-   press conferences
-   fireside chat
-   sound bites
-   media event

b. For each term you defined, explain its impact on the course of a presidential administration.

-   The First Amendment to the Constitution gives freedom to the press and allows media outlets to publish critical stories about the president of the United States. This freedom has an important impact on president because information both flattering and unflattering about the president is widely available in the United States. Presidents have access to the media and can use this power to improve their image. At the same time, the independent media is likely to publish stories that are negative in tone.

-   Press conferences are meetings held by the president with members of the press. They can have a negative impact on presidential approval. These meetings are not required by law or the Constitution, therefore presidents have some control over how many press conferences are held. Presidents can also ask their press secretary to hold the meetings for them. Press conferences are frequently confrontational in nature and can lead to discussions about scandals that have been published. For example, during Bill Clinton's presidency, he was directly asked about the Monica Lewinsky scandal in a press conference in spite of the fact that he had tried to turn the conversation to other topics. Because of the possibility of being questioned about scandals and unflattering events, modern presidents have tended not to hold press conferences.

-   The fireside chat began with FDR's presidency. These take place when presidents use the radio to communicate directly with citizens. They tend to have a positive impact on the president's term because there are no or few combative questions directed at the president. The president can set the tone of the talks and provide the information that he wants. Such "chats" are frequently used to attempt to change public opinion. FDR used fireside chats to change public opinion to favor the country's entry into World War II.

- Sound bites are short video clips of approximately 10 seconds, and are frequently all that are shown of a president's speech on the news. These can have a positive or negative impact on the president, depending on how the statements are portrayed in the media. A president may choose a particular sound bite and repeat it in order to generate a high likelihood that it is on the news, but also the media may choose a sound bite that the president is unhappy about.

8

Political Parties

☐ Chapter Overview

In his farewell address, President George Washington warned against the growing influence of political parties. From his perspective, parties represented a threat to democracy in the United States. But in spite of his caution, political parties today play a central role in American democracy. In this chapter, we analyze the role of political parties in American politics. We begin by outlining the functions that parties perform in American democracy. Then we explore the significance of party identification. We describe how parties are organized in the United States, and evaluate how well parties generally implement their platforms. Next, we examine the historical evolution of political parties in the United States. We conclude by evaluating the role of third parties in the American political system, and determine why the two-party system has persisted. By the end of the chapter, students should have a good understanding of the role of political parties in American politics.

☐ Study Outline

 Learning Objective 8.1: Identify the functions that political parties perform in American democracy. (p. 259)

The Meaning of Party

- A **political party** is a team of men and women seeking to control the governing apparatus by gaining office in an election.

- Political parties carry out several tasks, including choosing candidates, running campaigns, giving cues to voters, articulating policies, and coordinating policymaking.

- Political parties serve as **linkage institutions**, which are channels through which concerns become political issues on the government's policy agenda.

- **Rational choice theory** explains the actions of voters, politicians, and parties.

- It assumes that individuals act in their best interest and weigh the costs and benefits of possible alternatives.

- In order to win office, candidates select policies that are widely favored.

- The majority of voters are in the middle ideologically, so centrist parties win elections.

- This has led to criticism of the two major parties for being too similar.

8.2 Learning Objective 8.2: Determine the significance of party identification in America today. (p. 263)

The Party in the Electorate

- Many voters cast their ballots on the basis of **party identification**.

- For instance, people who consider themselves Democrats usually vote for Democratic candidates.

- Party identification is declining, however; as of 2000, the more voters considered themselves **Independent** than either Democratic or Republican.

- **Party image** is the voter's perception of what the Republicans and Democrats stand for, such as conservatism and liberalism.

- **Ticket splitting**, or voting for members of different parties for different offices in an election, is also on the rise.

- This practice leads to a divided party government—the president may be of a different party from the majority party in Congress, for example.

Learning Objective 8.3: Describe how political parties are organized in the United States. (p. 265)

The Party Organizations: From the Grass Roots to Washington

- Unlike the more formal parties of other countries, American political parties are fairly decentralized, with city, state, and national administrative bodies.

- State parties are becoming more formally organized, but most presidential campaigning is still conducted through the candidate's personal campaign organization.

- Holding elections is one important task performed by the states, each of which has its own unique party organization.

- Each state's parties go about the election process differently, such as by choosing which type of primary to hold. There are three main types of primaries: closed, open, and blanket.

- Until the 1930s, local parties had tremendous influence over city governments.

- These often-corrupt **party machines** maintained their power by using the **patronage system** to reward loyal members with important positions in the government.

- Today local parties have declined, while county-level organizations have increased their election activities.

- The national party organization, or **national committee**, writes the official party platform and holds the national convention through which a presidential and vice presidential candidate are nominated.

- The national committee maintains the party organization during nonelection years.

Learning Objective 8.4: Evaluate how well political parties generally do in carrying out their promises. (p. 268)

The Party in Government: Promises and Policy

- Parties help members of Congress form **coalitions** that support a particular policy objective; however, presidents do not need to rely on party support as much as they used to because they can gain the favor of the public directly through television.

Learning Objective 8.5: Differentiate the various party eras in American history. (p. 270)

Party Eras in American History

- Most democratic nations have multiparty systems that allow many interests to be represented.

- The United States, however, has always had a two-party system. Political scientists divide American history into **party eras** in which one party dominated politics for a significant period of time.

- Party eras change when a **critical election** reveals new issues and a failure of the traditional coalitions and this usually causes **party realignment**, when the party redefines itself and attracts a new coalition of voters.

- The **First Party System** (1796–1824) started with Alexander Hamilton's short-lived Federalist Party, the first American political party.

- For most of the period, though, Thomas Jefferson's Democratic-Republicans maintained control of the White House.

- During the period of the **Democrats and the Whigs** (1828–1856), Andrew Jackson appealed to the masses rather than to the elite.

- He formed a new coalition and, ultimately, the Democratic Party.

- The opposition party was the Whig Party, though it had little political success.

- The **Two Republican Eras** (1860–1928) were dominated by the Republican Party, but these eras saw a major realignment of party coalitions under the same name.

- The Republican Party formed out of a coalition of antislavery groups and nominated Abraham Lincoln as its first presidential candidate.

- The election of 1896 began another strongly Republican era during which industrialization and capitalism were advanced.

- The **New Deal Coalition** (1932–1964) formed when Franklin Roosevelt brought the Democratic Party back into favor by starting scores of federal programs to combat the Great Depression.

- The new Democratic coalition brought together the poor, Southerners, African Americans, city dwellers, Catholics, and Jews. Kennedy's New Frontier and

Johnson's Great Society and War on Poverty continued the Democratic New Deal tradition.

- Since 1968, we have seen **Southern realignment** and **divided party government**.

- The states in the South have realigned and are now strongholds of the Republican Party.

- President Nixon was able to capture the South, which had previously been solidly Democratic.

- When Nixon became president, there was divided government for the first time in the 20th century, with one party controlling Congress and another the White House.

- This became a frequent election pattern for most presidents that followed him.

- The trend in divided government has led many political scientists to believe that the party system has dealigned rather than realigned.

- **Party dealignment** means that people are gradually moving away from both parties.

 Learning Objective 8.6: Assess both the impact of third parties on American politics and their limitations. (p. 277)

Third Parties: Their Impact on American Politics

- **Third parties** occasionally arise to challenge the two major parties, but they rarely gain enough support to put a candidate in office.

- Some parties form around a specific cause; some are splinter parties, formed from smaller factions of the two major parties, and some form around a specific individual.

- Though they rarely win, third-party candidates do force particular issues onto the political agenda and allow Americans to express their discontent with the two major parties.

- They may also shift the votes of the electorate; for example, many political scientists think George W. Bush won the 2000 election because Green Party candidate Ralph Nader took votes away from Democrat Al Gore. The American **winner-take-all system** is an electoral system in which legislative seats are awarded to candidates who come in first.

- In presidential elections, the candidate who comes in first gets all of the state's electoral votes. This makes only two parties likely.

- **Proportional representation** is an electoral system in which seats in a legislative branch are awarded in proportion to the percentage of the vote received, making it likely that many parties will win seats.

- This often makes a **coalition government** necessary, in which two or more parties join together to form a majority in a national legislature.

 ## Learning Objective 8.7: Evaluate the advantages and disadvantages of responsible party government. (p. 279)

Understanding Political Parties

Democracy and Responsible Party Government

- Political parties today are considered to be essential to a democratic system and the prevention of totalitarian rule, although the framers of the Constitution were wary of political parties.

- Critics of the two-party system allege that there is little choice for voters because the two parties keep to the middle of the road, that there is less opportunity for political change, and that the party system is so decentralized that it fails to translate campaign promises into policy because politicians do not have to vote with the party line.

- Critics of the two-party system have proposed the **responsible party model**, which describes how parties should offer choices to voters, follow through with campaign promises, and accept responsibility as a party for the performance of the government.

- American officeholders do not always follow the platform planks of their party; for example, the **Blue Dog Democrats** are fiscally conservative Democrats who oppose the more liberal tendencies of the Democratic party.

American Political Parties and the Scope of Government

- American political parties do not require party discipline the way many European party systems do.

- The weak party structure of the United States makes it harder to pass legislation.

- Political parties have declined in strength.

- The political party is no longer the major source of information for citizens.

For Additional Review

Design a pyramid diagram depicting the top-down leadership structure within a political party (national level, state level, local level). Place the various party members on the pyramid along with a description of the role played by each. Use this pyramid diagram when reviewing and studying for the unit test and the AP Government and Politics exam.

Create a timeline depicting the evolution of political parties in the United States. Place the major eras of political party development on the timeline along with a description of each era, including the political parties, their platforms, and accomplishments. Use this timeline when reviewing and studying for the unit test and the AP Government and Politics exam.

❑ Review Questions

Multiple-Choice Questions

1. All of the following are functions of political parties EXCEPT
    a. dictating policies.
    b. choosing candidates.
    c. running campaigns.
    d. giving cues to voters.
    e. coordinating policymaking.

2. Which of the following is true of the Southern states?
    a. They have always leaned Republican.
    b. They have always leaned Democratic.
    c. They have no political leaning.
    d. They were once loyal to the Democratic Party but now are loyal to the Republican Party.
    e. They were once loyal to the Republican Party but now are loyal to the Democratic Party.

3. All of the following are true of the party machine EXCEPT
    a. they were successful in creating party loyalists.
    b. they provided jobs and favors for voters.
    c. they were corrupt.
    d. legislation has largely dismantled them.
    e. they relied on the merit principle when hiring employees.

4. Which of the following is true of an open primary?
   a. They allow crossover voting.
   b. They receive high turnout.
   c. They are the only system used to select a presidential candidate.
   d. They require that voters be registered with the party.
   e. They require voters to attend meetings in order to participate.

5. Which of the following is the best definition of "realignment"?
   a. the abandonment of citizens from the two major parties to be independent
   b. the requirement that members of a party vote together
   c. the party that controls the White House loses control in Congress
   d. a major ideological and demographic shift within a party
   e. the emergence of many third parties

6. Which of the following was least likely to join the New Deal coalition?
   a. minority voters
   b. blue-collar voters
   c. voters without a college education
   d. wealthy voters
   e. liberal voters

7. Obstacles to third parties' success include all of the following EXCEPT
   a. the winner-take-all rule.
   b. lack of funding from interest groups.
   c. inability to participate in the debate.
   d. lack of ballot access.
   e. inability to get media attention.

8. A two-party system differs from a multiparty system in that it
   a. encourages moderation in policymaking and discourages change.
   b. offers voters no choice among ideologies.
   c. usually includes a liberal and a conservative party.
   d. relies on popular elections to change the party in power.
   e. allows parties to choose their own leaders in the legislature.

9. Which of the following has led to ticket splitting in recent elections?
   a. partisan dealignment
   b. open primaries
   c. party realignment
   d. patronage system
   e. closed primaries

10. The event in which the parties formally nominate their candidate for the presidency is called
    a. a critical election.
    b. a national convention.
    c. an open primary.
    d. a closed primary.
    e. a national committee.

11. The U.S. has a "single member, plurality" system, often referred to as
    a. direct representation.
    b. proportional representation.
    c. winner-take-all.
    d. winner-take-most.
    e. winner-take-some.

12. Which of the following groups is likely to be Democratic?

    I. white-collar workers
    II. blue-collar workers
    III. trial lawyers
    IV. women who do not work outside the home

    a. I and IV
    b. II and III
    c. I, II, and III
    d. I and III
    e. I, II, III, and IV

13. A citizen's personal affinity for a political party, which results in the citizen voting for candidates of that political party, is known as party
    a. identification.
    b. registration.
    c. alignment.
    d. coalition.
    e. representation.

14. Which of the following statements about political parties is accurate?
    a. The U.S. has never had a third party.
    b. The Democratic and Republican parties have been on the presidential ballot for every election since the presidency of George Washington.
    c. Third parties are prohibited by the Constitution.
    d. Third parties have frequently captured the White House.
    e. While the Democrats and Republicans have dominated American politics, they have also seen competition from a wide variety of third parties.

15. Many Americans do not associate with either major political party and instead claim to "vote for the ___ and not the ___."
    a. party; person
    b. person; party
    c. challenger; incumbent
    d. free-rider; policy entrepreneur
    e. underdog; front-runner

16. A superdelegate is
    a. a spokesperson and arbitrator for the party during the four years between elections.
    b. a delegate to the Democratic Party's national convention that is reserved for an elected party official, whose vote at the convention is not pledged to individual candidates.
    c. someone elected in a winner-take-all system.
    d. someone selected by a proportional representation election.
    e. someone who won a seat by both proportional representation and winner-take-all district voting.

17. Even though the United States has many minor political parties, it remains
    a. a multiparty system.
    b. a two-party system.
    c. a third party system.
    d. a parliamentary system.
    e. a confederate system.

18. The political condition in which different political parties control the presidency and the Congress is called
    a. gridlock.
    b. dual federalism.
    c. cooperative federalism.
    d. divided government.
    e. apportionment.

19. Political party platforms can best be described as which of the following?
    a. They are strictly followed by elected officials.
    b. They are written by the president.
    c. They are intentionally vague.
    d. They are different from state-to-state.
    e. They are never followed by elected officials.

20. The gradual disengagement of people from the political parties in order to become Independents is known as
    a. realignment.
    b. misalignment.
    c. party patronage.
    d. dealignment.
    e. ticket splitting.

Free-Response Questions

1. The power of the political party has declined over the past fifty years.

    a. Define each of the terms below:

       - Dealignment
       - Political machine

- National party conventions

b. Choose two of the terms above and explain how they have contributed to the decline of political parties since 1960.

2. The Democratic and Republican parties have gone through several realignments.

a. Define realignment.

b. Identify one realignment for the Democratic Party and one for the Republican Party.

c. Explain the significance of realignments for American politics.

☐ Answers and Explanations

Multiple-Choice Questions

1. All of the following are functions of political parties EXCEPT

   (a) is correct because American political parties may articulate policy preferences, but they are unable to dictate policy.

   (b) is incorrect because political parties do choose candidates.

   (c) is incorrect because political parties do run campaigns.

   (d) is incorrect because political parties do give cues to voters.

   (e) is incorrect because political parties do coordinate policymaking.

   Page reference: 260–262, AP Topic: Political parties

2. Which of the following is true of the Southern states?

   (a) is incorrect because the South was historically Democratic.

   (b) is incorrect because the South now leans Republican.

   (c) is incorrect because the South does have political leanings.

   (d) is correct because the South was once "solidly Democratic" but now leans Republican.

   (e) is incorrect because it is an inaccurate description of southern party affiliation.

   Page reference: 275–276, AP Topic: Political parties

3.   All of the following are true of the party machine EXCEPT

(a) is incorrect because party machines were successful in creating party loyalists.

(b) is incorrect because party machines provided jobs and favors.

(c) is incorrect because party machines were corrupt.

(d) is incorrect because party machines have been limited by legislation.

(e) is correct because the party machines relied on the patronage system.

Page reference: 266, AP Topic: Political parties

4.   Which of the following is true of an open primary?

(a) is correct because open primaries allow citizens of either party to participate in the primary and this allows crossover voting, or a person of one party voting in another party's primary.

(b) is incorrect because open primaries do not necessarily receive a high turnout.

(c) is incorrect because open primaries are not the only means of selecting presidential candidates.

(d) is incorrect because open primaries do not require voters to be registered with the party.

(e) is incorrect because open primaries do not require voters to attend meetings in order to participate.

Page reference: 267, AP Topic: Political parties

5.   Which of the following is the best definition of "realignment"?

(a) is incorrect because it is an inaccurate description of realignment.

(b) is incorrect because it is an inaccurate description of realignment.

(c) is incorrect because it is an inaccurate description of realignment.

(d) is correct because realignments are major changes within a party. Change occurs both in the type of voters who are attracted to the party and the issues the party supports.

(e) is incorrect because it is an inaccurate description of realignment.

Page reference: 272, AP Topic: Political parties

6.   Which of the following was least likely to join the New Deal coalition?

(a) is incorrect because the New Deal attracted minorities.

(b) is incorrect because the New Deal attracted blue-collar voters.

(c) is incorrect because the New Deal attracted lower-educated voters.

(d) is correct because the New Deal coalition did not attract wealthy voters.

(e) is incorrect because the New Deal attracted liberal voters.

Page reference: 273–275, AP Topic: Political parties

7.   Obstacles to third parties' success include all of the following EXCEPT

(a) is incorrect because the winner-take-all rule is an obstacle to third parties.

(b) is incorrect because lack of funding from interest groups is an obstacle to third parties.

(c) is incorrect because televised debates are an obstacle to third parties.

(d) is incorrect because lack of ballot access is an obstacle to third parties.

(e) is correct because the inability to get media attention is not an obstacle to third parties.

Page reference: 277–278, AP Topic: Political parties

8.   A two-party system differs from a multiparty system in that it

(a) is correct because two-party systems encourage candidates to be more moderate and thereby discourage change.

(b) is incorrect because it is an inaccurate description of how a two-party system differs from a multiparty system.

(c) is incorrect because it is an inaccurate description of how a two-party system differs from a multiparty system.

(d) is incorrect because it is an inaccurate description of how a two-party system differs from a multiparty system.

(e) is incorrect because it is an inaccurate description of how a two-party system differs from a multiparty system.

Page reference: 258–278, AP Topic: Political parties

9. Which of the following has led to ticket splitting in recent elections?

(a) is correct because ticket splitting occurs because there are more citizens who are not loyal to one party over another.

(b) is incorrect because open primaries do not lead to ticket splitting.

(c) is incorrect because party realignment does not lead to ticket splitting.

(d) is incorrect because the patronage system does not lead to ticket splitting.

(e) is incorrect because closed primaries do not lead to ticket splitting.

Page reference: 264, AP Topic: Political parties

10. The event in which the parties formally nominate their candidate for the presidency is called

(a) is incorrect because presidential candidates are not selected in a critical election.

(b) is correct because candidates for the presidency are formally selected at a national convention.

(c) is incorrect because presidential candidates are not selected in an open primary.

(d) is incorrect because presidential candidates are not selected in a closed primary.

(e) is incorrect because presidential candidates are not selected by a national committee.

Page reference: 268, AP Topic: Political parties

11. The U.S. has a "single member, plurality" system, often referred to as

(a) is incorrect because it is an inaccurate selection for the definition provided.

(b) is incorrect because it is an inaccurate selection for the definition provided.

(c) is correct because national level elections in the U.S. use a system in which the party that receives at least one more vote than any other party wins the seat in question, which is known as winner-take-all.

(d) is incorrect because it is an inaccurate selection for the definition provided.

(e) is incorrect because it is an inaccurate selection for the definition provided.

Page reference: 278, AP Topic: Political parties

12. Which of the following groups is likely to be Democratic?

I. white-collar workers
II. blue-collar workers

III. trial lawyers

IV. women who do not work outside the home

(a) is incorrect because white-collar workers and women who do not work outside the home tend to favor Republicans.

(b) is correct because blue-collar workers and trial lawyers favor Democrats.

(c) is incorrect because white collar workers do not tend to be Democratic.

(d) is incorrect because I is an inaccurate choice.

(e) is incorrect because I and IV are inaccurate choices.

Page reference: 263–268, AP Topic: Political parties

13. A citizen's personal affinity for a political party, which results in the citizen voting for candidates of that political party, is known as party

(a) is correct because a citizen's personal affinity for a political party, usually expressed by a tendency to vote for the candidates of that party, is called the citizen's party identification.

(b) is incorrect because registration is an inaccurate choice for the definition provided.

(c) is incorrect because alignment is an inaccurate choice for the definition provided.

(d) is incorrect because coalition is an inaccurate choice for the definition provided.

(e) is incorrect because representation is an inaccurate choice for the definition provided.

Page reference: 263–264, AP Topic: Political parties

14. Which of the following statements about political parties is accurate?

(a) is incorrect because it is an inaccurate description of third parties.

(b) is incorrect because it is an inaccurate description of third parties.

(c) is incorrect because it is an inaccurate description of third parties.

(d) is incorrect because it is an inaccurate description of third parties.

(e) is correct because although third-party candidates rarely win elections, several have appeared on the ballot over the years and have had some effect on the political debate, and possibly the outcome of elections.

Page reference: 277–278, AP Topic: Political parties

15.   Many Americans do not associate with either major political party and instead claim to "vote for the ___ and not the ___."

(a) is incorrect because it is an inaccurate selection for the prompt.

(b) is correct because with the decline in party identification, the plurality of voters considered themselves Independent rather than Democratic or Republican, and many Americans insist that they vote for "the person, not the party."

(c) is incorrect because it is an inaccurate selection for the prompt.

(d) is incorrect because it is an inaccurate selection for the prompt.

(e) is incorrect because it is an inaccurate selection for the prompt.

Page reference: 263–264, AP Topic: Political parties

16.   A superdelegate is

(a) is correct because a superdelegate is a delegate to the Democratic Party's national convention that is reserved for an elected party official, whose vote at the convention is not pledged to individual candidates.

(b) is incorrect because it is an inaccurate description of a superdelegate.

(c) is incorrect because it is an inaccurate description of a superdelegate.

(d) is incorrect because it is an inaccurate description of a superdelegate.

(e) is incorrect because it is an inaccurate description of a superdelegate.

Page reference: 292, AP Topic: Political parties

17.   Even though the United States has many minor political parties, it remains

(a) is incorrect because the United States is not predominately a multiparty system.

(b) is correct because the United States still remains predominately a two-party system despite the existence of minor parties.

(c) is incorrect because the United States is not predominately a third party system.

(d) is incorrect because the United States is not a parliamentary system.

(e) is incorrect because the United States is not a confederate system.

Page reference: 259–278, AP Topic: Political parties

18.   The political condition in which different political parties control the presidency and the

(a) is incorrect because gridlock is an inaccurate choice for the definition provided.

(b) is incorrect because dual federalism is an inaccurate choice for the definition provided.

(c) is incorrect because cooperative federalism is an inaccurate choice for the definition provided.

(d) is correct because divided government is governance divided between the parties, as when one holds the presidency and the other controls one or both houses of Congress.

(e) is incorrect because apportionment is an inaccurate choice for the definition provided.

Page reference: 275–276, AP Topic: Political parties

19.   Political party platforms can best be described as which of the following?

(a) is incorrect because platforms are not strictly followed.

(b) is incorrect because platforms are not written by the president.

(c) is correct because party platforms are often written in vague terms to avoid controversy.

(d) is incorrect because platforms are not different from state-to-state.

(e) is incorrect because platforms are sometimes followed by elected officials.

Page reference: 268, 290–297, AP Topic: Political parties

20.   The gradual disengagement of people from the political parties in order to become Independents is known as

(a) is incorrect because realignment is an inaccurate choice for the definition provided.

(b) is incorrect because misalignment is an inaccurate choice for the definition provided.

(c) is incorrect because party patronage is an inaccurate choice for the definition provided.

(d) is correct because the gradual disengagement of people from parties, as seen in part by shrinking party identification is party dealignment.

(e) is incorrect because ticket-splitting is an inaccurate choice for the definition provided.

Page reference: 275–276, AP Topic: Political parties

Free-Response Questions

This rubric provides examples of many, but not all of the possible correct responses to the free-response questions.

1. The power of the political party has declined over the past fifty years.

    a. Define each of the terms below:

        - Dealignment
        - Political machine
        - National party conventions

    b. Choose two of the terms above and explain how they have contributed to the decline of political parties since 1960.

        - The power of the party has declined over the past one hundred years. This is due to a dealignment movement. Dealignment refers to the abandonment of citizen's affiliations with the two major political parties to become "independent" voters. Such independent or swing voters have hurt the power of the party because the members of the party must now battle for the ideological center rather than loyalists in order to win an election. The party can no longer depend on large numbers of citizens to vote a straight ticket, and thus the election results become a little more unpredictable. Also, presidents are less likely to staff government with all party loyalists and are more likely to turn to independents.

        - The decline of the party machine has also hurt the power of the party. The party machine can be described as a party organization with lots of power in large cities. Such a machine once guaranteed social services and jobs to new immigrants, ran conventions, and staffed city government. This created a group of party loyalists that lasted for generations. Some of these activities became illegal, causing the party to lose strength as the generations of party loyalists diminished.

        - Finally, the national party convention was once a source of party strength, but this strength has diminished greatly. The national party used to determine the nominee for the presidency, with no voter involvement at all. The progressive reforms stripped this power from the party at the state level and eventually all states began holding primaries and caucuses to determine the nominee, taking the power away from the party.

2. The Democratic and Republican parties have gone through several realignments.

a. Define realignment.

- A realignment usually occurs after a critical election. A realignment marks a major change in the nature of the political party. The change occurs in both the demographic groups that once supported the party as well as the agenda of the party. In a realignment, the party that was once the majority usually becomes the minority. The change is national as well as local, and the change is not simply marked by one election but has some permanence.

b. Identify one realignment for the Democratic Party and one for the Republican Party.

- Most political scientists argue that there have been four major realigning periods. Perhaps the most remembered realignment for the Republican Party took place after the election of 1860—sometimes referred to as the "birth of the Republican Party." The new president, Abraham Lincoln, had captured a new group of voters and his party dominated politics (the party realigned several times after that). Perhaps the most remembered realignment for the Democratic Party came after the election of 1932. Franklin D. Roosevelt began a "New Deal" coalition, which would unify the Democratic Party for years to come.

c. Explain the significance of realignments for American politics.

- Realignments are significant to American politics because they mark major changes in the nature of the party, and the party emerges as a completely different organization. Understanding realignments helps to explain how parties have changed. For example, it is surprising to some that Thomas Jefferson was a Democrat because he was a states' rights advocate, and the Democratic Party today has advocated federal power in most domestic policy areas. The explanation for this is that the Democratic Party has realigned since Thomas Jefferson was a member of the party.

9

Campaigns and Voting Behavior

☐ Chapter Overview

Elections form the foundation of the American system of democracy. They are the means by which citizens select the leaders of the government who, presumably, enact policies on behalf of constituents. But Americans often have a weak understanding of how campaigns, elections, and voting in the United States actually function, despite their importance. In this chapter, we explore the process of seeking elected office in the United States. We begin by exploring the fundamental election procedures—the rules of the game—that define how candidates are nominated and how winners are determined in American elections. We focus in particular on the fairness of our current system. Then we examine the key objectives of political campaigns and outline the benefits of incumbency and the role of money in the campaign process. Next, we consider the factors that influence the decisions of voters, focusing in particular on the role of party identification, candidate evaluation, and policy options on voting. We conclude by evaluating the advantages and disadvantages of the U.S. system of campaigns and elections. By the end of the chapter, students should have a good command of the formal structures and functions, as well as the behind-the-scenes politics, of campaigns and elections in the United States.

☐ Study Outline

9.1 **Learning Objective 9.1: Evaluate the fairness of our current system of presidential primaries and caucuses. (p. 290)**

The Nomination Game

- A nomination is a party's official endorsement of a candidate for office.

- Politicians begin their bid for a presidential nomination more than a year in advance of the election. In most other countries, campaigns are limited to only a few months.

- Most candidates have previously held a government post, such as representative, senator, governor, or military general.

- The master game plan candidates lay out to guide their electoral campaign is the **campaign strategy**.

Competing for Delegates

- Each state selects delegates to send to the Democratic and the Republican **national conventions**, which have the supreme power to select the presidential nominee for the party.

- A few states still use traditional **caucuses** to choose delegates, which are closed meetings of party regulars who participate in party building activities and select nominees.

- Most states now use **primaries** where voters can nominate a presidential candidate directly, or else they can choose delegates who have pledged to vote for that candidate.

- State parties may have open primaries, where any registered voter can fill out a party nomination ballot, or closed primaries, where advanced party registration is required.

- The political parties in each state decide how to divide its delegates' votes.

- Delegates are apportioned to each candidate based on their proportion of the vote in each state congressional district.

- The Republican Party gives all votes to the candidate with the majority vote in each district.

- The Democratic Party divides delegates proportionally by district and statewide. The rise of primaries has allowed the electorate to take control of the election process away from political parties.
- The primary system has raised numerous criticisms:
  - The early caucuses and primaries receive far too much media attention, which can distort campaigns and candidates who do not score early victories are likely to be dismissed by the media and the public and to be unable to raise funds to continue campaigning.
  - The lengthy campaign and rigors of the primary season discourage some capable politicians from running.
  - It requires and encourages an exorbitant amount of spending in campaigns.
  - Primaries are unrepresentative of the electorate because few people vote in them, and those who do are more likely to be older and wealthier than the majority of Americans.
  - It allows the media, which focuses on winners and dismisses losers early in the running, tremendous influence in shaping campaigns.
- One proposal by critics of the current system is a **national primary**, which would replace the extended primary calendar with a nationwide primary held on one day.
- Another proposal calls for **regional primaries**, which would allow regions to have primaries, with rotation of the order of regional primaries every four years.

The Convention Send-Off

- The delegates selected in each state's primary attend the **national convention**, where they cast their votes for their presidential candidate.
- The parties, especially the Democrats, have made efforts to **reform** delegate selection to ensure representation of youth, minorities, women, and organized labor at the convention.
- Some convention seats are reserved for **superdelegates**, party leaders and politicians who automatically earn a vote at the convention.
- The Democratic Party makes greater use of superdelegates than the Republican Party.

- The outcome of conventions today is usually predetermined by previous primary results, so conventions today are **media events**.

- At a national convention, delegates support their candidate, the party presents its official **party platform** for the next four years, the winning candidate formally accepts the party's nomination, and the party's vice-presidential nominee is chosen, usually based on the presidential nominee's preference for a running mate.

9.2 Learning Objective 9.2: Explain the key objectives of any political campaign. (p. 298)

The Campaign Game

- The two presidential candidates then embark on a **national campaign** to win the votes of different groups in different regions of the country.

- Modern campaign techniques include **television advertising**, televised **public appearances**, **direct mail** campaigns, and an official website to advance the candidate's platform and collect campaign contributions.

- The media closely follow campaigns and coverage focuses on the candidates' daily activities, **campaign strategies**, and poll results.

- Studies show that voters learn more about the candidates' positions on important issues from their advertisements than from the news.

- Critics fear that campaigns have become centered on candidates' images rather than their political beliefs.

- To coordinate a campaign, a candidate must hire a campaign team that serves to organize his or her daily activities and also conducts **public relations**, and this adds significantly to the enormous cost of a campaign.

Learning Objective 9.3: Outline how the financing of federal campaigns is regulated by campaign finance laws. (p. 301)

Money and Campaigning

- Candidates rely on television to communicate directly with the electorate, and airtime often translates into votes, and therefore, the necessity of television has made American campaigns extremely expensive.

- Politicians spend as much time fundraising as doing their jobs.

- In 1974, Congress passed the **Federal Election Campaign Act (FECA)** to attempt to control campaign costs and donations, which established the **Federal Election Commission** to enforce campaign laws, and initiated public financing of elections.

- Taxpayers can choose to donate $3 to a federal campaign fund that is divided among all candidates by checking a box on their income tax form (**Presidential Election Campaign Fund**).

- FECA also set limits for spending in each election by those who accept public funds.

- Under FECA, candidates are required to **report all campaign contributions and how the money was spent**, and individual campaign contributions are limited to $2,000.

- **Soft money** is one loophole through which businesses and wealthy individuals can make unlimited contributions.

- Soft money is intended for a party's general use; since it is therefore not a donation to a specific candidate, it can be channeled into presidential campaigns.

- The **Bipartisan Campaign Reform Act (BCRA or McCain–Feingold)** attempted to ban soft money, as the candidate often rewards contributors once he or she is in office.

- The Supreme Court upheld the act against a constitutional challenge in 2003.

- A loophole in the BCRA allowed 527 organizations to form and raise unlimited amounts of money to spend on advertising and voter mobilization efforts.

- **Political action committees (PACs)**, established in 1974 by the FECA, are another method through which interest groups try to influence policy through campaign contributions.

- To contribute to a campaign, an interest group must channel money through a PAC, which must be registered with the FEC so that it can be monitored.

- There is **no limit** to the amount PACs can spend.

- PACs can act independently of the candidate and his or her campaign team by running an advertisement without the candidate's approval.

- Created to provide unions and other groups the opportunity to contribute, PACs have been organized and used by businesses to affect elections.

- Candidates rely on PACs to help finance costly campaigns.

- PACs play a greater role in congressional elections than in presidential elections, which are partially funded by the public.

- Despite the massive amount of money spent on campaigns and the media's constant focus on them, campaigns rarely convert voters away from their predisposed party identification.

 Learning Objective 9.4: Determine why campaigns have an important yet limited impact on election outcomes. (p. 307)

The Impact of Campaigns

- In general, politicians tend to overestimate the impact of campaigns; political scientists have found that campaigning primarily reinforces citizens' views rather than changing views.

- Factors such as **selective perception**, party identification, and the incumbency advantage tend to weaken the ability of campaigns to influence voters' decisions.

 Learning Objective 9.5: Identify the factors that influence whether people vote. (p. 307)

Whether to Vote: A Citizen's First Choice

- **Suffrage** has been expanded several times throughout American history and, although the Constitution left the issue up to the states, generally only white, male, property owners had the right to vote.

- Today, almost **all Americans over the age of 18** can vote in elections.

- □ The Fifteenth Amendment granted suffrage to African Americans.
- □ The Nineteenth Amendment extended voting privileges to women.
- □ The Twenty-Sixth Amendment set the minimum voting age at 18.
- Although more people are able to vote, fewer people are exercising this right.
  - □ Some people do not vote because they believe that one vote in more than 100 million makes little difference.
  - □ Some people do not vote because they are unable to take time off of work to vote on a Tuesday; reformers have suggested moving Election Day to a Saturday.
  - □ Some people do not vote because **voter registration** is difficult or inconvenient in most states.
  - □ Procedures have been made easier, especially with the **Motor Voter Act**, but turnout has still decreased.
  - □ Some people do not vote because there is little ideological difference between the two parties' candidates.
  - □ Some people are more likely to vote because they perceive a significant ideological difference between the two parties' candidates.
  - □ Some people are more likely to vote because they have a sense of **political efficacy**—they believe their vote will make a difference.
  - □ Some people are more likely to vote because they want to perform their **civic duty** in a democracy.

Who Votes?

- People with a college education are more likely to vote.
- Older people, especially senior citizens, are more likely to vote.
- Hispanic Americans and African Americans are less likely to vote, but those with higher levels of education vote in greater percentages than educated Caucasians.
- More women than men have voted in recent elections.
- Union members are more likely to vote.
- People who are married are more likely to vote.
- Politicians who rely on these voters to be elected are more likely to address their concerns in the policy arena.

- Studies show that if turnout increased among groups with low turnout rates, Democrats would probably receive more votes.

- Reforms are unlikely because Republicans do not want to lose this advantage.

 Learning Objective 9.6: Assess the impact of party identification, candidate evaluations, and policy opinions on voting behavior. (p. 313)

How Americans Vote: Explaining Citizens' Decisions

- The idea that the winning candidate has a mandate from the people to carry out his or her platforms and politics is the **mandate theory of elections**.

- Some people vote according to their **party identification**.

- A candidate of their chosen party probably shares their political beliefs and they do not have to decide on or become informed about every issue.

- This trend is declining as parties have lost some significance in the political process.

- Some voters evaluate what they know and see of the **candidates' personalities** to make a decision.

- A candidate's appearance may play an unconscious role in voter decision making.

- People tend to value integrity, competence, and reliability in a candidate.

- Voters with a college education are actually more likely to base their decision on a candidate's personality, using it to make assumptions about the candidate's performance.

- Some people vote for candidates who share their **policy preferences**; this assumes that voters have firm policy convictions, they are familiar with each candidate's policy preferences, and that they are able to discern differences among candidates' stands on issues.

- A person may also **vote retrospectively** by choosing a candidate who vows to continue policies helpful to him or her, or by choosing the opposition candidate who promises to change the policy.

- Candidates may avoid taking a clear stand on a controversial issue, making **policy voting** difficult. This method requires a lot of effort on the part of voters.

9.7 Learning Objective 9.7: Evaluate the fairness of the Electoral College system for choosing the president. (p. 318)

The Last Battle: The Electoral College

- In the United States, the president is not chosen directly by the people in a popular election; the Electoral College casts the final vote.

- The writers of the Constitution created this institution to keep the presidency at a distance from the masses; it was intended to allow only the elite to choose the president.

- Each state's number of electors is equal to its total number of representatives and senators. Electors are chosen by the state party organizations.

- Almost all states are **winner-take-all**: The candidate who receives the highest popular vote in the state gets all of that state's electoral votes.

- The key states that the presidential campaigns focus on because they are most likely to decide the outcome of the Electoral College are known as **battleground states**.

- Electors convene in December and deliver their votes to the president of the Senate (the vice president), who officially announces the majority winner at the opening of the congressional session in January.

- If no candidate receives a majority of the electoral votes (at least 270), the members of the House of Representatives vote, with each state delegation having one vote.

- This system has received an enormous amount of criticism.

  □ It gives an unfair advantage to states with larger populations, because they have a greater number of electoral votes at stake; large states and their policy concerns receive more attention from presidential candidates.

  □ A candidate may need to win in only a few large states to win the election.

  □ This neglects the less populous states (although George W. Bush used a small-state strategy to win the presidency in 2000 and 2004).

  □ Because most large states also have large cities, the system is biased in favor of urban voters.

  □ It is possible to win the popular vote but lose the election because of the electoral votes. This happened to Al Gore, who won the popular vote in 2000.

Learning Objective 9.8: Assess the advantages and disadvantages of the U.S. system of campaigns and elections. (p. 321)

- American election campaigns are easily the most open and democratic in the world.

- They are extraordinarily long, perhaps excessively burdening politicians and leading politicians to make many promises that increase the scope of government.

- Long campaigns do give little-known candidates a chance to emerge and provide a strenuous test for all the candidates.

For Additional Review

Create a "Campaign Finance" graphic organizer (chart, etc.) to identify key legislation and Supreme Court decisions impacting the campaign finance process. Use this graphic organizer when reviewing and studying for the unit test and the AP Government and Politics exam.

Use the graphic organizer to create a timeline in order to examine the historical and current rules for campaign funding and finance. Place the rules, practices, etc. on the timeline and connect each change to the key legislation and Supreme Court decisions cited in the graphic organizer. Relate the timeline to the arguments for and against campaign finance reform. Use this information when reviewing and studying for the unit test and the AP Government and Politics exam.

☐ Review Questions

Multiple-Choice Questions

1. A caucus is
   a. held at the national level to select a nominee.
   b. a closed-door meeting of party regulars.
   c. open to all who want to participate.
   d. a meeting of members of Congress.
   e. a court hearing.

2. A primary is
   a. held at the national level to select a nominee.
   b. a closed-door meeting of party regulars.
   c. either open or closed.
   d. a meeting of members of Congress.
   e. a court hearing.

3. When the Democrats select delegates to their national convention, they
   a. require all delegates to vote based on a vote held at the state level.
   b. use a winner-take-all system to allocate delegates.
   c. mix use of proportional representation to select delegates with delegates who are not pledged.
   d. hold a series of closed primaries.
   e. open the convention to all who can afford a ticket.

4. Superdelegates are
   a. used more often by Republicans than by Democrats.
   b. used by Democrats to ensure a voice for party officials and for particular constituencies.
   c. not able to vote at the conventions.
   d. staff of the national parties.
   e. used to maintain party discipline.

5. The main loophole to the McCain-Feingold legislation is
   a. 527s.
   b. soft money.
   c. hard money.
   d. bundling.
   e. *Buckley v. Valeo.*

6. The goal of the Federal Election Campaign Act was to
   a. make delegate selection easier.
   b. make campaigns more fair and transparent.
   c. enforce party discipline.
   d. cause a realignment.
   e. limit the impact of the media.

7. PAC money gives the greatest advantage to
   a. the president's party.
   b. incumbents.
   c. Supreme Court justices.
   d. cabinet nominees.
   e. challengers.

8. Federal matching funds are available to
   a. governors.
   b. members of the House.
   c. senators.
   d. presidential candidates.
   e. judges.

9.   Where is the first caucus held?
      a. Iowa
      b. New Hampshire
      c. Washington, D.C.
      d. Florida
      e. South Carolina

10.   All of the following are criticisms raised against the primary system EXCEPT
      a. This process of selecting delegates is unfair because it prevents representation of minority groups at the national conventions.
      b. Too much weight is placed on the early primaries, especially because states like Iowa are not representative of the American electorate.
      c. It has extended the length of the campaign process to an impractical and unmanageable degree.
      d. It prevents many qualified politicians from running, because fundraising for and participating in primaries distracts them from their current office.
      e. It allows the media too much power in shaping presidential campaigns.

11.   For a candidate to gain office in a winner-take-all election, the candidate must
      a. receive a 2/3 majority of the votes.
      b. receive at least one vote more than any other competitor.
      c. receive a majority of the total votes cast.
      d. receive at least 10% more of the vote than his/her nearest competitor.
      e. receive an absolute majority of the votes.

12.   The Electoral College was created by the framers of the Constitution because they
      a. were skeptical of the influence of state governments in the election of the president.
      b. wanted to increase the states' influence in the election of the president.
      c. wanted to increase the influence of small states in the election of the president.
      d. wanted to decrease the influence of the large states in the election of the president.
      e. were skeptical of the direct influence of the people in the election of the president.

13.   The number of electoral votes a state has is determined by
      a. the number of male registered voters.
      b. the number of registered voters.
      c. the number of senators and representatives a state has.
      d. a formula devised by the first Congress.
      e. a formula devised by each state.

14.   Political contributions raised in unlimited amounts by political parties for party-building purposes is
      a. hard money.
      b. independent expenditures.
      c. illegal.
      d. loans.
      e. soft money.

15. A political party's statement of its goals, policies, and beliefs for the next four years is known as the party's
    a. platform.
    b. caucus.
    c. political culture.
    d. realignment.
    e. efficacy.

16. Spending for campaign activity that is not coordinated with a candidate's campaign is known as
    a. illegal.
    b. independent expenditures.
    c. hard money.
    d. loans.
    e. soft money.

17. This federal law banned soft money as a part of the election reform movement.
    a. Soft Money Reform Act
    b. Hard Money Reform Act
    c. Campaign Contributions Act
    d. Bipartisan Campaign Reform Act
    e. Political Action Reform Act

18. Candidates need money to do all of the following EXCEPT
    a. conduct political polls.
    b. ask their party for support.
    c. purchase television advertising.
    d. hire campaign managers.
    e. place advertising in newspapers.

19. Contributions given to candidates and party committees that are limited and committed to candidate-specific electoral activity are known as
    a. independent expenditures.
    b. soft money.
    c. salaries.
    d. illegal funds.
    e. hard money.

20. This system was created to reduce voter fraud and voting abuses.
    a. Internet voting
    b. mail-in-voting
    c. the 15th Amendment
    d. the Voting Rights Act
    e. registration

Free-Response Questions

1. Nominating a presidential candidate occurs through an indirect process.

    a. Describe the role of delegates in the nomination process.

    b. Define winner-take-all and proportional representation and identify where each system is used in the nomination process.

    c. Explain a campaign strategy that results from the indirect election process.

2. Despite the Supreme Court's decisions to uphold much of the Federal Election Campaign Act (FECA) and the Bipartisan Campaign Reform Act (BCRA), the fight to reverse this reform has continued.

    a. Define each of the following:

    -   Issue advocacy

    -   Independent expenditures

    -   Super PACs

    b. Explain how each of these is being used to attempt to reverse the reforms established in FECA and BCRA.

☐ Answers and Explanations

Multiple-Choice Questions

1. A caucus is

    (a) is incorrect because a caucus is not held to select a nominee.

    (b) is correct because in a caucus only members who are registered with the party can participate.

    (c) is incorrect because a caucus is not open to all who wish to participate.

    (d) is incorrect because a caucus is not a meeting of members of Congress.

    (e) is incorrect because a caucus is not a court hearing.

    Page reference: 292, AP Topic: Formation of policy agendas

2.   A primary is

(a) is incorrect because a primary is not held at the national level.

(b) is incorrect because a primary is not a closed door meeting of party regulars.

(c) is correct because primaries can be open to any citizen or they can be restricted to members who are registered with the party.

(d) is incorrect because a primary is not a meeting of members of Congress.

(e) is incorrect because a primary is not a court hearing.

Page reference: 293, AP Topic: Formation of policy agendas

3.   When the Democrats select delegates to their national convention, they

(a) is incorrect because delegates are not required to vote.

(b) is incorrect because they do not use a winner-take-all system.

(c) is correct because in most states, Democrats use proportional representation to select delegates. However, a large percentage of delegates to the national convention for the Democratic Party are unpledged delegates.

(d) is incorrect because they do not hold a series of primaries.

(e) is incorrect because the convention is not open to all.

Page reference: 290, AP Topic: Formation of policy agendas

4.   Superdelegates are

(a) is incorrect because superdelegates are not used more often by Republicans.

(b) is correct because superdelegates were instituted as part of a compromise between party regulars and those who wanted primaries to be the determinant of the nomination.

(c) is incorrect because superdelegates are able to vote.

(d) is incorrect because superdelegates are not staff.

(e) is incorrect because superdelegates are not used to maintain party discipline.

Page reference: 292, AP Topic: Formation of policy agendas

5. The main loophole to the McCain-Feingold legislation is

(a) is correct because 527 groups are able to advertise for an issue and thus enable some to thwart the goal of the McCain-Feingold legislation.

(b) is incorrect because soft money is not the main loophole to the McCain-Feingold legislation.

(c) is incorrect because hard money is not the main loophole to the McCain-Feingold legislation.

(d) is incorrect because bundling is not the main loophole to the McCain-Feingold legislation.

(e) is incorrect because *Buckley v. Valeo* is not the main loophole to the McCain-Feingold legislation.

Page reference: 304, AP Topic: Linkages between party processes and elections

6. The goal of the Federal Election Campaign Act was to

(a) is incorrect; the Federal Election Campaign Act does not make delegate selection easier.

(b) is correct because the goal of the Federal Election Campaign Act was to make campaigns more fair and transparent.

(c) is incorrect; the Federal Election Campaign Act does not enforce party discipline.

(d) is incorrect; the Federal Election Campaign Act does not cause realignment.

(e) is incorrect; the Federal Election Campaign Act does not limit the impact of the media.

Page reference: 302, AP Topic: Linkages between party processes and elections

7. PAC money gives the greatest advantage to

(a) is incorrect because PAC money does not give the greatest advantage to the president's party.

(b) is correct because PAC money benefits incumbents.

(c) is incorrect because PAC money does not give money to Supreme Court Justices.

(d) is incorrect because PAC money does not give the greatest advantage to cabinet nominees.

(e) is incorrect because PAC money does not give the greatest advantage to challengers.

Page reference: 302, AP Topic: Linkages between party processes and elections

8.   Federal matching funds are available to

(a) is incorrect because matching funds are not available to governors.

(b) is incorrect because matching funds are not available to members of the House.

(c) is incorrect because matching funds are not available to senators.

(d) is correct because federal matching funds are available for presidential candidates who meet certain rules.

(e) is incorrect because matching funds are not available to judges.

Page reference: 303, AP Topic: Linkages between party processes and elections

9.   Where is the first caucus held?

(a) is correct because the first caucus is held in Iowa.

(b) is incorrect because the first caucus is not held in New Hampshire.

(c) is incorrect because the first caucus is not held in Washington, D.C.

(d) is incorrect because the first caucus is not held in Florida.

(e) is incorrect because the first caucus is not held in South Carolina.

Page reference: 292, AP Topic: Linkages between party processes and elections

10.   All of the following are criticisms raised against the primary system EXCEPT

(a) is correct because Democrats mandate minority participation at the national convention and Republicans have made efforts to include minorities.

(b) is incorrect because it is a criticism of the primary system and therefore an inaccurate choice for the question.

(c) is incorrect because it is a criticism of the primary system and therefore an inaccurate choice for the question.

(d) is incorrect because it is a criticism of the primary system and therefore an inaccurate choice for the question.

(e) is incorrect because it is a criticism of the primary system and therefore an inaccurate choice for the question.

Page reference: 295–297, AP Topic: Linkages between party processes and elections

11. For a candidate to gain office in a winner-take-all election, the candidate must

(a) is incorrect because it is an inaccurate description of a winner-take-all election.

(b) is correct because a winner-take-all system is an electoral system in which the party that receives at least one more vote than any other party wins the election.

(c) is incorrect because it is an inaccurate description of a winner-take-all election.

(d) is incorrect because it is an inaccurate description of a winner-take-all election.

(e) is incorrect because it is an inaccurate description of a winner-take-all election.

Page reference: 319, AP Topic: Linkages between party processes and elections

12. The Electoral College was created by the framers of the Constitution because they

(a) is incorrect because it is an inaccurate description of why the framers established the Electoral College.

(b) is incorrect because it is an inaccurate description of why the framers established the Electoral College.

(c) is incorrect because it is an inaccurate description of why the framers established the Electoral College.

(d) is incorrect because it is an inaccurate description of why the framers established the Electoral College.

(e) is correct because the Founders wanted the president to be elected by the nation's elite, not directly by the people, therefore they established the Electoral College.

Page reference: 319, AP Topic: Linkages between party processes and elections

13. The number of electoral votes a state has is determined by

(a) is incorrect because electoral votes are not determined by the number of male voters.

(b) is incorrect because electoral votes are not determined by the number of registered voters.

(c) is correct because each state, according to the Constitution, has as many electoral votes as it has U.S. senators and representatives.

(d) is incorrect because electoral votes are not determined by the first Congress.

(e) is incorrect because electoral votes are not determined by each state.

Page reference: 319, AP Topic: Linkages between party processes and elections

14. Political contributions raised in unlimited amounts by political parties for party-building

(a) is incorrect because hard money is an inaccurate selection for the prompt.

(b) is incorrect because independent expenditures are an inaccurate selection for the prompt.

(c) is incorrect because illegal is an inaccurate selection for the prompt.

(d) is incorrect because loans are an inaccurate selection for the prompt.

(e) is correct because soft money involves unlimited political contributions earmarked for party-building expenses at the grassroots level or for generic party advertising.

Page reference: 303, AP Topic: Linkages between party processes and elections

15. A political party's statement of its goals, policies, and beliefs for the next four years is known as the party's

(a) is correct because a party platform is a political party's statement of its goals and policies for the next four years. The platform is drafted prior to the party convention by a committee whose members are chosen in rough proportion to each candidate's strength.

(b) is incorrect because a caucus is an inaccurate choice for the description provided.

(c) is incorrect because political culture is an inaccurate choice for the description provided.

(d) is incorrect because realignment is an inaccurate choice for the description provided.

(e) is incorrect because efficacy is an inaccurate choice for the description provided.

Page reference: 297, AP Topic: Linkages between party processes and elections

16. Spending for campaign activity that is not coordinated with a candidate's campaign is known as

(a) is incorrect because independent expenditures are not illegal.

(b) is correct because independent expenditures are expenses on behalf of a political message that are made by groups that are uncoordinated with any candidate's campaign.

(c) is incorrect because hard money is an inaccurate selection for the prompt.

(d) is incorrect because independent expenditures are not loans.

(e) is incorrect because soft money is an inaccurate selection for the prompt.

Page reference: 302, AP Topic: Linkages between party processes and elections

17. This federal law banned soft money as a part of the election reform movement.

(a) is incorrect because the Soft Money Reform Act is inaccurate.

(b) is incorrect because the Hard Money Reform Act is inaccurate.

(c) is incorrect because the Campaign Contributions Act is inaccurate.

(d) is correct because the Bipartisan Campaign Reform Act, also known as the McCain-Feingold Act, largely banned soft money, restored a long-standing prohibition on corporations and labor unions for using general treasury funds for electoral purposes, and narrowed the definition of issue advocacy.

(e) is incorrect because the Political Action Reform Act is inaccurate.

Page reference: 303, AP Topic: Linkages between party processes and elections

18. Candidates need money to do all of the following EXCEPT

(a) is incorrect because candidates do need money to conduct polls.

(b) is correct because candidates do not need funds in order to ask to support from their political party.

(c) is incorrect because candidates do need money to purchase television advertising.

(d) is incorrect because candidates do need money to hire campaign managers.

(e) is incorrect because candidates do need money to place advertising in newspapers.

Page reference: 300–301, AP Topic: Linkages between party processes and elections

19. Contributions given to candidates and party committees that are limited and committed to candidate-specific electoral activity are known as

(a) is incorrect because independent expenditures is an inaccurate selection for the prompt.

(b) is incorrect because soft money is an inaccurate selection for the prompt.

(c) is incorrect because salary is an inaccurate selection for the prompt.

(d) is incorrect because illegal funds is an inaccurate selection for the prompt.

(e) is correct because hard money refers to political contributions given to a party, candidate, or interest group that are limited in amount and fully disclosed. Raising such funds is harder than raising unlimited soft money, hence the term hard money.

Page reference: 302–305, AP Topic: Linkages between party processes and elections

20.	This system was created to reduce voter fraud and voting abuses.

(a) is incorrect because Internet voting is an inaccurate selection for the question.

(b) is incorrect because mail-in-voting is an inaccurate selection for the question.

(c) is incorrect because the 15th Amendment is an inaccurate selection for the question.

(d) is incorrect because the Voting Rights Act is an inaccurate selection for the question.

(e) is correct because a system adopted by the states that requires voters to register prior to voting. Some states require citizens to register as much as 30 days in advance, whereas others permit Election Day registration.

Page reference: 309, AP Topic: Linkages between party processes and elections

Free-Response Questions

This rubric provides examples of many, but not all of the possible correct responses to the free-response questions.

1.	Nominating a presidential candidate occurs through an indirect process.

a.	Describe the role of delegates in the nomination process.

- The selection of candidates for the presidency occurs through an indirect election. Voters are allowed to participate in primaries or caucuses at the state level. Their votes, however, translate into delegates that attend a national convention and cast an official vote for the nominee.

b.	Define winner-take-all and proportional representation and identify where each system is used in the nomination process.

- For the Democratic Party, most states allocate their delegates in proportion to voters' choices, which is proportional representation. The Republican Party mostly allocates their delegates on a winner-take-all basis, meaning that the candidate who wins the most votes in a state gets all of that states delegates to the national convention.

c.	Explain a campaign strategy that results from the indirect election process.

- There are several campaign strategies that result from the rules of this contest. One is known as frontloading, in which the candidates will put all their time, money, and resources into states with earlier primaries and caucuses in an effort to gain momentum. Another strategy is to concentrate on states that award more delegates for the effort, such as Texas, which holds a lot of delegates in both conventions. Candidates may not campaign at all in states with nonbinding primaries.

2.   Despite the Supreme Court's decisions to uphold much of the Federal Election Campaign Act (FECA) and the Bipartisan Campaign Reform Act (BCRA), the fight to reverse this reform has continued.

   a.   Define each of the following:

   - Issue advocacy
   - Independent expenditures
   - Super PACs

   - **Issue advocacy** is promoting a particular position or an issue paid for by interest groups or individuals but not candidates.
   - **Independent expenditures** refer to money spend by individuals or groups not associated with candidates to elect or defeat candidates for office.
   - A **Super PAC** is an independent expenditure only first allowed in 2010 after court decisions allowing unlimited contributions to such PACs.

   b.   Explain how each of these is being used to attempt to reverse the reforms established in FECA and BCRA.

   - Issue advocacy attempts to challenge the restrictions on campaign finance by running ads for or against candidates without specifically expressing advocacy of election or defeat. Issue advocacy is able to circumvent the controls of FECA and BCRA by not using the words "vote for," "elect," "cast your vote for," "vote against," "defeat" or any other such words. Ads that do not use these words are considered to be ads that deal with issues and not candidates, therefore, they do not violate FECA or BCRA.
   - The Supreme Court ruled, in 1996, that FECA did not limit individual or group spending for or against candidates. BCRA also does not constrain independent expenditures as long as those expenditures are independent of the candidate and

fully disclosed by the FCC. This allows individuals or groups to attempt to influence elections independently instead of going through a political party.

- In 2010, the Supreme Court rejected the ban on unions and corporations using their general funds on ads about the election or the defeat of a candidate. This allows Super PACs to receive unlimited funds from individuals, unions, and corporations.

10

Interest Groups

☐ Chapter Overview

Interest groups have long been central to American politics. During the debate over ratification, James Madison discussed the role of "factions" in a democratic polis. His writings, particularly in *The Federalist No. 10*, outlined a vision of a political system that checked the power of factions. Today, we generally refer to these "factions" as "interest groups," the topic of this chapter. We begin our analysis of interest groups by describing the role of interest groups in American politics and contrasting the three leading theories of interest group politics: pluralism, elitism, and hyperpluralism. Then, we analyze the factors that make some interest groups more successful than others in the political arena and assess the four basic strategies that interest groups use to try to shape policy. Next, we contrast the various types of interest groups. We conclude by evaluating ideas to limit the reach and influence of interest groups. By the end of the chapter, students should have a good understanding of the nature and role of interest groups in the United States.

☐ Study Outline

Learning Objective 10.1: Describe the role of interest groups in American politics. (p. 332)

The Role Interest Groups

- Interest groups may pursue any kind of policy, in all levels and branches of government.
- They differ from political parties in several ways.

- They pursue their agenda through the **political process**, whereas parties advance their agendas through elections.
- Interest groups specialize in one or two policy areas, whereas parties focus on general policies to win a majority.

 Learning Objective 10.2: Compare and contrast the theories of pluralism, elitism, and hyperpluralism. (p. 333)

Theories of Interest Group Politics

- **Pluralist theory:** Interest groups are important to democracy because they allow people to organize themselves to change policies.
- Because hundreds of interest groups must compete for influence, no one group will dominate the others.
- Groups put up a fair fight; they do not engage in illegal activities to surpass other groups. Groups are equal in power because they have different resources at their disposal.
- **Elite theory:** There may be hundreds of interest groups, but only a select few have any real power.
  - The interests of only a handful of elites, usually business people, are almost always favored over other interests.
  - The policy battles that smaller interests do win are usually minor.
  - Power rests mostly with large multinational corporations.
  - The system of elite control is maintained by a well-established structure of interlocking policy players.
- **Hyperpluralist theory** or **interest group liberalism: Subgovernments**, or **iron triangles**, form around specific policy areas.
- These are composed of an **interest group**, a **federal agency**, and any **legislative committees** or **subcommittees** that handle the policy area.
- By avoiding having to choose between policy initiatives, the government creates conflicting policies that waste time and money.
- Groups have too much political influence because they usually get what they want.
- Competing subgovernments only add to the confusion.

10.3   **Learning Objective 10.3: Analyze the factors that make some interest groups more successful than others in the political arena. (p. 336)**

What Makes an Interest Group Successful?

- **Smaller groups** are more effective than large groups because they can organize more easily.

- A member of a small group is more likely to experience the group's success and, therefore, is more likely to work harder than a member of a large group.

- However, groups do experience the **free rider problem**, where individuals can benefit from the work of the group without actually joining the group.

- According to Olson's law of large groups, this problem is greater with larger groups.

- Intensity is another important factor.

- **Single-issue groups** form around a specific policy and tend to pursue it uncompromisingly.

- Single-issue groups often deal with moral issues that people feel strongly about and members of single-issue groups often vote according to a candidate's stand on the group's issue.

- Politicians are most likely to serve the needs of people or groups with money.

- Money allows groups to mobilize, conduct research, and maintain an administration.

10.4   **Learning Objective 10.4: Assess the four basic strategies that interest groups use to try to shape policy. (p. 339)**

How Groups Try to Shape Policy

- **Lobbying:** Professional lobbyists attempt to persuade lawmakers to act on behalf of their group.

- The more helpful a lobbyist is, the more power he or she has with a politician.

- Lobbyists serve as policy experts in their interest area, act as consultants who advise legislators on how to approach policy issues and debates, mobilize support for politicians during reelection, and suggest innovative policy ideas.

- **Electioneering:** Interest groups endorse a candidate who supports their interests and work to get that candidate elected.

- The groups encourage people to vote for the candidate and help finance the candidate's campaign through **PACs**.

- Congressional candidates have become largely dependent on PAC money, and most PAC money goes to **incumbents** rather than challengers.

- **Litigation:** Interest groups use lawsuits to change policies that have already gone through the legislative process.

- Even the threat of a lawsuit may be enough to influence policymaking.

- Groups can file *amicus curiae* **briefs** to state their side in a court case and to assess the consequences of the decisions the court might make.

- Groups can also file **class action lawsuits**—suits on behalf of a larger group in the electorate.

- **Mobilizing public opinion:** Interest groups try to influence the public because they know that politicians' careers depend on public opinion.

- Groups cultivate a positive image of themselves in the eyes of the public and they encourage public participation to advance interests from the point of view of the constituency.

 Learning Objective 10.5: Identify the various types of interest groups and their policy concerns. (p. 347)

Types of Interest Groups

- **Economic interests** such as business, labor, and farmers are often against regulations and tax increases, and want tax advantages, subsidies, and contracts for work.

- Organized labor is the second largest group (e.g., the AFL-CIO, the National Education Association).

- The interest group with the largest membership is the American Association for the Advancement of Retired Persons (**AARP**), which represents the interests of older Americans.

- Businesses are the most widely represented interests in Washington.

- **Environmental interests** are the fastest-growing type of interest group, favoring wilderness protection, pollution control, and energy alternatives, while opposing policies that damage the environment; examples include the Sierra Club and the Nature Conservancy.

- **Equality interests** such as civil rights, women's rights, and social welfare groups' concerns center on fair treatment in jobs, housing, and education.
    - Examples include the American Civil Liberties Union (ACLU) and the Southern Poverty Law Center.

- **Consumers' interests** and **public interests** address issues in which the whole public benefits from certain policy actions, such as product safety, which was introduced by Ralph Nader, and also represent groups that cannot assert their interests themselves: children, the mentally ill, or animals, for example.

- Some groups advocate for fair and open government or government reform. Examples include Consumer Alert and the Children's Defense Fund.

For Additional Review

Create a graphic organizer, in chart form, for interest groups. At the top of the graph, put the definition of interest groups and describe the entities through which interest groups work. Next, create 3 columns for the chart: Classification, Purpose, and Example. In the Classification column, list the TYPES of interest groups; in the Purpose column, describe the PURPOSE of that type of interest group; and in the third column, list EXAMPLES of the type of interest group identified in the first column. Use this organizer when studying for the unit test and the AP Exam.

Create a second graphic organizer, this time in diagram form, explaining how interest groups influence. In the center circle, place the main topic of the diagram. In smaller circles, write the methods by which interest groups exercise influence, including an explanation of each method identified. Use this organizer when studying for the unit test and the AP Exam.

☐ Review Questions

Multiple-Choice Questions

1. Which of the following is the best definition of pluralism?
    a. A multitude of groups compete for and share power at any given time.
    b. A multitude of interest groups have the ability to form and survive.
    c. Several small, single-issue groups tend to hold power.
    d. The number of groups continues to increase as society becomes more complicated.
    e. Groups are multiplying and getting more intense.

2. Elite theorists believe that the power of interest groups
    a. is derived from their equal access to the government.
    b. comes mostly from public support.
    c. is evenly distributed among them.
    d. reinforces a more democratic government.
    e. is held by only a few wealthy groups.

3. The hyperpluralist theory holds that
    a. interest group intensity places pressure on members of Congress.
    b. the large number of groups slows down the policymaking process.
    c. it is common for one group to rapidly split up into other groups.
    d. many groups compete for and share power.
    e. salient issues cause a plurality of groups to form.

4. Lawmakers often rely on lobbyists for all of the following reasons EXCEPT
    a. to come up with new policy ideas that they can introduce in Congress.
    b. for advice on strategies to advance or prevent a piece of legislation.
    c. for money that would allow them to travel to their constituencies.
    d. to encourage group members to vote for them during reelection.
    e. for expertise on a certain issue.

5. Iron triangles are composed of
    a. a cabinet department, a legislative committee, and a federal judge.
    b. a corporate board, an interest group, and the Speaker of the House.
    c. a PAC, an interest group, and a congressional candidate.
    d. an interest group, a legislative committee, and a federal agency.
    e. a local civic group, a state legislator, and a federal department.

6. Proponents of the pluralist theory argue that, for the most part, power is evenly distributed among interest groups because
    a. the public participates equally in different types of interest groups.
    b. all interest groups receive the same amount of federal funds.
    c. each policy area is assigned a limited number of related interest groups.
    d. interest groups each get the same attention from politicians.
    e. competition prevents any one group from becoming more influential.

7. Which of the following statements accurately describes methods interest groups employ to influence policymaking?

    I. Class action lawsuits allow interest groups to sue in the name of a larger section of the public.

    II. Interest groups meet with judges about cases that affect their policy area.

    III. Interest groups make almost all of their PAC contributions to incumbents rather than challengers.

    IV. Lobbyists use their policy expertise to make themselves indispensable to politicians.

    V. Interest groups pay committee members to review proposed legislation from a legislative point of view.

    a. III only
    b. I and IV only
    c. II and V only
    d. I, III, and IV only
    e. II, IV, and V only

8. Interest groups do all of the following EXCEPT
    a. link the public to the political process.
    b. nominate candidates for elective office.
    c. try to shape specific policy goals.
    d. play a part in political campaigns.
    e. unite politicians with the same political ideology.

9. Which of the following interest groups is known to be the largest in membership size?
    a. National Rifle Association (NRA)
    b. League of Conservation Voters
    c. Christian Coalition
    d. American Association of Retired Persons (AARP)
    e. National Association for the Advancement of Colored People (NAACP)

10. Which of the following groups has primarily used litigation to advance its issues?
    a. National Rifle Association (NRA)
    b. League of Conservation Voters
    c. Christian Coalition
    d. American Association of Retired Persons (AARP)
    e. National Association for the Advancement of Colored People (NAACP)

11. The groups that, according to James Madison, arose from the unequal distribution of property or wealth and had the potential to cause instability in government are known as
    a. politiques.
    b. factions.
    c. cliques.
    d. parties.
    e. interests.

12. Interest groups are sometimes negatively referred to as
    a. radicals.
    b. elitists.
    c. cliques.
    d. demagogues.
    e. special interests.

13. When interest groups find the popular political channels closed to them, they may turn to
    a. celebrities.
    b. the president.
    c. litigation.
    d. governors.
    e. Congress.

14. Interest groups often create political action committees (PACs) to
    a. get the support of the national and state courts.
    b. create a new political party.
    c. nominate a candidate for political office.
    d. overturn executive orders.
    e. contribute money to candidates and political parties.

15. The U.S. government attempts to regulate interest groups by
    a. regulating membership requirements.
    b. banning some specific groups considered too extreme.
    c. regulating media access to the groups.
    d. regulating their access to the president.
    e. regulating the practice of lobbying.

16. The activities of a group or organization that seek to persuade political leaders to support the group's position are known as
    a. pluralism.
    b. free-riding.
    c. hyperpluralism.
    d. elitism.
    e. lobbying.

17. All of the following are appropriate lobbying strategies EXCEPT
    a. litigation.
    b. threatening members of Congress.
    c. electioneering.
    d. helping formulate campaign strategy.
    e. providing information to a congressional committee.

18. This is considered to be the most important resource interest groups and PACs can provide to candidates.
    a. strategies
    b. volunteers
    c. campaign workers
    d. money
    e. votes

19. Labor unions and trade associations are examples of what type of interest group?
    a. grassroots
    b. single-issue
    c. public
    d. economic
    e. occupational

20. Most political action committees represent
    a. government groups.
    b. labor unions.
    c. citizens' groups.
    d. business groups.
    e. potential groups.

Free-Response Questions

1. Interest groups use a variety of techniques to pursue their goals. For each of the interest groups below, identify a technique that has been important to the group's success in the policy process and explain why the group used this technique.

    a. NAACP

    b. AARP

    c. NRA

2. Interest groups are often criticized for hurting the political process by making PAC contributions.

    a. Identify one argument against allowing PACs to make contributions.

    b. Identify one argument in favor of allowing PACs to make contributions.

    c. Identify one law that regulates PACs and explain why it has or has not been effective.

☐ Answers and Explanations

Multiple-Choice Questions

1. Which of the following is the best definition of pluralism?

    (a) is correct because pluralists argue that political power is shared among many groups.

    (b) is incorrect because it is an inaccurate description of pluralism.

    (c) is incorrect because it is an inaccurate description of pluralism.

    (d) is incorrect because it is an inaccurate description of pluralism.

    (e) is incorrect because it is an inaccurate description of pluralism.

    Page reference: 333, AP Topic: Linkages between institutions and interest groups

2. Elite theorists believe that the power of interest groups

    (a) is incorrect because it is an inaccurate description of elitism.

    (b) is incorrect because it is an inaccurate description of elitism.

    (c) is incorrect because it is an inaccurate description of elitism.

    (d) is incorrect because it is an inaccurate description of elitism.

    (e) is correct because elitists argue that political power is primarily held by the wealthy.

    Page reference: 333, AP Topic: Linkages between institutions and interest groups

3. The hyperpluralist theory holds that

    (a) is incorrect because it is an inaccurate definition of hyperpluralism.

    (b) is correct because hyperpluralists argue that the number of interest groups can slow down our system as members of Congress are bombarded with competing information.

    (c) is incorrect because it is an inaccurate definition of hyperpluralism.

    (d) is incorrect because it is an inaccurate definition of hyperpluralism.

    (e) is incorrect because it is an inaccurate definition of hyperpluralism.

Page reference: 333, AP Topic: Linkages between institutions and interest groups

4.   Lawmakers often rely on lobbyists for all of the following reasons EXCEPT

(a) is incorrect because lobbyists do create new policy ideas for lawmakers.

(b) is incorrect because lobbyists do provide advice on strategies to lawmakers.

(c) is incorrect because lobbyists do provide money for travel to lawmakers.

(d) is correct because lawmakers do not depend on interest groups for votes since votes must come from their district.

(e) is incorrect because lobbyists do provide expertise to lawmakers.

Page reference: 341–343, AP Topic: Linkages between institutions and interest groups

5.   Iron triangles are composed of

(a) is incorrect because it is an inaccurate description of what composes an iron triangle.

(b) is incorrect because it is an inaccurate description of what composes an iron triangle.

(c) is incorrect because it is an inaccurate description of what composes an iron triangle.

(d) is correct because iron triangles are the relationship between congressional committees, government agencies, and interest groups who work together on policies.

(e) is incorrect because it is an inaccurate description of what composes an iron triangle.

Page reference: 335, AP Topic: Linkages between institutions and interest groups

6.   Proponents of the pluralist theory argue that, for the most part, power is evenly distributed among interest groups because

(a) is incorrect because it is an inaccurate description of the pluralist theory of interest groups.

(b) is incorrect because it is an inaccurate description of the pluralist theory of interest groups.

(c) is incorrect because it is an inaccurate description of the pluralist theory of interest groups.

(d) is incorrect because it is an inaccurate description of the pluralist theory of interest groups.

(e) is correct because pluralists believe that power is shared and that interest groups will check one another in the policy arena.

Page reference: 333–334, AP Topic: Linkages between institutions and interest groups

7.   Which of the following statements accurately describes methods interest groups employ to influence policymaking?

(a) is incorrect because choices I and IV are also correct.

(b) is incorrect because choice III is also correct.

(c) is incorrect because interest groups do not meet with judges about cases in their policy area.

(d) is correct because interest groups frequently file class action lawsuits in an attempt to reverse policy decisions. They also solidify their relationships with members of Congress by channeling most of their campaign contributions to incumbents. Interest groups also know that policymakers are more easily influenced if they must rely on a lobbyist for information and advice about a policy.

(e) is incorrect because selections II and V are incorrect choices.

Page reference: 339–347, AP Topic: Linkages between institutions and interest groups

8.   Interest groups do all of the following EXCEPT

(a) is incorrect because interest groups do link the public to the policy process.

(b) is correct because interest groups do not run candidates for office but, instead, attempt to influence policymakers.

(c) is incorrect because interest groups do try to shape specific policy goals.

(d) is incorrect because interest groups do play a part in political campaigns.

(e) is incorrect because interest groups do unite politicians with the same policy agenda.

Page reference: 339–347, AP Topic: Linkages between institutions and interest groups

9.   Which of the following interest groups is known to be the largest in membership size?

(a) is incorrect because the National Rifle Association is not the largest interest group.

(b) is incorrect because the League of Conservation Voters is not the largest interest group.

(c) is incorrect because the Christian Coalition is not the largest interest group.

(d) is correct because the AARP is the largest interest group in the United States.

(e) is incorrect because the National Association for the Advancement of Colored People is not the largest interest group.

Page reference: 347–352, AP Topic: Linkages between institutions and interest groups

10. Which of the following groups has primarily used litigation to advance its issues?

(a) is incorrect because the NRA does not typically use litigation to advance its issues.

(b) is incorrect because the League of Conservation Voters does not typically use litigation to advance its issues.

(c) is incorrect because the Christian Coalition does not typically use litigation to advance its issues.

(d) is incorrect because the AARP does not typically use litigation to advance its issues.

(e) is correct because the NAACP has used litigation in cases such as *Brown v. Board of Education* when other techniques were not useful.

Page reference: 347–352, AP Topic: Linkages between institutions and interest groups

11. The groups that, according to James Madison, arose from the unequal distribution of property or wealth and had the potential to cause instability in government are known as

(a) is incorrect because politiques refers to groups in power during the 16th and 17th centuries.

(b) is correct because James Madison, in *The Federalist No. 10*, described factions as working adverse to the interests of the nation as a whole and he tried to design the constitutional system to prevent such groups from having too much power.

(c) is incorrect because cliques are exclusive social groups.

(d) is incorrect because parties are political organizations organized to run candidates for office.

(e) is incorrect because interests are not necessarily organized groups.

Page reference: 330–331, AP Topic: Linkages between institutions and interest groups

12. Interest groups are sometimes negatively referred to as

(a) is incorrect because interest groups are not necessarily radical.

(b) is incorrect because interest groups are not necessarily elitist.

(c) is incorrect because interest groups are not necessarily cliques.

(d) is incorrect because interest groups are not demagogues.

(e) is correct because an interest group is an organization of people with shared policy goals entering the policy process at several points to try to achieve those goals.

Because these groups share a specific agenda they are also known as special interest groups.

Page reference: 332–335, AP Topic: Linkages between institutions and interest groups

13. When interest groups find the popular political channels closed to them, they may turn to

(a) is incorrect because using celebrities is not a typical channel for an interest group.

(b) is incorrect because using the president is not a typical channel for an interest group.

(c) is correct because if an interest group fails in Congress or gets only a vague piece of legislation, the next step is to go to court in the hope of getting specific rulings in its favor. Using the courts to achieve its goal is referred to as litigation.

(d) is incorrect because using governors is not a typical channel for an interest group.

(e) is incorrect because interest groups use litigation when their attempt to use Congress has failed.

Page reference: 345–346, AP Topic: Linkages between institutions and interest groups

14. Interest groups often create political action committees (PACs) to

(a) is incorrect because PACs do not lobby the courts.

(b) is incorrect because PACs do not create new political parties.

(c) is incorrect because PACs do not nominate candidates for office.

(d) is incorrect because PACs do not overturn executive orders.

(e) is correct because political action committees are groups that raise money from individuals and then distribute it in the form of contributions to candidates that the group supports.

Page reference: 339–347, AP Topic: Linkages between institutions and interest groups

15. The U.S. government attempts to regulate interest groups by

(a) is incorrect because the U.S. government does not regulate interest group membership requirements.

(b) is incorrect because the U.S. government does not ban certain interest groups.

(c) is incorrect because the U.S. government does not regulate interest group media access.

(d) is incorrect because the U.S. government does not regulate interest group presidential access.

(e) is correct because the U.S. government has passed legislation to regulate lobbying in order to regulate interest groups.

Page reference: 341–342, AP Topic: Linkages between institutions and interest groups

16. The activities of a group or organization that seek to persuade political leaders to support the group's position are known as:

(a) is incorrect because it is an inaccurate selection for the definition provided.

(b) is incorrect because it is an inaccurate selection for the definition provided.

(c) is incorrect because it is an inaccurate selection for the definition provided.

(d) is incorrect because it is an inaccurate selection for the definition provided.

(e) is correct because lobbying, according to Lester Milbrath, is a communication by someone other than a citizen acting on his or her own behalf, directed to a governmental decision maker with the hope of influencing his or her decision.

Page reference: 341, AP Topic: Linkages between institutions and interest groups

17. All of the following are appropriate lobbying strategies EXCEPT

(a) is incorrect because litigation is an appropriate lobbying strategy.

(b) is correct because threatening a member of Congress is an illegal activity and therefore would not be an appropriate lobbying strategy.

(c) is incorrect because electioneering is an appropriate lobbying strategy.

(d) is incorrect because helping to formulate campaign strategy is an appropriate lobbying strategy.

(e) is incorrect because providing information to a member of Congress is an appropriate lobbying strategy.

Page reference: 339–347, AP Topic: Linkages between institutions and interest groups

18. This is considered to be the most important resource interest groups and PACs can provide to candidates.

(a) is incorrect because even though strategy is an important resource, it is not as important as money.

(b) is incorrect because even though volunteers are an important resource, they are not as important as money.

(c) is incorrect because even though campaign workers are an important resource, they are not as important as money.

(d) is correct because even though interest groups and PACs can provide many important resources to candidates, due to the increasing expense associated with running for office, money is considered to be the most important resource that can be provided.

(e) is incorrect because even though votes are an important resource, they are not as important as money.

Page reference: 339, AP Topic: Linkages between institutions and interest groups

19.   Labor unions and trade associations are examples of what type of interest group?

(a) is incorrect because grassroots is an inaccurate description of the groups provided.

(b) is incorrect because single-issue is an inaccurate description of the groups provided.

(c) is incorrect because public is an inaccurate description of the groups provided.

(d) is correct because the primary purpose of an economic interest group is to promote the financial interests of its members. Labor unions work for the interest of their workers, while trade associations work to advance the economic good for the firms in their industry; hence both would be examples of economic interest groups.

(e) is incorrect because occupational is an inaccurate description of the groups provided.

Page reference: 332–339, AP Topic: Linkages between institutions and interest groups

20.   Most political action committees represent

(a) is incorrect because it is an inaccurate selection for the prompt.

(b) is incorrect because it is an inaccurate selection for the prompt.

(c) is incorrect because it is an inaccurate selection for the prompt.

(d) is correct because PACs can be categorized according to the type of interest they represent, and the greatest growth has been seen in the PACs representing corporations and trade organizations.

(e) is incorrect because it is an inaccurate selection for the prompt.

Page reference: 336–347, AP Topic: Linkages between institutions and interest groups

Free-Response Questions

This rubric provides examples of many, but not all of the possible correct responses to the free-response questions.

1. Interest groups use a variety of techniques to pursue their goals. For each of the interest groups below, identify a technique that has been important to the group's success in the policy process and explain why the group used this technique.

   a. NAACP

      - The NAACP is best known for using litigation to pursue its goals. In particular, the NAACP made history when its attorneys took on a class action lawsuit that reached the Supreme Court, *Brown v. Board of Education*, in 1954. Litigation is advantageous to groups like the NAACP, after attempts to use more traditional lobbying techniques are unsuccessful. Federal judges hold their positions for life, and are therefore not swayed by public opinion. Supreme Court case rulings are the final legal authority in the U.S., unless overturned by a constitutional amendment.

   b. AARP

      - The AARP is best known for its extraordinary large membership base. The members are also very active in grassroots lobbying: calling members of Congress, e-mailing, and making other similar types of contact with lawmakers. The AARP is powerful because elected officials depend on their votes to win, so their large membership base gains the attention of politicians.

   c. NRA

      - The NRA is known for making large campaign contributions. Campaign contributions are useful because elected officials rely on such contributions to run effective campaigns, and try to give as much as they can to their contributors to keep the contributions flowing.

2. Interest groups are often criticized for hurting the political process by making PAC contributions.

   a. Identify one argument against allowing PACs to make contributions.

- One argument against allowing PACs to make contributions is that it can lead to corruption. Those who subscribe to this view would argue that PACs essentially buy legislation by making contributions.

b. Identify one argument in favor of allowing PACs to make contributions.

- One argument in favor of allowing PACs to make contributions is that making a contribution is a type of expression, which is protected by the First Amendment of the Constitution.

c. Identify one law that regulates PACs and explain why it has or has not been effective.

- There are several laws that regulate PACs. The most recent law is called the Bipartisan Campaign Reform Act, also referred to as the McCain-Feingold Act. This law was designed to stop PACs from making unlimited contributions to the political party and thus banned so-called soft money. This law has been somewhat effective; however, one of the loopholes in this law is citizens' ability to make unlimited contributions to 527 groups. These groups support issues, not specific parties, and are identified by their status in the federal tax code. By making unlimited contributions to these groups, PACs have gotten around the McCain-Feingold law because the groups run similar ads to support candidates that the parties once did.

11

Congress

☐ Chapter Overview

Congress was intended by the founders to be the "people's branch." Its members are directly elected by the people to make decisions on their behalf. In this chapter, we examine the role of Congress in U.S. politics. We begin by considering the electoral politics of Congress, exploring both how representative members of Congress are of the U.S. population in general and identifying the factors that influence congressional elections. Then we examine the committee structures, leadership positions, and support staff that shape Congress's business. We consider in particular the role of the Congress in lawmaking, appropriations, and oversight. By the end of the chapter, students should understand the complex role and functions of Congress in the context of American government.

☐ Study Outline

 Learning Objective 11.1: Characterize the backgrounds of members of Congress and assess their impact on the ability of members of Congress to represent average Americans. (p. 361)

The Representatives and Senators

- Congress is composed of 435 representatives and 100 senators, for a total of 535 members.
- Congress is not a very diverse place.
- Most members are lawyers or businesspeople.
- The members of both houses have always been largely Caucasian.

- The House is more diverse than the Senate, which is almost exclusively white.

- The ratio of men to women in both the House and the Senate is about five to one.

- Most election years leave both houses about **evenly split** between Democrats and Republicans, with one or two independents in each.

11.2 Learning Objective 11.2: Identify the principal factors influencing the outcomes in congressional elections. (p. 364)

Congressional Elections

- Congressional elections are held every two years in November.

- The most important factor that determines which candidate wins an election is incumbency.

- **Incumbents** are elected officials who already hold office and are running for reelection. Incumbents win reelection more than 90 percent of the time.

- Incumbency allows senators and representatives to gain valuable experience and bring some stability to Congress; however, this may also work to insulate members of Congress from change, making it more difficult for constituents to effect change.

- Senatorial races are usually intense because incumbents, who tend to have **higher profiles**, are more likely to be held accountable for public policy successes or failures.

- Their challengers are also more likely to be known already in the political arena because senatorial races often draw former representatives or governors.

- Still, incumbents usually win, though by a narrower margin. In fact, turnover in Congress usually occurs only when members retire.

The Advantages of Incumbents

- Incumbents engage in three activities that increase the probability of being elected:
  - **Advertising:** Advertising makes a candidate visible to many constituents and name recognition is an important advantage for incumbents.
    - The number of votes a candidate receives is fairly proportional to his or her airtime on television and the frequency of his or her public appearances.

- Advertising requires a great deal of campaign funds, particularly for senators, which explains in part why Congress is composed mostly of wealthy men.
  - **Credit claiming:** Incumbents have the benefit of being able to present their **congressional record** to their constituents to demonstrate their hard work in service of the district or state.
    - They may have helped specific people or groups sidestep bureaucratic red tape (**casework**), or they have helped with federal programs and institutions (**pork barrel**).
    - From this record of service to the constituency, incumbents can build a more clearly defined **public image**, whereas challengers new to politics are less likely to be able to convey their position on issues to the public.
  - **Position taking:** Incumbents' public image is strengthened because they have already taken a stand on issues relevant to their constituency; and at election time, this can work in their favor to identify them in the minds of the public.

The Role of Party Identification

- **Party identification:** Voters for the most part cast their ballots along **party lines**; therefore, a predominantly Democratic district, for example, is most likely to elect and then reelect a Democratic candidate.

Defeating Incumbents

- While defeating an incumbent is very difficult, it does happen occasionally.
- Sometimes redistricting can occur, forcing incumbents to attempt to win over an unfamiliar constituency, or even making them compete against another incumbents.
- Sometimes incumbents are involved in scandals that are visible in the media, which tarnishes their name.
- Occasionally, the unpopularity of a president of the same party as the incumbent can have a negative impact on the incumbent's chances of success.

Open Seats/Stability and Change

- When an incumbent leaves a seat open, there is more likely to be competition; however, the competition usually occurs within the primary, as most seats are safe for one party or the other.
- Because real competition for seats is unusual, Congress does not change very much or very often.

 Learning Objective 11.3: Compare and contrast the House and Senate, and describe the roles of congressional leaders, committees, caucuses, and staff. (p. 370)

How Congress Is Organized to Make Policy: American Bicameralism

- A **bicameral legislature** is divided into two houses.
- Legislation must pass both houses of Congress to become law.
- The Senate is designed to represent states and the House is designed to represent the population.

The House

- A state's **population** determines how many representatives it has.
- A state is divided into **congressional districts**, each with an equal population.
- Every ten years, district lines must be redrawn according to the population data supplied by the national **census**.
- The political party in power in each state will try and draw district lines to their advantage, a process called gerrymandering.
- States therefore can lose or gain a seat in the House, but total membership remains at 435.
- Other characteristics of the House:
  - Members tend to vote along party lines.
  - Power is usually hierarchical.
  - Special responsibilities include introducing revenue bills and articles of impeachment.
- Key to agenda setting in the House is the **House Rules Committee**.

- The House Rules Committee gives each bill a rule for debate, schedules the bill on a calendar, allows time for debate, and may specify what types of amendments can be offered.
- The Speaker of the House chairs the Rules Committee.

The Senate

- Power is more evenly distributed among senators.
- Senators act more independently of their parties.
- Special responsibilities include approving presidential nominations, ratifying treaties, and the trial of impeached federal officials.
- Senators can **filibuster** and this power of unlimited debate means that they can talk so long that they delay or even prevent voting on a piece of legislation.
- Senators can stop a filibuster by voting for **cloture**, which halts debate.
- This rarely happens because it requires 60 votes; the majority party usually holds fewer than 60 seats, making cloture nearly impossible.

Congressional Leadership

- There are several elected positions in the House of Representatives. At the beginning of each congressional term, the parties will meet in caucus to elect these leaders.
- The leader of the House is the **Speaker of the House**, who is chosen by the majority party, and who presides over each session and is largely responsible for assigning representatives to committees or party positions.
- The vice president of the United States is president of the Senate, however, this role is more formal than active because most authority rests with party leaders in the Senate.
- In the House, the **majority leader** assists the Speaker of the House in assigning majority party members to committees and scheduling legislation.
- The **minority leader** leads the minority party in opposing the agenda of the majority, and in choosing minority party members for committees.
- The **majority leader** in the Senate is usually the most active or seasoned member of the majority party.

- The majority leader manages the schedule of debate and rallies party votes for party legislation or against proposals of the minority party.

- The **minority leader** rallies the support of the minority party around legislation and acts as its spokesperson.

- The majority and minority **whips** are responsible for "counting votes" for proposed legislation, working with members of their party to get enough votes to pass or defeat a piece of legislation.

The Committees and Subcommittees

- Committees are the nuts and bolts of Congress.

- Most members serve on at least five committees and subcommittees; senators usually serve on more committees than representatives do.

- There are four basic types of committees.

  - **Standing committees** handle a **specific policy area**, such as agriculture, finance, energy, and commerce; both the House and Senate have standing committees and each committee is often divided into **subcommittees**.

  - **Joint committees** are composed of both senators and representatives and are responsible for legislation that **overlaps policy areas**.

  - **Select committees** are appointed to handle a **specific issue**, such as an investigation or impeachment trial.

  - **Conference committees** are composed of members of both houses and they iron out the differences between the House and Senate version of a bill.

- Committees are responsible for researching, assessing, and revising the thousands of bills that are introduced by members of Congress each year.

- Committees also conduct **legislative oversight**, which is the monitoring of federal agencies and their execution of the law.

- Oversight usually takes the form of investigation—often committees **hold hearings** to question agency officials about the activities of their departments.

- As the federal bureaucracy has grown over the last few decades, so has the process of legislative oversight.

- One key to a new member of Congress's success is getting on a high-profile committee.

- Members seek committees that will help them to assist their constituency, or provide publicity to help them get reelected.
- Committee placement is decided by the chamber leadership.
  - **Committee chairs** influence the agenda of the committee.
  - The chair is always a member of the majority party, and usually is the most senior member of the majority party on the committee.
  - The minority party member of the committee with the longest tenure is called the ranking member.
  - The **seniority system** was a formal rule used to select chairs, but is no longer a requirement.

Caucuses: The Informal Organization of Congress

- A **caucus** is a group of members of Congress who share a similar interest.
- Each party has a caucus, and there are hundreds of caucuses, some more active than others.
- The Congressional Black Caucus and the Congressional Caucus for Women's Issues are two examples.
- Caucuses may hold hearings and put pressure on committees to try to influence legislation.

Congressional Staff (Personal Staff, Committee Staff, Staff Agencies)

- Senators and members of the House of Representatives each have a number of staff who assist them in serving their constituencies, researching legislation, and communicating with those who contact the office.
- The Committees also employ staff to organize hearings, draft reports, and perform other duties.
- Finally, Congress has staff agencies such as the *Congressional Research Service (CRS)* to track the progress of bills and perform research for members of Congress.

Learning Objective 11.4: Outline the path of bills to passage and explain the influences on congressional decision making. (p. 381)

The Congressional Process and Decision Making

- Policymaking is a slow and laborious process, and often a final bill has changed significantly from the original.

- The authors of the Constitution intentionally devised a complicated legislative system as a means to prevent hasty decisions and to encourage compromise in policymaking. The following diagram shows how proposed legislation usually follows a path through Congress.

1. A single member of Congress or a small group in either the House or Senate formally introduces a bill.

2. The bill goes to a subcommittee of the appropriate standing committee.

3. The subcommittee conducts research and holds hearings on the proposal and rewrites it as necessary.

4. The approved bill then moves to the standing committee, which assesses the legislation in a formal report, rewrites the bill as necessary, and ultimately decides whether to pass it on for debate or to kill it.

5. The bill is introduced for debate on the floor of the chamber. Committee members usually serve as authorities on the proposal to whom their colleagues turn, and they often rally support for it. Amendments may be added to the bill.

6. If passed by both houses, the bill goes to the president for final approval as law. If different versions are passed in each house, the two bills go to a conference committee that resolves the differences between them. Then both houses vote on the final version of the bill and it is sent to the president.

- Some important committees to know:
  - The **House Rules Committee** reviews all bills submitted by committees before they go to the House floor, assigns them a slot on the calendar, allocates time for debate, and even decides whether the bill may be amended or not. This committee is unique to the House and has a significant degree of power.
  - The **House Ways and Means Committee** writes bills concerning tax and other public revenue, which are subject to the approval of both houses.
  - The **Senate Finance Committee** works in conjunction with the House Ways and Means Committee to write **tax and revenue bills**.
  - The **Appropriations Committee in each house** decides how government money will be **apportioned** to federal agencies. This is the largest committee on each side, and divides into many subcommittees that attach to each of the standing committees.

Party, Constituency, and Ideology

- Members of Congress do not always vote with their party.
- Partisanship tends to be strongest on economic and welfare issues, however, on other issues, members of Congress may act more independently, especially to fulfill the needs of their constituents.
- When representatives or senators do act independently, what influences their vote?
  - If the issue is of significance to their constituency, or is likely to be highly publicized, members of Congress tend to vote as the constituency would want them to.
  - On the many other issues about which the public is less informed, representatives and senators are more likely to vote according to their own personal views and convictions.
- Over the past three decades, Republicans in Congress have become consistently more conservative, Democrats have become consistently more liberal, and the distance from the center of each party has increased.
- As a result of these ideological differences between the parties in Congress, it has been more difficult to reach any compromises.

- Increasingly divergent electoral coalitions and districts, which are more one-sided, have played an important role in this.

Lobbyists and Interest Groups

- With lobbyists dominating Washington, how effective is Congress in representing the people? You should be familiar with both sides of this debate.

Congress Represents the Interests of the Electorate

- Interest groups are organized by groups of "the people" to make their views known so that policymakers will act on their behalf.
- As pluralists contend, the competition among groups for the support of members of Congress ensures that compromise will play a part in policymaking.
- The issues on which Congress focuses are as diverse as the interests pushing them to the forefront, thereby decentralizing the political agenda and power in each house.

Congress Serves the Interest Groups, Not the Public

- Critics argue that those interest groups with enough money to buy influence dominate the policy agenda and distract policymakers from the needs of the public.
- So many competing interests prevent the formation of cohesive policy. In fact, different committees may handle the same policy issue in drastically different ways.
- Ultimately the government wastes a significant amount of money by attempting to appease so many interests.

For Additional Review

As you read your textbook, keep a list of all the committees you come across. For each committee, jot down what kind of committee it is and its role or policy specialty. Not only will this information help you prepare for Section I of the AP Government and Politics: United States Exam, but also, it may contain good examples for use in your free-response answers.

Create a chart comparing and contrasting the qualifications, organization, and powers of the House and the Senate. Use this chart when studying and preparing for the unit test and for the AP United States Government and Politics exam.

☐ Review Questions

Multiple-Choice Questions

1. Which demographic group is the most underrepresented in Congress?
    a. African Americans
    b. Latinos
    c. Asians
    d. women
    e. upper income

2. Which of the following is most likely to determine a candidate's chance of getting elected to Congress?
    a. their personal wealth
    b. their connections to the media
    c. their incumbency status
    d. their campaign style
    e. the promises they make to their constituents

3. Riders are frequently unpopular with the general public because
    a. the public does not understand them.
    b. they funnel federal money into targeted areas.
    c. they are secret.
    d. lobbyists oppose them.
    e. they are unconstitutional.

4. Which of the following would be an attractive committee for a member of Congress from Montana looking to serve his or her constituency?
    a. Ways and Means
    b. Rules
    c. Education
    d. Government Reform
    e. Agriculture

5. Descriptive representation refers to
    a. representing the interests of groups.
    b. serving constituents through pork barrel projects.
    c. representing constituents by mirroring their personal, politically relevant characteristics.
    d. living in the geographical area of one's constituents.
    e. All of the above.

6. A senator can effectively prevent the Senate from voting by
   a. conducting oversight.
   b. filibustering.
   c. introducing another bill.
   d. holding hearings.
   e. no known process, because the rules are very structured.

7. Which of the following ends debate in the Senate?
   a. cloture
   b. vote by the Rules Committee
   c. conference committee
   d. markup
   e. rider

8. Most of the time, members of Congress vote with
   a. the president.
   b. their state.
   c. celebrities.
   d. their party.
   e. the lobbyists.

9. After a House committee reviews a bill and writes its report, the bill goes to the
   a. Senate.
   b. appropriate subcommittee.
   c. president.
   d. floor for debate.
   e. House Rules Committee.

10. Which of the following is the best example of legislative oversight?
    a. The vice president presides over the Senate.
    b. The Rules Committee amends a bill.
    c. Debate is limited.
    d. A hearing is held to investigate misuse of funds within a federal agency.
    e. Riders are not allowed.

11. All of the following is true of Congress EXCEPT
    a. Most members of Congress today are professional politicians.
    b. The majority of incumbents get reelected.
    c. More than 50% of legislators are women.
    d. About 1/3 have studied law.
    e. Congress was not a career for most of the members during the 19th century.

12. The second most powerful official in Washington, D.C., after the president is the
    a. U.S. Senate *pro tempore*.
    b. chief justice of the Supreme Court.
    c. Speaker of the House of Representatives.
    d. vice president.
    e. majority party whip.

13. Most of the work in Congress is done
    a. on the floor of the House.
    b. in conjunction with the president.
    c. in meetings with lobbyists.
    d. in select committees.
    e. in standing committees.

14. Differences in House and Senate bills are resolved by
    a. the President.
    b. the Speaker of the House.
    c. the Senate Rules committee.
    d. the standing committee chairs.
    e. conference committees.

15. All of the following are true of congressional oversight EXCEPT
    a. Members tend to spend more time on things other than oversight.
    b. Oversight is administered through the committee system.
    c. Members spend less time on oversight when there is a scandal.
    d. The biggest obstacle of oversight is the lack of electoral advantage.
    e. Members spend more time on oversight when there is a scandal.

16. The term for redrawing Congressional districts to favor a particular political party is
    a. apportionment paradox.
    b. gerrymandering.
    c. redistricting.
    d. redlining.
    e. malapportionment.

17. This office is involved in the preparation of Congress' budget.
    a. Office of Management and Budget
    b. General Accounting Office
    c. Congressional Accounting Office
    d. Office of Congressional Management and Budget
    e. Congressional Budget Office

18. In the House of Representatives, the _____ controls the scheduling of bills for debate.
    a. House Ways and Means Committee
    b. Speaker of the House
    c. House Rules Committee
    d. Chief Administrative Officer
    e. House Administration Committee

19. The power of impeachment belongs to
    a. the Senate.
    b. the House.
    c. a Federal Grand Jury.
    d. the Supreme Court.
    e. the Chief Justice of the Supreme Court.

20. The custom followed in Congress specifying that majority party members with the longest record of service will become committee chairs is
    a. senatorial courtesy.
    b. ageism.
    c. the seniority rule.
    d. elder custom.
    e. senior incumbency.

Free-Response Questions

1. Occasionally, one party will have control of Congress and the presidency. This will give the majority party advantages in Congress, yet passing legislation is still difficult.

    a. Describe the legislative advantages of the majority party in Congress with respect to both committee structure and leadership.

    b. Explain why, even with single-party control, passing legislation is difficult. Use two examples to support your explanation.

2. Congress has several nonlegislative functions. Describe the relevance of each of the following and provide an example.

    a. oversight of the bureaucracy

    b. confirmation of political appointees

    c. impeachment

☐ Answers and Explanations

Multiple-Choice Questions

1. Which demographic group is the most underrepresented in Congress?

    (a) is incorrect because African Americans are not as underrepresented in Congress as are women.

    (b) is incorrect because Latinos are not as underrepresented in Congress as are women.

(c) is incorrect because Asians are not as underrepresented in Congress as are women.

(d) is correct because women make up a small percentage of both the House and the Senate that is far lower than the percentage of women in the general population.

(e) is incorrect because upper income individuals are overrepresented in Congress.

Page reference: 362, AP Topic: Congress

2.   Which of the following is most likely to determine a candidate's chance of getting elected to Congress?

(a) is incorrect because wealth is not as likely to determine a candidate's chance of getting elected to Congress.

(b) is incorrect because connections to the media are not as likely to determine a candidate's chance of getting elected to Congress.

(c) is correct because incumbency is the most important determinant in a candidate's chance of getting elected.

(d) is incorrect because campaign style is not as likely to determine a candidate's chance of getting elected to Congress.

(e) is incorrect because promises made to constituents are not as likely to determine a candidate's chance of getting elected to Congress.

Page reference: 368, AP Topic: Congress

3.   Riders are frequently unpopular with the general public because

(a) is incorrect because the public does understand what a rider is.

(b) is correct because riders are unpopular with the general public when the targeted money does not benefit them.

(c) is incorrect because riders are not secret.

(d) is incorrect because lobbyists do not necessarily oppose riders.

(e) is incorrect because riders are not unconstitutional.

Page reference: 381–382, AP Topics: Congress and The major formal and informal arrangements of power

4.   Which of the following would be an attractive committee for a member of Congress from Montana looking to serve his or her constituency?

(a) is incorrect because a representative from Montana would better serve his constituency on the Agricultural committee rather than the Ways and Means committee.

(b) is incorrect because a representative from Montana would better serve his constituency on the Agricultural committee rather than the Rules committee.

(c) is incorrect because a representative from Montana would better serve his constituency on the Agricultural committee rather than the Education committee.

(d) is incorrect because a representative from Montana would better serve his constituency on the Agricultural committee rather than the Government Reform committee.

(e) is correct because being on the Agriculture Committee would enable a member of Congress to assist his or her constituents in farming and ranching.

Page reference: 374–375, AP Topic: Congress

5.   Descriptive representation refers to

(a) is incorrect because representing the interests groups does not accurately relate to descriptive representation.

(b) is incorrect because serving constituents through pork barrel projects does not accurately relate to descriptive representation.

(c) is correct because the idea behind descriptive representation is that citizens are best represented by people like themselves.

(d) is incorrect because living in the geographical area of one's constituents does not accurately relate to descriptive representation.

(e) is incorrect because all of the choices are not correct.

Page reference: 361–364, AP Topic: Congress

6.   A senator can effectively prevent the Senate from voting by

(a) is incorrect because conducting oversight does not stall debate.

(b) is correct because the filibuster stalls the debate process and therefore prevents the Senate from voting.

(c) is incorrect because introducing another bill does not stall debate.

(d) is incorrect because holding hearings does not stall debate.

(e) is incorrect because it is an inaccurate representation of the senate.

Page reference: 371, AP Topic: Congress

7.   Which of the following ends debate in the Senate?

(a) is correct because cloture (which requires 60 votes) ends a filibuster.

(b) is incorrect because a vote by the Rules committee will not stop a filibuster.

(c) is incorrect because a conference committee cannot stop a filibuster.

(d) is incorrect because a markup cannot stop a filibuster.

(e) is incorrect because a rider cannot stop a filibuster.

Page reference: 371, AP Topic: Congress

8.   Most of the time, members of Congress vote with

(a) is incorrect because party affiliation influences member of Congress' vote more than the president.

(b) is incorrect because party affiliation influences member of Congress' vote more than his or her state.

(c) is incorrect because party affiliation influences member of Congress' vote more than celebrities.

(d) is correct because while party discipline is not required, on most legislative issues members of Congress will vote with their party.

(e) is incorrect because party affiliation influences member of Congress' vote more than lobbyists.

Page reference: 367–368, AP Topics: Congress and The major formal and informal institutional arrangements of power

9.   After a House committee reviews a bill and writes its report, the bill goes to the

(a) is incorrect because a bill does not go to the Senate until it has been passed by the House.

(b) is incorrect because a bill does not have to go to a subcommittee.

(c) is incorrect because a bill only goes to the president when it has passed both houses in identical form.

(d) is incorrect because a bill in the House must go to the Rules committee before going to the floor.

(e) is correct because after being discussed and marked up in committee, a bill goes to the Rules Committee, which will schedule it for debate on the floor of the House.

Page reference: 381, AP Topic: Congress

10. Which of the following is the best example of legislative oversight?

(a) is incorrect because the vice president presiding over the Senate is not an example of oversight.

(b) is incorrect because the vice president presiding over the Senate is not an example of oversight.

(c) is incorrect because the vice president presiding over the Senate is not an example of oversight.

(d) is correct because oversight committees routinely hold hearings and ask questions of members of an agency to investigate claims of misuse of funds.

(e) is incorrect because the vice president presiding over the Senate is not an example of oversight.

Page reference: 376–377, AP Topic: Congress

11. All of the following is true of Congress EXCEPT

(a) is incorrect because most members of Congress are professional politicians.

(b) is incorrect because the majority of incumbents get reelected.

(c) is correct because women make up significantly less than 50% in both houses of Congress, with only 78 women in the House and only 20 in the Senate.

(d) is incorrect because 1/3 of the members of Congress have studied the law.

(e) is incorrect because being a member of Congress was not a career for most of the members during the 19th century.

Page reference: 362, AP Topic: Congress

12. The second most powerful official in Washington, D.C., after the president is

(a) is incorrect because the U.S. Senate *pro tempore* has fewer powers than the Speaker of the House.

(b) is incorrect because the chief justice of the Supreme Court has fewer powers than the Speaker of the House.

(c) is correct because the Speaker of the House is a member of the majority party who has both formal and informal powers and is second in line in presidential succession. The Speaker is the most powerful member of Congress.

(d) is incorrect because the vice president has fewer powers than the Speaker of the House.

(e) is incorrect because the majority party whip has fewer powers than the Speaker of the House.

Page reference: 372, AP Topics: Congress and The major formal and informal institutional arrangements of power

13. Most of the work in Congress is done

(a) is incorrect because not all bills make it to the floor.

(b) is incorrect because not all bills make it to the president.

(c) is incorrect because lobbyists are not part of Congress.

(d) is incorrect because select committees have a focused, but limited area of responsibility.

(e) is correct because standing committees are permanent, subject-matter committees that handle bills in different policy areas and through which all bills must pass in both houses.

Page reference: 374, AP Topic: Congress

14. Differences in House and Senate bills are resolved by

(a) is incorrect because a bill cannot go to the president until the differences are resolved.

(b) is incorrect because the Speaker of the House cannot resolve the differences alone.

(c) is incorrect because the Senate Rules Committee deals with the rules of that body and does not resolve differences in bills.

(d) is incorrect because standing committee chairs cannot resolve the differences.

(e) is correct because conference committees are formed when the Senate and the House pass different versions of the same bill.

Page reference: 374, AP Topic: Congress

15. All of the following are true of congressional oversight EXCEPT

(a) is incorrect because even though oversight is important, members of Congress spend more time on other matters.

(b) is incorrect because oversight is administered through the committee system.

(c) is correct because oversight is Congress's monitoring of the bureaucracy and its administration of policy, performed mainly through hearings, and occurs especially in times of scandal.

(d) is incorrect because the biggest obstacle of oversight is the lack of electoral advantage.

(e) is incorrect because members do spend more time on oversight when there is a scandal.

Page reference: 375, AP Topic: Congress

16. The term for redrawing Congressional districts to favor a particular political party is

(a) is incorrect because apportionment paradox is not an accurate term for the description.

(b) is correct because gerrymandering is the drawing of congressional districts to produce a particular electoral outcome (usually in favor of a particular party) without regard to the shape of the district.

(c) is incorrect because redistricting is not an accurate term for the description.

(d) is incorrect because redlining is not an accurate term for the description.

(e) is incorrect because malapportionment is not an accurate term for the description.

Page reference: 361–369, AP Topic: Congress

17. This office is involved in the preparation of Congress' budget.

(a) is incorrect because the Office of Management and Budget prepares the president's budget.

(b) is incorrect because the General Accounting Office is the audit and investigative arm of Congress.

(c) is incorrect because the Congressional Accounting Office does not deal with the budget.

(d) is incorrect because the Office of Congressional Management and Budget does not deal with the budget.

(e) is correct because the Congressional Budget Office advises Congress on the probable consequences of its decisions, and forecasts revenues.

Page reference: 375, AP Topics: Congress and The major formal and informal institutional arrangements of power

18. In the House of Representatives, _____ controls the scheduling of bills for debate.

(a) is incorrect because the House Ways and Means Committee does not control the scheduling of bills for debate.

(b) is incorrect because the Speaker of the House does not control the scheduling of bills for debate.

(c) is correct because the House Rules Committee reviews most bills coming from a House committee before they go to the full House.

(d) is incorrect because the Chief Administrative Officer does not control the scheduling of bills for debate.

(e) is incorrect because the chief justice of the Supreme Court does not control the scheduling of bills for debate.

Page reference: 374, AP Topics: Congress and The major formal and informal institutional arrangements of power

19.   The power of impeachment belongs to

(a) is incorrect because the Senate does not possess the power of impeachment.

(b) is correct because the power of impeachment, the political equivalent of indictment in criminal law, was given to the House of Representatives by the Constitution.

(c) is incorrect because a federal grand jury does not possess the power of impeachment.

(d) is incorrect because the Supreme Court does not possess the power of impeachment.

(e) is incorrect because the Chief Justice of the Supreme Court does not possess the power of impeachment.

Page reference: 403–405, AP Topics: Congress and The major formal and informal institutional arrangements of power

20.   The custom followed in Congress specifying that majority party members with the longest record of service will become committee chairs is

(a) is incorrect because senatorial courtesy is a tradition related to the appointment of federal judges.

(b) is incorrect because ageism refers to discrimination based on age.

(c) is correct because the seniority rule is a legislative practice that assigns the chair of a committee or subcommittee to the member of the majority party with the longest continuous service on the committee.

(d) is incorrect because the elder custom is not an accurate term for the description.

(e) is incorrect because senior incumbency is not an accurate term for the description.

Page reference: 378, AP Topic: Congress

Free-Response Questions

This rubric provides examples of many, but not all of the possible correct responses to the free-response questions.

1. Occasionally, one party will have control of Congress and the presidency. This will give the majority party advantages in Congress, yet passing legislation is still difficult.

   a. Describe the legislative advantages of the majority party in Congress with respect to both committee structure and leadership.

      - The majority party in Congress has numerous advantages in the legislative process. All committee chairs come from the majority party and there are more members of the majority party on committees. The chair of the committee can decide to hold a vote on moving a piece of legislation to the next stage, and is usually successful since he has more members from his party on the committee. The majority party also selects the Speaker of the House, who chairs the Rules Committee, schedules legislation, oversees the rules for the legislation, and oversees the debate on the legislation.

   b. Explain why, even with single-party control, passing legislation is difficult. Use two examples to support your explanation.

      - Even when one party controls both the White House and Congress, passing legislation is still difficult. There are many things that can stop legislation from passing. First, there is no guarantee of party discipline. One defecting member of a political party has the potential to slow the legislation. Oftentimes members within a party will disagree significantly during the markup process. One committee chair can also essentially hold a piece of legislation hostage in committee. Finally, in the Senate, there are maneuvers that give the minority party power, such as filibustering. All a minority party senator has to do is declare their intent to filibuster, and then there is a requirement that 60 votes cut off the filibuster. If the majority party does not have 60 in the Senate, passing any legislation will be difficult.

2. Congress has several nonlegislative functions. Describe the relevance of each of the following and provide an example.

   a. oversight of the bureaucracy

- One nonlegislative function of Congress is oversight of the federal bureaucracy. This occurs when a committee investigates how a federal department or agency is doing its job. Normally, Congress does this by holding hearings and asking questions of federal employees. This information-gathering process results in reports, recommendations and, often, new legislation. This is done publicly, and video clips of these hearings are often shown on television. One example is the 9/11 Commission. This commission was created to try to figure out how our intelligence system could perform better and avoid another 9/11 catastrophe. Hearings were held and a major report was published, which resulted in the reorganization of U.S. intelligence services.

b. confirmation of political appointees

- Another nonlegislative function of Congress is confirming presidential appointees. Most often, the Senate Judiciary Committee performs this function. The committee holds a hearing and interviews the potential nominee. Former employers and those who know the nominee may also testify. The committee makes a recommendation about whether or not to approve the nominee and then the full Senate must vote by a simple majority in order for the nominee to be confirmed. One recent example is Michael Mukasey's nomination as U.S. attorney general.

c. impeachment

- Finally, impeachment is a nonlegislative function. If the president has committed a "high crime or misdemeanor," then the House may conduct an investigation of wrongdoing. The House then votes by simple majority and the Senate can conduct a trial to see if the allegations warrant removal of the president from office. The Senate is required to vote by a two-thirds majority in order to remove the president.

12

The Presidency

☐ Chapter Overview

In this chapter you will learn about the office of President of the United States, who serves both as the head of the government of the United States and the ceremonial representative of the country. We begin by considering how presidents are chosen. We then examine the formal and informal powers of the Office of the President, including the presidency itself, the vice president, the first lady, the cabinet, the Executive Office of the President, and the White House staff. Then we turn to consider how the president interacts with the Congress in the development of governmental policy. We conclude by exploring how presidential popularity and the president's relationship with the media influence the success of their term in office.

☐ Study Outline

 Learning Objective 12.1: Characterize the expectations for and the backgrounds of presidents and identify paths to the White House and how presidents may be removed. (p. 399)

The Presidents

- **Presidents** can reach the Oval Office in different ways:
    - Most are former governors or members of Congress who, after being nominated by their party, campaigned and won the election.
    - Some presidents were vice presidents who took over after the death or removal of a president.

- Vice presidents can also become president in the event the president resigns or is convicted in an impeachment trial.
- The **Twenty-Fifth Amendment** establishes the procedures for filling vacancies in both the offices of president and vice president, and it also makes provisions for presidential disability.

- The Constitution sets forth the process of **impeachment** of a president who has abused his powers or committed a "high crime or misdemeanor" worthy of removal from office.
- The **House** may vote for the impeachment of the president by a simple majority.
- The **Senate** conducts the impeachment trial and the chief justice of the Supreme Court presides over the trial.
- It takes a two-thirds vote in the Senate to remove the president from office.
- Only **two presidents** have been impeached, though neither was removed from office.
- Andrew Johnson was tried but not convicted in 1868, and Bill Clinton was acquitted by the Senate in 1999.

 Learning Objective 12.2: Evaluate the president's constitutional powers and the expansion of presidential power. (p. 405)

Presidential Powers

- The Constitution grants the president fairly limited powers that were designed to prevent him or her from gaining too much authority, thus maintaining the balance of power among government institutions.
- The power to "take care that the laws be faithfully executed," as specified in the Constitution, is one of the more overlooked responsibilities of the president.
- As the bureaucracy has grown, it has become nearly impossible for the president alone to execute and enforce all laws; instead, the president now appoints numerous administrative officials, including cabinet members and department heads.
- Some have argued that during the 1950s and 1960s the presidency became "imperial" in nature, taking nearly full control over American politics.

- Since then, the power waned considerably but grew again with concerns about national security after the September 11 attacks.

 Learning Objective 12.3: Describe the roles of the vice president, cabinet, Executive Office of the President, White House staff, and First Lady. (p. 408)

Running the Government: The Chief Executive

- **Vice presidents** traditionally have few responsibilities and little political prominence.
- Vice presidents are second in line to assume the presidency if the president is unable to fulfill the duties of office.
- The vice president is the president (presiding officer) of the Senate and casts a vote whenever there is a tie.
- Today, vice presidents assume more responsibilities, depending on how the president they are serving entrusts functions to them.
- Vice presidents may serve as diplomats representing the president, take part in important policy meetings, or help raise funds for their party.
- The **cabinet** is a group of officials who act as advisors to the president.
- The cabinet is not mentioned in the Constitution, but it quickly became an institution that has accompanied every presidency.
- The modern cabinet is composed of the attorney general and the heads, or secretaries, of the 13 executive departments.
- The president has the power to appoint all of these officials, but each appointment must be confirmed by the Senate.
- Each cabinet member heads a department that deals with a different policy area.
- The departments, created by Congress, carry out all the administrative work necessary to enforce laws or assist the president in his executive duties.
- The Executive Office of the President (E.O.P) is a collection of administrative and advisory bodies that assist the president in overseeing policy.
- The EOP includes the **National Security Council**, the **Council of Economic Advisors**, and the **Office of Management and Budget**.

- The White House Staff includes important personal and political advisors to the president, such as the legal counsel to the president, the president's personal secretary, and the chief of staff.

- This office takes care of the president's political needs and manages the press.

 Learning Objective 12.4: Assess the impact of various sources of presidential influence on the president's ability to win congressional support. (p. 414)

Presidential Leadership of Congress: The Politics of Shared Powers

- Though not a member of the legislative branch, presidents do have a role to play in the legislative process.

Chief Legislator

- The power to veto legislation can be an effective tool of intimidation.

- Because a veto rejects a bill in its entirety, the president can have a good deal of influence over the shaping of each specific provision.

- If the president does veto a bill, it goes back to Congress, which, by a two-thirds vote, can override the veto; however, this rarely happens.

- The president also has the power to reject any legislation submitted at the end of the congressional session without the possibility of his veto being overruled.

- If he does not sign a bill submitted by Congress within 10 days of its adjourning, the bill is automatically rejected, which is a **pocket veto**.

Party Leadership

- To influence policy, presidents must work closely with Congress.

- Specifically, they rely on close ties with members of Congress who are members of their political party.

- Political parties help bridge the gap between the legislative and executive branches.

- A president and a representative of the same party were most likely elected by the same body of people, or by voters who have similar political views, so they probably share political priorities.

- Members of Congress who support the president's legislative agenda are likely to receive support for some of their projects and initiatives in return.

- A close relationship with a popular president can also be beneficial to members of Congress during reelection (**presidential coattails**).

- The president must rely on members of Congress to introduce legislation for him or her and to win support for it during the legislative process; therefore, the president must work closely with party leaders to convince representatives to vote the party line.

- Even if a president's party is the majority party in either or both houses, he may not necessarily have the full support of representatives, who might not vote with the party line.

Public Support

- Public support for the president factors heavily in his congressional support.

- Representatives are much more likely to vote in favor of the initiatives of a president who is popular with the electorate, and presidents are well aware that public opinion is an incredibly powerful tool of persuasion.

- Public approval gives a president more leeway in pursuing policy goals, because representatives are more likely to support his objectives in the hope of being reelected by an electorate that has confidence in their president.

- Public support lends a president a greater degree of legitimacy. Congress is more likely to respond to the will of a president who was elected by a large margin, especially on legislation proposed early in his term.

- The policies of a president who is perceived as weak are more likely to be cast into doubt by Congress, making it harder for the president to garner legislative support.

Legislative Skills

- Presidents may also exert their influence over the political agenda by employing specific strategies at key times in the legislative process.

- To strengthen a presidential coalition, presidents often bargain with representatives by offering support on one piece of legislation in exchange for receiving it on another.

- Members of Congress may also receive certain presidential favors, such as joint public appearances during campaigns.

- Presidents present many proposals to Congress soon after their election during what is called the "honeymoon period," when there is a fresh sense of community in Washington.

- Presidents work hard to focus the attention of Congress on their own specific agendas.

- By setting priorities, they are able to concentrate their resources to push through a few key policy objectives.

 Learning Objective 12.5: Analyze the president's powers in making national security policy and the relationship between the president and Congress in this arena. (p. 422)

The President and National Security Policy

- The president is both the commander in chief of the armed forces and the chief U.S. diplomat.

- The diplomatic powers of the president include establishing formal recognition of other governments, negotiating treaties, formulating **executive agreements** with other foreign leaders (which, unlike treaties, do not require congressional approval; most executive agreements are administrative in nature), and using U.S. influence to arbitrate conflicts between other nations.

- Military powers include the decision to use weapons of mass destruction, authorizing military actions during war, and sending troops into specific areas of conflict.

- The **War Powers Resolution**, passed in 1973, was intended to limit this power by requiring that these troops be withdrawn within 60 days unless Congress declares war or issues an extension.

- Many believe that it is unconstitutional, and all presidents have treated it as such.

Learning Objective 12.6: Identify the factors that affect the president's ability to obtain public support. (p. 428)

Power from the People: The Public Presidency

- Because presidents know that public approval works enormously in their favor, they work hard to sell their agenda to the public.

- A voter's approval of the president is determined by whether the voter identifies with the political party of the president.

- A voter's approval of the president is determined by how the president responds to economic shifts or handles other current issues.

- A voter's approval of the president is determined by how effective a public speaker the president is, and his appearance in front of the cameras.

- A voter's approval of the president is determined by whether the president appeals to the public directly, in which case the public usually responds positively.

- A voter's approval of the president is determined by how the media interprets the actions of the president.

- The efforts of the White House to influence public opinion are not always successful, however. The public tends to be fickle in its approval, and the media often mislead the public by oversimplifying political and economic issues.

 Learning Objective 12.7: Characterize the president's relations with the press and news coverage of the presidency. (p. 434)

The President and the Press

- The press is the principal intermediary between the president and the public.

- Presidents and the press are frequently in conflict over the amount, nature, and tone of the coverage of the presidency.

- There has been an increase in the negativity of coverage and there are an increasing number of ideologically biased sources of news.

Learning Objective 12.8: Assess the role of presidential power in the American democracy and the president's impact on the scope of government. (p. 436)

Understanding the American Presidency

- There is always a fear of a presidential power that is harmful to democracy, however, there are many checks on presidential power.

For Additional Review

Take notes on the following areas of increased presidential power:

1. war powers
2. diplomacy by executive agreements
3. secrecy and executive privilege
4. government by veto

For each of the above areas of presidential power, explain how it has increased presidential power. Use these notes to help prepare for the unit test and the AP Government and Politics Exam.

Create a chart listing the roles of the president. Under each role, list the powers the president exercises when performing the duties for each role. Use this chart when reviewing and studying for the unit test and the AP Government and Politics Exam.

☐ Review Questions

Multiple-Choice Questions

1. Congress can override a presidential veto of legislation
   a. by appealing to the U.S. Supreme Court.
   b. by negotiating a deal with the vice president.
   c. by getting approval of the bill in three-fourths of the state legislatures.
   d. with a majority vote of the House Rules Committee.
   e. with a two-thirds vote in both houses of Congress.

2. According to the Constitution, the vice president
   a. chairs all cabinet meetings.
   b. is ineligible to run for president after two terms as vice president.
   c. is the president of the Senate.
   d. must be of the same party as the president.
   e. is an ex officio member of the Council of Economic Advisors.

3. Which of the following presidential appointments requires Senate confirmation?
   a. press secretary
   b. chief of staff
   c. White House counsel
   d. Council of Economic Advisors
   e. secretary of state

4. All of the following are true statements about the impeachment process EXCEPT
   a. the chief justice of the United States presides over the trial.
   b. the Supreme Court decides guilt or innocence.
   c. the trial must be held in public.
   d. the Senate serves as the jury.
   e. the House of Representatives brings the formal charges against the president.

5. A president is most likely to gain public support for a public policy proposal by
   a. sending the vice president out to conduct high-profile town hall meetings.
   b. placing ads in respected newspapers with large circulations.
   c. vetoing a bill passed by Congress.
   d. appealing to the public directly via the broadcast media.
   e. including the proposal in his or her party's campaign platform.

6. The Twenty-Fifth Amendment is significant because it
   a. clarifies the terms under which the vice president may become president if the president becomes disabled.
   b. defines the line of succession to the president.
   c. clarifies the formal roles, duties, and responsibilities of all parties involved in a presidential impeachment trial.
   d. defines the process to be used for creating new cabinet positions.
   e. clarifies Congress's role in the realm of U.S. foreign policy.

7. One of the primary tools presidents use to control the bureaucracy is
   a. the line-item veto.
   b. congressional oversight committees.
   c. campaign finance reform.
   d. the presidential power to appoint and remove top-level administrators.
   e. the presidential power to pardon.

8. Which of the following statements about the president as commander in chief is true?
   a. The president has the authority to declare war for up to 60 days without consulting Congress.
   b. The president decides if and when to use weapons of mass destruction in times of war.
   c. Presidents with no prior military experience are not allowed to make major military decisions alone.
   d. The president is required by law to consult with the Joint Chiefs of Staff before deploying the military.
   e. The president is a nonvoting member of the Senate Armed Services Committee.

9.	Which of the following are powers of the president?

I.	conducting diplomatic relations
II.	negotiating treaties
III.	dismissing Supreme Court justices
IV.	appointing cabinet officers

a.	IV only
b.	I, II, and III only
c.	I, II, and IV only
d.	I, III, and IV only
e.	II, III, and IV only

10.	Which of the following is NOT in the line of presidential succession?
a.	chief justice of the Supreme Court
b.	secretary of state
c.	secretary of the interior
d.	attorney general
e.	Speaker of the House

11.	The vice president possesses only one real constitutional duty, which is
a.	to break tie votes in the Senate.
b.	to serve as an advisor to the Supreme Court.
c.	to break tie votes in the House of Representatives.
d.	to act as chief diplomat.
e.	to serve as president of the House of Representatives.

12.	This is a formal agreement negotiated by the president of the United States and one or more nations, requiring approval of the Senate by a two-thirds vote.
a.	treaty
b.	executive order
c.	executive agreement
d.	executive memorandum
e.	mandate

13.	All of the following are powers of the president EXCEPT
a.	the power to convene Congress
b.	the power to nominate federal judges
c.	the power to veto legislation
d.	the power to declare war
e.	the power to recognize diplomats

14.	The President and Congress tend to agree
a.	during the first year of a president's first term.
b.	during the first year of a president's second term.
c.	when the president is a lame duck.
d.	when there is an unpopular president.
e.	when there is an unpopular Congress.

15. The body within the White House Staff of the President that advises the president on economic issues is
    a. the Treasury Office.
    b. the National Economic Council.
    c. the Office of Management and Budget.
    d. the Council of Economic Advisors.
    e. the Federal Reserve.

16. Which of the following are the formal constitutional qualifications for becoming president?

    I.   Must be a resident of the U.S. for at least 14 years.
    II. Must be at least 35 years old.
    III. Must be a white male.
    IV. Must be a natural born citizen.
    V.   Must have served in elective office.

    a. I and II
    b. II, III, and V
    c. I, IV, and V
    d. I, II, and IV
    e. II, IV and V

17. All of the following are in the Executive Office of the President EXCEPT
    a. the Council of Economic Advisors
    b. the General Accounting Office
    c. the National Security Council
    d. the Office of the Vice President
    e. the Office of Management and Budget

18. The annual statement the president presents to Congress and the nation is called the
    a. State of the Country Address.
    b. State of the Budget Address.
    c. State of the Union Address.
    d. State of the State Address.
    e. Congressional Oversight Address.

19. The director of which of the following departments is considered MOST central to the president's agencies?
    a. Energy
    b. Management and Budget
    c. Defense
    d. Homeland Security
    e. Treasury

20. This amendment to the Constitution established term limits for the president.
    a. Twelfth
    b. Twenty-Second
    c. Twenty-Fifth
    d. Twenty-First
    e. First

Free-Response Questions

1. The president is the single most powerful individual in government. Some of the president's most important responsibilities and powers fall in the area of national security.

    a. Identify and explain two national security powers or responsibilities granted to the president in the Constitution.

    b. Identify and describe two constitutional limitations on presidential national security power.

2. The president plays an important policymaking role in the federal system.

    a. Identify and explain two ways the president influences policy.

    b. Identify and describe two limitations on the president's policymaking power.

☐ Answers and Explanations

Multiple-Choice Questions

1. Congress can override a presidential veto of legislation

    (a) is incorrect because the power to override a veto belongs to Congress.

    (b) is incorrect because the vice-president does not have a role in overriding a veto.

    (c) is incorrect because state legislatures do not have a role in overriding a veto.

    (d) is incorrect because the House Rules committee does not have the power to override a veto.

    (e) is correct because, while a presidential veto usually effectively kills proposed legislation, Congress can override the veto with a two-thirds majority vote in both houses, and has done so in about four percent of the vetoes. The Constitution gives the president the power to veto as a means to check Congress, and it gives Congress the power to override a veto as a means of checking the president.

Page reference: 415, AP Topics: The Presidency and The major formal and informal institutional arrangements of power

2.   According to the Constitution, the vice president

(a) is incorrect because the vice president is not assigned the task of chairing cabinet meetings.

(b) is incorrect because the vice president is eligible to run for president after serving two terms as vice president.

(c) is correct because the Constitution assigns vice presidents the relatively minor tasks of presiding over the Senate and voting in case of a tie among the senators.

(d) is incorrect because there is no constitutional requirement for the vice president to be of the same party as the president.

(e) is incorrect because the vice president does not serve on the Council of Economic Advisors.

Page reference: 409, AP Topic: The Presidency

3.   Which of the following presidential appointments requires Senate confirmation?

(a) is incorrect because the press secretary is part of the president's personal staff of advisors and these appointments do not require Senate approval.

(b) is incorrect because the chief of staff is part of the president's personal staff of advisors and these appointments do not require Senate approval.

(c) is incorrect because the White House counsel is part of the president's personal staff of advisors and these appointments do not require Senate approval.

(d) is incorrect because the Council of Economic Advisors is part of the president's personal staff of advisors and these appointments do not require Senate approval.

(e) is correct, because they are a member of the president's cabinet, nominees for Secretary of State must be confirmed by the Senate.

Page reference: 410, AP Topic: The Presidency

4.   All of the following are true statements about the impeachment process EXCEPT

(a) is incorrect because the chief justice of the Supreme Court does preside over the presidential impeachment process.

(b) is correct because the Supreme Court plays no role in the presidential impeachment process.

(c) is incorrect because the presidential impeachment trial does have to be public.

(d) is incorrect because the Senate does serve as the jury in the presidential impeachment trial.

(e) is incorrect because the House of Representatives does bring the formal charges against the president in the presidential impeachment process.

Page reference: 403–404, AP Topics: The Presidency and The major formal and informal institutional arrangements of power

5. A president is most likely to gain public support for a public policy proposal by

    (a) is incorrect because having the vice president conduct high-profile town meetings is not as effective in gaining public support for a public policy proposal as the president appealing to the public directly.

    (b) is incorrect because placing ads in respected newspapers is not as effective in gaining public support for a public policy proposal as the president appealing to the public directly.

    (c) is incorrect because vetoing a bill is not as effective in gaining public support for a public policy proposal as the president appealing to the public directly.

    (d) is correct because public support is one of president's most important resources for getting their policy agenda enacted. Presidents who have the backing of the public have an easier time influencing Congress. Using the mass media to directly appeal to the public is an effective tool for gaining public support.

    (e) is incorrect because including the proposal in his or her party platform is not as effective in gaining public support for a public policy proposal as the president appealing to the public directly.

    Page reference: 420, AP Topic: The Presidency

6. The Twenty-Fifth Amendment is significant because it

    (a) is correct because the Twenty-Fifth Amendment, passed in 1967, is significant because it clarifies the terms under which the vice president may become president in the event that the president becomes disabled. It also outlines how a recuperated president can reclaim the job.

    (b) is incorrect because this is an inaccurate description of the 25th Amendment.

    (c) is incorrect because the 25th Amendment does not deal with impeachment.

    (d) is incorrect because the 25th Amendment does not deal with the creation of new cabinet positions.

(e) is incorrect because the 25th Amendment does not deal with the role of Congress in foreign policy.

Page reference: 401–403, AP Topic: The Presidency

7. One of the primary tools presidents use to control the bureaucracy is

(a) is incorrect because the line-item veto is not a tool of the president.

(b) is incorrect because congressional oversight committees are not tools the president uses to control the bureaucracy.

(c) is incorrect because campaign finance reform is not a tool the president uses to control the bureaucracy.

(d) is correct because the power to appoint and remove top-level administrators gives the president significant influence over what the federal bureaucracy does or does not do.

(e) is incorrect because the presidential power to pardon is not a tool the president uses to control the bureaucracy.

Page reference: 408–413, AP Topics: The Presidency and The major formal and informal institutional arrangements of power

8. Which of the following statements about the president as commander in chief is true?

(a) is incorrect because only Congress has the power to declare war.

(b) is correct because, as commander in chief of military forces, the president decides if and when American armed forces use weapons of mass destruction in times of war.

(c) is incorrect because a president's prior military experience is not a factor in the exercise of presidential power.

(d) is incorrect because the president does not have to consult with the Joint Chiefs of Staff before deploying the military.

(e) is incorrect because the president is not a member of the Senate Armed Services Committee.

Page reference: 424, AP Topics: The Presidency and The major formal and informal institutional arrangements of power

9. Which of the following are powers of the president?

(a) is incorrect because I and III are also powers belonging to the president.

(b) is incorrect because presidents nominate federal court judges, but they cannot remove them from their seats once the Senate has confirmed them because federal judges hold their positions for life.

(c) is correct because, according to the Constitution, presidents have the power to conduct diplomacy, negotiate treaties with foreign countries, and appoint members of their cabinet.

(d) is incorrect because III is not a power which belongs to the president.

(e) is incorrect because III is not a power which belongs to the president.

Page reference: 405–408, AP Topics: The Presidency and The major formal and informal institutional arrangements of power

10. Which of the following is NOT in the line of presidential succession?

(a) is correct because the chief justice is not in the line of presidential succession. The Constitution authorizes the vice president to take over the office of the presidency if the president dies, resigns, is impeached, or is otherwise unable to perform his duties.

(b) is incorrect because the Secretary of State, as a cabinet member, is in the line of presidential succession.

(c) is incorrect because the Secretary of the Interior, as a cabinet member, is in the line of presidential succession.

(d) is incorrect because the Attorney General, as a cabinet member, is in the line of presidential succession.

(e) is incorrect because the Speaker of the House is in the line of presidential succession.

Page reference: 401–403, AP Topics: The Presidency and The major formal and informal institutional arrangements of power

11. The vice president possesses only one real constitutional duty, which is

(a) is correct because the Constitution assigns vice presidents the minor tasks of presiding over the Senate and voting in case of a tie among senators.

(b) is incorrect because the Constitution does not give the vice president the task of serving as an advisor to the Supreme Court.

(c) is incorrect because the Constitution does not give the vice president the task of breaking tie votes in the House of Representatives.

(d) is incorrect because the Constitution does not give the vice president the task of serving as chief diplomat.

(e) is incorrect because the Constitution does not give the vice president the task of serving as the president of the House of Representatives.

Page reference: 409, AP Topics: The Presidency and The major formal and informal institutional arrangements of power

12. This is a formal agreement negotiated by the president of the United States and one or more nations, requiring approval of the Senate by a two-thirds vote.

(a) is correct because a treaty is a formal, public agreement between the United States and one or more nations that must be approved by two-thirds of the Senate.

(b) is incorrect because an executive order does not have to be approved by the Senate.

(c) is incorrect because an executive agreement does not have to be approved by the Senate.

(d) is incorrect because an executive memorandum does not have to be approved by the Senate.

(e) is incorrect because a mandate is a claim of public support and not a formal power of the president.

Page reference: 423, AP Topics: The Presidency and The major formal and informal institutional arrangements of power

13. All of the following are powers of the president EXCEPT

(a) is incorrect because the power to convene Congress is a power which belongs to the president.

(b) is incorrect because the power to nominate federal judges is a power which belongs to the president.

(c) is incorrect because the power to veto legislation is a power which belongs to the president.

(d) is correct because the power to declare war belongs to Congress and not to the president.

(e) is incorrect because the power to recognize diplomats is a power which belongs to the president.

Page reference: 405–408, AP Topics: The Presidency and The major formal and informal institutional arrangements of power

14. The President and Congress tend to agree

   (a) is correct because the "honeymoon" period occurs at the beginning of a new president's term and it is the period during which the president enjoys generally positive relations with the press and Congress, usually lasting about six months.

   (b) is incorrect because the "honeymoon" period is approximately the first six months of the president's first term.

   (c) is incorrect because the "honeymoon" period is approximately the first six months of the president's first term.

   (d) is incorrect because the "honeymoon" period is approximately the first six months of the president's first term.

   (e) is incorrect because the "honeymoon" period is approximately the first six months of the president's first term.

   Page reference: 420–421, AP Topics: The Presidency and The major formal and informal institutional arrangements of power

15. The body within the White House Staff of the President that advises the president on economic issues is

   (a) is incorrect because the Treasury Office is not part of the White House Staff.

   (b) is correct because the National Economic Council is a division of the policy offices housed in the White House Staff and it advises the president on economic issues.

   (c) is incorrect because the Office of Management and Budget is not part of the White House Staff.

   (d) is incorrect because the Council of Economic Advisors is not part of the White House Staff.

   (e) is incorrect because the Federal Reserve is not part of the White House Staff.

   Page reference: 412, AP Topic: The Presidency

16. Which of the following are the formal constitutional qualifications for becoming president?

   (a) is incorrect because I and II are only two of the three constitutional qualifications for president.

   (b) is incorrect because III and V are not constitutional qualifications for president.

   (c) is incorrect because V is not a constitutional qualification for president.

(d) is correct because the constitutional qualifications for becoming president are that the individual must be a resident of the U.S. for at least 14 years, must be at least 35 years old, and must be a natural born citizen.

(e) is incorrect because V is not a constitutional qualification for president.

Page reference: MyPoliSciLab/Constitution, AP Topics: The Presidency and The Constitution

17.	All of the following are in the Executive Office of the President EXCEPT

(a) is incorrect because the Council of Economic Advisors is part of the Executive Office of the president.

(b) is correct because the General Accounting Office is a congressional office and not part of the Executive Office of the president.

(c) is incorrect because the National Security Council is part of the Executive Office of the president.

(d) is incorrect because the Office of the Vice President is part of the Executive Office of the president.

(e) is incorrect because the Office of Management and Budget is part of the Executive Office of the president.

Page reference: 411, AP Topics: The Presidency and Congress

18.	The annual statement the president presents to Congress and the nation is called the

(a) is incorrect because the State of the Country Address is an inaccurate selection for the description provided.

(b) is incorrect because the State of the Budget Address is an inaccurate selection for the description provided.

(c) is correct because the State of the Union Address is the annual statement the president gives to Congress and to the nation.

(d) is incorrect because the State of the State Address is an inaccurate selection for the description provided.

(e) is incorrect because the Congressional Oversight Address is an inaccurate selection for the description provided.

Page reference: 415, AP Topics: The Presidency and Congress

19. The director of which of the following departments is considered MOST central to the president's agencies?

(a) is incorrect because, even though the Department of Energy provides important information to the president, it is not considered MOST central to the president's agencies.

(b) is correct because the director of the Office of Management and Budget heads the department that prepares the president's budget and also advises presidents on proposals from departments and agencies and helps review their proposed regulations.

(c) is incorrect because, even though the Department of Defense provides important information to the president, it is not considered MOST central to the president's agencies.

(d) is incorrect because, even though the Department of Homeland Security provides important information to the president, it is not considered MOST central to the president's agencies.

(e) is incorrect because, even though the Department of Treasury provides important information to the president, it is not considered MOST central to the president's agencies.

Page reference: 410, AP Topic: The Presidency

20. This amendment to the Constitution established term limits for the president.

(a) is incorrect because the Twelfth Amendment required the joint listing of the presidential and vice presidential candidates on the same ballot.

(b) is correct because the Twenty-second Amendment limits the president to two terms, or ten years total.

(c) is incorrect because the Twenty-fifth Amendment provided for presidential succession.

(d) is incorrect because the Twenty-first Amendment ended prohibition.

(e) is incorrect because the First Amendment provides for basic civil liberties.

Page reference: 401, AP Topics: The Presidency and the Constitution

Free-Response Questions

This rubric provides examples of many, but not all of the possible correct responses to the free-response questions.

1. The president is the single most powerful individual in government. Some of the president's most important responsibilities and powers fall in the area of national security.

   a. Identify and explain two national security powers or responsibilities granted to the president in the Constitution.

- **Commander in chief.** Because the framers wanted civilian control of the military, they made the president commander in chief of the armed forces. As commander in chief, the president controls where and how the military is deployed. The president also commands the vast arsenal of weapons of mass destruction. While only Congress can declare war, the president can interject U.S. troops into armed conflict on a limited basis.

- **Diplomatic powers.** The president alone extends diplomatic recognition to foreign governments. The president can also terminate relations with other countries.

- **Power to make treaties with other nations.** The president has the sole power to negotiate treaties with other countries, although the Constitution requires the Senate to approve them by a two-thirds vote.

b. Identify and describe two constitutional limitations on presidential national security power.

- Although the president has power to deploy U.S. troops, only Congress has the constitutional power to declare war.

- Treaties that presidents negotiate with foreign countries must be approved by a two-thirds vote in the Senate.

- Congress has the power of the purse. A president's national security agenda requires a willingness on the part of Congress to appropriate the necessary funds to support it.

2. The president plays an important policymaking role in the federal system.

a. Identify and explain two ways the president influences policy.

- **Executive orders.** The president can issue executive orders that have the effect of law. These can be powerful tools for the president to change the course of policy. For example, President Harry Truman used an executive order to desegregate the armed forces.

- **Setting the legislative agenda.** Many presidents play major roles in setting the agenda of Congress. They not only make policy proposals but also use lobbyists to steward proposals through the policymaking process.

b. Identify and describe two limitations on the president's policymaking power.

- **Congress has the power of the purse.** Although the president can make policy proposals, only Congress can appropriate funds.
- **The Supreme Court has judicial review.** The Supreme Court can review the constitutionality of executive orders or regulations promulgated by the bureaucracy.

13

The Budget: The Politics of Taxing and Spending

☐ Chapter Overview

As the popular saying "put your money where your mouth is" suggests, the federal budget process provides a powerful way to think about the priorities of the national government. In this chapter we examine the politics of the budget. We start by describing the sources of funding for the federal government and assess the consequences of tax expenditures and borrowing. Then we analyze federal expenditures and the growth of the budget, outline the budgetary process, and explain the role that politics plays. We conclude by assessing the impact of democratic politics on budgetary growth and of the budget on scope of government. By the end of the chapter, students should have a good understanding of the basic dynamics and controversies surrounding the federal budget.

☐ Study Outline

 Learning Objective 13.1: Describe the sources of funding for the federal government and assess the consequences of tax expenditure and borrowing. (p. 446)

Federal Revenue and Borrowing

- **Income taxes:** A percentage of what a person earns goes directly to the government.

- The **Sixteenth Amendment** (1913) officially authorized Congress to collect income taxes.

- The **Internal Revenue Service (IRS)** collects income taxes, monitors people's payments through **audits**, and investigates and prosecutes cases of tax evasion.

- The income tax is **progressive**—people with higher incomes pay a greater percentage in taxes.

- Opponents suggest a flat tax in which everyone pays an equal rate; such a tax is considered **proportional**.

- Others propose a sales tax to replace the income tax; because poorer people pay a higher percentage of their income in sales tax—they spend much more of their income than they save or invest—such a tax is called **regressive**.

- Corporations also pay taxes on their income, but most tax money comes from individual income taxes.

- **Social insurance taxes:** Social Security taxes are paid by both businesses and their employees.

  - Money collected from this tax is used specifically to pay current monthly benefits to senior citizens.

  - These taxes have grown significantly and now account for about one-third of the federal revenue.

  - As the population ages, more people will be expecting payments from the government. Economists are concerned that the baby boom generation may drain the system.

- **Borrowing:** The federal government has borrowed a huge amount of money over the years.

  - It borrows from foreign investors, foreign governments, and the American people by selling government bonds.

  - The government gets the money, but must pay it back to the bondholder with interest.

  - The money the government owes is the **national debt**.

  - About 7 percent of the federal budget is allocated to pay just the interest on the federal debt.

  - Future generations will have to pay for many policies enacted today.

- Lawmakers have considered proposing a **balanced budget amendment**, which would require Congress and the president to balance the budget each year.
- Critics argue that it is too difficult to predict a balanced budget because of the uncertainties of the economy.

Taxes and Public Policy

- **Tax loopholes** are any tax break that allows a person to benefit from not paying a part of his or her taxes. Deductions for specific items are considered loopholes.
- Not everyone has the same access to loopholes.
- **Tax expenditures** are the losses in federal revenues that result from tax breaks, deductions, and exemptions.
- They function as built-in subsidies—the government loses money by excusing a homeowner from paying taxes on a mortgage, but then the government does not have to pay for programs, such as a homeowners' assistance program.
- Middle- and upper-income people benefit the most because they usually have more deductions and write-offs.
- **Tax reform:** How much to tax is almost always a point of contention among Congress and the public.
  - President Clinton raised tax rates on the wealthy. President George W. Bush enacted a series of tax cuts across all income levels, but which particularly benefitted the wealthy.

 Learning Objective 13.2: Analyze federal expenditures and the growth of the budget. (p. 454)

Federal Expenditures

- The government must pay its own operational costs, which make up a significant percentage of its overall expenditures.
- **National security** was a large expenditure during the Cold War and Reagan era, but it had begun to decline before September 11, 2001.
- **Social services** are now the biggest expenditure: programs for people of low income and senior citizens make up one-third of the budget.

- Social Security began with the **Social Security Act**, part of the New Deal.

- **Medicare**, initiated in 1965, extends medical coverage to senior citizens.

- Because people are living longer and the current generation of senior citizens is large, Social Security taxes have risen.

- **Uncontrollable expenditures** are a form of mandatory spending.

- Pensions and payments toward the national debt are fixed, and thus not subject to budgetary cuts or changes.

- **Entitlements** are benefits the government must pay to people who are eligible according to federal rules, such as veterans' aid, Social Security, and welfare.

- **Incrementalism** is the basis on which the budget is adjusted every year.

- A budget is calculated by assuming that the expenditures included in the budget of the previous year will rise for the next year.

- One issue is how large the increment should be, and another concern is that this creates a system of an ever-increasing budgets.

 Learning Objective 13.3: Outline the budgetary process and explain the role that politics plays.

The Budgetary Process

- The budget affects and involves agencies and departments in the federal, state, and even local governments.

- Every year, the budget process begins with the "spring review," when the federal agencies review their programs and prepare their requests for the next fiscal year.

- Budget requests are submitted to the **Office of Management and Budget (OMB)**.

- During the "fall review," the OMB reviews the requests, and then submits the final requests to the president. Interest groups and agencies often team up when making budgetary requests.

- Based on all of the agency requests, the president formally proposes a budget plan to Congress in February.

- Since 1922, the president has been required to prepare and submit a budget to Congress.

- In 1974, the **Congressional Budget and Impoundment Control Act** was passed by Congress to reform and regain some control over the budgetary process.

- The **House Ways and Means Committee** and the **Senate Finance Committee** write the tax codes that will determine how much revenue the government will have for the year.

- The **Appropriations Committees** in both houses determine how federal funds within the total expenditure will be allotted among agencies and departments.

- The House and Senate Budget Committees and the **Congressional Budget Office** review the proposal for its feasibility.

- Congress must agree on a **budget resolution**, the final amount of expenditures not to be exceeded for the year.

- Congress might make changes to existing laws to meet the budget resolution.

- **Reconciliation bills** revise program authorizations.

- The **Authorization bill** allows the expenditures for discretionary programs or enacts the requirements for entitlement programs are changed.

- Congress must pass the final budget bill and the president must sign it for it to become law.

 Learning Objective 13.4: Assess the impact of democratic politics on budgetary growth and of the budget on scope of government. (p. 467)

Understanding Budgeting

- Budgets in democracies grow because the public and organized interests demand new and larger public services.

- Some politicians compete for votes by promising to limit budgets.

- Increasing budgets increase the scope of government, but decreases in taxes and increases in debt make it more difficult to add or expand programs.

For Additional Review

Make a table outlining the budgetary process. For each step, list the institutions involved and their specific responsibilities. Make a note of any political motivations that influence each participant's role in making the budget. Use this table when reviewing and studying for the unit test and for the AP Government and Politics exam.

Make a list of the sources of funding for the federal government. Include in this list the consequences of tax expenditures and borrowing. Use this list when reviewing and studying for the unit test and for the AP Government and Politics exam.

❑ Review Questions

Multiple-Choice Questions

1. Congress's authority to levy an income tax comes from which of the following?
    a. interstate commerce clause
    b. Sixteenth Amendment
    c. Budget Act (1974)
    d. Bill of Rights
    e. *Marbury v. Madison*

2. The institution responsible for compiling the president's budget proposal is the
    a. Department of the Treasury.
    b. Congressional Budget Office.
    c. Senate Appropriations Committee.
    d. Office of Management and Budget.
    e. Council of Economic Advisors.

3. The largest contribution to federal revenue comes from
    a. taxes on businesses.
    b. interest on foreign debt.
    c. entry fees at national parks.
    d. individual income taxes.
    e. capital gains taxes.

4. All of the following statements accurately describe the data in Figure 13.2 on page 448 of the textbook EXCEPT
    a. Individuals pay far more income taxes than corporations.
    b. Docial insurance taxes are the fastest-growing source of federal revenue.
    c. Excise taxes are the smallest source of federal revenue.
    d. Federal revenue increased very little between 2008 and 2010.
    e. The only time that federal revenue has dropped significantly since 1970 was during the early part of the George W. Bush administration (which began in 2003).

5. Which of the following statements is true about U.S. budget deficits?
    a. The first federal budget deficit did not occur until the 1990s.
    b. The Constitution requires a balanced federal budget.
    c. Large budget deficits make the U.S. government more financially dependent on foreign investors.
    d. Budget deficits have no practical effect on individual citizens.
    e. The Democratic and Republican parties have agreed that the deficit issue should not become an issue in presidential campaigns.

6. Two conditions associated with the dramatic government growth in the United States over the past half century are
    a. growth in the national security state and growth in the social service state.
    b. accelerated global warming and the rising cost of energy.
    c. growth in the number of cabinet offices and growth in the number of unfunded mandates.
    d. increased immigration and a growing birth rate.
    e. increased use of presidential vetoes and new public works projects.

7. Which of the following initiates the budget process?
    a. the House Ways and Means Committee
    b. the president
    c. the Senate Finance Committee
    d. the Congressional Budget Office
    e. the Council of Economic Advisors

8. The biggest category of federal expenditures is spending for
    a. foreign aid.
    b. salaries and benefits for public employees.
    c. interest on the national debt.
    d. national defense.
    e. aid to the elderly and the poor.

9. All of the following are examples of entitlement programs EXCEPT
    a. Social Security.
    b. Medicare.
    c. defense contracts.
    d. veterans' benefits.
    e. agricultural subsidies.

10. Which of the following conclusions may be drawn from the graph on page 450 of your textbook?
    a. The Clinton administration closed the budget deficit to reach a balanced budget in 1998.
    b. The federal deficit decreased dramatically during the Reagan administration.
    c. Between 1972 and 1992, the deficit grew by about five times the 1972 deficit.
    d. The federal deficit decreased significantly between 1975 and 1980.
    e. The administration of George W. Bush is primarily responsible for reversing the deficit and balancing the federal budget.

11. All the money borrowed by the federal government over the years and still outstanding is known as
    a. federal revenues.
    b. national debt.
    c. tax expenditures.
    d. tax reductions.
    e. entitlements.

12. Government spending determined by how many eligible beneficiaries there are for a program which cannot be easily controlled are known as
    a. entitlements.
    b. incrementalism.
    c. revenues.
    d. uncontrollable expenditures.
    e. controlled expenditures.

13. Policies for which Congress has obligated itself to pay a certain level of benefits to a certain number of recipients are known as
    a. entitlements.
    b. incrementalism.
    c. revenues.
    d. uncontrollable expenditures.
    e. controlled expenditures.

14. The body which advises Congress on the probable consequences of its budget decisions is the
    a. House Ways and Means Committee.
    b. Senate Finance Committee.
    c. Congressional Budget Office.
    d. Government Accountability Office.
    e. Executive Office of the President.

15. _____ is the description of the budget process in which the best predictor of this year's budget is last year's budget, plus a little more.
    a. Estimation
    b. Revenue sharing
    c. Deficit spending
    d. Incrementalism
    e. Reconciliation

16. _____ is the congressional process through which program authorizations are revised to achieve savings.
    a. Estimation
    b. Revenue sharing
    c. Deficit spending
    d. Incrementalism
    e. Reconciliation

17. When Congress is unable to pass appropriation bills, these allow agencies to continue spending at the level of the previous year.
    a. income taxes
    b. appropriation bills
    c. continuing resolutions
    d. budget resolutions
    e. authorization bills

18. An act of Congress that establishes, continues, or changes a discretionary government program or entitlement is known as
    a. reconciliation.
    b. appropriation bills.
    c. continuing resolutions.
    d. budget resolutions.
    e. authorization bills.

19. Losses in revenue which result from special exemptions, exclusions, or deductions are known as
    a. tax expenditures.
    b. tax reductions.
    c. uncontrollable expenditures.
    d. entitlements.
    e. refunds.

20. Tax expenditures were established by
    a. the Constitution.
    b. 1974 Budget Act.
    c. the Social Security Act.
    d. 16th Amendment.
    e. the Reagan Administration.

Free-Response Questions

1. The rise of the national security state and the rise of the social service state have long been associated with government growth and budget deficits in the United States.

    a. Briefly describe what is meant by "growth in the national security state."

    b. Briefly describe what is meant by "growth in the social service state."

    c. Identify one piece of legislation passed by Congress since 1970 that was designed to reform the budget process and control deficit spending by the government.

    d. For the legislation you identified in "c," briefly explain one goal it was designed to accomplish.

2. Budget deficits and increasing federal debt are perennial concerns for national policymakers.

   a. Define budget deficit.

   b. Define federal debt.

   c. Describe two negative consequences of a large federal debt.

☐ Answers and Explanations

Multiple-Choice Questions

1. Congress's authority to levy an income tax comes from which of the following?

   (a) is incorrect because the interstate commerce clause did not give Congress the authority to levy an income tax.

   (b) is correct because the Sixteenth Amendment, ratified in 1913, explicitly gives Congress the authority to levy a tax on income.

   (c) is incorrect because the Budget Act of 1974 did not give Congress the authority to levy an income tax.

   (d) is incorrect because the Bill of Rights did not give Congress the authority to levy an income tax.

   (e) is incorrect because the *Marbury v. Madison* did not give Congress the authority to levy an income tax.

   Page reference: 446, AP Topic: Policymaking in a federal system

2. The institution responsible for compiling the president's budget proposal is the

   (a) is incorrect because the Department of the Treasury is not responsible for compiling the president's budget proposal.

   (b) is incorrect because the Congressional Budget Office is not responsible for compiling the president's budget proposal.

   (c) is incorrect because the Senate Appropriations Committee is not responsible for compiling the president's budget proposal.

   (d) is correct because the Office of Budget and Management was established to coordinate the budget proposals of all government agencies into the president's final proposal. It has a significant amount of budgetary power, but this is checked by Congress's approval of the president's nominee for its director.

(e) is incorrect because the Council of Economic Advisors is not responsible for compiling the president's budget proposal.

Page reference: 461–466, AP Topic: Policymaking in a federal system

3. The largest contribution to federal revenue comes from

(a) is incorrect because it is an inaccurate response to the prompt.

(b) is incorrect because it is an inaccurate response to the prompt.

(c) is incorrect because it is an inaccurate response to the prompt.

(d) is correct because the three major sources of federal revenue are individual income, corporate, and social security insurance taxes. Of these, the individual income tax provides the most revenue for the federal government. Nearly half of all federal revenues are generated by personal income taxes.

(e) is incorrect because it is an inaccurate response to the prompt.

Page reference: 446–453, AP Topic: Policymaking in a federal system

4. All of the following statements accurately describe the data in Figure 13.2 on page 448 of the textbook EXCEPT

(a) is incorrect because it is an inaccurate description of the graph.

(b) is incorrect because it is an inaccurate description of the graph.

(c) is incorrect because it is an inaccurate description of the graph.

(d) is correct because the projected portion of the graph (with dashed lines) shows all sources of revenue increasing. The rapid rise in social insurance taxes is demonstrated by its greater slope compared to other sources of revenue. Federal revenue declined between 2001 and 2004.

(e) is incorrect because it is an inaccurate description of the graph.

Page reference: 448, AP Topic: Policymaking in a federal system

5. Which of the following statements is true about U.S. budget deficits?

(a) is incorrect because it is an inaccurate description of U.S. budget deficits.

(b) is incorrect because it is an inaccurate description of U.S. budget deficits.

(c) is correct because large budget deficits make the U.S. government more financially dependent on foreign investors, governments as well as individuals. Foreign investors currently hold one-fifth of the U.S. national debt.

(d) is incorrect because it is an inaccurate description of U.S. budget deficits.

(e) is incorrect because it is an inaccurate description of U.S. budget deficits.

Page reference: 445–460, AP Topic: Policymaking in a federal system

6. Two conditions associated with the dramatic government growth in the United States over the past half century are

    (a) is correct because two conditions associated with government growth in the U.S. are the rise in the national security state and the rise in the social service state. New military challenges and the cost of advanced technology are factors in the rising cost of the military state. Social service entitlements represent the largest expenditure in the federal budget.

    (b) is incorrect because it is an inaccurate response to the prompt.

    (c) is incorrect because it is an inaccurate response to the prompt.

    (d) is incorrect because it is an inaccurate response to the prompt.

    (e) is incorrect because it is an inaccurate response to the prompt.

    Page reference: 445–460, AP Topic: Policymaking in a federal system

7. Which of the following initiates the budget process?

    (a) is incorrect because the House Ways and Means Committee does not initiate the budget process.

    (b) is correct because budgets are produced through a long and complex process that begins and ends with the president and has Congress squarely in the middle. The president submits a budget to Congress for consideration and decides whether to accept or reject the budget that ultimately emerges from Congress.

    (c) is incorrect because the Senate Finance Committee does not initiate the budget process.

    (d) is incorrect because the Congressional Budget Office does not initiate the budget process.

    (e) is incorrect because the Council of Economic Advisors does not initiate the budget process.

    Page reference: 454–460, AP Topic: Policymaking in a federal system

8. The biggest category of federal expenditures is spending for

    (a) is incorrect because foreign aid is not the biggest category of federal expenditures.

(b) is incorrect because salaries and benefits for public employees is not the biggest category of federal expenditures.

(c) is incorrect because interest on the national debt is not the biggest category of federal expenditures.

(d) is incorrect because national defense is not the biggest category of federal expenditures.

(e) is correct because the biggest category of federal expenditures is spending for the elderly and the poor.

Page reference: 454–460, AP Topic: Policymaking in a federal system

9.   All of the following are examples of entitlement programs EXCEPT

(a) is incorrect because it is an example of an entitlement program.

(b) is incorrect because it is an example of an entitlement program.

(c) is correct because entitlement programs are a form of mandatory spending, as everyone entitled to the benefits of the program must be paid. Congress cannot control these expenditures unless it changes the eligibility requirements of the program, which it is unlikely to do unless such measures are absolutely necessary. Defense contracts clearly do not fit this definition.

(d) is incorrect because it is an example of an entitlement program.

(e) is incorrect because it is an example of an entitlement program.

Page reference: 460, AP Topic: Policymaking in a federal system

10.   Which of the following conclusions may be drawn from the graph on page 450 of your textbook?

(a) is correct because the deficit was at its peak when President Clinton was elected in 1992. It decreased dramatically throughout the 1990s, however, and disappeared completely in 1998, when the United States experienced its first budget surplus in 30 years. The deficit fluctuated significantly under President George W. Bush.

(b) is incorrect because it is an inaccurate assessment of the graph.

(c) is incorrect because it is an inaccurate assessment of the graph.

(d) is incorrect because it is an inaccurate assessment of the graph.

(e) is incorrect because it is an inaccurate assessment of the graph.

Page reference: 450, AP Topic: Policymaking in a federal system

11. All the money borrowed by the federal government over the years and still outstanding is known as

(a) is incorrect because federal revenue is an inaccurate selection for the prompt.

(b) is correct because the national debt is the total from the first presidency down to the present, which today totals about \$17.5 trillion.

(c) is incorrect because tax expenditure is an inaccurate selection for the prompt.

(d) is incorrect because tax reduction is an inaccurate selection for the prompt.

(e) is incorrect because entitlement is an inaccurate selection for the prompt.

Page reference: 449, AP Topic: Policymaking in a federal system

12. Government spending determined by how many eligible beneficiaries there are for a program which cannot be easily controlled are known as

(a) is incorrect because entitlements is an inaccurate selection for the description provided.

(b) is incorrect because incrementalism is an inaccurate selection for the description provided.

(c) is incorrect because revenue is an inaccurate selection for the description provided.

(d) is correct because uncontrollable expenditures are expenditures that are determined by how many eligible beneficiaries there are for a program or by previous obligations of the government and that Congress therefore cannot easily control.

(e) is incorrect because controlled expenditures is an inaccurate selection for the description provided.

Page reference: 460, AP Topic: Policymaking in a federal system

13. Policies for which Congress has obligated itself to pay a certain level of benefits to a certain number of recipients are known as

(a) is correct because entitlements are a claim for government funds that cannot be changed without violating the rights of the claimant. Social Security benefits are an example.

(b) is incorrect because incrementalism is an inaccurate selection for the prompt.

(c) is incorrect because revenue is an inaccurate selection for the prompt.

(d) is incorrect because uncontrollable expenditure is an inaccurate selection for the prompt.

(e) is incorrect because controlled expenditure is an inaccurate selection for the prompt.

Page reference: 460, AP Topic: Policymaking in a federal system

14. The body which advises Congress on the probable consequences of its budget decisions is the

(a) is incorrect because it is an inaccurate selection for the definition provided.

(b) is incorrect because it is an inaccurate selection for the definition provided.

(c) is correct because the Congressional Budget Office is an agency of Congress that analyzes presidential budget recommendations and estimates the costs of proposed legislation. It is a counterweight to the president's Office of Management and Budget.

(d) is incorrect because it is an inaccurate selection for the definition provided.

(e) is incorrect because it is an inaccurate selection for the definition provided.

Page reference: 462, AP Topic: Policymaking in a federal system

15. _____ is the description of the budget process in which the best predictor of this year's budget is last year's budget, plus a little more.

(a) is incorrect because it is an inaccurate selection for the prompt.

(b) is incorrect because it is an inaccurate selection for the prompt.

(c) is incorrect because it is an inaccurate selection for the prompt.

(d) is correct because incrementalism is the process of preparing a budget using the previous year's budget or actual performance as a basis with incremental amounts added for the new budget period.

(e) is incorrect because it is an inaccurate selection for the prompt.

Page reference: 459, AP Topic: Policymaking in a federal system

16. _____ is the congressional process through which program authorizations are revised to achieve savings.

(a) is incorrect because estimation is an inaccurate selection for the definition provided.

(b) is incorrect because revenue sharing is an inaccurate selection for the definition provided.

(c) is incorrect because deficit spending is an inaccurate selection for the definition provided.

(d) is incorrect because incrementalism is an inaccurate selection for the definition provided.

(e) is correct because reconciliation is the Congressional process through which program authorizations are revised to achieve required savings. It usually also

includes tax or other revenue adjustments. **This usually comes near the end of the budgetary process, although occasionally the president and Congress have sought to use it in place of the regular lawmaking process.**

Page reference: 464, AP Topic: Policymaking in a federal system

17. When Congress is unable to pass appropriation bills, these allow agencies to continue spending at the level of the previous year.

    (a) is incorrect because it is an inaccurate response to the prompt.

    (b) is incorrect because it is an inaccurate response to the prompt.

    (c) is correct because when Congress has not been able to reach agreement and pass appropriations bills at all, it has instead resorted to continuing resolutions, which are laws that allow agencies to spend at the previous year's level.

    (d) is incorrect because it is an inaccurate response to the prompt.

    (e) is incorrect because it is an inaccurate response to the prompt.

    Page reference: 466, AP Topic: Policymaking in a federal system

18. An act of Congress that establishes, continues, or changes a discretionary government program or entitlement is known as

    (a) is incorrect because reconciliation is an inaccurate selection for the definition provided.

    (b) is incorrect because appropriation bill is an inaccurate selection for the definition provided.

    (c) is incorrect because continuing resolution is an inaccurate selection for the definition provided.

    (d) is incorrect because budget resolution is an inaccurate selection for the definition provided.

    (e) is correct because an authorization bill is an act of Congress that establishes or changes a government program. Authorizations specify program goals and, for discretionary programs, set the maximum amount that they may spend.

    Page reference: 465, AP Topic: Policymaking in a federal system

19. Losses in revenue which result from special exemptions, exclusions, or deductions are known as

    (a) is correct because revenue losses that result from special exemptions, exclusions, or deductions allowed by federal tax law. These expenditures represent the difference

between what the government actually collects in taxes and what it would have collected without special exemptions.

(b) is incorrect because tax reduction is an inaccurate selection for the definition provided.

(c) is incorrect because uncontrollable expenditure is an inaccurate selection for the definition provided.

(d) is incorrect because entitlement is an inaccurate selection for the definition provided.

(e) is incorrect because refund is an in accurate selection for the definition provided.

Page reference: 451, AP Topic: Policymaking in a federal system

20.   Tax expenditures were established by

(a) is incorrect because the Constitution did not establish tax expenditures.

(b) is correct because the Budget Act of 1974 defined tax expenditures, which amount to the subsidies for different activities.

(c) is incorrect because the Social Security Act did not establish tax expenditures.

(d) is incorrect because the 16th Amendment did not establish tax expenditures.

(e) is incorrect because the Reagan Administration did not establish tax expenditures.

Page reference: 451, AP Topic: Policymaking in a federal system

Free-Response Questions

This rubric provides examples of many, but not all, of the possible correct responses to the free-response questions.

1.   The rise of the national security state and the rise of the social service state have long been associated with government growth and budget deficits in the United States.

   a.   Briefly describe what is meant by "growth in the national security state."

   ▪   "Growth in the national security state" refers to the costs of supporting the military and national security establishment. The U.S. devoted a large share of its budget to military expenditures during World War II, the Cold War, and the immediate post–9/11 period.

   b.   Briefly describe what is meant by "growth in the social service state."

- "Growth in the social service state" refers to dramatic increases in social welfare expenditures since the 1960s. Social welfare entitlement programs now make up the largest share of the federal budget.

c. Identify one piece of legislation passed by Congress since 1970 that was designed to reform the budget process and control deficit spending by the government.

- The Congressional Budget and Impoundment Act and the Gramm-Rudman-Hollings Act were designed to reform the budget process and control deficit spending by the government. The Congressional Budget and Impoundment Act was designed to make Congress less dependent on the president by giving it some independent expertise on budget matters. It allows Congress to set and meet its own budget goals and bring spending in line with revenues.

d. For the legislation you identified in "c," briefly explain one goal it was designed to accomplish.

- The Balanced Budget and Emergency Deficit Control Act was an attempt by Congress to gain control over growing budget deficits. It set maximum allowable deficits for each year. If Congress failed to meet the deficit goals, automatic across-the-board spending cuts were to be ordered by the president.

2. Budget deficits and increasing federal debt are perennial concerns for national policymakers.

a. Define budget deficit.

- A budget deficit occurs when expenditures exceed revenues.

b. Define federal debt.

- The federal debt is the cumulative amount of money borrowed by the federal government that is still outstanding.

c. Describe two negative consequences of a large federal debt.

- A large federal deficit can cause several problems:
  - Government borrowing to service the debt may make it harder for individuals and businesses to get loans at favorable rates. The competition to borrow money increases interest rates, which makes it more difficult for businesses to invest in

new equipment and buildings and create more jobs. Higher interest rates raise the costs to individuals of financing mortgages and credit card purchases.

□ Large deficits make the American government dependent on foreign investors, individuals, and governments to fund its debt. This is not a favorable position for a global superpower.

14

The Federal Bureaucracy

☐ Chapter Overview

Bureaucracies are probably the most misunderstood system of the American government. Most of the public views bureaucracies in negative terms, yet the work of the bureaucracy is essential to meeting all of the needs and requirements demanded by the American public. In this chapter, we examine the role and functions of the federal bureaucracy and consider the growth and evolution of the bureaucracy over time. Next, we evaluate the role of the bureaucracy in public policymaking. We conclude by exploring contending approaches for overseeing and reforming the federal bureaucracy. By the end of the chapter, students should have a solid understanding of the historical and contemporary nature and debates surrounding the federal bureaucracy.

☐ Study Outline

  Learning Objective 14.1: Describe the federal bureaucrats and the ways in which they obtain their jobs. (p. 475)

The Bureaucrats

Bureaucrats are hired in one of two ways:

- Bureaucrats are hired through the **civil service system**. The system relies on entrance exams, and civil servants are promoted by **merit** rather than **patronage (Pendleton Civil Service Act)**.

- Civil servants must be politically impartial and treated as such (**Hatch Act**).

- The Civil Service Reform Act of 1978 created the **Office of Personnel Management (OPM),** which recruits and recommends individuals and oversees promotions and other employee issues.

- **Bureaucrats are hired through presidential recruitment.** Each new administration fills about 3,000 of the top posts; the president chooses people who will support the administration's policies.

- Cabinet department heads are presidential nominees who must be **approved by the Senate**.

- The **Department of Defense** has the largest number of civil employees, followed by the U.S. Postal Service.

- Overall, federal civilian employment has not increased in decades, indicating that the federal bureaucracy is not actually growing.

 Learning Objective 14.2: Differentiate the four types of agencies into which the federal bureaucracy is organized. (p. 480)

How the Federal Bureaucracy Is Organized

- Fifteen **cabinet departments** oversee and administer various policy areas, and each is supervised by a secretary (with the exception of the Justice Department, which is headed by the attorney general).

- **Regulatory agencies** oversee a particular aspect of the economy, creating regulations that protect people.

- They can enforce regulations by judging disputes, and are usually headed by a commission (confirmed by Congress) rather than a secretary and they are often closely involved with interest groups that want to influence regulations.

- **Government corporations** perform services for a fee, like a private business; the U.S. Postal Service is the largest; other examples include Amtrak and the Tennessee Valley Authority.

- **Independent executive agencies** include all other executive bodies and most are created for specific purposes, such as the national Aeronautics and Space Administration (NASA).

- Heads are appointed by the president, so these usually have some partisan motivation.

 Learning Objective 14.3: Identify the factors that influence the effectiveness of bureaucratic implementation of public policy. (p. 484)

Bureaucracies as Implementers

- Bureaucracies enact and enforce rules and procedures for putting Congress's policy decisions into practice.
- Bureaucracies work out details and guidelines, assign responsibilities among bureaucrats, and oversee the day-to-day operation of the federal government.
- **Policy implementation** is not always successful for various reasons.
  - Program design is sometimes flawed or Congress may not be clear enough about policy goals.
  - A department may lack staff or resources to carry out implementation.
  - An agency is sometimes so mired in its **standard operating procedures** that it fails to see what else needs to be done.
  - Administrators use their discretion differently when the standard operating procedures do not sufficiently address a particular situation.
  - There can be confusion when several departments are involved in the implementation of a particular policy.
- Reorganization of the bureaucracy for the sake of efficiency is unlikely, because this would disrupt well-established **iron triangles** of congressional committees, the agencies they oversee, and the affiliated interest groups.

 Learning Objective 14.4: Describe how bureaucracies regulate and assess deregulation and alternative approaches to regulation. (p. 493)

Bureaucracies as Regulators

- Bureaucracies oversee policies once they are in place through regulation.

- They establish guidelines for a program or project, and enforce guidelines through a combination of complaints registered by the public, inspections, and by issuing permits and licenses to people who meet the guidelines.

- Bureaucratic institutions have the authority to change rules of a policy and apprehend violators.

- All products, and even many daily activities, are shaped by regulation.

14.5 Learning Objective 14.5: Identify the means of controlling the bureaucracy and assess the role of iron triangles. (p. 496)

Controlling the Bureaucracy

- The governmental bureaucracy hires the most civilians but is not elected by the public.

- Ultimately answering to the president, who appoints agency heads that will support his or her policies, the governmental bureaucracy issues **executive orders** to change or implement statutes, manage the budget of each agency (at least in his budget proposal), and can reorganize an agency.

- The governmental bureaucracy is partially controlled by Congress.

- Congress ultimately determines each agency's budget, can refuse to confirm a presidential appointment, performs legislative oversight through hearings, and can change the legislation behind a program.

- In 1996, Congress introduced special procedures in the Congressional Review Act, allowing them to express disapproval of the actions of agencies.

- The governmental bureaucracy is full of **iron triangles**, which may produce conflicting guidelines or regulations.

- The president and Congress can control the bureaucracy, including appointments, budgets, reorganization, investigations, and direct orders and specific legislation.

14.5 Learning Objective 14.6: Assess the role of unelected bureaucrats in American democracy and the impact of the bureaucracy on the scope of government. (p. 500)

Understanding Bureaucracies

Bureaucracy and Democracy

- Although bureaucrats are not elected, bureaucracies may be controlled by elected decision makers.

- Bureaucrats are competent and reasonably representative of Americans.

- The role of government and the size of the bureaucracy ultimately depends more on voters than bureaucrats.

For Additional Review

Create a timeline of the bureaucracy. On this timeline, put the history and goals of the bureaucracies within the government departments under the executive office. Use this timeline when studying and reviewing this material for the unit test and for the AP Government and Politics Exam.

Create an organizational chart of the bureaucracy. Be sure to include the individual members and sub-departments, committees, or bureaus. Use this visual depiction of the bureaucracy to aid your understanding of the organization of the bureaucracy and refer to this when studying and reviewing for the unit test and the AP Government and Politics Exam.

☐ Review Questions

Multiple-Choice Questions

1. All of the following are important official services performed by the federal bureaucracy EXCEPT
    a. implementing laws passed by Congress.
    b. implementing the president's policy initiatives.
    c. solving disputes between the executive and legislative branches of government.
    d. distributing information about public programs and services.
    e. issuing rules and regulations.

2. The Pendleton Civil Service Act is significant because
   a. it instituted an affirmative action policy for hiring and promoting federal bureaucrats.
   b. it created the federal civil service and prescribed that the hiring of civil servants be based on merit.
   c. it gave the president more control over federal agencies.
   d. it reduced the number of federal civil servants working outside of Washington, D.C.
   e. it established clear boundaries between state and federal bureaucracies.

3. Bureaucracies are often criticized as being undemocratic because
   a. they are not directly accountable to the people.
   b. they utilize a merit system for hiring.
   c. citizens tend to have low opinions of them.
   d. the courts have no influence over their actions.
   e. they are overly influenced by campaign contributions.

4. Presidents attempt to exercise control over the bureaucracy through which of the following means?

   I. appointing loyal supporters as the heads of federal agencies
   II. issuing executive orders
   III. altering agencies' budgets
   IV. providing incentive pay to senior agency administrators

   a. I only
   b. I and III only
   c. III and IV only
   d. I, II, and III only
   e. all of the above

5. Which of the following statements represent a prevalent myth about the federal bureaucracy?

   I. The bureaucracy is growing larger each year.
   II. Most federal bureaucrats work in Washington, D.C.
   III. Citizens are generally dissatisfied with the bureaucracy.
   IV. The bureaucracy makes government inefficient and cumbersome.

   a. I only
   b. IV only
   c. I and II only
   d. II, III, and IV only
   e. all of the above

6. An important tool Congress uses to influence the bureaucracy is
   a. submitting amicus curiae briefs to the federal courts.
   b. issuing executive orders.
   c. hiring civil servants to head federal agencies.
   d. frequently removing administrators from office.
   e. requiring agency heads to routinely appear before congressional committees.

7. Iron triangles are made up of which of the following?
   a. congressional committees, independent executive agencies, and private corporations
   b. bureaucratic agencies, congressional committees, and interest groups
   c. regulatory commissions, the Office of Management and Budget, and interest groups
   d. the executive, legislative, and judicial branches of government
   e. the president's cabinet, interest groups, and private corporations

8. All of the following are independent regulatory commissions EXCEPT the
   a. Federal Reserve Board.
   b. National Labor Relations Board.
   c. Securities and Exchange Commission.
   d. Office of Management and Budget.
   e. Federal Trade Commission.

9. The Hatch Act helps maintain a nonpartisan bureaucracy because it
   a. creates a federal commission on which half the members are Democrats and half are Republican.
   b. ensures that federal employees are hired based on merit.
   c. requires all federal employees to register to vote as independents.
   d. requires all federal agencies to have staffs that are balanced along party lines.
   e. prohibits government employees from active participation in partisan politics.

10. Implementation of public policy is most successful when
    a. the goals of the policy and the authority of the implementers are clear.
    b. there is a court order mandating compliance with the policy.
    c. the executive branch has precleared the policy with the federal judiciary.
    d. multiple agencies and bureaucrats are involved.
    e. the policy originated in the executive branch as opposed to the legislative branch.

11. The federal bureaucracy handles all of the following activities EXCEPT
    a. issuing rules and regulations.
    b. holding hearings to obtain information about proposed policies.
    c. implementing policies passed by Congress.
    d. appropriating funds to pay for federal government programs.
    e. acting as a quasi-judicial body.

12. Government entities that resemble a Cabinet department but have narrower areas of responsibility are called a(n)
    a. independent department.
    b. government corporation.
    c. independent executive agency.
    d. department.
    e. independent regulatory commissions.

13. The civil service is defined as
    a. a system of hiring and promotion based on the merit principle and the desire to create a nonpartisan government service.
    b. a system in which jobs and promotions are awarded for political reasons rather than for merit or competence.
    c. a system of government employment in which selection and promotion depend on seniority rather than political patronage.
    d. an independent agency that oversees merit in the federal government personnel system.
    e. a judicial agency that administers civil service laws, rules, and regulations.

14. The spoils system is defined as
    a. the dispensing of government jobs to persons based on a competitive, non-partisan process.
    b. the dispensing of government jobs to persons who belong to the winning political party.
    c. the dispensing of government job promotions based on the seniority system.
    d. an independent agency that oversees merit in government departments.
    e. an independent agency that oversees the Food and Drug Administration.

15. Which of the following was NOT established by the Pendleton Act?
    a. higher minimum salaries for federal employees
    b. a requirement that applicants demonstrate their qualifications for employment
    c. creation of the Civil Service Commission
    d. retention and promotion of federal employees based on job performance, not political loyalty
    e. competitive exams to qualify for employment

16. The main task of the federal bureaucracy is to
    a. implement and administer federal laws and programs.
    b. interpret and apply federal laws and programs.
    c. implement and administer the orders of the president.
    d. implement and administer the orders of the cabinet.
    e. implement and administer state laws and programs.

17. The president's choice of cabinet members is limited by the fact that
    a. he must make selections based on applicants approved by his political party.
    b. he must make selections based on applicants approved by the House of Representatives.
    c. his selections must be confirmed by the House of Representatives.
    d. his selections must be confirmed by the Senate.
    e. he must make selections based on applicants approved by the Supreme Court.

18. The president has the most direct control over which of the following?
    a. independent regulatory commissions
    b. government corporations
    c. departments
    d. executive corporations
    e. independent executive agencies

19. Though similar to independent executive agencies, independent regulatory commissions are
    a. under direct control of the president.
    b. under direct control of the Senate.
    c. in operation at the state level.
    d. in operation within the judiciary.
    e. free of direct control by the president.

20. These agencies were created to engage in commercial activities that could be provided by the private sector, and they typically charge for their services.
    a. independent executive agencies
    b. government corporations
    c. independent regulatory commissions
    d. Federal Reserve banks
    e. cabinet departments

Free-Response Questions

1. Many political scientists believe that having a nonpartisan civil service increases the likelihood that government will operate in an effective and efficient manner.

    a. Define the merit principle and explain how it helps to ensure that the civil service remains nonpartisan.

    b. Define the Hatch Act and explain how it helps to ensure that the civil service remains nonpartisan.

    c. Although the federal bureaucracy is nonpartisan, the president is nominally in charge of it. Identify and describe two ways a president attempts to control the bureaucracy.

2. Policy implementation involves translating the goals and objectives of a policy into an operating, ongoing program. When policies are not successful, it is often due to problems at the implementation stage of the policy process.

    a. Identify three reasons that policy implementation might fail.

    b. Explain how each reason could contribute to the failure of policy implementation.

☐ Answers and Explanations

Multiple-Choice Questions

1. All of the following are important official services performed by the federal bureaucracy EXCEPT

    (a) is incorrect because implementing laws passed by Congress is an official service performed by the federal bureaucracy.

    (b) is incorrect because implementing the president's policy initiatives is an official service performed by the federal bureaucracy.

    (c) is correct because the bureaucracy does not referee or solve disputes between the executive and legislative branches of government. Bureaucracies are essentially implementers of policy.

    (d) is incorrect because distributing information about public programs and services is an official service performed by the federal bureaucracy.

    (e) is incorrect because issuing rules and regulations is an official service performed by the federal bureaucracy.

    Page reference: 484–493, AP Topics: The role of institutions in the enactment of policy and policymaking in a federal system

2. The Pendleton Civil Service Act is significant because

    (a) is incorrect because the Pendleton Civil Service Act did not institute affirmative action policy.

    (b) is correct because the Pendleton Civil Service Act of 1883 created the federal civil service system. Hiring and promotions in this system are based on the merit system. With regards to hiring, applicants must take an exam, and those individuals in the highest scoring group are hired. Most federal bureaucratic positions are filled this way, though the president does appoint some people to high-level positions.

    (c) is incorrect because the Pendleton Civil Service Act did not give the president more control over federal agencies.

    (d) is incorrect because the Pendleton Civil Service Act did not reduce the number of civil servants working outside Washington, D.C.

    (e) is incorrect because the Pendleton Civil Service Act did not establish clear boundaries between federal and state bureaucracies.

Page reference: 478, AP Topic: The role of institutions in the enactment of policy and policymaking in a federal system

3.   Bureaucracies are often criticized as being undemocratic because

(a) is correct although they make vital decisions and perform essential services for government and the people, bureaucrats are not directly accountable to citizens, just as the president and Congress are. This has led to the criticism that the bureaucracy is an undemocratic branch of government.

(b) is incorrect because the merit system is not a source of criticism concerning the undemocratic nature of bureaucracies.

(c) is incorrect because popular criticism is not necessarily related to the undemocratic nature of bureaucracies.

(d) is incorrect because the influence of the courts is not related to the criticisms of the bureaucracy.

(e) is incorrect because the bureaucracies are not elected.

Page reference: 476–479, AP Topics: The role of institutions in the enactment of policy and policymaking in a federal system

4.   Presidents attempt to exercise control over the bureaucracy through which of the following means?

(a) is incorrect because II and III are also accurate.

(b) is incorrect because I is also accurate.

(c) is incorrect because IV is an inaccurate choice.

(d) is correct because presidents have no control over the compensation bureaucrats receive. There is a fairly rigid federal pay scale that is used to determine the level of pay and benefits to which federal employees are entitled.

(e) is incorrect because all of the answers are not accurate.

Page reference: 479–480, AP Topics: The role of institutions in the enactment of policy and policymaking in a federal system

5.   Which of the following statements represent a prevalent myth about the federal bureaucracy?

(a) is incorrect because the federal bureaucracy is not growing bigger and bigger each year.

(b) is incorrect because only about 12 percent of federal bureaucrats work in Washington, D.C. California, with more than 245,000 federal employees, leads the nation in the number of federal bureaucrats.

(c) is incorrect because both selections are inaccurate.

(d) is incorrect because most citizens are generally satisfied with the service they receive from the bureaucracy.

(e) is correct because all of these statements are false or misleading.

Page reference: 476–478, AP Topics: The role of institutions in the enactment of policy and policymaking in a federal system

6.   An important tool Congress uses to influence the bureaucracy is

(a) is incorrect because amicus curiae briefs are not used by Congress to influence bureaucracy.

(b) is incorrect because executive orders are not used by Congress to influence bureaucracy.

(c) is incorrect because Congress cannot hire the heads of the departments.

(d) is incorrect because Congress cannot remove administrators from office.

(e) is correct because Congress uses oversight committee hearings as a means to ensure that federal agencies are meeting the goals and objectives set in the laws it passes, as well as to help keep federal agencies free of fraud, waste, and abuse.

Page reference: 497–500, AP Topics: The role of institutions in the enactment of policy and policymaking in a federal system

7.   Iron triangles are made up of which of the following?

(a) is incorrect because iron triangles are not made up of congressional committees, independent executive agencies, and private corporations.

(b) is correct because an iron triangle is the mutually dependent relationship between bureaucratic agencies, interest groups, and congressional committees. These relationships are often detrimental to the interests of taxpayers and ordinary citizens.

(c) is incorrect because iron triangles are not made up of regulatory commissions, the Office of Management and Budget, and interest groups.

(d) is incorrect because iron triangles are not made up of the executive, the legislative, and the judicial branches.

(e) is incorrect because iron triangles are not made up of the president's cabinet, interest groups, and private corporations.

Page reference: 498–500, AP Topics: The role of institutions in the enactment of policy and policymaking in a federal system

8.   All of the following are independent regulatory commissions EXCEPT the

(a) is incorrect because the Federal Reserve Board is an independent regulatory agency.

(b) is incorrect because the National Labor Relations Board is an independent regulatory agency.

(c) is incorrect because the Securities and Exchange Commission is an independent regulatory agency.

(d) is correct because the Office of Management and Budget is part of the Executive Office of the President and is not an independent regulatory commission.

(e) is incorrect because the Federal Trade Commission is an independent regulatory agency.

Page reference: 481–483, AP Topics: The role of institutions in the enactment of policy and policymaking in a federal system

9.   The Hatch Act helps maintain a nonpartisan bureaucracy because it

(a) is incorrect because the Hatch Act does not create a bipartisan commission.

(b) is incorrect because the Hatch Act does not insure merit based hiring.

(c) is incorrect because the Hatch Act does not require employees to register to vote.

(d) is incorrect because the Hatch Act does not require politically balanced staffs.

(e) is correct because the Hatch Act, originally passed in 1939 and amended most recently in 1993, prohibits civil service employees from actively participating in partisan politics while on duty. The act was intended to help ensure a fair and impartial bureaucracy, and to protect bureaucrats from coercion on the part of superiors or political appointees.

Page reference: 478, AP Topics: The role of institutions in the enactment of policy and policymaking in a federal system

10.   Implementation of public policy is most successful when

(a) is correct because if the goals of a policy are not clear to those who have to implement it, and if those who have to implement it lack the authority to act definitively, then the policy in question is not likely to be well implemented or received.

(b) is incorrect because court orders do not necessarily insure compliance with a policy.

(c) is incorrect because the president preclearing a policy does not necessarily insure compliance with a policy.

(d) is incorrect because having multiple agencies and bureaucrats involved does not necessarily insure compliance with a policy.

(e) is incorrect because having a policy originate in the executive branch does not necessarily insure compliance with a policy.

Page reference: 484–493, AP Topics: The role of institutions in the enactment of policy and policymaking in a federal system

11. The federal bureaucracy handles all of the following activities EXCEPT

(a) is incorrect because the federal bureaucracy does issue rules and regulations.

(b) is incorrect because the federal bureaucracy does hold hearings to obtain information on proposed policies.

(c) is incorrect because the federal bureaucracy does implement policies passed by Congress.

(d) is correct because only Congress can appropriate funds to be spent by the federal government. The bureaucracy engages in all of the other activities listed.

(e) is incorrect because the federal bureaucracy does act as a quasi-judicial body.

Page reference: 484–493, AP Topics: Public policy, The role of institutions in the enactment of policy

12. Government entities that resemble a Cabinet department but have narrower areas of responsibility are called a(n)

(a) is incorrect because an independent department is an inaccurate selection for the description.

(b) is incorrect because a government corporation is an inaccurate selection for the description.

(c) is correct because independent executive agencies are not accounted for by cabinet departments, independent regulatory commissions, and government corporations, and which have a narrower area of responsibility.

(d) is incorrect because a department is an inaccurate selection for the description.

(e) is incorrect because an independent regulatory commission is an inaccurate selection for the description.

Page reference: 483, AP Topics: Public Policy, The role of institutions in the enactment of policy

13.   The civil service is defined as

(a) is correct because civil service is the system for hiring and promoting federal employees through a competitive, not political selection process.

(b) is incorrect because civil service jobs and promotions are not awarded for political reasons.

(c) is incorrect because civil service jobs and promotions are not awarded based on seniority.

(d) is incorrect because the civil service is not an agency that oversees the federal personnel system.

(e) is incorrect because the civil service is not a judicial agency that administers laws.

Page reference: 478, AP Topics: Public Policy, The role of institutions in the enactment of policy

14.   The spoils system is defined as

(a) is incorrect because it is an inaccurate description of the spoils system.

(b) is correct because the spoils system, also known as patronage, is a system of public employment based on rewarding political party loyalists and friends.

(c) is incorrect because it is an inaccurate description of the spoils system.

(d) is incorrect because it is an inaccurate description of the spoils system.

(e) is incorrect because it is an inaccurate description of the spoils system.

Page reference: 478, AP Topic: Policymaking in a federal system

15.   Which of the following was NOT established by the Pendleton Act?

(a) is correct because the Pendleton Act is a reform measure that established the principle of federal employment on the basis of open, competitive exams and created the Civil Service Commission, but it did not establish a higher minimum wage for federal employees.

(b) is incorrect because this is a correct description of the Pendleton Act.

(c) is incorrect because this is a correct description of the Pendleton Act.

(d) is incorrect because this is a correct description of the Pendleton Act.

(e) is incorrect because this is a correct description of the Pendleton Act.

Page reference: 478, AP Topic: Policymaking in a federal system

16. The main task of the federal bureaucracy is to

(a) is correct because a bureaucracy is a form of organization that operates through impersonal, uniform regulations which uses task specialization to implement and administer federal laws and programs.

(b) is incorrect because a bureaucracy does not interpret and apply federal laws and programs.

(c) is incorrect because a bureaucracy does not implement and administer orders of the president.

(d) is incorrect because a bureaucracy does not implement and administer orders of the cabinet.

(e) is incorrect because a bureaucracy does not implement and administer state laws and programs.

Page reference: 475, AP Topic: Policymaking in a federal system

17. The president's choice of cabinet members is limited by the fact that

(a) is incorrect because the president is not limited by political party when selecting cabinet members.

(b) is incorrect because the president is not limited by the House of Representatives when selecting cabinet members.

(c) is incorrect because the president is not limited by the House of Representatives when selecting cabinet members.

(d) is correct because each of the 15 cabinet departments is headed by a secretary (except for the Department of Justice, which is headed by the attorney general), who has been chosen by the president but who must also be approved by the Senate.

(e) is incorrect because the president is not limited by the Supreme Court when selecting cabinet members.

Page reference: 480–483, AP Topic: Public policy

18. The president has the most direct control over which of the following?

(a) is incorrect because independent regulatory commissions are not as directly controlled by the president as independent executive agencies.

(b) is incorrect because government corporations are not as directly controlled by the president as independent executive agencies.

(c) is incorrect because departments are not as directly controlled by the president as independent executive agencies.

(d) is incorrect because executive corporations are not an accurate selection for this question.

(e) is correct because independent executive agencies' administrators are appointed by the president and serve at his will.

Page reference: 482–483, AP Topic: Public policy

19. Though similar to independent executive agencies, independent regulatory commissions are

(a) is incorrect because independent regulatory commissions are not under the direct control of the president.

(b) is incorrect because independent regulatory commissions are not under the direct control of the Senate.

(c) is incorrect because independent regulatory commissions are not in operation at the state level.

(d) is incorrect because independent regulatory commissions are not in operation with the judiciary.

(e) is correct because independent regulatory commissions are agencies whose independence is protected by Congress and are therefore free from direct control by the president.

Page reference: 481–482, AP Topic: Public policy

20. These agencies were created to engage in commercial activities that could be provided by the private sector, and they typically charge for their services.

(a) is incorrect because independent executive agencies do not operate like businesses.

(b) is correct because government corporations are government agencies that are designed like a business corporation and engage in commercial activities that could be provided by the private sector; they typically charge for their services.

(c) is incorrect because independent regulatory commissions do not operate like businesses.

(d) is incorrect because Federal Reserve banks do not operate like businesses.

(e) is incorrect because cabinet departments do not operate like businesses.

Page reference: 483, AP Topic: Public policy

Free-Response Questions

This rubric provides examples of many, but not all of the possible correct responses to the free-response questions.

1. Many political scientists believe that having a nonpartisan civil service increases the likelihood that government will operate in an effective and efficient manner.

    a. Define the merit principle and explain how it helps to ensure that the civil service remains nonpartisan.

        ■   The merit principle calls for the use of entrance exams and promotion ratings to hire and reward qualified civil servants. Under this principle, individuals are hired and promoted based on their qualifications, rather than patronage or partisan ties.

    b. Define the Hatch Act and explain how it helps to ensure that the civil service remains nonpartisan.

        ■   The Hatch Act is a federal law that prohibits government employees from participating in partisan political activities while on duty. The law helps to protect civil service employees from pressures from political appointees and others to behave in a partisan manner in carrying out their professional duties.

    c. Ways a president attempts to control the bureaucracy.

        ■   **Appoint the right people to head agencies.** Presidents control the appointments of federal agency heads and subheads. Appointing individuals with shared ideology and goals is one effective way presidents can influence agencies.
        ■   **Issue executive orders.** Executive orders carry the force of law and can be used to get agencies to take, or not take, certain actions.
        ■   **Alter an agency's budget.** The Office of Management and Budget (OMB) is instrumental in determining an agency's budget. Threats to cut or add to a budget usually get an agency's attention.

2. Policy implementation involves translating the goals and objectives of a policy into an operating, ongoing program. When policies are not successful, it is often due to problems at the implementation stage of the policy process.

    a. Identify three reasons that policy implementation might fail.

    b. Explain how each reason could contribute to the failure of policy implementation.

There are several reasons that policy implementation might fail.

- **Flawed program design:** It is difficult to implement a policy or program that is defective in its basic theoretical conception. In this case, policy fails because the policy itself cannot be successfully implemented even with the best effort.

- **Lack of clarity:** Congress often states a broad policy goal in legislation and leaves the implementation of the policy to bureaucrats. Congress does this so that it can claim to be responsive to its constituents, while reserving the ability to blame others if specific policies fail to meet constituents' expectations. Similarly, bureaucrats sometimes receive unclear or even contradictory instructions from Congress. This makes knowing what to implement and how best to do it quite difficult.

- **Lack of resources:** If agencies have insufficient funds to carry out assigned tasks, successful policy implementation will be difficult to achieve. For example, the IRS is required to catch people who cheat on their taxes, but this is impossible if they cannot hire enough auditors.

15

The Federal Courts

☐ Chapter Overview

The observation that all political questions eventually move into the judicial system was made in the nineteenth century. It was a true statement at the time, and it is even more accurate today. The judicial system extends into the lives of almost all Americans. In this chapter, we explore how the judiciary operates in the United States. We begin by outlining the basic elements and structure of the courts in the United States. Then, we consider the politics of the judicial nomination and confirmation process. We examine the backgrounds and qualifications for judges, assessing how background and judicial philosophy affect judicial decision-making. Next we trace the evolution of judicial review and the dynamics of the court. We conclude by evaluating limits on the power of the courts. By the end of the chapter, students should be able to assess the role of the courts in American democracy.

☐ Study Outline

 Learning Objective 15.1: Identify the basic elements of the American judicial system and the major participants in it. (p. 509)

The Nature of the Judicial System

- **Criminal law** is used when a person has violated a law.
- **Civil law** is used to settle disputes between private parties.
- Only about 3 percent of all cases actually go to trial; most are settled out of court.

- **Litigants** are the parties involved in a case.

- The **plaintiff** brings the charges (the plaintiff's name is listed first in the name of the case), and in matters of criminal law, the government is the plaintiff.

- The **defendant** is the party who has been charged (this name is listed second).

- Plaintiffs must have **standing to sue**, or sufficient legal reason to bring charges.

- Plaintiffs in a **class action suit** sue on behalf of all citizens who are in the same situation.

- **Interest groups** become involved with court cases to influence decisions about the law, and they may have their lawyers take up an appropriate litigant's case.

- They often submit *amicus curiae* briefs to influence a judge's decision in cases where the group is not itself a litigant, which often explain the possible effects of the judge's decision, bring new points of view to the case, or provide additional information not presented in the case.

- **Attorneys** present a case in court, and every citizen is guaranteed a lawyer in a criminal case.

- **Public interest lawyers** and **legal aid groups** may represent poor people in some civil and criminal cases.

- State and local governments hire public defenders to represent poor defendants in criminal cases.

 Learning Objective 15.2: Outline the structure of the federal court system and the major responsibilities of each component. (p. 511)

The Structure of the Federal Judicial System

- Courts of **original jurisdiction** are the first courts to hear a case, usually when it goes to **trial**.

- The court assesses and decides a case based on the facts of the case, and most cases do not continue after their first ruling.

- There are 94 federal **district courts**, which have original jurisdiction and hold trials in which the litigants appear before the court.

- Federal district courts primarily handle cases violating federal law or involving federal civil law, civil suits in which the litigants are of different states, bankruptcy proceedings, and process of naturalization.

- The **U.S. attorney** in each district serves as the government's lawyer.

- The federal government is a plaintiff when prosecuting violators of federal laws; the government can be a plaintiff or defendant in a civil suit.

- Courts of **appellate jurisdiction** hear cases that have been **appealed**.

- The court interprets the case as it relates to the law; it does not review the facts and the litigants do not appear before the court (only their lawyers appear), and there is no jury.

- Thirteen **circuit courts of appeal** review cases appealed from the district courts; they have appellate jurisdiction.

- They do not focus on the facts of the case, but evaluate the treatment of the case in the district court in terms of errors of procedure or the law.

- Usually three judges hear a case, and their ruling sets a **precedent** for the district courts within their geographic circuit.

- The **Supreme Court** is the ultimate authority on the law.

- It has original jurisdiction in cases between two states, the federal government and a state, or a state and a foreign country, but most cases fall under its appellate jurisdiction.

- It can choose which cases to hear and it consists of nine justices who rule on cases together.

 Learning Objective 15.3: Explain the process by which judges and justices are nominated and confirmed. (p. 516)

The Politics of Judicial Selection

- All federal judges and justices are appointed by the president. Nominations must be confirmed by the Senate.

- Confirmation of district and circuit court judges is influenced by **senatorial courtesy**, by which senators of the president's party from the state where the district is located, or in which a circuit court nominee resides, can stop confirmation.

- Justices are carefully selected by the president when there is a vacancy on the Supreme Court.

- Justices serve much longer than a president's term.

- If the president's choice is confirmed by the Senate, the court will be more closely aligned with the president's ideology for a longer period of time.

- Nomination was routine for most of the 20th century, but since the 1960s nominations have become much more contentious, especially with regard to issues like abortion, affirmative action, and other socially divisive issues.

15.4 **Learning Objective 15.4: Describe the backgrounds of judges and justices and assess the impact of background on their decisions. (p. 521)**

The Backgrounds of Judges and Justices

- Judges and justices are not a representative sample of the American people; they are lawyers and disproportionately white males.

- They usually share the partisan and ideological views of the president who nominated them, and these views are often reflected in their decisions.

- Other characteristics, such as gender and race, are also seen to influence decisions.

15.5 **Learning Objective 15.5: Outline the judicial process at the Supreme Court level and assess the major factors influencing decisions and their implementation. (p. 525)**

The Courts as Policymakers

- The Supreme Court shapes policy by selecting which cases to hear.

- It is most likely to choose cases involving civil rights and civil liberties, a discrepancy in the lower courts' interpretation of the law, or disagreements between justices and the lower courts.

- The Supreme Court follows a regular process for making decisions.

- Justices read briefs pertaining to the case, hear **oral arguments**, meet to discuss cases, vote on the decision, and write and announce opinions.

- Opinions that have the support of the majority, called "opinions of the court," establish law that is binding on lower courts.

- Decisions are based heavily on **precedent**; lower courts must follow precedents set by higher courts. Justices usually rule *stare decisis*: "let the decision stand."

- Decisions must be translated into policy, which is accomplished by policymakers, the president, lower courts, lawyers, and administrators.

- The public must become aware of its rights under the new decision.

- Often implementers disagree with the decision and try to hinder implementation.

 Learning Objective 15.6: Trace the Supreme Court's use of judicial review in major policy battles in various eras of American history. (p. 532)

The Courts and Public Policy: A Historical View

- Some courts (usually referred to by the name of the chief justice at the time) have had a significant impact on the shaping of policy.

- **John Marshall** initiated the practice of judicial review in the case of *Marbury v. Madison* and expanded the power of the Supreme Court significantly.

- The **Warren court** became actively involved in expanding civil rights and civil liberties.

- The **Burger court** became somewhat more conservative than the Warren court, though it still allowed abortion in *Roe v. Wade*.

- The **Rehnquist and Roberts courts** became even more conservative, with mainly Republican presidents' appointments, and began to limit (though not reverse) previous rulings.

- Some critics think the Supreme Court is too powerful, and favor **judicial restraint**.

- Others favor **judicial activism** to allow justices the freedom to forge new policies, especially concerning people largely underrepresented in the political process.

- Power of the courts is checked by the president's appointments, and also by Congress's ability to amend the Constitution, despite—or in order to overrule—a Supreme Court decision.

15.7 **Learning Objective 15.7: Assess the role of unelected courts and the scope of judicial power in American democracy. (p. 536)**

Understanding the Courts

- Judges and justices are not elected and are difficult to remove.

- They are not completely insulated from politics and often have acted to promote openness in the political system.

- They have a number of tools to avoid making controversial decisions.

- There are a number of means more democratically elected officials can use to overturn Court decisions.

For Additional Review

Create a chart of the following information concerning the judiciary:

- What powers are given to the judiciary in the Constitution?

- Why is judicial independence necessary?

- What constitutional provisions assure this independence?

- Why does the federal judiciary include several levels of courts?

- What are the differences among these three levels?

Use this chart when reviewing and studying for the unit test and the AP Government and Politics Exam.

Create a diagram which demonstrates how a case finds its way to the Supreme Court. Compare and contrast judicial restraint versus judicial activism and list cases which apply to each. Use this information when reviewing and studying for the unit test and the AP Government and Politics Exam.

☐ Review Questions

Multiple-Choice Questions

1. Which of the following statements is true of the judicial system in the United States?
   a. It is unitary court system.
   b. Interest groups are forbidden from participating in criminal proceedings.
   c. The system prescribes that criminal cases be decided by juries, and civil cases be decided by judges.
   d. The U.S. Constitution established all federal courts.
   e. It is an adversarial system in which justice is supposed to emerge from the struggle between two contending points of view.

2. Which of the following is part of the federal court system?

   I. U.S. Supreme Court
   II. State Supreme Courts
   III. Court of Military Appeals
   IV. U.S. Court of Appeals

   a. I only
   b. IV only
   c. I and IV only
   d. I, II, and IV only
   e. I, III, and IV only

3. Federal district courts are the only federal courts in which
   a. the facts are presented by both parties in the case.
   b. *amicus curiae* briefs are registered with the court.
   c. the solicitor general appears for oral argument.
   d. juries are impaneled to decide cases.
   e. three judge panels decide the outcome of cases.

4. Which of the following statements is true about Congress's influence over Supreme Court decision making?
   a. Congress can pass laws to prohibit judicial activism.
   b. The Senate can filibuster court decisions.
   c. Congress has significant control over the court's appellate jurisdiction.
   d. The Senate can decide which cases the Supreme Court will hear.
   e. District court judges are reviewed by Congress every 10 years.

5. Senatorial courtesy is
   a. the custom of the Supreme Court sharing its docket with the Senate Judiciary Committee before it is made public.
   b. a tradition whereby nominees for federal judgeships must meet the approval of senators of the president's party from the state in which the nominee will serve.
   c. the tradition of the full Senate approving all judicial nominees who win a majority vote in the Judiciary Committee.
   d. the practice of the Senate filling judicial vacancies with judges who share the same judicial philosophy as their most immediate predecessor.
   e. the tradition of the vice president hosting a formal reception to introduce Supreme Court nominees to members of the Senate.

6. All of the following influence the selection of federal judges and Supreme Court justices EXCEPT
   a. campaign contributions.
   b. partisanship.
   c. ideology.
   d. experience.
   e. judicial philosophy.

7. Which of the following is true about the vast majority of cases decided by the Supreme Court?
   a. They are decided by unanimous decision.
   b. The decisions tend to significantly alter current policy.
   c. They tend to reverse the decision of the lower courts.
   d. They result in the payout of larger damage awards than decisions rendered by lower courts.
   e. They are decided based on how similar past cases have been decided.

8. One major weakness of federal courts as policymakers is that
   a. judges are term-limited, which affects their ability to implement their decisions.
   b. lower courts are not required to follow the decisions of superior courts.
   c. the courts must rely on other institutions to implement their decisions.
   d. they are shielded from the pressures of electoral politics.
   e. courts tend to lack legitimacy in the eyes of most citizens.

9. Interest groups play a role in the federal judicial process in all of the following ways EXCEPT by
   a. running advertisements endorsing a judicial nominee.
   b. lobbying the Judiciary Committee about a judicial nominee.
   c. filing *amicus curiae* briefs.
   d. having their lawyers represent a plaintiff.
   e. filing a class action suit.

10. The power of courts to determine which acts of Congress, the executive branch, and state legislatures are constitutional is known as
   a. precedent.
   b. *stare decisis.*
   c. original jurisdiction.
   d. judicial implementation.
   e. judicial review.

11. These petitions are filed by individuals who do not have the funds to file a lawsuit.
   a. *writs of certiorari*
   b. *writs of habeas corpus*
   c. *amicus curiae* briefs
   d. *in forma pauperis*
   e. precedents

12. All of the following are true about the Supreme Court EXCEPT
   a. Cases are not allowed to be televised.
   b. Members are seated in alphabetical order.
   c. There were originally six members in the court.
   d. There have been as many as ten members in the court.
   e. Their members are the only ones to be called justice.

13. The philosophy of the courts where judges play a minimal policymaking role and defer to legislatures whenever possible is known as
   a. judicial implementation.
   b. senatorial courtesy.
   c. judicial activism.
   d. judicial review.
   e. judicial restraint.

14. This is a request for the Supreme Court to order up the records from a lower court to review the case.
   a. *in forma pauperis*
   b. concurrent opinion
   c. *writ of certiorari*
   d. *stare decisis*
   e. *writ of habeas corpus*

15. The "rule of four" is a Supreme Court practice which permits four of the nine justices to
   a. overrule senatorial courtesy.
   b. grant a *writ of certiorari.*
   c. adjourn the court.
   d. establish a precedent.
   e. hand down a decision on the case.

16. *Stare decisis* is a judicial principle which states that the courts will decide cases largely based on
    a. earlier court decisions.
    b. economic and social conditions of the day.
    c. equality and justice.
    d. the intention of Congress when the law was written.
    e. the opinions and attitudes of the judges.

17. Legal briefs submitted by a "friend of the court" for the purpose of influencing the court's decision by raising additional arguments and points of view is a(n)
    a. *writ of certiorari.*
    b. *writ of habeas corpus.*
    c. *amicus curiae* brief.
    d. *stare decisis* ruling.
    e. concurring opinion.

18. A decision written by one or more judges expressing disagreement with the majority opinion of the Supreme Court is a(n)
    a. judicial review.
    b. "rule of four."
    c. concurring opinion.
    d. judicial disputes.
    e. dissenting opinion.

19. The Supreme Court's power is strengthened by its ability to
    a. exercise senatorial courtesy.
    b. nominate its own replacements.
    c. impeach the president.
    d. decide on the constitutionality of laws as soon as they are passed by Congress.
    e. select the cases it will hear.

20. The philosophy of the courts where judges make decisions based on the spirit of the times and needs of the nation is known as
    a. *stare decisis.*
    b. a dissenting opinion.
    c. judicial activism.
    d. judicial implementation.
    e. judicial restraint.

Free-Response Questions

1. The framers of the Constitution desired a federal judiciary that was removed from the pressures and direct consequences of electoral politics.

    a. Identify and describe two provisions in the Constitution that were intended to shield the judiciary from electoral politics.

b. The framers' intent notwithstanding, the federal judiciary is not free of the influence of electoral politics. Identify and describe two ways electoral politics affect the federal judiciary.

2. The Constitution provides each of the three branches of government with the capacity to limit and trump the powers of the other two.

   a. Describe one way the president can check and balance the powers of the federal judiciary.

   b. Describe one way Congress can check and balance the powers of the federal judiciary.

   c. Describe one way the Supreme Court can check and balance the powers of the executive branch.

   d. Describe one way the Supreme Court can check and balance the powers of Congress.

☐ Answers and Explanations

Multiple-Choice Questions

1. Which of the following statements is true of the judicial system in the United States?

   (a) is incorrect because the U.S. judicial system is not a unitary court system.

   (b) is incorrect because interest groups are not forbidden from participating in criminal proceedings.

   (c) is incorrect because civil cases can be decided by juries, as well.

   (d) is incorrect because not all federal courts were established by the Constitution.

   (e) is correct because a bedrock principle underlying the American court system is that justice will emerge from an adversarial system in which there is a struggle between two contending points of view.

   Page reference: 509–511, AP Topic: Federal courts

2. Which of the following is part of the federal court system?

   (a) is incorrect because the Supreme Court is only one of the correct answers provided.

   (b) is incorrect because the U.S. Court of Appeals is only one of the correct answers provided.

   (c) is incorrect because I and IV are only two of the accurate choices.

(d) is incorrect because state courts are not part of the federal court system.

(e) is correct because all of the courts listed except state supreme courts are part of the federal judiciary.

Page reference: 512–516, AP Topic: Federal courts

3. Federal district courts are the only federal courts in which

(a) is incorrect because facts are not presented by both sides in a trial.

(b) is incorrect because *amicus* briefs are not registered with district courts.

(c) is incorrect because the solicitor general does not appear for an oral argument in district courts.

(d) is correct because federal district courts have original jurisdiction and operate as trial courts where juries may be impaneled; there are no juries in the courts of appeal, the Supreme Court, or any other federal courts.

(e) is incorrect because a three judge panel is not used in a district court.

Page reference: 512–513, AP Topic: Federal courts

4. Which of the following statements is true about Congress's influence over Supreme Court decision making?

(a) is incorrect because Congress cannot pass laws to prohibit judicial activism.

(b) is incorrect because the Senate cannot filibuster court decisions.

(c) is correct because in many instances, federal courts' jurisdiction derives from Congress and not the Constitution. The Constitution provides Congress with the discretion to determine which category of cases appellate courts may hear.

(d) is incorrect because the Senate cannot decide which cases the Supreme Court will hear.

(e) is incorrect because district court judges are not reviewed by Congress.

Page reference: 514–529, AP Topics: Federal courts and Relationships among institutions and varying balances of power

5. Senatorial courtesy is

(a) is incorrect because senatorial courtesy does not deal with the sharing of the Supreme Court docket.

(b) is correct because senatorial courtesy is a tradition whereby nominees for federal judgeships must meet the approval of senators of the president's party from the state

in which the nominee will serve. **This tradition began under George Washington, and since that time the Senate has tended not to confirm nominations for district court judges when senators of the president's party from the state in which the nominee will serve oppose them.**

(c) is incorrect because senatorial courtesy is not a tradition involving the full Senate.

(d) is incorrect because senatorial courtesy does not involve appointment based on judicial philosophy.

(e) is incorrect because senatorial courtesy does not involve a formal reception held by the vice president.

Page reference: 516, AP Topics: Federal courts and Relationships among institutions and varying balances of power

6.   All of the following influence the selection of federal judges and Supreme Court justices EXCEPT

(a) is correct because there is no evidence that campaign contributions to presidential races are a major factor in determining who a president nominates for federal judgeships.

(b) is incorrect because partisanship does influence the selection of federal judges and Supreme Court justices.

(c) is incorrect because ideology does influence the selection of federal judges and Supreme Court justices.

(d) is incorrect because experience does influence the selection of federal judges and Supreme Court justices.

(e) is incorrect because judicial philosophy does influence the selection of federal judges and Supreme Court justices.

Page reference: 516–521, AP Topics: Federal courts and Relationships among institutions and varying balances of power

7.   Which of the following is true about the vast majority of cases decided by the Supreme Court?

(a) is incorrect because most Supreme Court cases are not unanimous decisions.

(b) is incorrect because most decisions do not significantly alter policy.

(c) is incorrect because most decisions do not overturn state court decisions.

(d) is incorrect because most decisions do no result in the payout of larger damage rewards.

(e) is correct because most Supreme Court rulings uphold the decision made by the lower court. This is the principle of *stare decisis*, meaning "let the decision stand."

Page reference: 527–532, AP Topics: Federal courts and Relationships among institutions and varying balances of power

8.   One major weakness of federal courts as policymakers is that

(a) is incorrect because judges' terms do not relate to the role of policymaking.

(b) is incorrect because it does not relate to policymaking.

(c) is correct because unlike legislatures and the executive branch, the courts must always rely on other units of government to implement and enforce their rulings. This is widely viewed as a weakness for the courts as policymakers.

(d) is incorrect because political insulation does not relate to policymaking.

(e) is incorrect because courts do not lack legitimacy.

Page reference: 530–532, AP Topics: Federal courts and Relationships among institutions and varying balances of power

9.   Interest groups play a role in the federal judicial process in all of the following ways EXCEPT by

(a) is correct because interest groups do attempt to influence the appointment of federal judges, but not by running advertisements. The process of filling judgeships is far removed from the public—the only means of influence it has is by influencing the election of the president and members of the Senate, who, in turn, choose judges. Advertisements aimed at swaying public opinion therefore have little use in this case.

(b) is incorrect because interest groups do attempt to influence the appointment of federal judges by lobbying the Judiciary Committee.

(c) is incorrect because interest groups do attempt to influence the appointment of federal judges by filing *amicus curiae* briefs.

(d) is incorrect because interest groups do attempt to influence the appointment of federal judges by having their lawyers represent a plaintiff.

(e) is incorrect because interest groups do attempt to influence the appointment of federal judges by filing a class action suit.

Page reference: 510, AP Topics: Federal courts and Interest groups

10.   The power of courts to determine which acts of Congress, the executive branch, and state legislatures are constitutional is known as

(a) is incorrect because a precedent is how similar cases have been decided in the past.

(b) is incorrect because *stare decisis* means let the decision stand.

(c) is incorrect because original jurisdiction is a court's ability to hear the case first.

(d) is correct because judicial review is the power of the courts to determine whether acts of Congress, the executive branch, and the states are constitutional. This power was established by the Supreme Court's decision in *Marbury v. Madison*.

(e) is incorrect because judicial implementation is how and whether a court's decision will be enacted.

Page reference: 532–536, AP Topics: Federal courts and Relationships among institutions and varying balances of power

11.   These petitions are filed by individuals who do not have the funds to file a lawsuit.

(a) is incorrect because *writs of certiorari* are requests from the Supreme Court to a lower court to send up the records of a case.

(b) is incorrect because *writs of habeas corpus* are orders requiring an explanation of why a prisoner is being held.

(c) is incorrect because *amicus curiae* briefs are filed to give the Supreme Court more information pertaining to a case.

(d) is correct because petitions which allow a party to file "as a pauper" and avoid paying Court fees is an *in forma pauperis* petition.

(e) is incorrect because precedents are decisions made in previous cases.

Page reference: 511, AP Topics: Federal courts and Relationships among institutions and varying balances of power

12.   All of the following are true about the Supreme Court EXCEPT

(a) is incorrect because cases cannot be televised.

(b) is correct because members of the Supreme Court do not sit in alphabetical order, but instead, sit according to seniority.

(c) is incorrect because there were originally six members of the Court.

(d) is incorrect because there have been as many as ten members of the Court.

(e) is incorrect because judges on the Supreme Court are the only ones to be called justices.

Page reference: 518–519, AP Topics: Federal courts and Relationships among institutions and varying balances of power

13. The philosophy of the courts where judges play a minimal policymaking role and defer to legislatures whenever possible is known as

(a) is incorrect because judicial implementation deals with how judicial decisions are translated into policy.

(b) is incorrect because senatorial courtesy relates to the appointment process of judges.

(c) is incorrect because judicial activism calls for judges to make bold policy decisions.

(d) is incorrect because judicial review is the power of the courts to determine the constitutionality of laws and acts.

(e) is correct because judicial restraint is a philosophy proposing that judges should allow the decisions of other branches of government to stand, even if they offend a judge's own principles, unless the clearly violate the Constitution.

Page reference: 538, AP Topics: Federal courts and Relationships among institutions and varying balances of power

14. This is a request for the Supreme Court to order up the records from a lower court to review the case.

(a) is incorrect because an *in forma pauperis* appeal is a request to have court fees waived for poor people.

(b) is incorrect because a concurrent opinion is a written decision on a case.

(c) is correct because a *writ of certiorari* is a formal writ used to bring a case before the Supreme Court.

(d) is incorrect because *stare decisis* is a judicial philosophy based on ruling on precedent.

(e) is incorrect because a *writ of habeas corpus* is a court order requesting an explanation of why a prisoner is being held in custody.

Page reference: 526, AP Topics: Federal courts and Relationships among institutions and varying balances of power

15. The "rule of four" is a Supreme Court practice which permits four of the nine justices to

(a) is incorrect because the Court cannot overrule senatorial courtesy.

(b) is correct because the "rule of four" is the practice of the Supreme Court where at least four justices must vote to consider a case before a *writ of certiorari* can be issued.

(c) is incorrect because the "rule of four" does not relate to adjournment.

(d) is incorrect because the "rule of four" does not relate to establishing precedents.

(e) is incorrect because the "rule of four" does not relate to decision making.

Page reference: 526, AP Topics: Federal courts and Relationships among institutions and varying balances of power

16. *Stare decisis* is a judicial principle which states that the courts will decide cases largely based on

    (a) is correct because *stare decisis* means that court rulings will rely on past decisions or precedents to formulate decisions in new cases.

    (b) is incorrect because it is the opposite of the principle stated in the question.

    (c) is incorrect because *stare decisis* does not relate to equality and justice.

    (d) is incorrect because *stare decisis* does not relate to the original intent of Congress.

    (e) is incorrect because it is the opposite of the principle stated in the question.

    Page reference: 528, AP Topics: Federal courts and Relationships among institutions and varying balances of power

17. Legal briefs submitted by a "friend of the court" for the purpose of influencing the court's decision by raising additional arguments and points of view is a(n)

    (a) is incorrect because a *writ of certiorari* is an order for a lower court to send up a case.

    (b) is incorrect because a *writ of habeas corpus* is an order for an explanation for why an individual is being held.

    (c) is correct because an *amicus curiae* brief is filed by an individual or organization urging the Supreme Court to hear a case (or discouraging it from doing so) or, at the merits stage, to present arguments in addition to those presented by the immediate parties to a case.

    (d) is incorrect because a *stare decisis* ruling does not relate to this question.

    (e) is incorrect because a concurring opinion does not relate to this question.

    Page reference: 527, AP Topics: Federal courts and Relationships among institutions and varying balances of power

18. A decision written by one or more judges expressing disagreement with the majority opinion of the Supreme Court is a(n)

    (a) is incorrect because judicial review is declaring an act unconstitutional.

    (b) is incorrect because "rule of four" is used when deciding to hear a case.

    (c) is incorrect because a concurring opinion is written when justices agree with the majority opinion, but for different reasons.

(d) is incorrect because judicial disputes do not relate to this question.

(e) is correct because a dissenting opinion is an opinion written when justices are opposed to all or part of the majority's decision.

Page reference: 528, AP Topics: Federal courts and Relationships among institutions and varying balances of power

19. The Supreme Court's power is strengthened by its ability to

   (a) is incorrect because the Court does not exercise senatorial courtesy.

   (b) is incorrect because the Court does not nominate its own replacements.

   (c) is incorrect the Court cannot impeach the president.

   (d) is incorrect because the Court cannot rule on laws until they have been appealed to them.

   (e) is correct because the power of the Supreme Court is strengthened by its ability to control its agenda. Of the approximately 8,000 cases appealed to the Supreme Court, the Court actually places fewer than 100 cases on the docket.

   Page reference: 526, AP Topics: Federal courts and Relationships among institutions and varying balances of power

20. The philosophy of the courts where judges make decisions based on the spirit of the times and needs of the nation is known as

   (a) is incorrect because *stare decisis* is the opposite of the accurate response.

   (b) is incorrect because a dissenting opinion is not a judicial philosophy.

   (c) is correct because judicial activism is a philosophy of judicial decision making that posits judges should use their power broadly to further justice by making decisions based on the spirit of the times and needs of the nation.

   (d) is incorrect because judicial implementation relates to how decisions are translated into policy.

   (e) is incorrect because judicial restraint is the opposite of the accurate response.

   Page reference: 528, AP Topics: Federal courts and Relationships among institutions and varying balances of power

Free-Response Questions

This rubric provides examples of many, but not all of the possible correct responses to the free-response questions.

1.　The framers of the Constitution desired a federal judiciary that was removed from the pressures and direct consequences of electoral politics.

　　a.　Identify and describe two provisions in the Constitution that were intended to shield the judiciary from electoral politics.

- **Federal judges are appointed, not elected.** This feature allows judges to make reasoned decisions based on the rule of law without the fear of losing their jobs because some of their decisions may be unpopular with a group of constituents or the general public.

- **Lifetime appointment for federal judges.** Once confirmed by the Senate, federal judges have lifetime tenure on the bench, so long as they do not commit impeachable offenses. This lifetime tenure allows judges to make reasoned decisions based on the rule of law without the fear of losing their jobs, since some of their decisions may be unpopular with other government officials or the general public.

- **Federal judges' salaries cannot be reduced.** The Constitution expressly prohibits the reduction of judges' salaries during their time on the bench. This constitutional provision allows judges to make decisions without fear of reprisal from the executive and legislative branches.

　　b.　The framers' intent notwithstanding, the federal judiciary is not free of the influence of electoral politics. Identify and describe two ways electoral politics affect the federal judiciary.

- **The president, who is a political partisan, nominates federal judges.** Presidents seek to appoint judges to the bench who share their party affiliations, ideologies, judicial philosophies, and stances on specific issues. This makes federal judges products of a partisan political process.

- **The confirmation process.** The confirmation process for federal judges is sometimes highly partisan, with Democrats and Republicans seemingly using the process as a continuation of the last election or a precursor for the next.

- **Congress controls the appellate jurisdiction of federal courts.** Because of this authority, Congress has the capacity to prohibit the courts from hearing specific categories or classes of cases.

2. The Constitution provides each of the three branches of government with the capacity to limit and trump the powers of the other two.

   a. Describe one way the president can check and balance the powers of the federal judiciary.

      - **Appointment power.** The president nominates Supreme Court and other federal judges.

   b. Describe one way Congress can check and balance the powers of the federal judiciary.

      - **Confirmation process.** The Senate must confirm Supreme Court justices and all other federal judicial nominees.
      - **Impeachment power.** Congress can impeach federal judges.
      - **Jurisdiction authority over lower federal courts.** The Constitution created just one federal court, the U.S. Supreme Court. It gave Congress the authority to create any other subordinate courts that it saw fit to create. Thus, in theory, Congress could disband all federal courts except the Supreme Court. Congress also has the capacity to prohibit the courts from hearing specific categories or classes of cases.
      - **Power of the purse.** Although the Constitution expressly prohibits the reduction of judges' salaries during their time on the bench, Congress determines if federal judges receive pay raises and how much any raise will be.

   c. Describe one way the Supreme Court can check and balance the powers of the executive branch.

      - **Judicial review.** Courts can declare acts of the president and federal agencies to be unconstitutional or unlawful.

   d. Describe one way the Supreme Court can check and balance the powers of Congress.

      - **Judicial review.** Courts can declare laws passed by Congress to be unconstitutional.

16

Economic and Social Welfare Policymaking

☐ Chapter Overview

Domestic economic and social policy is at the heart of many contemporary political debates in the United States. From health care and education to Social Security and the budget deficit, American politics is often characterized by sharp differences in policy preferences. In this chapter, we examine some of these contemporary debates. We begin by exploring the economic policies of the American government. We then turn to analyze domestic social policy in the United States. We contrast entitlement and means-tested welfare programs. We assess the extent of economic inequality in the United States and consider the role of the government in militating against growing inequality. Next, we consider the politics of public policy, examining both the major welfare programs in the United States and the politics of Social Security and welfare reform. We conclude by distinguishing the American social welfare system from those of other established democracies and by exploring the impact of social and economic policy on democracy in the United States. By the end of the chapter, students should have a well-rounded understanding of domestic economic and social policy in the United States across a wide variety of issues.

☐ Study Outline

 Learning Objective 16.1: Identify the main policy tools that American government can employ to address economic problems, and contrast Keynesian and supply-side economics. (p. 550)

Economic Policymaking

- The new U.S. economy is deep in the challenges and opportunities of globalization, but, through rules and regulations, the federal government plays a major role as well.

- Economic conditions affect both voting behavior and presidential approval; they are the best single predictor of voters' evaluation of how the president is doing his job.

- But voters tend to assess the overall rate of employment and unemployment more than their individual circumstances.

- Democrats are more likely to stress the importance of keeping unemployment low, whereas Republicans are worried about inflation.

- This difference in priorities reflects their constituencies.

- Unemployment occurs when there are not enough jobs and it is measured by the **unemployment rate**.

- The Democratic coalition consists of groups concerned with unemployment (labor and the lower classes).

- Democrats generally sacrifice higher inflation to keep unemployment down.

- **Inflation** occurs when prices rise and inflation is measured by the **Consumer Price Index (CPI)**.

- The Republican coalition includes businesspeople who are concerned about the cost of goods and services.

- Republicans generally try to prevent inflation, even at the risk of rising unemployment.

Policies for Controlling the Economy

Monetary Policy and the "Fed"

- **Monetary policy** is monitoring and controlling the amount of money in circulation; based on the economic theory known as monetarism, which states that controlling the money supply is the key to controlling the economy.

- **Monetarism** is an economic theory holding that the supply of money is the key to a nation's economic health; if there is too much available cash or credit, inflation occurs.

- The **Federal Reserve System** (the Fed) was created to manage monetary policy.

- Its board of governors is appointed by the president and confirmed by the Senate, but operates fairly independently.

- The Federal Open Market Committee is the most important body within the Federal Reserve; it decides how monetary policy is carried out.

- The Fed regulates monetary policy by influencing the rate at which loans are given, which influences decisions about borrowing; by controlling the amount of money banks have available, and, in turn, the rate at which people can borrow; and by adding to the money supply by selling bonds.

Fiscal Policy: Keynesian Versus Supply-Side Economics

- **Fiscal policy** is regulating revenues and expenditures through the federal budget; determined by Congress and the president.

- **Keynesian economic theory** encourages government's active participation in the economy.

- Keynesians argue that government spending and tax cuts stimulate the economy by creating demand. This is known as expansionary fiscal policy.

- The government can decrease demand to control inflation by cutting spending and increasing taxes, which is known as contractionary fiscal policy.

- **Supply-side economics** holds that by decreasing government involvement in the economy, people will be forced to work harder and save more.

- Cutting taxes increases investment and the supply of goods, which promotes growth.

- The economic philosophy which is in direct contradiction to monetary and fiscal policy is known as **laissez-faire**, which is the principle that government should not meddle in the economy.

Why It Is Hard to Control the Economy

- Some believe that presidents manipulate the economy for short-run advantage to win elections, called the "political business cycle."
- It is difficult to predict the economy far enough in advance to make and implement policy.
- Also, the economy is grounded in billions of private sector decisions, which are harder to regulate than government policy.

 Learning Objective 16.2: Compare and contrast entitlement and means-tested social welfare programs. (p. 558)

Types of Social Welfare Policies

- Most government funds are given through **entitlement programs** to people who are not poor.
- These programs provide benefits to individuals regardless of need.
- The two main entitlement programs, Social Security and Medicare, are the largest and most expensive social welfare programs in America.
- **Means-tested programs**, such as the Food Stamp Program and Medicaid, provide benefits only to people with specific needs.
- Eligibility for these depends on how narrowly "poverty" is defined.
- Means-tested programs generate much political controversy, with the positions taken depending largely on how people see the poor and the causes of poverty.

Learning Objective 16.3: Assess the extent of economic inequality in America and the role of government in lessening it. (p. 559)

Income, Poverty, and Public Policy

- **Income distribution** is the way the national income is divided into "shares" ranging from the poor to the rich.

- A perception by an individual that he or she is not doing well economically in comparison to others is known as **relative deprivation**.

- The rich have not only more **income** (the amount of money collected between two points in time) but also greater **wealth** (the value of assets including bank accounts, stocks, homes, and other assets).

- A small number of Americans—1 percent of the total population—possess more than one-third of all wealth in the United States.

- The assets of that 1 percent are actually higher than the total worth of 90 percent of Americans.

- Poverty is defined by the government as family income that falls below the **poverty line**.

- Counts underestimate poverty, because millions of people hover around the line and continually fall just below or rise just above it.

- African Americans, Hispanic Americans, people living in inner cities, and unmarried women tend to be the groups most afflicted with poverty.

- The increase in the incidents of women and their children living in poverty is referred to as the **feminization of poverty**.

How Public Policy Affects Income

- There are three main types of taxes.
  - **Progressive** taxes tax the wealthy at a higher rate.
  - Everyone is taxed at the same rate in **proportional taxes**.
  - **Regressive taxes** tax people of lower incomes at a higher rate.
- **State sales taxes** are somewhat regressive, but the effect is counterbalanced by progressive federal income taxes.

- **Earned Income Tax Credit:** This program provides very low-income workers with a cash credit, even if they paid no federal income tax.

- Through **expenditures, transfer payments** are given directly to citizens by the government.

  - Examples are food stamps, financial aid grants, and Social Security and Medicare benefits.

  - The elderly receive the most in transfer payments through Social Security.

 Learning Objective 16.4: Trace the changes over time in major federal welfare programs. (p. 566)

Helping the Poor? Social Policy and the Needy

- The **Great Depression** proved that poverty can be beyond anyone's control and encouraged the government to become more involved in welfare.

- Social Security began under the **New Deal (Social Security Act of 1935)**; the poor become a part of the Democratic Party coalition.

- President Johnson initiated many **Great Society** programs to fight the **War on Poverty** during the civil rights era.

- President Reagan cut the growth of many of these programs in the 1980s.

- The system underwent a major overhaul during the Clinton administration **(Personal Responsibility and Work Opportunity Reconciliation Act of 1996)**.

- Under the reforms, families receive small payments with a maximum of two years to find employment, people have a lifetime maximum of five years on welfare, and states have more latitude and discretion in operating their own welfare programs.

- Welfare reform brought with it a name change for the cash payments to families from Aid to Families with Dependent Children (AFDC) to **Temporary Assistance for Needy Families (TANF)**.

Learning Objective 16.5: Outline how America's Social Security program works and the challenge of keeping it financially solvent in the coming years. (p. 569)

Social Security: Living on Borrowed Time

- Social Security has lifted many elderly out of poverty.

- The government taxes employees and their employers a percentage of the employee's income, up to a maximum contribution, and these are deposited into the **Social Security Trust Fund**.

- Both employee and employer contributions are paid into the Social Security Trust Fund, from which benefits are paid.

- Currently, there are about three workers per recipient, and benefits and contributions are balanced.

- But it is possible that the system will go bankrupt during the 21st century.

- More people will be of retirement age, fewer people will be working, and the cost of living is rising, so monthly payments will increase.

- Either taxes will have to be raised or benefits will have to be cut.

 Learning Objective 16.6: Distinguish American social welfare policy from that of other established democracies. (p. 571)

Social Welfare Policy Elsewhere

- Most established democracies have more expensive and generous social welfare programs than does the United States.

- In particular, European governments provide citizens with benefits, such as paid parental leave upon the birth of a child, that are unheard of in the United States.

- Taxes in Europe have to be higher than taxes in the United States in order to pay for these benefits.

Learning Objective 16.7: Assess the impact of economic and social welfare policies on democracy and the scope of government in America. (p. 572)

Understanding Economic and Social Welfare Policymaking

- As in most policy arenas, groups with ample political resources tend to get more of what they want in the battle over social welfare policies.

- The elderly have been very successful in preserving their Social Security and Medicare benefits, whereas the poor have faced difficulties in preserving welfare funding.

- The growth in social welfare spending, particularly for Social Security and Medicare, accounts for much of the increase in the scope of government in recent decades.

For Additional Review

Create a list of the main policy tools the government can use to address economic problems in the United States. For each tool, describe HOW and WHEN that tool can be used to address economic problems. Use this list when studying for the unit test and when preparing for the AP Government and Politics exam.

Create a chart demonstrating the economic inequality which exists in the United States, i.e. groups living below the poverty level. List the ways the government attempts to lessen this inequality and identify the program as an entitlement or a means-tested social welfare program. Use this list chart when studying for the unit test and when preparing for the AP Government and Politics exam.

☐ Review Questions

Multiple-Choice Questions

1. _____ refer(s) to the "shares" of the national income earned by various groups.
   a. Entitlements
   b. Income distribution
   c. Wealth
   d. Taxable income
   e. Profits

2. Which of the following groups has consistently had the highest rates of poverty?
   a. Asian Americans
   b. African Americans
   c. Hispanic Americans
   d. Southern whites
   e. Non-Hispanic white Americans

3. The Social Security program is endangered primarily because
   a. the U.S. birth rate has increased dramatically over the past decade.
   b. the program has lost public support in recent years.
   c. the number of contributors to the program is growing at a much slower rate than the number of recipients.
   d. large federal budget deficits have reduced the amount of tax revenue collected in support of the program.
   e. the program has become more identified with racial minorities.

4. All of the following are examples of means-tested programs EXCEPT
   a. Temporary Assistance for Needy Families (TANF).
   b. Children's Health Insurance Program (CHIP).
   c. Food Stamp Program.
   d. Medicaid.
   e. Social Security.

5. The most expensive social welfare program in the United States is
   a. Social Security.
   b. Aid to Families with Dependent Children (AFDC).
   c. Food Stamps.
   d. Supplemental Security Income (SSI).
   e. Children's Health Insurance Program (CHIP).

6. Senior citizens fare better than the poor in social welfare budget battles for which of the following reasons?
   a. The Constitution requires a certain amount of spending for senior citizens, but not the poor.
   b. Most social services for senior citizens come from state governments.
   c. Lobbyists representing the poor are not allowed to make campaign contributions.
   d. Senior citizens are more organized and better represented politically than the poor.
   e. There are more senior citizens in the U.S. than there are poor people.

7. The value of all goods and services produced by an economy during a specific period of time, such as a year, is called the
   a. budget production.
   b. growth rate.
   c. economic output.
   d. gross national product.
   e. consumer price index.

8.   One way the government attempts to overcome inflation is by
        a. decreasing loan rates to make money more available to the public.
        b. increasing the amount of credit available to the public.
        c. decreasing the amount of money in banks, which raises loan rates and discourages people from borrowing.
        d. limiting the number of bonds sold to the public.
        e. increasing the amount of money in banks to help individuals and businesses acquire spending capital.

9.   The economic theory that opposes governmental interference in economic affairs beyond what is necessary to protect life and property is known as
        a. trickle-down theory.
        b. protectionism.
        c. laissez-faire economics.
        d. socialism.
        e. Keynesianism.

10.   Which of the following statements best describes the significance of the National Labor Relations Act?
        a. It prohibits labor unions within the federal bureaucracy.
        b. It guarantees workers the right to unionize and bargain collectively.
        c. It allows mediation to solve conflicts between public and private workers.
        d. It allows companies to disband labor unions after giving 30 days advanced notice.
        e. It prohibits labor unions from collecting union dues from federal workers.

11.   All of the following are affected by actions of the Federal Reserve Board EXCEPT
        a. the federal budget deficit.
        b. the money supply.
        c. interest rates.
        d. the availability of jobs.
        e. inflation.

12.   The economic theory holding that the key task for fiscal policy is to stimulate the supply of goods, as by cutting tax rates, is known as
        a. supply side economics.
        b. protectionism.
        c. laissez-faire economics.
        d. socialism.
        e. Keynesianism.

13.   Monetary policy refers to government control of
        a. the banking and computer industries.
        b. the money supply and interest rates.
        c. taxing and spending policies.
        d. equities and securities.
        e. bonds and deficits.

14. A recession is
    a. a short-term decline in the economy that occurs as investment sags, production falls off, and unemployment increases.
    b. caused by high levels of government debt.
    c. a decrease in the amount of money in banks, which raises loan rates and discourages people from borrowing.
    d. a time when monetary policy is used to increase interest rates to keep people from going further into debt.
    e. a time of increasing amounts of imports that displace American workers.

15. Which of the following would be an example of fiscal policy?
    a. intentionally running a budget deficit to spur economic growth
    b. cutting the prime interest rate to encourage investment
    c. engaging in open market operations
    d. inflating the value of government assets to increase real estate prices
    e. purchasing consumers' credit card debt to prevent personal bankruptcies

16. Government programs providing benefits to qualified individuals regardless of need are known as
    a. means tested programs.
    b. income distribution.
    c. entitlement programs.
    d. earned income tax credit.
    e. supply side economics.

17. A Federal Reserve open-market operation involves
    a. protecting people against loss of income because of retirement, disability, unemployment, or death or absence of the family breadwinner.
    b. government benefits that all citizens meeting eligibility criteria—such as age, income level, or unemployment—are legally "entitled" to receive.
    c. the buying and selling of government securities by the Federal Reserve Bank in the securities market.
    d. government requirements that a portion of member banks' deposits must be retained to back loans made.
    e. the setting of the rate of interest at which member banks can borrow money from their regional Federal Reserve Bank.

18. Which of the following indicates that the United States has a mixed economy?
    a. The Supreme Court regulates interstate commerce.
    b. The federal government owns the means of production.
    c. Congress plays no role in setting tariffs on imported goods.
    d. The Justice Department can sue monopolistic companies.
    e. Federal workers are not allowed to unionize.

(e) is incorrect because both I and III are inaccurate descriptions of Republicans.

Page reference: 550–565, AP Topic: Policymaking in a federal system

20. One way the government attempts to overcome inflation is by

(a) is incorrect because it is not a way the government controls inflation.

(b) is incorrect because it is not a way the government controls inflation.

(c) is correct because one way the government attempts to overcome inflation is by decreasing the amount of money in banks, which raises loan rates and discourages people from borrowing. The Federal Reserve Board controls how much money is issued from the Federal Reserve Bank to all other banks. When it limits those available funds, banks are forced to offer loans at higher rates. This discourages people from applying for loans, which are one cause of the over-circulation of money.

(d) is incorrect because it is not a way the government controls inflation.

(e) is incorrect because it is not a way the government controls inflation.

Page reference: 550–558, AP Topic: Policymaking in a federal system

Free-Response Questions

1. The two major tools for macroeconomic policy are monetary and fiscal policies.

    a. Define monetary policy and fiscal policy.

    - Fiscal policy and monetary policy are the two main policy tools for the macroeconomy. Fiscal policy is policy regarding taxing and spending. By taxing, the government takes money out of consumers' hands and reduces consumption. Spending does the opposite. By spending too much, the government might create high inflation, but spending too little would keep people from buying goods and services. Fiscal policy is established by the president and Congress through the process of making the budget.

    b. Describe how each policy is made at the federal level.

    - Monetary policy is policy regulating the amount of money in the economy. More money in the economy lowers interest rates, increasing borrowing and consumption. Less money reduces consumption and, if the economy is overheating, can keep inflation under control. But lowering inflation tends to increase unemployment, and vice-versa. Monetary policy is made by the Federal Reserve Board of Governors, mainly by setting interest rates.

    c.   Describe the major trade-offs in each policy area.

- *Note that the trade-offs for fiscal and monetary policy are not addressed in the textbook. No one source will give you all of the information that you need to answer every question. You should look at as many possible sources as you can in preparing for the AP Exam.*

2.   Taxation is as much a social policy as it is a fiscal policy.

    a.   Describe the difference between progressive and regressive taxes.

    b.   Identify an example of each.

    c.   Identify one argument for and one against each type of tax policy.

- There are several types of tax policies. Progressive taxes are taxes in which the percentage of income that one pays increases with the amount of money one makes. The individual income tax is a good example. Some people believe that progressive taxes are unfair to the rich, but others argue that the rich should pay more because they get more benefits from the government. For example, the police protect everyone's property, but the rich have more property to protect.
- Regressive taxes are taxes in which the poor pay a higher percentage of their income than the rich. Sales taxes are a good example. Even though everyone pays the same tax rate, poor people spend a larger proportion of their income than the rich, who save more of their income. So poor people are taxed on more of their income. Many people believe that this is unfair, but some kinds of economic activity can only be taxed in this way.

17

Policymaking for Health Care, the Environment, and Energy

☐ Chapter Overview

Health care, the environment, and energy represent three important areas of domestic policymaking. In this chapter, we examine how the government makes policy across these three areas. We begin by exploring the problems of health care in America and the role of government in health care, focusing in particular on the debate over the Patient Protection and Affordable Care Act (PPACA) of 2010. Then we analyze the conflicts between economic growth and environmental protection and identify the major national environmental protection policies. Along the way we evaluate the advantages and disadvantages of each of the principal sources of energy in the United States. We conclude by assessing the role of democratic politics in making health care, environmental, and energy policy and the effect of these policies on the scope of government. By the end of the chapter, students should have a well-rounded understanding of social policy in the United States across a wide variety of issues.

☐ Study Outline

 Learning Objective 17.1: Outline the problems of health care in America and the role of government in health care. (p. 581)

Health Care Policy

- The cost of health care in the United States is very high and is growing.

- Funding has focused on **technological advances** that are extremely expensive.

- More health care facilities have been built than are being used, but their upkeep must be paid for.

- New drugs and procedures have been developed to treat more illnesses than ever before.

- The public is not pressed to be concerned about the cost of health care, since most of it is paid for by the government, employers, and insurance companies.

- Malpractice lawsuits are becoming more common, which raises doctors' insurance premiums and, in turn, raises the cost of their services.

- Companies feel they are bearing too much of the health care burden, but they do get significant tax breaks for contributing to their employees' insurance policies. Part-time employees are usually not eligible for benefits. Many small companies cannot afford to pay for their employees' health care.

- Americans do not all have equal access to health care. Health care and insurance are mostly privatized, not nationalized, so they are not provided for everyone. Most people get insurance through their jobs. Unemployed people have to pay for health care themselves, and most cannot afford to pay.

- **Health maintenance organizations (HMOs)** have lowered the cost of health care but have not alleviated the problem of inaccessibility.

- Accessibility is unequal among people of different races and incomes.

- A greater percentage of minorities and lower-income families do not have insurance.

- Members of minority groups and lower classes have poorer health because they often do not have regular family doctors.

- In some cases, policymakers and insurance companies choose which medical procedures to fund because the money necessary to perform just a few very expensive procedures could be distributed more widely to provide basic services to more people.

The Role of Government in Health Care

- Debate continues over who should pay for health care.
- The government pays for 42 percent of health care costs. The government pays for **Medicare** and part of **Medicaid**, but the Medicare system is in danger of running out of money in the next decade.
- Senior citizens actively pursue federal funding for Medicare.
- Lawmakers must fulfill the needs of their constituents, especially of those who vote.
- Interest groups representing the medical profession and insurance companies are well-funded and very active in the political arena.
- Business groups try to persuade the government to take on more responsibility for health care so that businesses do not have to pay for it.
- Many groups, particularly the poor, are largely underrepresented in the health care policy debate.

Reform Efforts

- In the 1940s, Harry S. Truman called for **national health insurance**, a compulsory insurance program to finance all Americans' medical care.
- The idea was strongly opposed by the American Medical Association, which disparaged it as "socialized medicine."
- While every other industrial nation in the world adopted some form of national health insurance, the United States remained the exception.
- President Clinton made health care reform the centerpiece of his first administration.
- Particularly, his plan would have guaranteed health coverage for all Americans by requiring that employers provide health insurance for their employees or pay a premium into a public fund.

- Opponents labeled it a government takeover of the health care system, and the middle class felt its health care threatened. After a long and tortuous battle, the plan died in Congress.

- Early in his administration, Barack Obama made comprehensive health care reform a top priority in domestic policy.

- His plan would create a new insurance marketplace that would allow people without insurance, as well as small businesses, to compare plans and buy insurance at competitive prices, and provided new tax credits to help people buy insurance and to help small businesses cover their employees.

- It also required large employers to cover their employees and individuals who could afford it to buy insurance.

- Despite opposition from businesses and the public, the White House and the Democratic majorities in Congress pushed through an historic comprehensive health care reform bill in 2010.

 Learning Objective 17.2: Analyze the conflicts between economic and environmental protection, and identify the major national environmental protection policies. (p. 592)

Environmental Policy

- **Environmental policy** and **economic policy** often conflict with each other.

- Industrial processes can harm the environment. Environmental restrictions may inhibit economic growth and expansion.

- Environmental and business interest groups lobby strongly for conflicting policies.

- Environmental groups call for preservation of wildlife and natural resources and for greater regulation of pollution.

- Business groups demand fewer regulations and restrictions that inhibit industrial expansion.

- The **EPA** was created in 1970 and is responsible for administering the government's environmental legislation.

- Under the **National Environmental Policy Act** (1969), private companies and federal agencies must file an **Environmental Impact Statement** with the EPA, citing the possible effects on the environment of every project they plan to undertake.

- Interest groups have access to the reports, and even the threat of a lawsuit brought by one of them deters many companies from proposing projects that may be challenged by the environmental lobby.

- There are around 20 major pieces of federal environmental legislation. Among them are the **Clean Air Act of 1970**, the **Water Pollution Control Act of 1972**, the **Endangered Species Act of 1973**, and the EPA's **Superfund**, which was created in 1980 to clean up toxic waste sites throughout the United States.

- One of the most intractable—and potentially the most serious—environmental issue is **global warming**.

- Most scientists agree that the Earth is warming at a rapid rate, with potentially disastrous consequences.

- The principal way to reduce greenhouse gases is to burn less fuel or find alternative sources of energy, which opponents fear will cost a staggering sum.

- President Obama has proposed to stem carbon dioxide emissions through a market-based cap-and-trade system.

 Learning Objective 17.3: Evaluate the advantages and disadvantages of each of the principal sources of energy in the United States. (p. 600)

Energy Policy

- Fossil fuels such as coal, petroleum, and natural gas are the bulk of America's energy sources.

- Coal is America's most abundant, but also dirtiest, fuel.

- Natural gas and petroleum are somewhat cleaner than coal, but they both contribute to global warming.

- In addition, transporting oil can result in spills that cause serious environmental damage, and refining oil pollutes the air.

- Dependence on foreign oil and natural gas also places the United States at the mercy of actions of other nations.

- One way to minimize the effects of an oil supply disruption is to ensure that our domestic production of oil is maintained.

- Oil exploration on public lands and offshore in coastal waters has the potential to increase America's oil supplies; however, this drilling also raises issues of environmental protection.

- The most controversial energy source is nuclear power.

- Nuclear energy met with increasing skepticism in the light of the accidents at Three Mile Island and Chernobyl, in 1979 and 1986, respectively.

- No new nuclear power plants have been started in the United States since 1978, but interest is growing because nuclear energy does not produce greenhouse gases.

- Renewable energy sources include water, wind, the sun, geothermal sources, hydrogen, and biomass.

- These provide between 7 percent (according to Figure 19.2) and 10 percent (according to page 567) of America's energy, but the contribution of renewable sources of energy to America's energy supply is likely to remain small for the foreseeable future.

17.4 | Learning Objective 17.4: Assess the role of democratic politics in making health care, environmental, and energy policy and the effect of these policies on the scope of government. (p. 603)

- High-tech issues strain the limits of public participation in a democracy, but most Americans do not leave these issues to "experts" to decide.

- The scope of the federal government has grown as it has provided health care for the elderly, the poor, and, more recently, those who simply cannot afford health insurance.

- Health is the most rapidly growing public policy area and poses a long-term challenge for budgeters.

- Concerns for environmental protection have placed additional demands on the federal government, increasing its regulatory reach.

- The public also expects the government to ensure a sufficient supply of energy and to deal with its polluting byproducts.

For Additional Review

Make a table of the advantages and disadvantages of the current health care system. Then, in a third column, note reforms that have been attempted or suggested. Use this table when reviewing and studying for the unit test and the AP Government and Politics exam.

Make a chart depicting the steps in the policymaking process. List the possible participants for each stage of the process. Finally, put the specific information on the chart for the policymaking processes for both health care and environmental policies. Use this table when reviewing and studying for the unit test and the AP Government and Politics exam.

☐ Review Questions

Multiple-Choice Questions

1. An interesting paradox about American health care is that
    a. the U.S. spends more money on health care than any other country, yet it is far from having the healthiest population.
    b. Americans are healthier than people in most other countries, even though the U.S. devotes relatively few resources to health care.
    c. the cost of health care has been declining, even though inflation in general is becoming more of a problem.
    d. expenditures for health care for the elderly exceed expenditures for health care for the young.
    e. the rising costs of health care do not directly affect individuals because nearly all Americans have private insurance.

2. Most people in the U.S. get health insurance
    a. from the federal government.
    b. from state governments.
    c. from private policies.
    d. through their jobs.
    e. through special cooperatives established by Congress.

3. Which of the following groups has the least access to health care?
    a. federal employees
    b. blue-collar workers
    c. the elderly
    d. children
    e. racial and ethnic minorities

4. All of the following are major pieces of federal environmental legislation EXCEPT
   a. the Endangered Species Act.
   b. the Environmental Protection Agency.
   c. the Clean Air Act.
   d. the Superfund.
   e. the Water Pollution Control Act.

5. All of the following are accurate statements about the health care policy debate EXCEPT
   a. Business interest groups represent employers who want the government to take greater responsibility for health care.
   b. Groups like the American Medical Association lobby successfully for privatized health care because they are well-funded and highly organized.
   c. Senior citizens are the most active portion of the electorate in the health care debate because they stand to gain the most.
   d. Many new interest groups have arisen to lobby for more health care assistance to people in poverty.
   e. Disagreement between the government and private employers is pervasive.

6. Environmental concerns often become hotly contested political issues because
   a. the number of environmental interest groups is shrinking.
   b. the federal courts refuse to get involved in disputes involving the environment.
   c. environmental concerns often conflict with other concerns like foreign trade and economic growth.
   d. Congress has failed to enact any major environmental protection laws.
   e. large corporations support any efforts by the government to clean up the environment.

7. Which federal program was designed to provide health care for poor Americans?
   a. Medicare
   b. National Health Insurance
   c. Managed Care
   d. Endangered Species Act
   e. Medicaid

8. One major reason that many groups' health needs go unmet is
   a. there are too few well-organized groups that insist the government meets these needs.
   b. there is confusion about what their health needs are.
   c. the health care industry is overly centralized.
   d. there are too few doctors in the United States.
   e. the states have failed to reach agreements over what constitutes proper treatment.

9. Which of the following is the United States' most abundant fuel?
   a. natural gas
   b. coal
   c. greenhouse gas
   d. oil
   e. nuclear energy

10. The first step of the policy process is
    a. problem recognition.
    b. agenda setting.
    c. policy implementation.
    d. policy evaluation.
    e. policy formulation.

11. The exchanges in the Patient Protection and Affordable Care Act of 2010 will be fully implemented in
    a. 2011.
    b. 2014.
    c. 2018.
    d. 2020.
    e. 2023.

12. In 1993, under the provisions of the Clean Air Act, an emissions trading system was created and the first sales of allowances for the discharge of sulfur dioxide were held. This illustrates which stage of the public policy process?
    a. agenda setting
    b. policy evaluation
    c. budgeting
    d. policy adoption
    e. implementation

13. Which of the following programs provides medical care to elderly Social Security recipients?
    a. Old Age, Survivors, and Disability Insurance
    b. veterans disability benefits
    c. Medicare
    d. Medicaid
    e. the National Health Service

14. Due to the steep rise in oil prices in the early 1970s, energy policy
    a. was put on the backburner.
    b. was placed on the governmental agenda.
    c. began to focus on renewable energy over fossil fuels.
    d. relied almost exclusively on renewable portfolio standards to increase domestic production.
    e. was declared a "national security event" that enabled the president to tap into the Strategic Petroleum Reserve.

15. The funding for Social Security comes from
    a. individual property taxes.
    b. payroll taxes on employers and employees.
    c. individual income taxes.
    d. individual state taxes.
    e. a special savings account.

16. Public schools are the responsibility of
    a. local governments.
    b. the states.
    c. state and local governments.
    d. the Department of Education.
    e. the federal government.

17. The Great Society legislation is associated with which president?
    a. Theodore Roosevelt
    b. Jimmy Carter
    c. Lyndon B. Johnson
    d. Franklin D. Roosevelt
    e. John Kennedy

18. The act, passed in 2002, which allowed the federal government to become more involved in local education is the
    a. Head Start Act.
    b. Education Improvement Act.
    c. U.S. Education Act.
    d. Project Lead the Way Act.
    e. No Child Left Behind Act.

19. Which of the following has NOT contributed to the rise in health care costs?
    a. new technology
    b. stronger environmental regulations
    c. unnecessary tests and procedures
    d. excessive record keeping
    e. cost of malpractice insurance

20. Which of the following was NOT part of the Great Society?
    a. Social Security
    b. Medicare
    c. Medicaid
    d. Head Start
    e. Food Stamps

Free-Response Questions

Some AP Free-Response Questions will ask you to address one specific policy area. It is, however, important that you understand the public policymaking process in general and to be able to draw appropriate examples from a variety of policy areas, because some questions will ask you to address several policy areas in one question.

1. One of the most pressing issues in public policy is health care.

    a. Describe how health care is provided in the United States, and how this shapes access to health care.

b. Identify two advantages and two disadvantages to a national health care system.

2. One of the biggest environmental challenges is reconciling environmental policy with policy goals in other areas.

a. Describe two major environmental policies.

b. Describe how environmental policies conflict with policies in two other areas.

☐ Answers and Explanations

Multiple-Choice Questions

1. An interesting paradox about American health care is that

    (a) is correct because there is a paradox about American health care: The U.S. spends more money on health care than any other country, yet it is far from having the healthiest population.

    (b) is incorrect because it is an inaccurate description of the American health care system.

    (c) is incorrect because it is an inaccurate description of the American health care system.

    (d) is incorrect because it is an inaccurate description of the American health care system.

    (e) is incorrect because it is an inaccurate description of the American health care system.

    Page reference: 581–592, AP Topic: The formation of policy agendas

2. Most people in the U.S. get health insurance

    (a) is incorrect because most people do not get their health insurance from the government.

    (b) is incorrect because most people do not get their health insurance from state government.

    (c) is incorrect because most people do not get their health insurance from private policies.

    (d) is correct because most Americans who have health insurance get it through their job.

    (e) is incorrect because most people do not get their health insurance from cooperatives.

    Page reference: 581–592, AP Topic: The formation of policy agendas

3.   Which of the following groups has the least access to health care?

(a) is incorrect because "federal employees" is an inaccurate response to the prompt.

(b) is incorrect because "blue collar workers" is an inaccurate response to the prompt.

(c) is incorrect because "the elderly" is an inaccurate response to the prompt.

(d) is incorrect because "children" is an inaccurate response to the prompt.

(e) is correct because there is uneven access to health care in the United States. Access to insurance and quality care is closely tied to race and income. Of the groups listed, racial and ethnic minorities have the worst access to health care.

Page reference: 586–589, AP Topic: The formation of policy agendas

4.   All of the following are major pieces of federal environmental legislation EXCEPT

(a) is incorrect because it is a major piece of environmental legislation.

(b) is correct because the Environmental Protection Agency (EPA) is not a piece of federal legislation. It is the federal agency charged with administering the government's environmental policies.

(c) is incorrect because it is a major piece of environmental legislation.

(d) is incorrect because it is a major piece of environmental legislation.

(e) is incorrect because it is a major piece of environmental legislation.

Page reference: 592–597, AP Topic: The formation of policy agendas

5.   All of the following are accurate statements about the health care policy debate EXCEPT

(a) is incorrect because it is an accurate statement about the health care policy debate.

(b) is incorrect because it is an accurate statement about the health care policy debate.

(c) is incorrect because it is an accurate statement about the health care policy debate.

(d) is correct because although there are many different interest groups who are extremely active in the health care debate, there has not been a significant rise in the number of such groups advocating for the poor.

(e) is incorrect because it is an accurate statement about the health care policy debate.

Page reference: 584–592, AP Topic: The formation of policy agendas

6. Environmental concerns often become hotly contested political issues because

    (a) is incorrect because the number of interest groups is not shrinking.

    (b) is incorrect because the federal courts do get involved in environmental disputes.

    (c) is correct because environmental concerns often become heated political issues because the environmental concerns often conflict with other concerns like foreign trade and economic growth. For example, environmental restrictions may inhibit economic growth. As a consequence, business interest groups often oppose environmental groups on specific policy proposals.

    (d) is incorrect because Congress has enacted environmental legislation.

    (e) is incorrect because large corporations do not always support environmental clean up.

    Page reference: 592–597, AP Topic: The formation of policy agendas

7. Which federal program was designed to provide health care for poor Americans?

    (a) is incorrect because Medicare is not health care for the poor.

    (b) is incorrect because National Health Insurance is not health care for the poor.

    (c) is incorrect because Managed Care is not health care for the poor.

    (d) is incorrect because the Endangered Species Act is not health care for the poor.

    (e) is correct because Medicaid is a public assistance program designed to provide health care for the poor. Medicaid is funded by both the national and state governments. It is often confused with Medicare, which is the part of the Social Security Program that provides hospitalization insurance for the elderly.

    Page reference: 589, AP Topic: The formation of policy agendas

8. One major reason that many groups' health needs go unmet is

    (a) is correct because one major reason that many groups' health needs go unmet is because there are relatively few advocacy groups pressuring the government to meet these needs. Single women, racial minorities, and the poor are worst off in this regard.

    (b) is incorrect because it is an inaccurate reason for why many groups' health needs go unmet.

    (c) is incorrect because it is an inaccurate reason for why many groups' health needs go unmet.

    (d) is incorrect because it is an inaccurate reason for why many groups' health needs go unmet.

(e) is incorrect because it is an inaccurate reason for why many groups' health needs go unmet.

Page reference: 584–591, AP Topic: The formation of policy agendas

9. Which of the following is the United States' most abundant fuel?

(a) is incorrect because natural gas is not the most abundant fuel in the U.S.

(b) is correct because coal is the United States' most abundant fuel. About 90 percent of the country's energy resources are in coal deposits—enough to last hundreds of years.

(c) is incorrect because greenhouse gas is not the most abundant fuel in the U.S.

(d) is incorrect because oil is not the most abundant fuel in the U.S.

(e) is incorrect because nuclear energy is not the most abundant fuel in the U.S.

Page reference: 600–603, AP Topic: The formation of policy agendas

10. The first step of the policy process is

(a) is correct because the correct order of stages in the policymaking process is: problem recognition, agenda setting, policy formulation, policy adoption, budgeting, policy implementation, and policy evaluation.

(b) is incorrect because agenda setting is not the first step in the policy process.

(c) is incorrect because policy implementation is not the first step in the policy process.

(d) is incorrect because policy evaluation is not the first step in the policy process.

(e) is incorrect because policy formulation is not the first step in the policy process.

Page reference: 421–422, 484–493, AP Topic: The formation of policy agendas

11. The exchanges in the Patient Protection and Affordable Care Act of 2010 will be fully implemented in

(a) is incorrect because it is an inaccurate choice for the question.

(b) is correct because the primary purpose of the Patient Protection and Affordable Care Act is to establish government-operated health insurance exchanges to ensure that all Americans would have access to health care coverage. These exchanges will not be fully implemented until 2014.

(c) is incorrect because it is an inaccurate choice for the question.

(d) is incorrect because it is an inaccurate choice for the question.

(e) is incorrect because it is an inaccurate choice for the question.

Page reference: 590–592, AP Topic: The formation of policy agendas

12. In 1993, under the provisions of the Clean Air Act, an emissions trading system was created and the first sales of allowances for the discharge of sulfur dioxide were held. This illustrates which stage of the public policy process?

(a) is incorrect because agenda setting is an inaccurate answer to the question.

(b) is incorrect because policy evaluation is an inaccurate answer to the question.

(c) is incorrect because budgeting is an inaccurate answer to the question.

(d) is incorrect because policy adoption is an inaccurate answer to the question.

(e) is correct because policy implementation is the process of carrying out public policy through governmental agencies and the courts. Actually creating an emissions trading system and selling allowances for the discharge of sulfur dioxide is carrying out the policies set forth in the Clean Air Act.

Page reference: 421–422, 484–493, 595, AP Topic: The formation of policy agendas

13. Which of the following programs provides medical care to elderly Social Security recipients?

(a) is incorrect because Old Age, Survivors, and Disability Insurance is another name for Social Security.

(b) is incorrect because this is a healthcare program for veterans.

(c) is correct because Medicare is the federal program established in the Lyndon B. Johnson administration that provides medical care to elderly Social Security recipients.

(d) is incorrect because Medicaid is the government program that subsidizes medical care for the poor.

(e) is incorrect because the National Health Service is the government-operated healthcare system in Britain.

Page reference: 584–589, AP Topic: The formation of policy agendas

14. Due to the steep rise in oil prices in the early 1970s, energy policy

(a) is incorrect because it is an inaccurate response to the prompt.

(b) is correct because the governmental agenda is the changing list of issues which government believes it should address. Prior to the steep rise in oil prices and the concomitant Arab oil embargo demonstrating America's vulnerability to heavy reliance on imported oil, energy policy was not an issue most government leaders

thought needed to be on the governmental agenda, but changes in the early 1970s worked to put it there.

(c) is incorrect because it is an inaccurate response to the prompt.

(d) is incorrect because it is an inaccurate response to the prompt.

(e) is incorrect because it is an inaccurate response to the prompt.

Page reference: 592–597, AP Topic: The formation of policy agendas

15.   The funding for Social Security comes from

(a) is incorrect because Social Security is not funded by individual property taxes.

(b) is correct because Social Security is funded through payroll taxes which are paid by employers and by employees.

(c) is incorrect because Social Security is not funded by income taxes.

(d) is incorrect because Social Security is not funded by state taxes.

(e) is incorrect because Social Security is not funded by a special savings account.

Page reference: 457, 566, AP Topic: The formation of policy agendas

16.   Public schools are the responsibility of

(a) is incorrect because local governments are only partly responsible for public education.

(b) is incorrect because states are only partly responsible for public education.

(c) is correct because public schools are the domain of the state and local governments due to the dual federalism established by the Constitution.

(d) is incorrect because the Department of Education is not responsible for public education.

(e) is incorrect because the federal government is not responsible for public education.

Page reference: 484–485, 453, 85–86, AP Topic: The formation of policy agendas

17.   The Great Society legislation is associated with which president?

(a) is incorrect because Theodore Roosevelt is not associated with the Great Society.

(b) is incorrect because Jimmy Carter is not associated with the Great Society.

(c) is correct because President Lyndon Johnson was responsible for the adoption of the Great Society legislation, which established much of the present-day welfare system.

(d) is incorrect because Franklin Roosevelt is not associated with the Great Society.

(e) is incorrect because John Kennedy is not associated with the Great Society.

Page reference: 275, 457, 546, 549, 566, AP Topic: The formation of policy agendas

18.   The act, passed in 2002, which allowed the federal government to become more involved in

(a) is incorrect because it is an inaccurate response to the question.

(b) is incorrect because it is an inaccurate response to the question.

(c) is incorrect because it is an inaccurate response to the question.

(d) is incorrect because it is an inaccurate response to the question.

(e) is correct because the education reform passed in 2002 that employs high standards and measurable goals as a method of improving American education is known as the No Child Left Behind Act (NCLB). This act allowed the federal government to become more involved in public education.

Page reference: 78, 85, 88, 92, AP Topic: The formation of policy agendas

19.   Which of the following has NOT contributed to the rise in health care costs?

(a) is incorrect because new technology is related to increased health care costs.

(b) is correct because stronger environmental regulations are unrelated to the rising cost of health care.

(c) is incorrect because unnecessary tests and procedures is related to increased health care costs.

(d) is incorrect because excessive record keeping is related to increased health care costs.

(e) is incorrect because the cost of malpractice insurance is related to increased health care costs.

Page reference: 581–592, AP Topic: The formation of policy agendas

20.   Which of the following was NOT part of the Great Society?

(a) is correct because Social Security was created through New Deal legislation and not through the legislation passed in conjunction with the Great Society.

(b) is incorrect because Medicare is part of the Great Society.

(c) is incorrect because Medicaid is part of the Great Society.

(d) is incorrect because Head Start is part of the Great Society.

(e) is incorrect because Food Stamps are part of the Great Society.

Page reference: 275, 457, 546, 549, 566, AP Topic: The formation of policy agendas

Free-Response Questions

This rubric provides examples of many, but not all of the possible correct responses to the free-response questions.

1. One of the most pressing issues in public policy is health care.

   a. Describe how health care is provided in the United States, and how this shapes access to health care.

      - In the United States, health care is provided in two ways. The government provides health care for a limited number of groups, especially children and the elderly. For most people, health care is provided through private insurance as a job fringe benefit. This means that unemployed and self-employed people often cannot get insurance. Many jobs, especially low-wage and part-time jobs, do not come with insurance. Many working poor must go without health care as a result.

   b. Identify two advantages and two disadvantages to a national health care system.

      - One proposed solution to this problem is a national health care system. This would give everyone access to health care, and might be able to keep costs down because of government controls. However, many believe that this would increase waiting times for health care and would take away people's ability to choose their health care providers.

2. One of the biggest environmental challenges is reconciling environmental policy with policy goals in other areas.

   a. Describe two major environmental policies.

      - There are many policies meant to deal with the environment. The National Environmental Policy Act requires that many private actors and federal agencies complete an Environmental Impact Statement describing the effects of their projects on the environment. The federal government also provides funding for developing alternative energy sources. *There are several other policies that could be included here, including the Endangered Species Act, air and water pollution legislation, and the Superfund system.*

b. Describe how environmental policies conflict with policies in two other areas.

- Environmental policies can conflict with both economic and energy policies. Environmental regulations can increase costs to many businesses that trade policies are trying to promote. They can also create conflicts with energy policy, as energy policies aimed at developing new sources of energy may promote the energy sources, such as nuclear or coal, that environmental policies aim to reduce. *Notice that this answer is specific about how the policies conflict, which is often necessary to receive credit for a question.*

18

National Security Policymaking

☐ Chapter Overview

Unlike domestic policy, which receives considerable attention and debate, foreign policy usually escapes popular attention. This is largely a reflection of the general apathy toward foreign policy expressed by the American public. In this chapter, we explore U.S. foreign policy. We begin by outlining the major foreign policy instruments and decision makers in the United States. Then we outline the evolution of and major issues in American foreign policy through the end of the Cold War, focusing in particular on the post-Cold War threat of terrorism. Next, we examine the major elements of U.S. defense policy and consider the challenges for national security policy in the United States. We conclude by assessing the role of democratic politics in making national security policy and the role of national security policy in expanding government. By the end of the chapter, students should have a good understanding of the major foreign policy issues and the policymaking process.

☐ Study Outline

 Learning Objective 18.1: Identify the major instruments and actors in making national security policy. (p. 611)

American Foreign Policy: Instruments, Actors, and Policymakers

Instruments

- The **military** is among the oldest instruments of foreign policy.

- The United States has been involved in only a few full-scale wars, but it has often employed force to influence actions in other countries.
- Today, economic instruments are becoming weapons almost as potent as those of war.
- Diplomacy, the quietest instrument of influence, is the process by which nations carry on relationships with each other.

Actors on the World Stage

- **International organizations** are becoming more necessary in today's global political and economic arenas.
- The **United Nations** is a global legislative body.
- Nearly 200 countries are members, each with one vote in the General Assembly.
- It is mainly responsible for **peacekeeping**, but also administers international economic, education, and welfare programs.
- The **Security Council** has the real power in the United Nations and therefore makes the most pressing decisions.
- Five permanent members each hold veto power: the United States, China, Russia, France, and Great Britain. Ten other seats are rotated each session.
- **Regional organizations** combine blocs of countries in military and economic alliances.
- The **North Atlantic Treaty Organization (NATO)** is a military alliance formed by the United States and Western European countries during the Cold War.
- Since the end of the Cold War, some former Eastern bloc countries have been admitted.
- Members pledge to support each other in times of war; NATO helps prevent the threat of war in Europe.
- The **European Union** is an economic alliance.
- Most Western European countries share a common currency and there are no trade barriers or employment restrictions among countries.
- **Multinational corporations** contribute to about one-fifth of the global economy.
- They have significant influence over taxes and trade regulations, and can be as powerful as governments.

- **Nongovernmental organizations (NGOs)** such as churches, labor unions, environmental groups, and human rights groups unite people globally for common causes or goals.

Policymakers

- The president serves as chief diplomat and as commander-in-chief of the armed forces.

- He negotiates treaties, makes executive agreements, and appoints ambassadors; he can act quickly and decisively.

- The bureaucratic arm of foreign policy is the **State Department**.
  - The **secretary of state** is the president's top foreign policy advisor.
  - American embassies fall under the jurisdiction of this department.

- The **Department of Defense** works closely with the State Department in matters of national security.

- The **Joint Chiefs of Staff** represent each branch of the armed forces in an advisory committee to the president.

- The **Central Intelligence Agency (CIA)** collects information in other countries to help the departments and the president make policy decisions.
  - It sometimes plays a covert role in the governmental affairs of other nations.

- **Congress** helps to oversee foreign policy, authorizes declarations of war, and appropriates funds for national security; the Senate ratifies treaties.

 Learning Objective 18.2: Outline the evolution of and major issues in American foreign policy through the end of the Cold War. (p. 618)

American Foreign Policy Through the Cold War

- Foreign policy is made up of a nation's external policies and positions and the techniques for achieving those policies and positions.

- The goal of foreign policy is to achieve peace and prosperity in the international community.

- Foreign policy is typically a struggle to achieve a middle ground between political idealism and political realism.

- The United States practiced **isolationism** until World War I.

- During the ideological **Cold War**, the United States focused on the **containment** of **communism**.

- The Department of Defense grew in terms of size and responsibilities.

- The **military-industrial complex** came to play a major role in politics.

- The **arms race** between the United States and the Soviet Union caused an international arms buildup.

- The United States became involved in the **Vietnam War** to contain the spread of communism in Asia.

   - The prolonged conflict resulted in massive troop commitments and heavy bombing of North Vietnam.

   - Protests erupted at home, and Americans' faith in the government was shaken.

   - Policy stances varied after the Vietnam War.

- The policy of *détente* brought greater cooperation between the U.S. and U.S.S.R. Defense spending went up enormously under Reagan, higher than it had been through the previous decades of the Cold War.

- The Cold War came to an end with the fall of the Soviet bloc in the late 1980s and early 1990s, but international relations have yet to stabilize completely in a new system.

Learning Objective 18.3: Explain the major obstacles to success in the war on terrorism. (p. 624)

American Foreign Policy and the War on Terrorism

- "Terrorism" is the use of violence to demoralize and frighten a country's population or government.

- It is difficult to defend against terrorism, especially in an open society.

- Terrorists have the advantage of stealth and surprise and, often, of a willingness to die for their cause.

- Following the September 11, 2001 attacks, the United States launched a military campaign against al Qaeda and on the Taliban regime that had been harboring them in Afghanistan.

- The president also declared that Iran, Iraq, and North Korea formed an "axis of evil" and he began laying plans to remove Iraqi president Saddam Hussein from power.

- In 2003, a U.S.-led coalition toppled Hussein.

- The United States faced first chaos and then a protracted insurrection in Iraq.

- Critics responded that the war proved a boon for extremists.

- The presence of foreign, non-Muslim occupiers made the country a magnet for militants who opposed their presence and welcomed an opportunity to kill Americans and other Westerners.

- Since the war in Afghanistan, al Qaeda has transformed itself into an umbrella organization that provides an inspirational focal point for loosely affiliated terrorist groups in dozens of countries worldwide.

- Because of the increasingly decentralized nature of the terrorist threat, the military component of the global counterterrorism campaign is more likely to resemble a war of attrition on multiple fronts, and it is unlikely that the use of military force alone will suffice.

Learning Objective 18.4: Identify the major elements of U.S. defense policy. (p. 627)

Defense Policy

- Defense spending has decreased to one-sixth of the federal budget.

- There is some concern that defense spending detracts from social spending.

- Decreasing spending means fewer jobs for weapons builders.

- The standing army is large and costly.

- The extremely costly arms buildup has stopped, but new expenditures are focused on engagements in Afghanistan and Iraq, and on high-tech weapons systems.

- Treaties have reduced nuclear weapons reserves among several nations with nuclear arms.

Learning Objective 18.5: Analyze the evolving challenges for U.S. national security policy. (p. 631)

The New National Security Agenda

The Changing Role of Military Power

- As policymakers have learned that there are limits to what military strength can achieve, attention has shifted away from long wars and formal military actions and alliances.

- "Soft power," the ability of a country to persuade others to do what it wants without force or coercion, is often crucial to national security.

- On various occasions in recent decades, the United States and its allies have used military force in **humanitarian interventions**.
    - Such interventions are often controversial, because they may involve violating a nation's sovereignty with the use of force.
    - And the United States is usually hesitant to intervene, as American lives may be lost and there may be no clear ending point for the mission.

- **Economic sanctions** have become a powerful tool of foreign policy.
    - Embargoes, cutting off economic aid, and restricting imports are all forms of sanctions.
    - They are safer and cheaper than military alternatives, and often initiated as a result of the efforts of human rights, environmental, and other political groups.

- Stopping the proliferation of **nuclear weapons** is high on the international agenda.

The International Economy

- International trade has increased dramatically in the past few decades.

- International economic treaties have attempted to address the issue of international trade through such ideas as most favored nation status, where equitable trade and tariff policies are observed by nations.

- The use of **tariffs** has declined to allow free trade among nations.

- Capital can also move more easily across borders with the Internet and advanced communications systems.

- Labor is cheaper in other countries and this leads to unemployment in the U.S., especially in blue-collar jobs.

- In the United States, imports exceed exports, so there is a **balance of trade deficit**.

- International protests against free trade have become common, because people fear the exploitation of less-developed countries by multinational corporations and because workers fear the loss of jobs.

- The North-South divide of wealthy nations and Third World countries is becoming increasingly apparent.

- Less-developed countries are millions of dollars in debt to developed countries.

- Many countries receive foreign aid from the developed world, but aid from the United States is usually tied to military considerations; most goes to Egypt and Israel.

- **Oil** and energy supplies are making economies more interdependent.

- The United States imports most of its oil from the Middle East.

- The policies of the **Organization of Petroleum Exporting Countries (OPEC)** are therefore of real importance to the United States.

 Learning Objective 18.6: Assess the role of democratic politics in making national security policy and the role of national security policy in expanding government. (p. 640)

Understanding National Security Policymaking

- There are different opinions over how much discretion to accord policymakers in national security policy, and policies at odds with the public wishes cannot be sustained.

- Congress provides a crucial check on the executive in the area of national security policymaking.

- The United States is fighting a war on terror, has treaty obligations to defend allies around the world, and participates actively in an interdependent global economy.

- As a result of these activities, the United States must deal with questions of energy supplies, global warming, and nuclear proliferation.

For Additional Review

Create a timeline demonstrating the evolution of foreign policy in the United States. Be sure to describe the key events which led to each of the foreign policy changes. Use this timeline when studying and reviewing for the unit test and the AP Government and Politics exam.

Create a diagram listing all the major foreign policy players within and outside of the American government including the United Nations. For each player listed, describe how that player is involved with American foreign policy and how specific players might interact at any given time. Use this diagram when studying and reviewing for the unit test and the AP Government and Politics exam.

◻ Review Questions

Multiple-Choice Questions

1.   Which of the following is the United Nations' most powerful policymaking entity?
     a.   Joint Chiefs of Staff
     b.   North Atlantic Treaty Organization (NATO)
     c.   European Union (EU)
     d.   Security Council
     e.   Organization of American States (OAS)

2.   American foreign policy is conducted mostly by the
     a.   Senate Foreign Relations Committee.
     b.   president and the Executive Branch.
     c.   National Security Agency.
     d.   Joint Chiefs of Staff.
     e.   House Foreign Affairs Committee.

3.   All of the following contribute directly to the development of U.S. foreign policy EXCEPT
     a.   the United Nations' General Assembly.
     b.   the Joint Chiefs of Staff.
     c.   the Central Intelligence Agency.
     d.   the State Department.
     e.   the Department of Defense.

4. Congress exercises influence over foreign policy in which of the following ways?

I. declaring war
II. confirming ambassadors
III. appropriating money
IV. ratifying treaties

a. I only
b. III only
c. I, II, and III only
d. I, III, and IV only
e. all of the above

5. Which of the following is an accurate statement about the role regional organizations have played in U.S. defense and foreign policy?
a. Regional organizations have contributed large sums of money to U.S. defense budgets.
b. In times of war, regional organizations have gained complete control over U.S. armed forces.
c. Regional organizations have largely been ignored by U.S. presidents.
d. The U.S. ended its involvement in most regional organizations after the Cold War ended.
e. Regional organizations have been used to promote economic as well as national security interests.

6. All of the following can be used to characterize U.S. foreign policy at various times during past century EXCEPT
a. isolationism.
b. unilateral disarmament.
c. *détente*.
d. containment.
e. arms race.

7. Which of the following is a true statement about the U.S. and foreign aid?
a. The Constitution limits the amount of money that can be spent on such aid.
b. The U.S. can only provide nonmilitary aid.
c. The U.S. is the world's largest donor of foreign aid.
d. The president can provide such aid without congressional approval.
e. The U.S. provides no foreign aid to European countries.

8. Which of the following is the most important national security issue the United States has faced since the end of the Cold War?
a. the spread of terrorism
b. a dramatic increase in nuclear proliferation
c. an increasing isolationist State Department
d. the inability to secure cooperation and commitments from allies
e. the strengthening of the Warsaw Alliance's military forces

9. Which of the following bureaucratic institutions has primary responsibility for coordinating U.S. foreign and military policies?
   a. Department of Defense
   b. Federal Bureau of Investigation
   c. Central Intelligence Agency
   d. National Security Council
   e. State Department

10. Which of the following statements best describes today's international economy?
    a. It is dominated by trade between the United States and the European Union.
    b. It is remarkably similar to the international economy prior to World War II.
    c. It is controlled and dominated by regional nongovernmental organizations.
    d. Mutually assured destruction is its underlying operating principle.
    e. It is characterized by greater interdependency than ever before.

11. The U.S. decision to continue with the planned invasion of Iraq even after failing to gain approval from the United Nations Security Council is an example of
    a. containment.
    b. isolationism.
    c. humanitarianism.
    d. unilateralism.
    e. deterrence.

12. President Jimmy Carter differed from his Cold War predecessors in operating foreign policy according to the principles of
    a. isolationism.
    b. unilateralism.
    c. moralism.
    d. containment.
    e. pragmatism.

13. All of the following can be used to characterize U.S. foreign policy at various times during the 20th century EXCEPT
    a. isolationism.
    b. unilateral disarmament.
    c. *détente.*
    d. containment.
    e. arms race.

14. The Constitution divided foreign policy powers between
    a. the Democrats and the Republicans.
    b. Congress and the Supreme Court.
    c. Congress and the president.
    d. the president and the Supreme Court.
    e. the states and the federal government.

15. Taxes on imports used to raise government revenue and to protect infant industries are
    a. domestication duties.
    b. excise taxes.
    c. revenue taxes.
    d. tariffs.
    e. embargo taxes.

16. Which of the following bureaucratic institutions has primary responsibility for advising the president about foreign and defense policy and events?
    a. Department of Defense
    b. National Security Agency
    c. Central Intelligence Agency
    d. National Security Council
    e. State Department

17. Which of the following is most consistent with the principle of isolationism?
    a. the Truman Doctrine
    b. the Marshall Plan
    c. the Bush Doctrine
    d. American involvement in the United Nations
    e. the Senate's refusal to join the League of Nations

18. Treaties in the United States are ratified by
    a. two-thirds vote in Congress.
    b. two-thirds vote in the House.
    c. two-thirds vote in the Senate.
    d. an executive order of the president.
    e. a ruling from the Supreme Court.

19. The foreign policy course the United States followed throughout most of its history, whereby it tried to stay out of other nations' conflicts, particularly European wars, is known as
    a. multilateralism.
    b. isolationism.
    c. unilateralism.
    d. multinational.
    e. humanitarianism.

20. A foreign policy strategy that called for the United States to isolate the Soviet Union and resist its encroachments by peaceful means if possible but by force if necessary is known as
    a. deterrence.
    b. *détente.*
    c. containment.
    d. interdependency.
    e. isolationism.

Free-Response Questions

1.   Foreign policy involves choices about relations with the rest of the world. The instruments or tools presidents use to conduct foreign policy are different from the instruments or tools they use to conduct domestic policy.

   a.   Identify three types of instruments or tools mostly commonly used by presidents to conduct foreign policy.

   b.   Choose two of the instruments or tools you identified in "a," and describe how they are used to help accomplish foreign policy objectives.

   c.   Identify two executive branch bureaucratic institutions involved in U.S. foreign policy and describe the role they play in the foreign policy process.

2.   Congress shares with the president constitutional authority over foreign and defense policy.

   a.   Identify and describe two constitutionally derived powers Congress has in foreign policymaking.

   b.   Identify and describe two constitutionally derived powers the president has in foreign policymaking.

   c.   Identify and describe a limitation on Congress in foreign policymaking.

☐ Answers and Explanations

Multiple-Choice Questions

1.   Which of the following is the United Nations' most powerful policymaking entity?

   (a) is incorrect because the Joint Chiefs of Staff is not a part of the U.N.

   (b) is incorrect because NATO is not a part of the U.N.

   (c) is incorrect because the EU is not a part of the U.N.

   (d) is correct because the Security Council is the seat of real power in the UN. Five of its 15 members (the United States, Great Britain, China, France, and Russia) are permanent members of the council; the other 10 are chosen on a rotating basis. The five permanent member states on the Security Council and have veto power over all Security Council decisions.

   (e) is incorrect because the OAS is not a part of the U.N.

Page reference: 612–613, AP Topics: The formation of policy agendas, The role of institutions in the enactment of policy

2.   American foreign policy is conducted mostly by the

(a) is incorrect because it is an inaccurate response to the question.

(b) is correct because the president is the chief initiator of foreign policy in the U.S. Presidents are aided in foreign policy decision making by several executive branch agencies including the State Department, the Department of Defense, the National Security Council, and the Central Intelligence Agency.

(c) is incorrect because it is an inaccurate response to the question.

(d) is incorrect because it is an inaccurate response to the question.

(e) is incorrect because it is an inaccurate response to the question.

Page reference: 614–618, AP Topics: The formation of policy agendas, The role of institutions in the enactment of policy

3.   All of the following contribute directly to the development of U.S. foreign policy EXCEPT

(a) is correct because the UN General Assembly plays no direct role in formulating American foreign policy.

(b) is incorrect because the Joint Chiefs of Staff do play a role in the development of U.S. foreign policy.

(c) is incorrect because the CIA does play a role in the development of U.S. foreign policy.

(d) is incorrect because the State Department does play a role in the development of U.S. foreign policy.

(e) is incorrect because the Department of Defense does play a role in the development of U.S. foreign policy.

Page reference: 614–618, AP Topics: The formation of policy agendas, The role of institutions in the enactment of policy

4.   Congress exercises influence over foreign policy in which of the following ways?

I.   declaring war
II. confirming ambassadors
III. appropriating money
IV. ratifying treaties
V.   all of the above

(a) is incorrect because it is an incomplete answer.

(b) is incorrect because it is an incomplete answer.

(c) is incorrect because it is an incomplete answer.

(d) is incorrect because it is an incomplete answer.

(e) is correct because although the president is the chief initiator of foreign policy in the U.S., Congress exercises influence over foreign policy through its powers to declare war, appropriate funds, ratify treaties, and confirm ambassadors to foreign nations. Congress has full authority over all military expenditures, including foreign aid and the budgets of the State Department, the Department of Defense, and the CIA.

Page reference: 614–618, AP Topics: The formation of policy agendas, The role of institutions in the enactment of policy

5. Which of the following is an accurate statement about the role regional organizations have played in U.S. defense and foreign policy?

    (a) is incorrect because it is an inaccurate response to the question.

    (b) is incorrect because it is an inaccurate response to the question.

    (c) is incorrect because it is an inaccurate response to the question.

    (d) is incorrect because it is an inaccurate response to the question.

    (e) is correct because regional organizations have proliferated since the end of World War II. The United States has used them to help to promote its economic and national security interests.

    Page reference: 613–614, AP Topics: The formation of policy agendas, The role of institutions in the enactment of policy

6. All of the following can be used to characterize U.S. foreign policy at various times during past century EXCEPT

    (a) is incorrect because the U.S. has engaged in isolationism.

    (b) is correct because although the U.S. has entered into several arms control agreements over the years, it has never had a foreign policy predicated on unilateral disarmament.

    (c) is incorrect because the U.S. has engaged in *détente*.

    (d) is incorrect because the U.S. has engaged in containment.

    (e) is incorrect because the U.S. has engaged in an arms race.

    Page reference: 618–624, AP Topics: The formation of policy agendas, The role of institutions in the enactment of policy

7. Which of the following is a true statement about the U.S. and foreign aid?

(a) is incorrect because it is an inaccurate statement about U.S. foreign aid.

(b) is incorrect because it is an inaccurate statement about U.S. foreign aid.

(c) is correct because the U.S. is the world's largest donor of foreign aid. However, the U.S. ranks lower than almost all other industrialized nations in the percentage of its gross domestic product it spends on economic development aid for needy nations.

(d) is incorrect because it is an inaccurate statement about U.S. foreign aid.

(e) is incorrect because it is an inaccurate statement about U.S. foreign aid.

Page reference: 618–624, AP Topics: The formation of policy agendas, The role of institutions in the enactment of policy

8. Which of the following is the most important national security issue the United States has faced since the end of the Cold War?

(a) is correct because the spread of terrorism is the most troublesome national security issue the U.S. has faced in the post-Cold War era. Terrorism takes on many forms, including bombing buildings and assassinating political leaders. It is difficult and costly to defend against terrorism, especially in an open society like the United States.

(b) is incorrect because nuclear proliferation is not the most important national security issue.

(c) is incorrect because isolationism is not the most important national security issue.

(d) is incorrect because lack of cooperation from allies is not the most important national security issue.

(e) is incorrect because a stronger Warsaw Alliance is not the most important national security issue.

Page reference: 624–641, AP Topics: The formation of policy agendas, The role of institutions in the enactment of policy

9. Which of the following bureaucratic institutions has primary responsibility for coordinating U.S. foreign and military policies?

(a) is incorrect because the Department of Defense is not the institution primarily responsible for coordinating U.S. foreign and military policies.

(b) is incorrect because the FBI is not the institution primarily responsible for coordinating U.S. foreign and military policies.

(c) is incorrect because the CIA is not the institution primarily responsible for coordinating U.S. foreign and military policies.

(d) is correct because created in 1947, the National Security Council (NSC) is charged with the responsibility of coordinating American foreign and military policies. The NSC is composed of the president, vice president, the secretary of defense, and the secretary of state. The president's national security advisor manages the NSC staff.

(e) is incorrect because the State Department is not the institution primarily responsible for coordinating U.S. foreign and military policies.

Page reference: 614–618, AP Topics: The formation of policy agendas, The role of institutions in the enactment of policy

10. Which of the following statements best describes today's international economy?

(a) is incorrect because it is an inaccurate description of today's international economy.

(b) is incorrect because it is an inaccurate description of today's international economy.

(c) is incorrect because it is an inaccurate description of today's international economy.

(d) is incorrect because it is an inaccurate description of today's international economy.

(e) is correct because interdependency is the word that best describes today's international economy. The health of the American economy depends increasingly on the prosperity of its trading partners and on the smooth flow of trade and finance across borders.

Page reference: 635–640, AP Topics: The formation of policy agendas, The role of institutions in the enactment of policy

11. The U.S. decision to continue with the planned invasion of Iraq even after failing to gain approval from the United Nations Security Council is an example of

(a) is incorrect because containment is an inaccurate selection for the scenario provided.

(b) is incorrect because isolationism is an inaccurate selection for the scenario provided.

(c) is incorrect because humanitarianism is an inaccurate selection for the scenario provided.

(d) is correct because unilateralism is acting without consulting with or gaining support from others. Invading a country after being denied support by others can be seen as acting unilaterally.

(e) is incorrect because deterrence is an inaccurate selection for the scenario provided.

Page reference: 618–631, AP Topics: The formation of policy agendas, The role of institutions in the enactment of policy

12. President Jimmy Carter differed from his Cold War predecessors in operating foreign policy according to the principles of

(a) is incorrect because isolationism does not describe President Carter's approach to foreign policy.

(b) is incorrect because unilateralism does not describe President Carter's approach to foreign policy.

(c) is correct because President Carter differed from his Cold War predecessors by emphasizing support for human rights as the moral and proper course of action to follow. Moralism is the policy of emphasizing morality in foreign affairs, thus emphasizing human rights would be an example of moralism.

(d) is incorrect because containment does not describe President Carter's approach to foreign policy.

(e) is incorrect because pragmatism does not describe President Carter's approach to foreign policy.

Page reference: 622, AP Topics: The formation of policy agendas, The role of institutions in the enactment of policy

13. All of the following can be used to characterize U.S. foreign policy at various times during the 20th century EXCEPT

(a) is incorrect because isolationism does describe U.S. foreign policy at times during the 20th century.

(b) is correct because, although the U.S. has entered into several arms control agreements over the years, it has never had a foreign policy predicated on unilateral disarmament. The U.S. followed isolationism in the period between WWI and WWII. *Détente* was the policy toward the Soviet Union for most of the 1970s, replacing the more conflict-based policy of the nuclear arms race and attempts to use containment to prevent further Soviet expansion.

(c) is incorrect because *détente* does describe U.S. foreign policy at times during the 20th century.

(d) is incorrect because containment does describe U.S. foreign policy at times during the 20th century.

(e) is incorrect because arms race does describe U.S. foreign policy at times during the 20th century.

Page reference: 618–626, AP Topics: The formation of policy agendas, The role of institutions in the enactment of policy

14. The Constitution divided foreign policy powers between

    (a) is incorrect because it is an inaccurate selection for how foreign policy powers are divided.

    (b) is incorrect because it is an inaccurate selection for how foreign policy powers are divided.

    (c) is correct because the Constitution divided authority for foreign and military policy functions between the president and Congress. The president is made commander-in-chief of the armed forces, but Congress has the power to fund the army and navy and to declare war. The president has authority to negotiate and sign treaties, but treaties only take effect after the Senate ratifies them by a two-thirds majority.

    (d) is incorrect because it is an inaccurate selection for how foreign policy powers are divided.

    (e) is incorrect because it is an inaccurate selection for how foreign policy powers are divided.

Page reference: 614–618, AP Topics: The formation of policy agendas, The role of institutions in the enactment of policy

15. Taxes on imports used to raise government revenue and to protect infant industries are

    (a) is incorrect because it is an inaccurate selection for the prompt provided.

    (b) is incorrect because it is an inaccurate selection for the prompt provided.

    (c) is incorrect because it is an inaccurate selection for the prompt provided.

    (d) is correct because tariff is defined in the root of the question.

    (e) is incorrect because it is an inaccurate selection for the prompt provided.

Page reference: 636, AP Topics: The formation of policy agendas, The role of institutions in the enactment of policy

16. Which of the following bureaucratic institutions has primary responsibility for advising the president about foreign and defense policy and events?

    (a) is incorrect because the Department of Defense runs the military.

    (b) is incorrect because the National Security Agency is in charge of gathering electronic intelligence.

(c) is incorrect because the Central Intelligence Agency is in charge of collecting human intelligence, analyzing all intelligence, and conducting the occasional covert operation.

(d) is correct because, created in 1947, the National Security Council (NSC) is charged with the responsibility of advising the president about foreign and defense policy and events. The other agencies mentioned play other roles in the foreign policy process.

(e) is incorrect because the State Department is in charge of conducting negotiations and relations with other countries.

Page reference: 614–618, AP Topics: The formation of policy agendas, The role of institutions in the enactment of policy

17.   Which of the following is most consistent with the principle of isolationism?

(a) is incorrect because the Truman Doctrine is not an example of isolationism.

(b) is incorrect because the Marshall Plan is not an example of isolationism.

(c) is incorrect because the Bush Doctrine is not an example of isolationism.

(d) is incorrect because involvement in the U.N. is not an example of isolationism.

(e) is correct because isolationism is a policy of avoiding participation in foreign affairs. Refusing to join the League of Nations would be a way of avoiding participation in foreign affairs.

Page reference: 619, AP Topics: The formation of policy agendas, The role of institutions in the enactment of policy

18.   Treaties in the United States are ratified by

(a) is incorrect because it is an inaccurate selection for the prompt.

(b) is incorrect because it is an inaccurate selection for the prompt.

(c) is correct because treaties entered into by the United States must be ratified by a two-thirds vote in the Senate.

(d) is incorrect because it is an inaccurate selection for the prompt.

(e) is incorrect because it is an inaccurate selection for the prompt.

Page reference: 614–618, AP Topics: The formation of policy agendas, The role of institutions in the enactment of policy

19. The foreign policy course the United States followed throughout most of its history, whereby it tried to stay out of other nations' conflicts, particularly European wars, is known as

(a) is incorrect because multilateralism is an inaccurate selection for the question.

(b) is correct because isolationism is the desire to avoid international entanglements altogether and this philosophy characterized the foreign policy course followed by the United States for most of its history.

(c) is incorrect because unilateralism is an inaccurate selection for the question.

(d) is incorrect because multinational is an inaccurate selection for the question.

(e) is incorrect because humanitarianism is an inaccurate selection for the question.

Page reference: 619, AP Topics: The formation of policy agendas, The role of institutions in the enactment of policy

20. A foreign policy strategy that called for the United States to isolate the Soviet Union and resist its encroachments by peaceful means if possible but by force if necessary is known as

(a) is incorrect because deterrence is an inaccurate selection for the description provided.

(b) is incorrect because *détente* is an inaccurate selection for the description provided.

(c) is correct because the U.S. policy of opposing Soviet expansion and communist revolutions around the world with military forces, economic assistance and political influence is known as containment.

(d) is incorrect because interdependency is an inaccurate selection for the description provided.

(e) is incorrect because isolationism is an inaccurate selection for the description provided.

Page reference: 620, AP Topics: The formation of policy agendas, The role of institutions in the enactment of policy

Free-Response Questions

This rubric provides examples of many, but not all of the possible correct responses to the free-response questions.

1. Foreign policy involves choices about relations with the rest of the world. The instruments or tools presidents use to conduct foreign policy are different from the instruments or tools they use to conduct domestic policy.

   a. Identify three types of instruments or tools mostly commonly used by presidents to conduct foreign policy.

- **Military instruments**
- **Diplomacy**
- **Economic instruments**

b. Choose two of the instruments or tools you identified in "a," and describe how they are used to help accomplish foreign policy objectives.

- **Military.** War and the threat of war are among the oldest instruments of foreign policy. Among other things, the United States has used its armed forces to help topple enemy governments, protect friendly governments, ensure the delivery of humanitarian aid, protect American business interests and prevent ethnic cleansing.

- **Diplomacy.** Diplomacy is the least obvious instrument of foreign policy. It takes place when national leaders meet in summit talks or when less prominent negotiators meet to work out treaties covering all kinds of national contracts, such as economic relations, arms control agreements, and cease fires in armed conflicts.

- **Economic.** Economic instruments can be as potent as war. For example, the control of oil can be a major source of power. Trade regulations, embargos, tariffs, and monetary policies can all be economic instruments of foreign policy.

c. Identify executive branch bureaucratic institutions involved in U.S. foreign policy and describe the role they play in the foreign policy process.

- **State Department.** The State Department is the main foreign policy agency of the U.S. government. It is the home of the diplomatic corps, and its head, the secretary of state, is the president's chief diplomatic advisor.

- **Department of the Defense.** The Department of Defense is a key foreign policy actor. It is the administrative home to the U.S. military, the army, air force, and navy. U.S. strategic and tactical military planning take place at the Department of the Defense.

- **National Security Council (NSC).** The NSC is the committee that links the president's key foreign and military policy advisors. Its formal members are the president, vice president, secretary of defense, and secretary of state. The NSC coordinates U.S. national security policy for the president.

- **Central Intelligence Agency (CIA).** The CIA is responsible for collecting and analyzing military, economic, and political data and information from foreign countries. This information can be used for both military and diplomatic planning. Information gathered by the CIA can also be used to prevent attacks on U.S. interests.

2. Congress shares with the president constitutional authority over foreign and defense policy.

    a. Identify and describe two constitutionally derived powers Congress has in foreign policymaking.

        - **Power to declare war.**

        - **Power of the purse.** A president's national security agenda requires a willingness on the part of Congress to appropriate the necessary funds to support it.

        - **Treaty ratification.** Treaties that presidents negotiate with foreign countries must be approved by a two-thirds vote in the Senate.

        - **Approval of key personnel.** The secretaries of state and defense, the director of the CIA, and ambassadors to foreign nations must be confirmed by the Senate.

    b. Identify and describe two constitutionally derived powers the president has in foreign policymaking.

        - **Commander-in-chief.** Because the framers wanted civilian control of the military, they made the president commander-in-chief of the armed forces. As commander in chief, the president controls where and how the military is deployed. The president also commands the vast arsenal of weapons of mass destruction.

        - **Appointment power.** The president selects the persons who serve in key foreign policy decision-making positions like the secretaries of state and defense, the national security advisor, and the director of the CIA.

        - **Diplomatic powers.** The president alone extends diplomatic recognition to foreign governments. The president can also terminate relations with other countries. The president is also responsible for choosing U.S. ambassadors to foreign countries.

        - **Power to make treaties with other nations.** The president has the sole power to negotiate treaties with other countries, although the Constitution requires the Senate to approve them by a two-thirds vote.

c. Identify and describe a limitation on Congress in foreign policymaking.

- Congress is a relative large and decentralized institution, which makes it difficult for it to speak with one unified voice.

- There is a common perception that the Constitution vests foreign policy decision making solely in the president. This often makes it difficult for Congress to effectively assert itself in matters of foreign policy.

- Congress has to rely on the president for important intelligence information about other countries. This can sometimes result in Congress receiving misleading or wrong information, as in the period leading up to the 2003 invasion of Iraq.

Part

III

Sample Exams with Answers and Explanations

Government and Politics: United States AP Exam Practice Test 1

☐ Government and Politics: United States

Section I
Time: 45 minutes
60 Questions

Directions: *Each of the questions or incomplete statements below is followed by five suggested answers or completions. Select the one that is best in each case and then fill in the corresponding oval on the answer sheet.*

1. Political action committees (PACs) were created by campaign reform laws to
    a. involve the public more directly in presidential campaigns.
    b. regulate how groups such as business and labor contribute to campaigns.
    c. finance challengers' campaigns to eliminate the advantages of incumbency.
    d. pay for candidates' air time because it has become the most expensive feature in a campaign.
    e. limit the influence of political parties over election outcomes.

2. All of the following are examples of entitlement programs EXCEPT
    a. Social Security.
    b. Medicare.
    c. defense contracts.
    d. veteran's benefits.
    e. agricultural subsidies.

Political Action Committees—Number of Committee Type:
1980 to 2001

(As of December 31)

Committee Type	1980	1985	1990	1995	1997	1998	1999	2000	2001
Total	2,551	3,992	4,172	4,016	3,844	3,798	3,835	3,706	3,907
Corporate	1,206	1,710	1,795	1,674	1,597	1,567	1,548	1,523	1,545
Labor	297	388	346	334	332	321	318	316	317
Trades/membership/health	576	695	774	815	825	821	844	812	860
Nonconnected	374	1,003	1,062	1,020	931	935	972	902	1,026
Cooperative	42	54	59	44	42	39	38	39	41
Corporation without stock	56	142	136	129	117	115	115	114	118

Source: U.S. Federal Election Commission, press release of January 2002.

3. Which of the following generalizations is supported by the information in the chart above?
   a. Nonconnected PACs grew in number more sharply between 1980 and 2001 than any other kind of PAC.
   b. The most dramatic change in the number of PACs occurred between 1985 and 1990.
   c. There are only a few cooperative PACs because these are the most difficult type to meet the approval of the Federal Election Commission.
   d. Business PACs spend the most money on congressional elections.
   e. All types of PACs have increased in number dramatically since 1980.

4. Federal district courts are the only federal courts in which
   a. the facts are presented by both parties in the case.
   b. *amicus curiae* briefs are registered with the court.
   c. the solicitor general appears for oral argument.
   d. juries are impaneled to decide cases.
   e. three-judge panels decide the outcome of cases.

5. The government began to pursue civil rights in the 1950s when
   a. Congress passed the Voting Rights Act.
   b. civil rights activists marched on Washington to demand government action.
   c. the Supreme Court declared public school segregation unconstitutional.
   d. states agreed to discontinue their use of poll taxes as a means of preventing people from voting.
   e. the president issued an executive order to desegregate all public transportation.

6. Which of the following statements about the president as commander in chief is true?
    a. The president has the authority to declare war for up to 60 days without consulting Congress.
    b. The president can decide if and when to use weapons of mass destruction in times of war.
    c. Presidents with no prior military experience are not allowed to make major military decisions alone.
    d. The president is required by law to consult with the Joint Chiefs of Staff before deploying the military.
    e. The president is a nonvoting member of the Senate Armed Services Committee.

7. Interest groups play a role in the federal judicial process in all of the following ways EXCEPT by
    a. giving campaign contributions to judicial nominees.
    b. lobbying the Judiciary Committee about a judicial nominee.
    c. filing *amicus curiae* briefs.
    d. having their lawyers represent a plaintiff.
    e. filing a class action suit.

8. Presidents exercise their influence over the ideology of federal courts by
    a. trying to appoint only judges who agree with their ideology and political views.
    b. ordering Congress to impeach judges who are too liberal or too conservative.
    c. demoting judges to lower courts.
    d. allowing them to hear only those cases on which judges are likely to agree with the president's point of view.
    e. meeting with members of the Senate Judiciary Committee when they are performing oversight.

9. The electoral votes of most states are allocated by which of the following methods?
    a. Each party's candidate receives electoral votes based on his or her percentage of the state's popular vote.
    b. Each elector chooses the candidate whom he or she feels is best suited to represent the needs of the state.
    c. The winner of the popular election in the state receives 75 percent of the state's electoral votes and the loser receives 25 percent.
    d. All of the state's electors cast their votes for whichever candidate won the state's popular vote.
    e. The loser in the popular election receives one electoral vote and the winner receives the rest of the state's electoral votes.

10. Which of the following groups is most likely to vote in elections?
    a. people under the age of 21
    b. senior citizens
    c. people without a college degree
    d. people with no party affiliation
    e. men with low-income jobs

11. The Supreme Court asserted which of the following principles in *Marbury v. Madison*?
    a. The Fourteenth Amendment guarantees all individual freedoms under state laws.
    b. Freedom of religion is guaranteed, but some religious practices may violate the establishment clause.
    c. Under the Tenth Amendment, the federal government can regulate commerce among states.
    d. The exclusionary rule must be upheld in all state court trials.
    e. The Supreme Court has the power to declare laws passed by Congress unconstitutional.

12. In the process of political socialization, individuals
    a. form their political beliefs.
    b. participate in a direct democracy.
    c. attend functions organized by political parties.
    d. evaluate and select their representatives.
    e. engage in political protest against a law.

13. The failure of the Articles of Confederation and necessity for a new Constitution were made evident by the
    a. success of the American Revolution.
    b. legislature's inability to select a president.
    c. need for a bicameral legislature.
    d. government's inability to subdue Shays' Rebellion.
    e. excess of centralized power in the national government.

14. Voter turnout in the United States is low in part because
    a. minority groups still struggle for the right to vote in Southern states.
    b. registering to vote has become more difficult.
    c. voters see little difference between the platforms of the two parties' candidates.
    d. many low-income people are not able to pass the literacy test required to vote.
    e. candidates do little to try to attract voters.

15. Which of the following statements is true about U.S. budget deficits?
    a. The first federal budget deficit did not occur until the 1990s.
    b. The Constitution requires a balanced federal budget.
    c. Large budget deficits make the U.S. government more financially dependent on foreign investors.
    d. Budget deficits have no practical effect on individual citizens.
    e. The Democratic and Republican parties have agreed that the deficit issue should not become an issue in presidential campaigns.

16. Congress performs legislative oversight over executive departments by
    a. hiring and firing department heads.
    b. determining departments' budgets.
    c. vetoing department proposals.
    d. issuing impoundment bills.
    e. coordinating department activities with the president.

17. Members of Congress most often vote according to
    a. their own policy preferences.
    b. the needs of their constituents.
    c. their relationship with the president.
    d. their party affiliation.
    e. the ideology of their geographic region.

18. Which of the following is NOT specifically prohibited by the Constitution?
    a. gender bias in the workplace
    b. self-incrimination
    c. slavery
    d. national religion
    e. cruel and unusual punishment

19. Regulatory agencies are most likely to turn to the industries they oversee when they
    a. have leaders who need campaign contributions.
    b. want to deregulate.
    c. have an unambiguous policy to implement.
    d. are making budget proposals to Congress.
    e. are trying to win general public approval.

20. The largest federal expenditure is
    a. national defense.
    b. public education.
    c. Social Security.
    d. grants to the states.
    e. political campaigns.

Entitlements and Discretionary Spending, 1963–2007

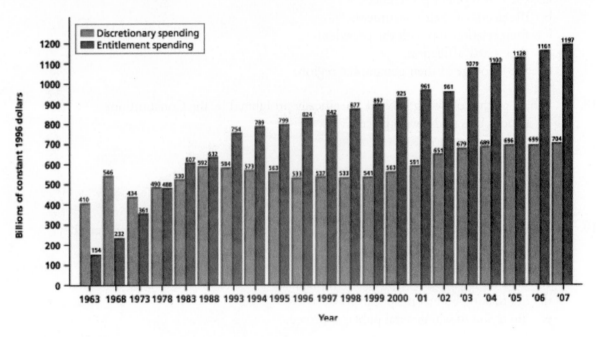

Source: United States Budget, Fiscal Year 2007, www.gpo.gov.

21. Which of the following are true of the data in the figure above?

    I. The government has always spent more on entitlements than on discretionary spending.
    II. Discretionary spending has declined over time.
    III. Entitlement spending has increased by more than 900 percent.
    IV. Entitlement and discretionary spending are at relatively equal levels.

    a. III only
    b. I and II only
    c. II and III only
    d. III and IV only
    e. I and IV only

22. The two main responsibilities of congressional committees are
    a. making and implementing policies.
    b. setting the dates for federal elections and confirming the appointment of federal judges.
    c. writing guidelines for federal programs and educating the public.
    d. reviewing proposed legislation and performing legislative oversight.
    e. suggesting candidates for cabinet positions and writing tax codes.

23. All of the following are recent trends in presidential nominations and campaigns EXCEPT
    a. declining party identification among voters.
    b. increasing costs of campaigning.
    c. decreasing importance of national conventions.
    d. increasing reliance on PACs to sustain campaigns.
    e. infrequency of presidential primaries among states.

24. Single-issue groups, as opposed to other types of groups, represent people in the electorate who
    a. have little political access and influence.
    b. donate money to political campaigns.
    c. pressure candidates to be less ambiguous about their ideology.
    d. feel strongly about a certain cause.
    e. advocate campaign finance reform.

25. Which of the following presidential appointments requires Senate confirmation?
    a. the National Security Council
    b. the Chief of Staff
    c. the White House Counsel
    d. the Council of Economic Advisors
    e. the Secretary of State

26. According to the Constitution, the vice president
    a. chairs all cabinet meetings.
    b. is ineligible to run for president after two terms as vice president.
    c. is the president of the Senate.
    d. must be of the same party as the president.
    e. is an ex officio member of the Council of Economic Advisors.

27. The Social Security program is endangered primarily because
    a. the U.S. birth rate has increased dramatically over the past decade.
    b. the program has lost public support in recent years..
    c. the number of contributors to the program is growing at a much slower rate than the number of recipients.
    d. large federal budget deficits have reduced the amount of tax revenue collected in support of the program..
    e. the program has become more identified with racial minorities.

28. The Supreme Court has upheld which of the following in its interpretation of the freedom of speech?
    a. All forms of speech, including obscenity, are protected under the First Amendment.
    b. The government cannot under any circumstances censor information.
    c. Protests against the government are not protected under the First Amendment.
    d. Forms of symbolic speech are protected under the First Amendment.
    e. The freedom of speech is guaranteed by federal law, but it does not have to be upheld by the states.

29. The rise of the primary election system has led to
    a. the increasing role of political parties in presidential elections.
    b. the public's more direct involvement in the election of the president.
    c. a decline in media coverage of presidential campaigns.
    d. a shift in power from national to state party organizations.
    e. fewer candidates seeking each party's nomination.

30. Congress exercises influence over foreign policy in which of the following ways?

   I. declaring war
   II. confirming ambassadors
   III. appropriating money
   IV. ratifying treaties

   a. I only
   b. III only
   c. I, II, and III only
   d. I, III, and IV only
   e. All of the above

31. Unlike members of the House of Representatives, senators can influence policy debates by
   a. relying on partisan support.
   b. calling for a vote.
   c. using a filibuster.
   d. forming a presidential coalition.
   e. running televised ads.

32. Bureaucracies are often criticized as being undemocratic because
   a. they are not directly accountable to the people.
   b. they utilized a merit system for hiring.
   c. citizens tend to have low opinions of them.
   d. the courts have no influence over their actions.
   e. they are overly influenced by campaign contributions.

33. All of the following influence the selection of federal judges and Supreme Court justices EXCEPT
   a. campaign contributions.
   b. partisanship.
   c. ideology.
   d. experience.
   e. judicial philosophy.

34. A president can be removed from office in which of the following ways?
   a. The Supreme Court rules that he is incompetent or has violated the law.
   b. In a recall, citizens can vote to remove the president from office.
   c. The House votes to impeach him, and the Senate tries and convicts him.
   d. The Senate votes to impeach him, and the Supreme Court tries the president.
   e. Both houses of Congress vote to remove the president by a simple majority.

35. Third parties rarely last in the American system because
   a. they encourage moderation in policymaking and discourage change.
   b. they offer voters no choice among ideologies.
   c. the rules of the U.S. political system make it hard for third parties to win elections.
   d. they deal with unimportant issues and political figures.
   e. citizens are more likely to be independents than to affiliate with a party.

36. Proponents of the pluralist theory argue that for the most part, power is evenly distributed among interest groups because
    a. the public participates equally in different types of interest groups.
    b. all interest groups receive the same amount of federal funds.
    c. each policy area is assigned a limited number of related interest groups.
    d. interest groups each get the same attention from politicians.
    e. competition prevents any one group from becoming more influential.

37. The government institution responsible for drawing congressional district lines is the
    a. state's governor.
    b. Senate Committee on Governmental Affairs.
    c. state's legislature, or its delegated body (Ohio has an apportionment board).
    d. House Rules Committee.
    e. Department of the Interior.

38. All of the following are true of two-party systems, EXCEPT
    a. They encourage extremism in policymaking and encourage change.
    b. They offer voters no choice among ideologies.
    c. They usually include a liberal and a conservative party.
    d. They rely on popular elections to change the party in power.
    e. They allow parties to choose their own leaders in the legislature.

39. The media has the most influence over which of the following aspects of the presidential selection process?
    a. the way electoral votes are distributed
    b. the outcome of the popular election
    c. who decides to run for office
    d. the outcome of primary elections
    e. the party's national convention

40. The framers' distrust of the public when writing the Constitution is best illustrated by the
    a. Electoral College.
    b. Bill of Rights.
    c. process of electing members to the House of Representatives.
    d. creation of a bicameral legislature.
    e. ability to amend the Constitution.

41. Congress increased the power of the federal government to enforce regulations in employment by passing the
    a. Fourteenth Amendment.
    b. Civil Rights Act.
    c. Fifteenth Amendment.
    d. Equal Rights Amendment.
    e. Voting Rights Act.

42. The Hatch Act helps maintain a nonpartisan bureaucracy because it
    a. creates a federal commission on which half the members are Democrats and half are Republican.
    b. ensures that federal employees are hired based on merit.
    c. requires all federal employees to register to vote as independents.
    d. requires all federal agencies to have staffs that are balanced along party lines.
    e. prohibits government employees in their official capacities from active participation in partisan politics.

43. In *Miranda v. Arizona*, the Supreme Court ruled that persons accused of a crime
    a. cannot be denied bail.
    b. have the right to a fair trial.
    c. have rights during police questioning.
    d. have equal protection under the law.
    e. cannot be searched illegally.

44. The principle that the Constitution gives states all powers that are neither granted to the federal government nor denied the states refers to
    a. states' rights.
    b. reserved powers.
    c. federal supremacy.
    d. concurrent powers.
    e. federalism.

45. Critical elections tend to occur under which of the following circumstances?
    a. when a third-party candidate wins some electoral votes
    b. after a presidential scandal has been exposed in the media
    c. when the United States engages in a military operation
    d. after a serious domestic crisis alters the political agenda
    e. when one of the parties suffers a major defeat in a congressional election

46. Which of the following statements is true about Congress' influence over Supreme Court decision making?
    a. Congress can pass laws to prohibit judicial activism.
    b. The Senate can filibuster court decisions.
    c. Congress has significant control over the court's appellate jurisdiction.
    d. The Senate can decide which cases the Supreme Court will hear.
    e. District court judges are reviewed by Congress every 10 years.

47. Which of the following statements are true of political parties?

    I. The United States has a multiparty system.
    II. The electorate is becoming increasingly independent of political parties.
    III. The use of television advertising allows candidates more independence from their political parties.
    IV. Political party organizations are exercising greater control over the choice of candidates.

    a. II only
    b. III only
    c. II and III only
    d. I, III, and IV only
    e. II, III, and IV only

48. Each of the following helps explain the incumbency advantage of members of Congress EXCEPT
    a. the franking privilege.
    b. the pattern of campaign contributions.
    c. casework.
    d. the low standing of Congress in public opinion.
    e. name recognition.

49. Implementation of public policy is most successful when
    a. the goals of the policy and the authority of the implementers are clear.
    b. there is a court order mandating compliance with the policy.
    c. the executive branch has precleared the policy with the federal judiciary.
    d. multiple agencies and bureaucrats are involved.
    e. the policy originated in the executive branch as opposed to the legislative branch.

50. Interest groups differ from political parties in which of the following ways?
    a. Interest groups link the public to the political process.
    b. Interest groups pursue general policy goals in the political arena.
    c. Interest groups try to shape specific policy goals.
    d. Interest groups are not allowed to play any part in political campaigns.
    e. Interest groups unite politicians with the same political ideology.

51. Which of the following is true of relationships between the president and Congress?
    a. Presidents usually have little success in forming presidential coalitions in Congress.
    b. Presidents work mostly with minority party leaders to win minority support.
    c. Policy gridlock results when the president's party is not the majority in Congress.
    d. Members of Congress almost always vote in favor of presidential initiatives.
    e. Presidents usually have closer relationships with members of the House than they do with senators.

52. The elderly fare better than the poor in social welfare budget battles for which of the following reasons?
   a. The Constitution requires a certain amount of spending for the elderly, but not the poor.
   b. Most social services for the elderly come from state governments.
   c. Lobbyists representing the poor are not allowed to make campaign contributions.
   d. The elderly are more organized and better represented politically than the poor.
   e. There are more elderly people in the US than there are poor people.

53. Which of the following statements accurately describes iron triangles?
   a. Iron triangles are composed of members of the military-industrial complex, Congress, and the Department of Defense.
   b. Iron triangles are formed in specific policy areas to advance policies among groups that benefit each other mutually.
   c. Iron triangles are formed to generate support for presidential proposals in Congress.
   d. Iron triangles help coordinate policy among the executive, legislative, and judicial branches.
   e. Iron triangles help perform policy implementation among the local, state, and federal levels of government.

54. Which of the following statements represent a prevalent myth about the federal bureaucracy?

   I. The bureaucracy is growing bigger and bigger each year.
   II. Most federal bureaucrats work in Washington, D.C.
   III. Citizens are generally dissatisfied with the bureaucracy.
   IV. The bureaucracy makes government inefficient and cumbersome.

   a. I only
   b. IV only
   c. I and II only
   d. II, III, and IV only
   e. All of the above

55. The establishment clause, as interpreted by the Supreme Court, prevents
   a. states from passing laws that conflict with federal laws.
   b. the government from violating the rights of individuals.
   c. Congress from exercising any powers beyond those necessary to execute the law.
   d. gender discrimination in the workplace.
   e. the incorporation of religion into policy.

56. *Regents of the University of California v. Bakke* is a Supreme Court case that addressed
   a. affirmative action.
   b. prayer in school.
   c. the rights of the accused.
   d. the right of privacy.
   e. desegregation through busing.

57. One of a president's most powerful tools for gaining support of his proposals is
    a. his financial resources.
    b. executive privilege.
    c. "going public" to sway public opinion.
    d. senatorial courtesy.
    e. his cabinet.

58. Which of the following statements accurately describe traditional Republican Party economic positions?

    I.   Republicans place greater emphasis on full employment than Democrats do.
    II. Republicans tend to worry about inflation more than Democrats do.
    III. Republican economic positions tend to appeal to the working class and unions.
    IV. Republicans tend to favor higher income tax rates.

    a. I only
    b. II only
    c. II and III only
    d. I and IV only
    e. I, II, and III only

59. Members of Congress are more likely to vote according to their personal ideology when
    a. the issue is not well known by their constituents.
    b. they are up for reelection.
    c. the piece of legislation was introduced by the president.
    d. they are on the committee responsible for the piece of legislation.
    e. interest groups have been actively involved with the piece of legislation.

60. In the era of globalization, which of the following presidential powers is becoming important?
    a. vetoing legislation
    b. negotiating economic agreements
    c. declaring war
    d. authorizing the use of weapons of mass destruction
    e. appointment of Supreme Court justices

END OF SECTION I.

IF YOU FINISH BEFORE TIME IS CALLED, YOU MAY CHECK YOUR WORK ON THIS SECTION.

DO NOT GO ON TO SECTION II UNTIL YOU ARE TOLD TO DO SO.

❑ Government and Politics: United States

Section II
Time: 100 minutes

Directions: *You have 100 minutes to answer all four of the following questions. It is suggested that you take a few minutes to plan and outline each answer.* Spend approximately one-fourth of your time (25 minutes) on each question. *Illustrate your essay with substantive examples where appropriate. Make certain to number each of your answers as the question is numbered below.*

1. In the American democracy, political parties use two different systems for selecting delegates to the national party conventions that nominate presidential candidates.

    a. Describe how caucuses select delegates to the national convention.

    b. Describe how primaries select delegates to the national convention.

    c. Explain one consequence of "frontloading" the delegate selection process.

2. The mass media has a major effect on politics in the United States. It has both positive and negative consequences for the political process.

    a. Describe two positives effects that the media has on the political process.

    b. Describe two negative effects that the media has on the political process.

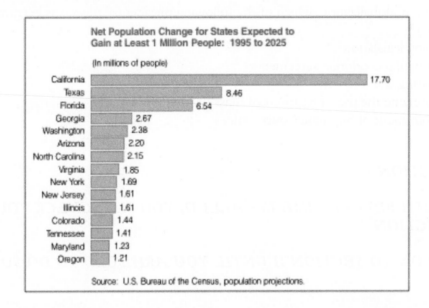

3. The above graph shows population projections for the first quarter of the 21st century. All of the states listed are expected to gain at least a million people in the next few decades. Using the data above and your knowledge of U.S. government and politics, identify and

explain THREE ways that these shifting populations will have an impact on government and politics.

4.   The Tenth Amendment reserves for the states all powers neither denied nor designated to the federal government in the Constitution. For decades, this afforded states a good deal of freedom in writing their state laws. However, the ratification of the Fourteenth Amendment allowed the Supreme Court to exercise its authority over the states in an attempt to advance the civil liberties of all Americans.

   a.   What provision of the Fourteenth Amendment has been used by the Supreme Court to exercise its authority over the states for the purpose of advancing civil liberties?

   b.   Identify two areas in which civil liberties protections have been extended to the states, and discuss the specific case(s) that accomplished this task in each area.

END OF EXAMINATION

☐ Answers and Explanations

Practice Test 1
Section I

1. Political action committees (PACs) were created by campaign reform laws to

    (a) is incorrect because PACs were created to limit the amount of money interest groups can contribute, not to increase public involvement in presidential campaigns.

    (b) is correct because political action committees were created by the Federal Election Campaign Act of 1974 to regulate how much business, labor, and other groups could contribute to a candidate's election.

    (c) is incorrect because PACs were created to limit the amount of money interest groups can donate to a campaign, not to limit the advantages of incumbency.

    (d) is incorrect because PACs were created to limit the amount of money interest groups can donate to a campaign, not specifically to pay for air time.

    (e) is incorrect because PACs were created to limit the amount of money interest groups can donate to a campaign, not to limit the influence of political parties.

    Page reference: 302, AP Topic: Interest Groups

2. All of the following are examples of entitlement programs EXCEPT

    (a) is incorrect because Social Security is an example of an entitlement program.

    (b) is incorrect because Medicare is an example of an entitlement program.

    (c) is correct because entitlement programs are a form of mandatory spending because everyone entitled to the benefits of the program must be paid. Congress cannot control these expenditures unless it changes the eligibility requirements of the program. Defense contracts clearly do not fit this definition.

    (d) is incorrect because veteran benefits are an example of an entitlement program.

    (e) is incorrect because agricultural subsidies are an example of an entitlement program.

    Page reference: 460, AP Topic: Political Parties

3. Which of the following generalizations is supported by the information in the chart above?

    (a) is correct because according to the data in the chart, the number of nonconnected PACs nearly tripled between 1980 and 1985 alone, increasing from 374 to 1,003.

(b) is incorrect because the most dramatic change in the number of PACs occurred between 1980 and 2001.

(c) is incorrect because the fact that there are only a few cooperative PACs does not answer the question.

(d) is incorrect because the fact that the business PACs spend the most money does not answer the question.

(e) is incorrect because all types of PACs have not grown dramatically since 1980.

Page reference: 302, AP Topic: Interest Groups

4.   Federal district courts are the only federal courts in which

(a) is incorrect because the facts are presented only by the prosecution in federal district court.

(b) is incorrect because *amicus curiae* briefs are use in the Supreme Court, not federal district courts.

(c) is incorrect because the solicitor general gives oral arguments before the Supreme Court, not in federal district courts.

(d) is correct because federal district courts function like state trial courts and use a jury to decide cases.

(e) is incorrect because a three-judge panel is used in the Court of Appeals, not in federal district courts.

Page reference: 513, AP Topic: Federal Courts

5.   The government began to pursue civil rights in the 1950s when

(a) is incorrect because the Voting Rights act was passed in 1965.

(b) is incorrect because the March on Washington was in 1963.

(c) is correct because the Supreme Court's 1954 landmark decision in *Brown v. Board of Education* overturned segregation in public education which began "the Second Reconstruction," in which the Court, Congress, and the executive took steps to advance civil rights.

(d) is incorrect because poll taxes were abolished by the 24th Amendment in 1964.

(e) is incorrect because public transportation was desegregated in the 1960s by a Supreme Court ruling, not an executive order.

Page reference: 180, AP Topic: Civil Rights

6. Which of the following statements about the president as commander in chief is true?

(a) is incorrect because the president cannot declare war.

(b) is correct because as commander in chief of military forces, the president decides if and when American armed forces use weapons of mass destruction in times of war.

(c) is incorrect because a president's past military experience does not affect the exercise of executive powers.

(d) is incorrect because the president does not have to consult the Joint Chiefs of Staff before deploying the military.

(e) is incorrect because the Senate Armed Services Committee is part of the legislative branch and the president is not a member of that committee.

Page reference: 419, AP Topics: Presidency

7. Interest groups play a role in the federal judicial process in all of the following ways EXCEPT by

(a) is correct because federal judges are appointed, not elected, and therefore do not receive campaign contributions from interest groups.

(b) is incorrect because interest groups can influence the federal judicial process by lobbying the judiciary Committee concerning a judicial nominee.

(c) is incorrect because interest groups can influence the federal judicial process by submitting *amicus curiae* briefs to the courts.

(d) is incorrect because interest groups can influence the federal judicial process by having attorneys represent a plaintiff in a case.

(e) is incorrect because interest groups can influence the federal judicial process by filing a class action suit with the court.

Page reference: 513, AP Topics: The Federal Courts and Interest Groups

8. Presidents exercise their influence over the ideology of federal courts by

(a) is correct because presidents work hard to seek and appoint judges who agree with their own political ideology. Not only would the judges be more likely to favor the president's agenda, but also (because they have no term limits) they would continue to influence policy long after the president's term has ended.

(b) is incorrect because the president cannot order Congress to impeach judges.

(c) is incorrect because the president cannot demote judges to lower courts.

(d) is incorrect because the president has no control over cases heard by the federal courts.

(e) is incorrect because the president does not meet with the Senate Judiciary Committee when it is performing its oversight function.

Page reference: 419, AP Topics: Federal Courts and the Presidency

9. The electoral votes of most states are allocated by which of the following methods?

(a) is incorrect because electoral votes are not cast on a percentage basis.

(b) is incorrect because electoral votes are typically cast according to party affiliation.

(c) is incorrect because electoral votes are cast "winner-take-all."

(d) is correct because most states award their electoral votes in a "winner-take-all" system which means the candidate who wins the popular vote in the state receives all of that state's electoral votes.

(e) is incorrect because the loser in a state election does not receive any electoral votes.

Page reference: 419, AP Topics: Presidency and Electoral laws and systems

10. Which of the following groups is most likely to vote in elections?

(a) is incorrect because young people do not have a high voter turnout percentage.

(b) is correct because senior citizens tend to be the most active and informed group in the electorate, especially because Social Security and health care have become major political issues, therefore they have the highest voter turnout.

(c) is incorrect because people who do not have a college degree also do not have a high voter turnout percentage.

(d) is incorrect because people who do not have a party affiliation also do not have a high voter turnout percentage.

(e) is incorrect because people of low income do not have a high voter turnout percentage.

Page reference: 311, AP Topic: Factors that influence citizens to differ from one another in terms of political beliefs and behaviors

11. The Supreme Court asserted which of the following principles in *Marbury v. Madison*?

(a) is incorrect because *Marbury v. Madison* did not relate to the individual freedoms in the 14th Amendment.

(b) is incorrect because *Marbury v. Madison* did not relate to the establishment clause.

(c) is incorrect because *Marbury v. Madison* did not relate to the 10th Amendment.

(d) is incorrect because *Marbury v. Madison* did not relate to the exclusionary rule.

(e) is correct because in the 1803 case of *Marbury v. Madison*, the Supreme Court under Chief Justice John Marshall first asserted its power of judicial review, which allows the Supreme Court, whose responsibility is to interpret the Constitution, to declare laws passed by Congress unconstitutional.

Page reference: 513, AP Topic: Federal Courts

12. In the process of political socialization, individuals

(a) is correct because political socialization is the process through which citizens learn about government and form their political beliefs. Family, school, the media, and religion play major parts in influencing how people see the government and with which party they identify themselves.

(b) is incorrect because political socialization is not related to any particular form of government.

(c) is incorrect because political socialization is not dependent upon participation in organized political parties.

(d) is incorrect because political socialization is not related to the evaluation and selection of representatives.

(e) is incorrect because political socialization is not dependent upon engaging in political protest against a law.

Page reference: 35, AP Topic: Beliefs that citizens hold about their government and its leaders

13. The failure of the Articles of Confederation and necessity for a new Constitution were made evident by the

(a) is incorrect because the American Revolution made it possible to create the Articles of Confederation.

(b) is incorrect because the Articles of Confederation lacked an executive branch.

(c) is incorrect because a bicameral legislature was not an issue related to the failure of the Articles of Confederation.

(d) is correct because under the Articles of Confederation, the national government was not able to raise a militia to stop Shays' Rebellion, and so the event was an embarrassing failure for the new government. It served as the final proof that the government established by the Articles lacked centralized power and legitimacy.

(e) is incorrect because under the Articles of Confederation there was no centralized government.

Page reference: 43, AP Topic: Considerations that influenced the formulation and adoption of the Constitution

14. Voter turnout in the United States is low in part because

(a) is incorrect because the right to vote has been secured for minorities in the Southern states and elsewhere.

(b) is incorrect because registering to vote has become less difficult, not more difficult.

(c) is correct because people who have not voted often cite the generally indistinguishable ideologies of the candidates of the two parties as one major reason for their inaction.

(d) is incorrect because literacy tests have been abolished.

(e) is incorrect because candidates spend enormous amounts of time and energy to attract voters.

Page reference: 314, AP Topic: The ways in which citizens vote and otherwise participate in political life

15. Which of the following statements is true about U.S. budget deficits?

(a) is incorrect because the U.S. has almost continually had a deficit.

(b) is incorrect because the Constitution does not have a provision requiring a balanced budget.

(c) is correct because large budget deficits make the U.S. government more financially dependent on foreign investors, other governments, and individuals.

(d) is incorrect because budget deficits impact the U.S. economy and therefore do have an effect on individual citizens.

(e) is incorrect because the deficit is typically a major issue in presidential campaigns.

Page reference: 445, AP Topic: Institutions of the National Government

16. Congress performs legislative oversight over executive departments by

(a) is incorrect because Congress cannot hire and fire department heads in the executive departments.

(b) is correct because one of the ways Congress oversees the activities of the departments in the executive branch is by determining their budgets and deciding how much each department can spend on its programs and activities.

(c) is incorrect because Congress does not have the power to veto proposals in the executive departments.

(d) is incorrect because the president has the power of impoundment, not Congress.

(e) is incorrect because Congress does not coordinate department activities with the president.

Page reference: 366, AP Topic: Relationships among the four institutions and varying balances of power

17. Members of Congress most often vote according to

(a) is incorrect because members of Congress only occasionally vote according to their own preferences.

(b) is incorrect because members of Congress only occasionally vote according to the needs of their constituents.

(c) is incorrect because members of Congress only occasionally vote according to their relationship with the president.

(d) is correct because members of Congress most often vote according to their party affiliation based on the presumption that in doing so, they may also be voting according to their constituency's preferences.

(e) is incorrect because members of Congress only occasionally vote according to the ideology of their geographic region.

Page reference: 366, AP Topics: The Congress and Political Parties

18. Which of the following is NOT specifically prohibited by the Constitution?

(a) is correct because gender discrimination is not specifically addressed in the Constitution or its amendments, however, it is prohibited by law as a form of civil rights discrimination.

(b) is incorrect because self-incrimination is prohibited by the 5th Amendment.

(c) is incorrect because slavery is prohibited by the 13th Amendment.

(d) is incorrect because a national religion is prohibited by the 1st Amendment.

(e) is incorrect because cruel and unusual punishment is prohibited by the 8th Amendment.

Page reference: 56, AP Topic: Constitutional Underpinnings of the United States Government

19. Regulatory agencies are most likely to turn to the industries they oversee when they

(a) is incorrect because leaders of regulatory agencies are appointed, not elected.

(b) is incorrect because regulatory agencies are involved in oversight, not deregulation.

(c) is incorrect because implementation policies are typically very specific.

(d) is correct because industries increase their lobbying pressure during the budgetary process to convince the relevant committees of their need for the money they have requested.

(e) is incorrect because regulatory agencies are typically not concerned with winning public approval.

Page reference: 495, AP Topic: Linkages between policy processes

20.   The largest federal expenditure is

(a) is incorrect because national defense represents a smaller percentage of the budget than Social Security.

(b) is incorrect because public education represents a smaller percentage of the budget than Social Security.

(c) is correct because in the past few decades, Social Security has become the largest federal expenditure. It alone accounts for nearly a quarter of all expenditures.

(d) is incorrect because grants to the states represent a smaller percentage of the budget than Social Security.

(e) is incorrect because public financing of political campaigns is rare and therefore represents a smaller percentage of the budget than Social Security.

Page reference: 445, AP Topic: Linkages between policy processes

21.   Which of the following are true of the data in the figure above?

(a) is correct because entitlement spending has increased exponentially since 1963 and today it encompasses a majority of the federal budget.

(b) is incorrect because discretionary spending has not declined over time and the government has not always spent more money on entitlements than on discretionary spending.

(c) is incorrect because discretionary spending has not declined over time and entitlement spending has not increased over 900 percent.

(d) is incorrect because entitlement spending has not increased over 900 percent and entitlement and discretionary spending are not at relatively equal levels.

(e) is incorrect because the government has not always spent more money on entitlements than on discretionary spending, and entitlement and discretionary spending are not at relatively equal levels.

Page reference: 445, AP Topic: The major formal and informal institutional arrangements of power

22. The two main responsibilities of congressional committees are

(a) is incorrect because making and implementing policies are not functions of congressional committees.

(b) is incorrect because setting the dates for federal elections and confirming appointments are not functions of congressional committees.

(c) is incorrect because writing guidelines for federal programs and educating the public are not functions of congressional committees.

(d) is correct because congressional committees review and assess bills for their feasibility and consequences and revise them, kill, them or pass them with a recommendation. Congressional committees also perform oversight of all the federal departments and agencies by setting their budgets and assessing their performance and activities in committee hearings.

(e) is incorrect because suggesting candidates for cabinet positions and writing tax codes are not functions of congressional committees.

Page reference: 366, AP Topic: Congress

23. All of the following are recent trends in presidential nominations and campaigns EXCEPT

(a) is incorrect because party identification among voters is declining.

(b) is incorrect because campaign costs are increasing.

(c) is incorrect because national conventions are decreasing in importance.

(d) is incorrect because reliance on PACs to sustain campaigns is increasing.

(e) is correct because the use of presidential primaries has been increasing, not decreasing.

Page reference: 419, AP Topics: Presidency and Elections

24. Single-issue groups, as opposed to other types of groups, represent people in the electorate who

(a) is incorrect because many groups have access and influence in the political process.

(b) is incorrect because many groups donate money to political campaigns to advance their issue.

(c) is incorrect because many groups pressure candidates to take a stand on their issue.

(d) is correct because single-issue groups attract people who feel very strongly about one particular issue, such as abortion or gun control, which often incite emotional responses.

(e) is incorrect because many groups advocate campaign finance reform.

Page reference: 387, AP Topic: Interest Groups

25. Which of the following presidential appointments requires Senate confirmation?

(a) is incorrect because the National Security Council is part of the president's personal staff of advisors and does not need to be approved by the Senate.

(b) is incorrect because the chief of staff is part of the president's personal staff of advisors and does not need to be approved by the Senate.

(c) is incorrect because the White House counsel is part of the president's personal staff of advisors and does not need to be approved by the Senate.

(d) is incorrect because the Council of Economic Advisors is considered to be part of the president's personal staff of advisors and does not need to be approved by the Senate.

(e) is correct because the secretary of state is a member of the president's cabinet and nominees for this post must be confirmed by the Senate.

Page reference: 419, AP Topics: Presidency and Congress; Relationships among these four institutions and varying balances of power

26. According to the Constitution, the vice president

(a) is incorrect because the vice president does not chair cabinet meetings.

(b) is incorrect because the vice president is eligible to run for president even after serving two terms as vice president.

(c) is correct because the Constitution assigns vice presidents the relatively minor tasks of presiding over the Senate and voting in case of a tie among the senators.

(d) is incorrect because the vice president is not required to belong to a particular political party.

(e) is incorrect because the vice president is not a member of the Council of Economic Advisors.

Page reference: 409, AP Topics: Presidency and Constitution

27. The Social Security program is endangered primarily because

(a) is incorrect because the U.S. birth rate has not increased over the past decade.

(b) is incorrect because Social Security has not lost support in recent years.

(c) is correct because the Social Security dilemma is that the number of Social Security contributors (the workers) is growing slowly, while the number of recipients (the retired) is growing rapidly.

(d) is incorrect because tax revenues collected to support the program have not significantly declined.

(e) is incorrect because the program is identified with the elderly and not with racial minorities.

Page reference: 457, AP Topics: Public Policy and the role of institutions in the enactment of policy

28.   The Supreme Court has upheld which of the following in its interpretation of the freedom of speech?

(a) is incorrect because obscenity is not a protected form of speech.

(b) is incorrect because under certain circumstances, the government can censor information.

(c) is incorrect because protests against the government are protected under the First Amendment.

(d) is correct because in the 1989 case of *Texas v. Johnson*, the Supreme Court determined that flag burning, a form of symbolic speech, is protected under the First Amendment.

(e) is incorrect because the freedom of speech does have to be upheld by the states.

Page reference: 527, AP Topics: Constitution, Federal Courts, and Civil Rights

29.   The rise of the primary election system has led to

(a) is incorrect because primaries decrease the role of political parties in presidential elections.

(b) is correct because primary elections give voters the opportunity to participate more directly in the presidential election process which circumvents the traditional role of political parties in the nomination process, especially when a blanket primary is used.

(c) is incorrect because media coverage of presidential campaigns has increased, not decreased.

(d) is incorrect because primaries have not shifted power to state party organizations, but to the people.

(e) is incorrect because the number of candidates seeking each party's nomination is increasing.

Page reference: 292, AP Topics: Presidency and Elections

30.   Congress exercises influence over foreign policy in which of the following ways?

(a) is incorrect because declaring war is only one way Congress exercises influence over foreign policy.

(b) is incorrect because appropriating money is only one way Congress exercises influence over foreign policy.

(c) is incorrect because declaring war, confirming ambassadors and appropriating money are only three of the ways Congress influences foreign policy.

(d) is incorrect because declaring war, appropriating money and ratifying treaties are only three of the ways Congress influences foreign policy.

(e) is correct because Congress exercises influence over foreign policy through its powers to declare war, appropriate funds, ratify treaties, and confirm ambassadors to foreign nations.

Page reference: 366, AP Topics: Congress and the Presidency

31.   Unlike members of the House of Representatives, senators can influence policy debates by

(a) is incorrect because members of the House can also use partisan support to influence policy debates.

(b) is incorrect because members of the House can also call for a vote to influence policy debates.

(c) is correct because only senators have the ability to use a filibuster to hold up debate on a bill. The Senate imposes no restrictions on the length of time for debate over a piece of legislation, so senators are free to talk as long as it takes for their colleagues to lose interest and choose not to vote on the bill.

(d) is incorrect because members of the House can also for a presidential coalition to influence policy debates.

(e) is incorrect because member of the House can also run television ads to influence policy debates.

Page reference: 489, AP Topics: Congress and Public Policy

32.   Bureaucracies are often criticized as being undemocratic because

(a) is correct because although they make vital decisions and perform essential services for government and the people, bureaucrats are not directly accountable to citizens the way the president and Congress are. This has led to the criticism that the bureaucracy is an undemocratic branch of government.

(b) is incorrect because the merit based system is democratic.

(c) is incorrect because low opinions do not relate to being undemocratic.

(d) is incorrect because the fact that the courts have no control over bureaucracies is not relevant.

(e) is incorrect because bureaucracies are not influenced by campaign contributions.

Page reference: 489, AP Topics: The role of institutions in the enactment of policy and the role of the Bureaucracy

33.   All of the following influence the selection of federal judges and Supreme Court justices EXCEPT

(a) is correct because there is no evidence that campaign contributions to presidential races are a major factor in determining a president's nominees for federal judgeships.

(b) is incorrect because partisanship does influence the selection of judges.

(c) is incorrect because ideology does influence the selection of judges.

(d) is incorrect because experience does influence the selection of judges.

(e) is incorrect because judicial philosophy does influence the selection of judges.

Page reference: 527, AP Topics: The Presidency and the Courts

34.   A president can be removed from office in which of the following ways?

(a) is incorrect because the Supreme Court does not rule in impeachment proceedings.

(b) is incorrect because the president cannot be removed by a recall vote.

(c) is correct because the impeachment process set forth in the Constitution provides that the House votes to impeach the president then the Senate tries the president and can convict and remove with a two-thirds vote.

(d) is incorrect because the Senate tries the president but does not impeach.

(e) is incorrect because only the Senate votes to remove the president from office.

Page reference: 419, AP Topics: The Presidency and the Congress

35.   Third parties rarely last in the American system because

(a) is incorrect because third parties encourage change and discourage moderation.

(b) is incorrect because third parties do offer a choice among ideologies.

(c) is correct because the winner-take-all system used in American legislative elections and in apportioning most states' Electoral College votes makes it very hard for third parties to win substantial representation in government.

(d) is incorrect because third parties deal with important issues and political figures.

(e) is incorrect because the fact that third parties are independents does not cause them to fail.

Page reference: 277, AP Topic: Political Parties

36. Proponents of the pluralist theory argue that for the most part, power is evenly distributed among interest groups because

(a) is incorrect because the public does not participate equally in interest groups.

(b) is incorrect because interest groups do not receive equal federal funding.

(c) is incorrect because interest groups are not limited in number nor are they assigned to particular policy areas.

(d) is incorrect because interest groups do not get the same attention from politicians.

(e) is correct because pluralist believe that interest groups have about the same amount of power because they must compete with each other for influence.

Page reference: 16, AP Topics: Interest Groups and Policymaking

37. The government institution responsible for drawing congressional district lines is the

(a) is incorrect because a state's governor does not draw congressional district lines.

(b) is incorrect because a Senate committee does not draw congressional district lines.

(c) is correct because state legislatures have the task of drawing congressional district lines for their state and if seats must be reapportioned or redistricted, bases on the census, the state legislature, or a body it designates, redraws district lines.

(d) is incorrect because the House Rules Committee does not draw congressional district lines.

(e) is incorrect because the Department of the Interior does not draw congressional district lines.

Page reference: 489, AP Topics: Elections, Congress, Federalism

38. All of the following are true of two-party systems, EXCEPT

(a) is correct because with only two parties offering policy alternatives, there is little opportunity or incentive for political change. Each party, to draw in a majority of the electorate, stays toward the middle of the road and maintains the status quo.

(b) is incorrect because offering no choice of ideologies is a correct description of the two-party system.

(c) is incorrect because including a liberal and conservative party is a correct description of the two-party system.

(d) is incorrect because relying on popular elections to change the party in power is a correct description of the two-party system.

(e) is incorrect because allowing parties to choose their own legislative leadership is a correct description of the two-party system.

Page reference: 277, AP Topic: Political Parties

39.   The media has the most influence over which of the following aspects of the presidential selection process?

(a) is incorrect because the media does not influence the way electoral votes are distributed.

(b) is incorrect because the media does not have as much influence over the popular election as the primary elections.

(c) is incorrect because the media does not have as much impact on who decides to run for office as it has on primary elections.

(d) is correct because one of the major criticisms held against the primary system is that it allows the media too much influence over election results, particularly in the early primaries. Media attention skews the results by branding winners and losers so early in the campaign process that losers have little chance to score victories in later primaries.

(e) is incorrect because the media does not have as much impact on a party's national convention as it has on primary elections.

Page reference: 246, AP Topics: Elections and the Media

40.   The framers' distrust of the public when writing the Constitution is best illustrated by the

(a) is correct because the authors of the Constitution were a group of elite intellectuals who distrusted leaving government too much in the hands of the uneducated masses. Therefore, they arranged for the president to be chosen by the Electoral College, a group of chosen electors, rather than by the public at large.

(b) is incorrect because the Bill of Rights lists the rights of the public at large and does not indicate a sense of mistrust.

(c) is incorrect because House members are directly elected by the people and does not indicate a sense of mistrust.

(d) is incorrect because the creation of a bicameral legislature does not directly relate to the people.

(e) is incorrect because the ability to amend the Constitution requires input from the state level and does not indicate a sense of mistrust.

Page reference: 35, AP Topic: The Constitution

41. Congress increased the power of the federal government to enforce regulations in employment by passing the

(a) is incorrect because the 14th amendment does not specifically relate to employment.

(b) is correct because by passing the Civil Rights Act of 1964, Congress outlawed discrimination in the workplace, and consequently, the Justice Department was granted authority to enforce equality in employment and to pursue violators of the Civil Rights Act.

(c) is incorrect because the 15th amendment does not relate to employment.

(d) is incorrect because the Equal Rights amendment was not ratified.

(e) is incorrect because the Voting Rights Act does not relate to employment.

Page reference: 366, AP Topic: Civil Rights

42. The Hatch Act helps maintain a nonpartisan bureaucracy because it

(a) is incorrect because the Hatch Act does not create a partisan commission.

(b) is incorrect because the Hatch Act does not create a merit-based hiring system.

(c) is incorrect because the Hatch Act does not require employees to register as independents.

(d) is incorrect because the Hatch Act does not require a party balance among employees.

(e) is correct because the Hatch Act, originally passed in 1939 and amended most recently in 1993, prohibits civil service employees from actively participating in partisan politics while on duty.

Page reference: 493, AP Topic: Bureaucracy

43. In *Miranda v. Arizona*, the Supreme Court ruled that persons accused of a crime

(a) is incorrect because the *Miranda* decision did not address bail.

(b) is incorrect because the *Miranda* decision did not address the right to a fair trial.

(c) is correct because the Supreme Court enhanced the rights of the accused in its decision in *Miranda v. Arizona*, which required that all people arrested for a crime be informed of their rights before questioning.

(d) is incorrect because the *Miranda* decision did not guarantee equal protection under the law.

(e) is incorrect because the *Miranda* decision did not address searches.

Page reference: 134, AP Topic: Civil Rights

44. The principle that the Constitution gives states all powers that are neither granted to the federal government nor denied the states refers to

(a) is incorrect because states' rights is a doctrine of strict interpretation of the Constitution as opposed to the specific creation of reserved powers by the 10th Amendment.

(b) is correct because the Tenth Amendment articulates the reserved powers of the states by stating all powers not denied by the Constitution or specifically designated to the federal government are held by the states.

(c) is incorrect because federal supremacy is the opposite of reserved powers.

(d) is incorrect because concurrent powers are those shared with the national government and not the powers which belong only to the states.

(e) is incorrect because federalism relates to the geographic division of government and not specifically to the powers of the government.

Page reference: 40, AP Topics: The Constitution and Federalism

45. Critical elections tend to occur under which of the following circumstances?

(a) is incorrect because a third party candidate winning electoral votes does not constitute a critical election.

(b) is incorrect because a presidential scandal does not constitute a critical election.

(c) is incorrect because a military operation does not constitute a critical election.

(d) is correct because most critical elections follow a serious domestic problem that significantly alters the political landscape, such as The Great Depression.

(e) is incorrect because a major party defeat in a congressional election does not constitute a critical election.

Page reference: 364, AP Topic: Elections

46. Which of the following statements is true about Congress' influence over Supreme Court decision making?

(a) is incorrect because Congress cannot pass a law to prohibit judicial activism.

(b) is incorrect because Congress cannot filibuster court decisions.

(c) is correct because in many instances federal courts' jurisdiction derives from Congress and not the Constitution due to the fact that the Constitution provides Congress with the discretion to determine which category of cases appellate courts may hear.

(d) is incorrect because the Senate cannot decide which cases the Supreme Court hears.

(e) is incorrect because district court judges are not reviewed by Congress.

Page reference: 366, AP Topics: Congress and the Courts

47. Which of the following statements are true of political parties?

(a) is incorrect because it provides only one true statement about political parties.

(b) is incorrect because it provides only one true statement about political parties.

(c) is correct because political parties are losing power due to the fact that both candidates and voters have come to rely less on them. Because candidates can address voters directly through television, the public does not have to fall back on party identification to choose candidates. At the same time, candidates who use television do not need their party to help attract voters as much as in the past.

(d) is incorrect because statements I and IV are not true statements about political parties.

(e) is incorrect because statement IV is not a true statement about political parties.

Page reference: 381, AP Topics: Elections and Political Parties

48. Each of the following helps explain the incumbency advantage of members of Congress EXCEPT

(a) is incorrect because the franking privilege deals with free postage and not incumbency advantage.

(b) is incorrect because the pattern of campaign contributions does not relate to incumbency advantage.

(c) is incorrect because casework does not guarantee or negate incumbency advantage.

(d) is correct because more than 90 percent of all congressional incumbents seeking reelection win and this occurs in spite of the fact that people hold a low opinion of Congress as an institution.

(e) is incorrect because name recognition does not guarantee or negate incumbency advantage.

Page reference: 366, AP Topic: Public Opinion and Voters

49. Implementation of public policy is most successful when

(a) is correct because if the goals of a policy are not clear to those who have to implement it, and if those who have to implement lack the authority to act definitively, then the policy in question is not likely to be well implemented or received.

(b) is incorrect because a court order mandating compliance does not guarantee ease of implementation.

(c) is incorrect because the executive preclearing the policy does not guarantee ease of implementation.

(d) is incorrect because the fact that there are multiple agencies and bureaucrats involved makes it more difficult to implement policies.

(e) is incorrect because the origin of the policy does not impact the implementation of a policy.

Page reference: 248, AP Topic: Bureaucracy

50. Interest groups differ from political parties in which of the following ways?

(a) is incorrect because interest groups do not necessarily link the public to the political process.

(b) is incorrect because interest groups pursue specific policy goals.

(c) is correct because interest groups concentrate most of their efforts on shaping policy during the political process and they maintain frequent contact with lawmakers while Congress is in session. Political parties, on the other hand, try to shape the policy agenda by having their candidates elected to office and they therefore apply their efforts mostly to campaigns.

(d) is incorrect because interest groups due play a part in political campaigns.

(e) is incorrect because interest groups do not necessarily unite politicians.

Page reference: 387, AP Topics: Interest Groups and Political Parties

51. Which of the following is true of relationships between the president and Congress?

(a) is incorrect because presidents have been successful forming coalitions in Congress.

(b) is incorrect because presidents do not necessarily work successfully with minority party leaders.

(c) is correct because the relationship between the president and Congress tends to be strained when the president's party is not the majority party in Congress. The two often have conflicting policy goals and work together less often than do a president and Congress of the same political party.

(d) is incorrect because members of Congress do not always vote in favor of presidential initiative.

(e) is incorrect because do not necessarily have closer relationships with the House than with the Senate.

Page reference: 365, AP Topics: The Presidency and the Congress

52.   The elderly fare better than the poor in social welfare budget battles for which of the following reasons?

(a) is incorrect because there is no constitutional requirement for spending for the elderly.

(b) is incorrect because most social services for the elderly come from the national government.

(c) is incorrect because lobbyist for the elderly are allowed to make campaign contributions.

(d) is correct because the elderly fare better than the poor in social welfare budget battles due to being more organized, more politically active and better represented than the poor. The elderly are also widely considered to be among the deserving poor.

(e) is incorrect there are not more elderly people in the U.S. than poor people.

Page reference: 442, AP Topics: Interest Groups and Public Policy

53.   Which of the following statements accurately describes iron triangles?

(a) is incorrect because the military-industrial complex is not necessarily a part of iron triangles.

(b) is correct because iron triangles are unofficial political entities composed of interest groups, agencies, and legislative committees that are all concerned with the same policy area, and each group helps the others to help itself in the policy arena.

(c) is incorrect because iron triangles are not formed to generate support for presidential proposals.

(d) is incorrect because iron triangles do not coordinate policy among the three branches.

(e) is incorrect because iron triangles do not perform policy implementation functions.

Page reference: 498, AP Topics: Public Policy and Policymaking

54. Which of the following statements represent a prevalent myth about the federal bureaucracy?

(a) is incorrect because the federal bureaucracy is not growing bigger and bigger each year.

(b) is incorrect because the federal bureaucracy does not make government inefficient and cumbersome.

(c) is incorrect because only about 12 percent of federal bureaucrats work in Washington, D.C., and I. is also incorrect.

(d) is incorrect because most citizens are generally satisfied with the service they receive from the bureaucracy, and I, II, and III are also incorrect.

(e) is correct because all of these statements are false or misleading.

Page reference: 489, AP Topic: Bureaucracy

55. The establishment clause, as interpreted by the Supreme Court, prevents

(a) is incorrect because the establishment clause deals with religion and not supremacy of national law.

(b) is incorrect because the establishment clause deals specifically with religion and not with prohibition of the rights of the individual.

(c) is incorrect because the establishment clause deals specifically with religion and not with lawmaking in general.

(d) is incorrect because the establishment clause deals with religion and not with gender discrimination.

(e) is correct because the establishment clause, located in the First Amendment of the Constitution, establishes the separation of church and state in all levels of government which means that religious qualifications cannot be imposed on public officials, and the government cannot regulate, restrict, or endorse religious worship.

Page reference: 109, AP Topics: The Constitution and Civil Rights

56. *Regents of the University of California v. Bakke* is a Supreme Court case that addressed

(a) is correct because in *Bakke*, the Supreme Court upheld the principle of affirmative action but banned the use of quotas to establish racial diversity.

(b) is incorrect because the *Bakke* case did not address prayer in school.

(c) is incorrect because the *Bakke* case did not address the rights of the accused.

(d) is incorrect because the *Bakke* case did not address the right of privacy.

(e) is incorrect because the *Bakke* case did not address desegregation through busing.

Page reference: 181, AP Topic: Civil Rights

57. One of a president's most powerful tools for gaining support of his proposals is

(a) is incorrect because a president does not use money to obtain public support.

(b) is incorrect because a president does not use executive privilege to obtain public support.

(c) is correct because a president relies heavily on the power of public opinion because, with the backing of the public, members of Congress have little recourse but to support him as well.

(d) is incorrect because a president does not use senatorial courtesy to obtain public support.

(e) is incorrect because a president does not use the cabinet to obtain public support.

Page reference: 419, AP Topic: The Presidency

58. Which of the following statements accurately describe traditional Republican Party economic positions?

(a) is incorrect because republicans to not emphasize full employment more than democrats.

(b) is correct because republicans tend to worry about inflation more than Democrats do and. republicans generally try to prevent inflation, even at the risk of rising unemployment.

(c) is incorrect because republican economic positions do not appeal to the working class and unions.

(d) is incorrect because republicans do not emphasize full employment more than democrats do, nor do they support higher taxes.

(e) is incorrect because choices I, II, and III are all false.

Page reference: 368, AP Topic: Political Parties

59. Members of Congress are more likely to vote according to their personal ideology when

(a) is correct because their constituents usually are familiar with only the most publicized issues, members of Congress have many opportunities to vote according to their own ideology on smaller, less publicized issues.

(b) is incorrect because members of Congress up for reelection are more likely to vote in accordance with the wishes of constituents.

(c) is incorrect because the origin of the legislation does not necessarily impact a member's vote.

(d) is incorrect because committee involvement does not necessarily impact a member's vote.

(e) is incorrect because interest group involvement does not necessarily impact a member's vote.

Page reference: 366, AP Topic: Congress

60.   In the era of globalization, which of the following presidential powers is becoming important?

(a) is incorrect because vetoing is not part of the president's diplomatic powers.

(b) is correct because in the recent era of globalization, foreign policy is shifting toward economic concerns and the president, as chief diplomat, has both increasing power and responsibility as the nation's negotiator of treaties and executive agreements.

(c) is incorrect because declaring war is not part of negotiating economic agreements.

(d) is incorrect because authorizing weapons of mass destruction is not part of negotiating economic agreements.

(e) is incorrect because appointing Supreme Court justices is not part of the president's diplomatic powers.

Page reference: 419, AP Topic: The Presidency

Free-Response Questions

This rubric provides examples of many, but not all of the possible correct responses to the free-response questions.

1.   In the American democracy, political parties use two different systems for selecting delegates to the national party conventions that nominate presidential candidates.

a.   Describe how caucuses select delegates to the national convention.

- In some states, delegates are chosen for the national conventions by caucuses. Caucuses are when members of political parties meet (i.e., caucus) in town hall-like meetings to discuss and debate about their party's nominees for the presidency.

Individuals attending the caucus vote for their preferred candidate. Candidates are awarded delegates to the state and national party conventions based on the number of votes they receive.

b. Describe how primaries select delegates to the national convention.

- In some states, delegates are elected for the national party conventions in a primary vote. In states that have primaries, voters go to the poll to vote for a particular candidate. When people vote for the presidential candidate they prefer, they are most often voting for a delegate to the state or national convention who, at the convention, is obligated to vote for the candidate they represent.

c. Explain one consequence of "frontloading" the delegate selection process.

- Frontloading is when several states hold their primary or caucus early in the primary election cycle. With frontloading, one candidate often is able to gain an insurmountable lead in the delegate count long before primaries and caucuses are held in other states. Frontloading has led to a race to the front of the line, with many states moving their primary or caucus to earlier dates.

2. The mass media has a major effect on politics in the United States. It has both positive and negative consequences for the political process.

a. Describe two positives effects that the media has on the political process.

- Citizens have access to important information about candidates for public office, elected officials, and public policy.
- Through investigative reporting, the media performs a watchdog role for the political process. In this role the media uncovers governmental fraud, waste, and abuse and helps voters hold public officials accountable for their actions.

b. Describe two negative effects that the media has on the political process.

- The media tend to provide superficial coverage of complex public policy issues.
- Because mass media outlets tend to be owned by profit-seeking corporations, the choice of what news they cover might be influenced by how well it will sell rather than how important it is to the public.

- The media (especially television) are biased towards stories that generate good pictures.

- In political campaigns the media tends to focus more on the horse race than the issues positions of the candidates.

3. The above graph shows population projections for the first quarter of the 21st century. All of the states listed are expected to gain at least a million people in the next few decades. Using the data above and your knowledge of U.S. government and politics, identify and explain THREE ways that these shifting populations will have an impact on government and politics.

- The graph clearly indicates that Florida, Texas, and especially California are expected to see the largest increase in population in the next 20 to 25 years. These states will therefore experience a significant increase in political clout as well. With more seats in the House, they will have more influence over national policy and may bring new issues that are pertinent to them to the federal agenda.

- A state's number of electors is equal to the total of its representatives and senators, so if these states gain seats, they will also gain electoral votes. As a result, presidential candidates will focus their campaign efforts on these states.

- The increasing power as a result of migration to these three states in particular may have other political consequences, because all three of these states have sizable populations of Hispanic Americans. This minority group, which is itself growing, may therefore win a greater voice in government. More Hispanic Americans may be elected to public office to represent largely Hispanic constituencies. They may also bring new social and economic issues particular to Hispanic Americans to the political agenda.

4. The Tenth Amendment reserves for the states all powers neither denied nor designated to the federal government in the Constitution. For decades, this afforded states a good deal of freedom in writing their state laws. However, the ratification of the Fourteenth Amendment allowed the Supreme Court to exercise its authority over the states in an attempt to advance the civil liberties of all Americans.

   a. What provision of the Fourteenth Amendment has been used by the Supreme Court to exercise its authority over the states for the purpose of advancing civil liberties?

   - The due process clause of the Fourteenth Amendment was used to make the provisions of the federal Bill of Rights applicable to state governments.

b. Identify two areas in which civil liberties protections have been extended to the states, and discuss the specific case(s) that accomplished this task in each area.

- **Freedom of speech** (*Gitlow v. New York*)

- **Freedom of press** (*Near v. Minnesota*)

- **Right of Privacy** (*Griswold v. Connecticut*)

- **Right to Counsel in felony cases** (*Gideon v. Wainwright*)

Government and Politics: United States AP Exam Practice Test 2

☐ Government and Politics: United States

Section I
Time: 45 minutes
60 Questions

Directions: *Each of the questions or incomplete statements below is followed by five suggested answers or completions. Select the one that is best in each case and then fill in the corresponding oval on the answer sheet.*

1. In which of the following elections are voters allowed to choose candidates from either party for different offices?
   a. open primary
   b. initiative
   c. closed primary
   d. blanket primary
   e. recall election

2. All of the following play a role in the impeachment of a president, EXCEPT the
   a. court of appeals.
   b. Judiciary Committee.
   c. U.S. House of Representatives.
   d. chief justice of the United States.
   e. U.S. Senate.

3. Popular elections are held for all of the following governmental offices EXCEPT
   a. senator.
   b. president.
   c. federal judge.
   d. member of the House of Representatives.
   e. governor.

4. In general, Democrats are more likely than the Republicans to advocate for which of the following?
   a. lower capital gains tax rates
   b. reduced spending for social services
   c. prayer in public schools
   d. increased military spending
   e. restrictions on handgun ownership

5. The federal bureaucracy handles all of the following activities EXCEPT
   a. issuing rules and regulations.
   b. holding hearings to obtain information about proposed policies.
   c. implementing policies passed by Congress.
   d. appropriating funds to pay for federal government programs.
   e. acting as a quasi-judicial body.

6. The elastic clause grants Congress the authority to
   a. amend the president's budget proposal as it sees fit.
   b. make any laws that enable it to carry out its assigned responsibilities.
   c. raise taxes.
   d. create any number of legislative committees and subcommittees.
   e. reapportion seats based on the nation's changing population.

7. The most common way that ordinary citizens participate in politics is by
   a. participating in political protests.
   b. writing letters to the editor of a local newspaper.
   c. voting in elections.
   d. contacting their elected representatives.
   e. joining an interest group.

8. The Constitution authorizes Supreme Court justices to be appointed for life for which of the following reasons?
   a. to shield judges from political influence and pressure
   b. to reward judges for their distinguished careers
   c. to create a strong relationship between the court and Congress
   d. to allow politicians to use the patronage system
   e. to limit the power of presidents to appoint judges too frequently

9. One common criticism of the media's participation in politics is
   a. its bias in favor of outsiders and third parties.
   b. its focus on the Supreme Court to the exclusion of the other branches.
   c. its live and uncensored coverage of committee hearings.
   d. its tendency to focus more on personalities than on issues.
   e. its failure to shape the public agenda through its news coverage.

10. Which of the following groups is the least likely to participate in politics?
    a. 65- to 75-year-olds
    b. high school graduates
    c. women
    d. Protestants
    e. 18- to 25-year-olds

11. Which of the following statements about the budgetary process is true?
    a. The president submits a budget proposal to Congress, which ultimately decides how to allocate money.
    b. The president assigns a spending minimum and maximum to each agency in the executive branch.
    c. Interest groups have little influence over this aspect of policymaking.
    d. The Office of Management and Budget handles the entire budgetary process.
    e. Committees submit their internal budget requests to the Congressional Budget Office.

12. According to the Supreme Court's decision in *Lemon v. Kurtzman* (1971), which of the following is true about public aid to church-related schools?
    a. Any use of public funds for church-related schools violates the separation of church and state doctrine.
    b. Only local governments may allocate public money to church-related schools.
    c. Public aid to church-related schools must be matched by an equal amount of privately raised funds.
    d. Public aid to church-related schools must have a primary effect that neither advances nor inhibits religion.
    e. Religious schools are not allowed to receive any public funds.

13. Which of the following powers are granted to Congress by the Constitution?

    I. appropriate money
    II. confirm justices
    III. send troops into war
    IV. enforce laws
    V. regulate commerce

    a. I and IV only
    b. II and III only
    c. III and V only
    d. I, II, and V only
    e. III, IV, and V only

14. Which of the following authorized the Justice Department to send federal officials to oversee state elections?
    a. Fifteenth Amendment
    b. Voting Rights Act
    c. Motor Voter Act
    d. Thirteenth Amendment
    e. Civil Rights Act

15. In which of the following cases is a congressional candidate most likely to be elected?
    a. if he or she has a good television presence
    b. when a state has just gained seats due to reapportionment
    c. if he or she is new to politics
    d. after a critical election for the presidency
    e. if he or she is an incumbent

16. Which of the following is true of iron triangles?
    a. An iron triangle is composed of the president, the Speaker of the House, and the chief justice.
    b. Iron triangles inhibit the policy process by interfering with the debate over a piece of legislation.
    c. Iron triangles help unify the three branches of government in pursuit of a single, clear policy agenda.
    d. Iron triangles help advance legislation and implementation in a particular policy area.
    e. Iron triangles rarely form in government at the federal level because they lack sufficient resources for sustainability.

17. An environmental lobby would be LEAST likely to exert its influence by meeting with a
    a. federal judge hearing a case on the constitutionality of an environmental regulation.
    b. member of the House committee that authorizes money for the building of power plants.
    c. staff member of the Environmental Protection Agency.
    d. newspaper in the town where environmental laws are being violated.
    e. staff member of the White House who is known to be sympathetic to environmental concerns.

18. A voter's choice of candidate is most influenced by
    a. campaign finance laws.
    b. political advertisements.
    c. party identification.
    d. the media.
    e. radio talk shows.

19. Many Supreme Court cases of the 1960s involved issues of
    a. gender discrimination.
    b. economic regulation.
    c. constitutional powers of the president.
    d. rights of the accused.
    e. campaign finance reform.

20. If the Supreme Court rules that a newly passed law is unconstitutional, Congress can
    a. ask the president to appoint new justices.
    b. try to amend the Constitution to override the Supreme Court's interpretation.
    c. appeal the Court's decision to the Senate Judiciary Committee.
    d. issue a referendum to allow the public to vote on the Supreme Court's decision.
    e. vote to override the Supreme Court's decision.

21. Which of the following are types of elections held in the U.S.?

    I. run-off election
    II. national primary
    III. general election
    IV. initiative petition
    V. referendum

    a. III only
    b. II and III only
    c. I, II and III only
    d. I, III, IV, and V only
    e. All of the above

22. If the House and Senate pass two different versions of a bill,
    a. the Senate version has seniority and is sent to the president.
    b. the Supreme Court chooses the better version.
    c. the two versions are sent to a conference committee to work out a compromise bill.
    d. the president has the authority to choose which version will be signed into law.
    e. each house must amend its bill and take another vote.

23. One tool that allows the president to sidestep congressional approval of his diplomatic duties is the
    a. power to negotiate treaties.
    b. authority to enter into executive agreements.
    c. ability to send troops into war.
    d. freedom to appoint ambassadors.
    e. privilege of receiving foreign diplomats.

24. Which of the following is an accurate statement about the caseload of the Supreme Court?
    a. Only a small portion of cases seeking review are heard by the Supreme Court.
    b. The Senate Judiciary Committee selects which cases will be placed on the docket.
    c. Most cases that reach the Supreme Court are appealed from state courts.
    d. The solicitor general is responsible for assigning cases to the Supreme Court.
    e. The Supreme Court attempts to hear every case appealed to it.

25. The Supreme Court has extended federal supremacy over state laws through its interpretation of the
    a. Tenth Amendment.
    b. eminent domain clause.
    c. First Amendment.
    d. Fourteenth Amendment.
    e. establishment clause.

26. Which of the following is an incumbent's greatest advantage during an election?
   a. automatic endorsement from the president
   b. a clean political record
   c. name recognition
   d. more campaign resources and funding
   e. a large number of undecided voters in the constituency

27. Television has had which of the following effects on political parties?
   a. It has helped lower the cost of campaigning, thereby saving the parties money.
   b. It has forced candidates to rely more heavily on their parties.
   c. It has caused a decrease in party identification among the electorate.
   d. It has led to the declining importance of national conventions.
   e. It has caused party realignment because parties can appeal to new groups in the electorate.

28. Articles of impeachment must be passed by
   a. either the House or the Senate.
   b. both the House and the Senate.
   c. the Senate.
   d. the House.
   e. the Supreme Court.

29. What happens if no presidential candidate receives an Electoral College majority?
   a. The election is decided by the U.S. House of Representatives.
   b. The winner is decided by a conference of the state governors.
   c. A run-off election is held to determine the winner.
   d. The U.S. Supreme Court determines the winner.
   e. The winner is decided by a vote of superdelegates.

30. Which of the following is a trend in American elections?
   a. Fewer candidates are seeking elective office.
   b. Campaigns are becoming less expensive to run.
   c. Political pundits are becoming more influential.
   d. Fewer citizens are making financial contributions to candidates.
   e. More states are allowing early voting.

31. Article II of the Constitution grants the president power to do all of the following EXCEPT
   a. authorizing troop movements during war.
   b. appropriating funds for agencies.
   c. vetoing proposed legislation.
   d. appealing to Congress and making legislative requests in a state of the union address.
   e. establishing or discontinuing relations with foreign governments.

32. The Civil Rights Act of 1964 articulated which of the following?
    a. the requirement that all public schools desegregate
    b. a prohibition of states' institution of poll taxes or literacy tests when administering elections
    c. he illegality of discrimination in employment and public accommodations
    d. the creation of the Justice Department to investigate civil rights violations
    e. the right of all Americans, regardless of race or gender, to vote in federal elections

33. Which of the following statements accurately describes the procedure of debate in the House?
    a. The Rules Committee determines the order in which bills will be heard and the length of debate for each one.
    b. Representatives who are introducing a bill are allowed the privilege of unlimited debate.
    c. The Speaker and the sergeant at arms together determine the schedule of debate.
    d. The minority party is allowed an automatic 10 minutes of debate time to refute legislation introduced by the majority party.
    e. Only members of the party whose representative introduced the bill are allowed time on the floor to discuss it.

34. Which of the following statements characterize the relationship between congressional committees and federal agencies?

    I. Committees appropriate funds for each agency to spend during the year.
    II. Agencies regulate committees by holding hearings to assess their performance.
    III. Committees perform oversight of the agencies that fall under their jurisdiction.
    IV. Both committees and agencies can be influenced by the lobbying efforts of interest groups.

    a. II only
    b. III only
    c. I and III only
    d. II and IV only
    e. I, III, and IV only

35. In *Texas v. Johnson*, the Supreme Court determined that
    a. the drawing of unreasonable school district lines cannot be used as a means of integrating schools.
    b. symbolic speech is protected under the First Amendment.
    c. affirmative action quotas are unconstitutional.
    d. the death penalty is not a form of cruel and unusual punishment.
    e. obscenity is not protected by the First Amendment.

36. Which of the following is usually a result of a critical election?
    a. party dealignment
    b. divided government
    c. policy implementation
    d. party realignment
    e. policy gridlock

37. A weakness of the Articles of Confederation was that they established a government that was unable to
    a. remain a democracy.
    b. be recognized by foreign governments.
    c. represent the views of the various states.
    d. centralize its powers.
    e. make decisions through a legislative process.

38. The Federal Reserve Board oversees which of the following policy areas?
    a. social welfare policy
    b. foreign policy
    c. monetary policy
    d. health care policy
    e. domestic policy

39. Which of the following is a major difference between the Democratic and Republican parties?
    a. The Democratic Party campaigns fairly, but the Republican Party does not.
    b. A wider variety of groups in the electorate vote for Republican candidates.
    c. The Republican Party is much older than the Democratic Party.
    d. The Republican Party endorses raising taxes, whereas the Democratic Party favors cutting taxes.
    e. The Democratic Party has a more liberal ideology, whereas the Republican Party has a more conservative ideology.

40. Legislation that forbids labor contracts from requiring workers to join unions in order to hold their jobs is known as
    a. unfair labor practice legislation.
    b. right-to-work laws.
    c. right-to-choose laws.
    d. right-to-unionize laws.
    e. fair share laws.

41. A unitary system of government is one in which
    a. an executive, legislative, and judicial branch share equal powers.
    b. political officials are elected by the public in a popular election.
    c. legislative committees and federal agencies work together to make and implement policy.
    d. more than one level of government oversees a body of people.
    e. all power resides in a central government.

42. The rise of the Social Security system has had which of the following effects on the federal budget?
    a. It has led to cutbacks in defense spending and the building of new weapons.
    b. It has become the largest federal expenditure.
    c. It has increased Americans' trust in a government that provides for all Americans.
    d. It has caused income tax rates to double since its initiation.
    e. It has discouraged senior citizens from participating in politics.

43. One way federal agencies regulate an industry is by
    a. hiring corporate leaders in the industry.
    b. issuing bonds to the industry.
    c. fixing stock prices in the industry.
    d. limiting its ability to trade internationally.
    e. sending inspectors to investigate an industry's regular activity.

44. Members of Congress are most likely to endorse a president's proposal when
    a. one party holds the majority in Congress by only a slim margin.
    b. the congressional session is nearing its end.
    c. the president has a high public approval rating.
    d. the issue at hand is not well publicized.
    e. it involves amending the federal tax codes.

45. Which of the following is a basic weakness inherent in the presidency?
    a. Except in military affairs, presidents must rely on the support of other people to influence policy decisions.
    b. Because they are limited to only two terms, presidents rarely have enough time to achieve any of their policy goals.
    c. Media attention focuses heavily on the president, which leads the public to hold him accountable and, in turn, deprives him of power.
    d. The president is commander in chief, yet he cannot act in military situations without congressional approval.
    e. Because the Electoral College officially elects the president, presidents usually lack legitimacy among the electorate.

46. Despite their influence over the political agenda, interest groups may be seen as democratic institutions in that they
    a. help voters decide how to cast their ballots in an election.
    b. fund campaigns through political action committees.
    c. run advertisements to generate public support for a presidential proposal.
    d. promote equal representation of citizens' political beliefs.
    e. represent the concerns of groups in the electorate in the political arena.

47. The power of the president has expanded for which of the following reasons?

    I. increasing importance of foreign relations
    II. the shift toward candidate-centered politics as a result of television
    III. the use of primaries in presidential elections
    IV. the easing of tensions among social groups as a result of the civil rights movement

    a. II only
    b. IV only
    c. I and II only
    d. III and IV only
    e. I, II, and III only

48. Which of the following is true of federal systems of government?
    a. The central government completely regulates the activities of state governments.
    b. Citizens vote for central government officials only.
    c. The central government shares power with the states.
    d. Most democracies are federal systems.
    e. Federal systems tend to have just two major political parties.

49. The House of Representatives differs from the Senate in all of the following ways EXCEPT
    a. House seats are distributed according to each state's population, whereas each state has the same number of senators.
    b. House debates are scheduled, whereas the Senate allows unlimited debate.
    c. Representatives tend to act more independently, whereas senators usually vote according to party lines.
    d. Power is distributed more hierarchically in the House than it is in the Senate.
    e. Senators have the ability to filibuster, but representatives do not.

50. An American citizen's approval of the president depends most heavily on
    a. the president's ability to stand up to Congress.
    b. whether the president is of the same party with which the citizen identifies himself or herself.
    c. whether the president has balanced his attention between foreign and domestic policy.
    d. how accessible the president is to members of the public.
    e. the media's bias in favor of or against the president.

51. One way the executive branch may attempt to influence the outcome of a Supreme Court case is by
    a. filing an *amicus curiae* brief.
    b. selecting which justices will hear the case.
    c. having the solicitor general preside over the justices.
    d. requesting the chief justice to meet with the president.
    e. issuing an opinion on the case.

52. The president may exercise authority over the federal bureaucracy in all of the following ways EXCEPT by
    a. advising cabinet members and agency heads on department activities.
    b. proposing budgets for each department to Congress.
    c. appointing department secretaries who share his political goals.
    d. creating or dismantling agencies and departments.
    e. holding hearings on the departments' activities and performance.

53. In some states, citizens can participate directly in lawmaking by
    a. appointing legislators to committees.
    b. presenting a budget proposal in the state legislature.
    c. approving legislation through referenda.
    d. writing letters to the governor.
    e. setting the requirements for who can run for office.

54. Which of the following is a true statement about the Voting Rights Act of 1965?
    a. It resulted in increased discrimination against women voters.
    b. It allowed literacy tests to be administered as a prerequisite for voting.
    c. It gave the states more control over federal elections.
    d. It was the first voting rights law to pass Congress with no opposition.
    e. It resulted in dramatic increases in the number of African American voters.

55. In a state that has six electoral votes, the Republican candidate wins the popular vote, earning 54 percent to the Democratic candidate's 46 percent. The electoral votes would most likely be allocated in which of the following ways?
    a. The Republican and Democrat would each get three electoral votes.
    b. The Republican would get five electoral votes, and the one electoral vote reserved for a third-party candidate would go unused.
    c. The Republican would get four electoral votes, and the Democrat would get two.
    d. The Republican would get six electoral votes.
    e. The Republican would get five electoral votes, and the Democrat would get one.

56. Senators are often more willing to allow a filibuster than they are to vote for cloture because
    a. voting for cloture looks bad on the senator's congressional record.
    b. they want to ensure that their colleagues will not vote for cloture when they choose to filibuster.
    c. voting for cloture does little to stop a filibuster.
    d. they fear losing public approval by refusing to hear the full debate.
    e. filibusters often generate well-developed, successful policies.

57. The president exercises the most influence over policymaking by
    a. vetoing legislation passed by Congress.
    b. setting the congressional agenda.
    c. introducing legislation for debate.
    d. participating in committee hearings.
    e. appointing party leaders in both houses of Congress.

58. Which of the following sets of states has the most Electoral College votes?
    a. California, New York, and Texas
    b. Iowa, New Hampshire, and South Carolina
    c. Florida, New Jersey, and Ohio
    d. Maine, Massachusetts, and Vermont
    e. North Carolina, Oregon, and Pennsylvania

59. If one sees candidates from more than one political party on a ballot, one may be voting in

   I. an open primary.
   II. a closed primary.
   III. a blanket primary.
   IV. a general election.

   a. I only
   b. I and III only
   c. I, III, and IV only
   d. III and IV only
   e. IV only

60. Which of the following is the presiding officer of the U.S. Senate?
   a. Speaker
   b. majority leader
   c. majority whip
   d. chief clerk
   e. vice president

END OF SECTION I.

IF YOU FINISH BEFORE TIME IS CALLED, YOU MAY CHECK YOUR WORK ON THIS SECTION.

DO NOT GO ON TO SECTION II UNTIL YOU ARE TOLD TO DO SO.

☐ Government and Politics: United States

Section II
Time: 100 minutes

Directions: You have 100 minutes to answer all four of the following questions. It is suggested that you take a few minutes to plan and outline each answer. Spend approximately one-fourth of your time (25 minutes) on each question. *Illustrate your essay with substantive examples where appropriate. Make certain to number each of your answers as the question is numbered below.*

1. The writers of the Constitution favored the ideals of democracy, yet they feared putting too much power in the hands of the people.

    a. Identify TWO changes from the original Constitution that increased the democratic nature of government.

    b. Explain how each of the two factors identified in part *a*, above, has resulted in a more democratic nation.

2. Incumbent members of Congress have a tremendous advantage over challengers in elections. But the many advantages notwithstanding, incumbents do sometimes lose elections.

    a. Identify three possible sources of incumbency advantage.

    b. Describe how each of the items you identified in part *a*, above, works to an incumbent's advantage.

    c. Identify and explain two reasons why incumbents tend to lose elections.

Race and Ethnicity in America, 1967–2008

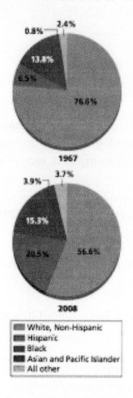

Source: U.S. Census Bureau, Statistical Abstract of the United States.

3.   The above graph details how the composition of the American population has changed over the last 40 years. Using the data above and your knowledge of U.S. government and politics, identify and explain THREE ways that these shifting populations will have an impact on government and politics.

   a.   Identify one way the geographic distribution of the population has changed according to the chart above, and explain why that shift occurred.

   b.   Describe THREE ways that these shifting populations will have an impact on government and politics.

4.   During the budgetary process, Congress weighs revenues and expenditures to determine how to allocate money within the federal government. Social spending has become a major component of the federal budget in recent decades, but in some cases Congress is not able to adjust spending for it.

   a.   Identify TWO items in the budget that cannot usually be amended during the budgetary process.

   b.   For each one, explain why spending is not cut.

END OF EXAMINATION

☐ Answers and Explanations

Practice Test 2
Section I

1. In which of the following elections are voters allowed to choose candidates from either party for different offices?

    (a) is incorrect because an open primary does not allow for ticket splitting.

    (b) is incorrect because an initiative involves proposing legislation.

    (c) is incorrect because a closed primary allows only party members to participate.

    (d) is correct because in a blanket primary, candidates of all parties are listed on the ballot and a voter may choose a candidate from one party for one office and a candidate from another party for a different office.

    (e) is incorrect because a recall election involves removing an incumbent from office.

    Page reference: 364, AP Topics: Political Parties and Elections

2. All of the following play a role in the impeachment of a president, EXCEPT the

    (a) is correct because the court of appeals plays no role in the impeachment process.

    (b) is incorrect because the Judiciary Committee decides whether to proceed with impeachment.

    (c) is incorrect because the U.S. House votes to impeach.

    (d) is incorrect because the chief justice presides over the impeachment trial.

    (e) is incorrect because the U.S. Senate tries the president.

    Page reference: 419, AP Topics: The Presidency and the Federal Courts

3. Popular elections are held for all of the following governmental offices EXCEPT

    (a) is incorrect because senators are chosen by popular election.

    (b) is incorrect because the president is chosen by popular election.

    (c) is correct because federal judges are not elected by the public—they are appointed by the president and confirmed by the Senate.

    (d) is incorrect because a member of the House is chosen by popular election.

(e) is incorrect because a governor is chosen by popular election.

Page reference: 364, AP Topic: Federal Courts

4. In general, Democrats are more likely than the Republicans to advocate for which of the following?

    (a) is incorrect because Republicans are more likely to favor lower capital gains tax rates.

    (b) is incorrect because Republicans are more likely to favor reduced spending for social services.

    (c) is incorrect because Republicans are more likely to favor prayer in public schools.

    (d) is incorrect because Republicans are more likely to favor increased military spending.

    (e) is correct because Democrats more than Republicans tend to favor polices like background checks and mandatory safety classes that make it more difficult for individuals to own handguns.

    Page reference: 368, AP Topic: Political Parties

5. The federal bureaucracy handles all of the following activities EXCEPT

    (a) is incorrect because bureaucracies can issue rules and regulations.

    (b) is incorrect because bureaucracies can hold hearing to obtain information about proposed policies.

    (c) is incorrect because bureaucracies can implement policies passed by Congress.

    (d) is correct because only Congress can appropriate funds to be spent by the federal government.

    (e) is incorrect because bureaucracies can act as quasi-judicial bodies.

    Page reference: 489, AP Topic: Bureaucracy

6. The elastic clause grants Congress the authority to

    (a) is incorrect because the budget is part of the delegated powers of Congress.

    (b) is correct because, located in Article I of the Constitution, the elastic clause enumerates the implied powers of Congress and it gives the legislature full authority to make any laws "necessary and proper" to carry out those responsibilities assigned to it by the Constitution.

    (c) is incorrect because taxing is part of the delegated powers of Congress.

(d) is incorrect because creating committees and subcommittees is part of the delegated powers of Congress.

(e) is incorrect because reapportionment is part of the delegated powers of Congress.

Page reference: 366, AP Topic: Constitution

7. The most common way that ordinary citizens participate in politics is by

(a) is incorrect because participating in political protests is not a common method of participation.

(b) is incorrect because writing letters to the editor is not a form of participation for the majority of citizens.

(c) is correct because voting is the most common way people express their political views and by participating in an election, voters choose those candidates whom they feel agree with their political beliefs.

(d) is incorrect because contacting elected representatives is not a form of participation for the majority of citizens.

(e) is incorrect because joining an interest group is not a form of participation for the majority of citizens.

Page reference: 314, AP Topic: Political Participation

8. The Constitution authorizes Supreme Court justices to be appointed for life for which of the following reasons?

(a) is correct because Supreme Court justices are granted life terms which allows them to make judicial decisions objectively without the pressures of political influence.

(b) is incorrect because a life term is not related to distinguished careers.

(c) is incorrect because a life term is not related to the relationship between Congress and the courts.

(d) is incorrect because a life term does not allow politicians to use the patronage system.

(e) is incorrect because a life term is not intended to place limits on the presidential appointment power.

Page reference: 513, AP Topic: Federal Courts

9. One common criticism of the media's participation in politics is

(a) is incorrect because the media is not biased in favor of outsiders and third parties.

(b) is incorrect because the media is not focused on the Supreme Court.

(c) is incorrect because the media does not provide live and uncensored coverage of committee hearings.

(d) is correct because the media tends to focus more heavily on candidates' personality than their policy platforms for the sake of achieving higher viewer ratings and this may distort the public's perception both of candidates and the party they represent.

(e) is incorrect because the media does shape the public agenda.

Page reference: 246, AP Topic: Media

10.   Which of the following groups is the least likely to participate in politics?

(a) is incorrect because 65 to 75 year-olds have a relatively high participation rate.

(b) is incorrect because high school graduates are more likely to participate than young people.

(c) is incorrect because women are more likely to participate than young people.

(d) is incorrect because Protestants are more likely to participate than young people.

(e) is correct because young people (18- to 25-year-olds) are the least likely group in the electorate to vote and this is partially because young people have not yet formed their political beliefs or determined their needs from government.

Page reference: 314, AP Topic: Political Participation

11.   Which of the following statements about the budgetary process is true?

(a) is correct because the president sends his proposed budget to Congress, which, through its committees, ultimately decides how much money each department or agency gets to spend in the coming year.

(b) is incorrect because it is not an accurate description of the budgetary process.

(c) is incorrect because interests do have an influence over the budgetary process.

(d) is incorrect because the OMB handles only a part of the budgetary process.

(e) is incorrect because it is not an accurate description of the budgetary process.

Page reference: 445, AP Topic: Relationships among the four institutions and varying balances of power.

12.   According to the Supreme Court's decision in *Lemon v. Kurtzman* (1971), which of the following is true about public aid to church-related schools?

(a) is incorrect because ALL use of public funds is not prohibited.

(b) is incorrect because local governments are restricted by the *Lemon* case, as well.

(c) is incorrect because matching funds are prohibited, as well.

(d) is correct because in *Lemon v. Kurtzman* the Supreme Court ruled that aid to church-related schools must (1) have a secular purpose (2) must have a primary effect that neither advances nor inhibits religion and (3) not foster excessive government entanglement with religion.

(e) is incorrect because religious schools may receive some public funds.

Page reference: 513, AP Topic: Civil Rights

13. Which of the following powers are granted to Congress by the Constitution?

(a) is incorrect because enforcing laws is not an enumerated power of Congress.

(b) is incorrect because sending troops into war is not an enumerated power of Congress.

(c) is incorrect because sending troops into war is not an enumerated power of Congress.

(d) is correct because some of Congress's enumerated powers are to appropriate money, confirm the appointment of justices, and regulate commerce.

(e) is incorrect because sections III and IV are not enumerated powers of Congress.

Page reference: 366, AP Topic: Congress

14. Which of the following authorized the Justice Department to send federal officials to oversee state elections?

(a) is incorrect because the 15th Amendment gave African Americans the right to vote, but did not give the Justice Department the power to send in federal officials.

(b) is correct because the Voting Rights Act was passed to enable the government to enforce African Americans' right to vote as guaranteed by the Fifteenth Amendment and as a result of its new power to enforce the law, the Justice Department sent in federal officials to oversee elections in Southern states.

(c) is incorrect because the Motor Voter Act made voter registration easier.

(d) is incorrect because the 13th Amendment abolished slavery.

(e) is incorrect because the Civil Rights Act did not deal with voting rights.

Page reference: 477, AP Topics: Elections and Civil Rights

15. In which of the following cases is a congressional candidate most likely to be elected?

(a) is incorrect because a good television presence is not as important as incumbency.

(b) is incorrect because addition of new seats does not relate to election advantages.

(c) is incorrect because being new to politics does not relate to election advantages.

(d) is incorrect because a critical election for the president does not relate to a congressional candidates election.

(e) is correct because incumbents have better exposure, a political record with the constituency, and more campaign money with which to eliminate any chance of their challengers' success, and as a result of these advantages, usually more than 50 percent of congressional incumbents are reelected.

Page reference: 366, AP Topics: Congress and Elections

16. Which of the following is true of iron triangles?

(a) is incorrect because this is an incorrect description of iron triangles.

(b) is incorrect because iron triangles do no inhibit the policy process.

(c) is incorrect because iron triangles do not work as a unifying force.

(d) is correct because iron triangles, or subgovernments, often work like well-oiled machines to produce and implement policies in a specific policy area.

(e) is incorrect because iron triangles are common.

Page reference: 498, AP Topic: Relationships among the four institutions and varying balances of power

17. An environmental lobby would be LEAST likely to exert its influence by meeting with a

(a) is correct because lobbyists have the least influence over judges because they have no leverage with which to influence judges who hold their offices for life. However, interest groups can file *amicus curiae* briefs to try to influence a judge's decision.

(b) is incorrect because lobbyists do exert influence over House members.

(c) is incorrect because lobbyists do exert influence over agency staff.

(d) is incorrect because lobbyists do use newspapers to exert influence.

(e) is incorrect because lobbyists do exert influence over White House staff members.

Page reference: 302, AP Topics: Public Policy, Interest Groups

18.   A voter's choice of candidate is most influenced by

(a) is incorrect because campaign finance laws have little influence over a voter's choice of candidate.

(b) is incorrect because political ads do not influence a voter's choice as much as party identification does.

(c) is correct because political science research has consistently found party identification to be the strongest predictor of vote choice.

(d) is incorrect because the media does not influence a voter's choice as much as party identification does.

(e) is incorrect because radio talk shows do not influence a voter's choice as much as party identification does.

Page reference: 314, AP Topics: Political Participation

19.   Many Supreme Court cases of the 1960s involved issues of

(a) is incorrect because gender was not the focus of the 1960s cases.

(b) is incorrect because economic regulation was not the focus of the 1960s cases.

(c) is incorrect because the president's constitutional powers were not the focus of the 1960s cases.

(d) is correct because many important and controversial Supreme Court cases in the 1960s addressed the rights of the accused such as extending the right of protection from self-incrimination, the right of counsel to the poor and confirmed the exclusionary rule, preventing the use of evidence gained through unreasonable search and seizure from being used in trials.

(e) is incorrect because campaign finance reform was not the focus of the 1960s cases.

Page reference: 513, AP Topics: The Federal Courts and Civil Rights

20.   If the Supreme Court rules that a newly passed law is unconstitutional, Congress can

(a) is incorrect because the president cannot appoint new justices unless there is a vacancy on the Court.

(b) is correct because if the Supreme Court finds a law unconstitutional, Congress has the authority to amend the Constitution to suit the law, then the Supreme Court would have no choice but to interpret the law in light of the amendment to the Constitution.

(c) is incorrect because the Supreme Court is the court of last resort.

(d) is incorrect because people cannot vote to overrule a Supreme Court decision.

(e) is incorrect because Congress cannot vote to override the Supreme Court's decision.

Page reference: 513, AP Topics: Institutions of the National Government

21. Which of the following are types of elections held in the U.S.?

(a) is incorrect because a general election is only one type of election held in the U.S.

(b) is incorrect because there is no national primary election in the United States.

(c) is incorrect because selection II is incorrect.

(d) is correct because general and run-off elections are elections to select governing officials and initiative petitions and referenda are elections in which voters play a role in deciding whether a specific policy proposal becomes law.

(e) is incorrect because selection II is incorrect.

Page reference: 364, AP Topic: Elections

22. If the House and Senate pass two different versions of a bill,

(a) is incorrect because the Senate version of the bill does not have seniority.

(b) is incorrect because the Supreme Court is not involved in the lawmaking process.

(c) is correct because it is often the case that the two houses pass different versions of the same bill and when this happens, the bill is sent to a conference committee composed of members of both houses. The committee works to develop a compromise between the bill's two versions.

(d) is incorrect because the president cannot select the version of a bill to sign.

(e) is incorrect because each house has already amended its bill, which resulted in the problem.

Page reference: 366, AP Topics: Institutions of the National Government

23. One tool that allows the president to sidestep congressional approval of his diplomatic duties is the

(a) is incorrect because treaties must be approved by Congress.

(b) is correct because the president has the power to negotiate executive agreements as well as treaties. Treaties are more formal require the approval of Congress, but executive agreements, however, deal with smaller matters, so it is often easier for the president to handle them independently.

(c) is incorrect because sending troops into war is not a diplomatic duty.

(d) is incorrect because the appointment of ambassadors requires Congressional approval.

(e) is incorrect because receiving diplomats is not an explicitly stated power of the president.

Page reference: 419, AP Topics: The President and The Congress

24. Which of the following is an accurate statement about the caseload of the Supreme Court?

(a) is correct because thousands of cases are appealed to the Supreme Court each year, but only a few are actually placed on the docket due to the fact that the justices choose to hear only those cases they feel are most deserving of appeal or may have the greatest impact on the interpretation of the law.

(b) is incorrect because the Senate Judiciary Committee does not play a role in setting the caseload for the Court.

(c) is incorrect because even though most cases reach the Court on appeal, it does not answer the question.

(d) is incorrect because the solicitor general does not play a role in setting the caseload for the Court.

(e) is incorrect because the Court does not attempt to hear every case appealed to it.

Page reference: 513, AP Topic: The Federal Courts

25. The Supreme Court has extended federal supremacy over state laws through its interpretation of the

(a) is incorrect because the 10th amendment provides for reserved powers of the states.

(b) is incorrect because the eminent domain clause does not allow the Court to assert federal supremacy over state law.

(c) is incorrect because the 1st amendment does not relate to the supremacy of federal law.

(d) is correct because the Fourteenth Amendment offered the Supreme Court the opportunity to assert federal supremacy over state laws in order to grant to all people the right to due process of the law and the court has cited the Fourteenth Amendment in numerous civil liberties and civil rights cases.

(e) is incorrect because the establish clause deals with religion.

Page reference: 513, AP Topics: The Court and Federalism

26. Which of the following is an incumbent's greatest advantage during an election?

(a) is incorrect because a presidential endorsement is not the greatest advantage.

(b) is incorrect because a clean political record is not the greatest advantage.

(c) is correct because the *greatest* advantage of an incumbent in an election is name recognition due to the fact that incumbents receive a great deal of press coverage from local media outlets, and as a consequence, their names are more easily recognized by voters.

(d) is incorrect because more campaign resources and funding are not the greatest advantage.

(e) is incorrect because a large number of undecided voters is not the greatest advantage.

Page reference: 364, AP Topic: The Congress [1]

27. Television has had which of the following effects on political parties?

(a) is incorrect because television has increased the cost of campaigning.

(b) is incorrect because television has decreased reliance on parties.

(c) is correct because television allows viewers to see and judge political candidates without the structure of a political party and candidates too can address the public directly without having to channel their campaigns through the party machine.

(d) is incorrect because television has no led to the declining importance of national conventions.

(e) is incorrect because television has not caused party realignment.

Page reference: 259, AP Topics: Media and Campaigning

28. Articles of impeachment must be passed by

(a) is incorrect because the Senate cannot impeach.

(b) is incorrect because the Senate cannot impeach.

(c) is incorrect because the Senate cannot impeach.

(d) is correct because Articles of Impeachment are the formal charges brought by the House.

(e) is incorrect because the Supreme Court cannot impeach.

Page reference: 419, AP Topics: The Presidency, The Congress, The Federal Courts

29. What happens if no presidential candidate receives an Electoral College majority?

(a) is correct because if no candidate receives an Electoral College majority, then the election moves to the House of Representatives, which must choose from among the top three electoral vote winners.

(b) is incorrect because the presidential winner is not decided by a conference of state governors.

(c) is incorrect because there is no presidential run-off.

(d) is incorrect because the Supreme Court cannot decide the presidential election.

(e) is incorrect because superdelegates cannot decide the presidential election.

Page reference: 419, AP Topics: Institutions of the National Government

30.   Which of the following is a trend in American elections?

(a) is incorrect because the number of candidates is not decreasing.

(b) is incorrect because campaigns are becoming more expensive.

(c) is incorrect because the influence of political pundits is not increasing.

(d) is incorrect because the number of citizens making contributions to candidates is not decreasing.

(e) is correct because more and more states are allowing early voting, which is voting that takes place before the announced Election Day and allows registered voters to either vote by mail or show up at specially designated polling places to cast their votes.

Page reference: 314, AP Topic: Elections

31.   Article II of the Constitution grants the president power to do all of the following EXCEPT

(a) is incorrect because authorizing troop movements is a power of the president.

(b) is correct because even though residents do have a significant amount of influence over the federal budget, Article II does not grant them the power to appropriate funds for agencies.

(c) is incorrect because vetoing legislation is a power of the president.

(d) is incorrect because giving the state of the union address is a power of the president.

(e) is incorrect because relations with foreign governments is a power of the president.

Page reference: 56, AP Topics: The Constitution and The Presidency

32.   The Civil Rights Act of 1964 articulated which of the following?

(a) is incorrect because the Civil Rights Act did not deal with desegregation of schools.

(b) is incorrect because the Civil Rights Act did not deal with poll taxes or literacy tests.

(c) is correct because the Civil Rights Act officially prohibited discrimination in any public facilities and in employment and it authorized the Justice Department to enforce the act by investigating and suing any company that violated civil rights as outlined by the law.

(d) is incorrect because the Civil Rights Act did not create the Justice Department.

(e) is incorrect because the Civil Rights Act did not deal with the right to vote.

Page reference: 90, AP Topic: Civil Rights

33. Which of the following statements accurately describes the procedure of debate in the House?

   (a) is correct because the Rules Committee is very influential on legislation because it determines the length of debate for each piece of legislation and the order in which the bills will be heard .

   (b) is incorrect because it is an incorrect statement concerning the procedures for debate in the House.

   (c) is incorrect because the Speaker and sergeant at arms do not set debate.

   (d) is incorrect because it is an incorrect statement concerning the procedures for debate in the House.

   (e) is incorrect because it is an incorrect statement concerning the procedures for debate in the House.

   Page reference: 366, AP Topic: The Congress

34. Which of the following statements characterize the relationship between congressional committees and federal agencies?

   (a) is incorrect because agencies do not regulate committees.

   (b) is incorrect because III is not the only correct statement describing the relationship between committees and agencies.

   (c) is incorrect because I and III are not the only correct statements describing the relationship between committees and agencies.

   (d) is incorrect because II is not a correct statement describing the relationship between committees and agencies.

   (e) is correct because committees oversee agencies, both by holding hearings and by setting their budgets. These are two ways the legislative branch checks the power of the executive branch. However, both committees and agencies are lobbied regularly

by interest groups that hope to influence either policymaking or policy implementation.

Page reference: 366, AP Topics: Congress and the Bureaucracy

35.   In *Texas v. Johnson*, the Supreme Court determined that

(a) is incorrect because the case does not deal with school district lines.

(b) is correct because in *Texas v. Johnson* the court ruled that flag burning is protected under the First Amendment as a form of speech; and therefore set a precedent that symbolic speech is considered "free speech" in the eyes of the law.

(c) is incorrect because the case does not deal with affirmative action quotas.

(d) is incorrect because the case does not deal with the death penalty.

(e) is incorrect because the case does not deal with obscenity.

Page reference: 32, AP Topic: Civil Rights

36.   Which of the following is usually a result of a critical election?

(a) is incorrect because party dealignment is the opposite of the correct answer.

(b) is incorrect because divided government does not relate to a critical election.

(c) is incorrect because policy implementation does not relate to a critical election.

(d) is correct because party realignment often accompanies a critical election due to the fact that they initiate a new party era and such major changes often are a result of new party affiliations among the electorate.

(e) is incorrect because policy gridlock does not relate to a critical election.

Page reference: 364, AP Topics: Elections and Political Parties

37.   A weakness of the Articles of Confederation was that they established a government that was unable to

(a) is incorrect because the government under the Articles was democratic.

(b) is incorrect because the government under the Articles was recognized by foreign governments.

(c) is incorrect because the government under the Articles clearly represented the views of the various states.

(d) is correct because the Articles did prevent the new United States from raising militias and paying its war debts and these were consequences of the fact that the

government simply was too weak—it did not have enough centralized power to give it legitimacy and, ultimately, to allow it to function.

(e) is incorrect because the government under the Articles did have a legislative branch

Page reference: 35, AP Topics: The Constitution

38. The Federal Reserve Board oversees which of the following policy areas?

(a) is incorrect because the Federal Reserve does not oversee social welfare policy.

(b) is incorrect because the Federal Reserve does not oversee foreign policy.

(c) is correct because the Federal Reserve Board is an executive institution that oversees monetary policy by controlling the flow of currency.

(d) is incorrect because the Federal Reserve does not oversee health care policy.

(e) is incorrect because the Federal Reserve does not oversee domestic policy.

Page reference: 554, AP Topic: Public Policy

39. Which of the following is a major difference between the Democratic and Republican parties?

(a) is incorrect because the campaign strategies of the parties are basically the same.

(b) is incorrect because the wider variety of groups tend to gravitate toward the democratic party.

(c) is incorrect because the Democratic party is older than the Republican party.

(d) is incorrect because the Republican party favors cutting taxes and the Democratic party raising them.

(e) is correct because Democrats tend to favor liberal policies such as social spending, whereas Republicans usually endorse more conservative policies, such as those that limit the role of the federal government.

Page reference: 277, AP Topic: Political Parties

40. Legislation that forbids labor contracts from requiring workers to join unions in order to hold their jobs is known as

(a) is incorrect because unfair labor practice legislation does not relate to unions.

(b) is correct because right-to-work laws are a key tactic of businesses in trying to weaken labor unions by preventing mandatory membership.

(c) is incorrect because right to choose laws do not relate to unions.

(d) is incorrect because right to union laws is the opposite of the correct answer.

(e) is incorrect because fair share laws do not relate to unions.

Page reference: 277, AP Topics: The Congress and Public Policy

41.   A unitary system of government is one in which

(a) is incorrect because a unitary government does not share powers among branches.

(b) is incorrect because elections can take place in all forms of government.

(c) is incorrect because it does not relate to the question of location of power.

(d) is incorrect because it a unitary government does not divide power among levels of government.

(e) is correct because in a unitary system all power resides in a central government and state and local governments have duties and powers that are delegated to them by the central government.

Page reference: 75, AP Topics: Federalism

42.   The rise of the Social Security system has had which of the following effects on the federal budget?

(a) is incorrect because defense spending and new weapons have not been affected by the increase in Social Security spending.

(b) is correct because Social Security has replaced national defense as the government's biggest expenditure.

(c) is incorrect because spending for Social Security has not impacted the trust in the government.

(d) is incorrect because spending for Social Security has not caused income taxes to double.

(e) is incorrect because spending for Social Security has encouraged senior citizen participation in government.

Page reference: 457, AP Topics: The Budget and Political Participation

43.   One way federal agencies regulate an industry is by

(a) is incorrect because federal agencies do not hire corporate leaders.

(b) is incorrect because federal agencies do not issue bonds to industry.

(c) is incorrect because federal agencies do not fix stock prices.

(d) is incorrect because federal agencies do limit an industry's international trade.

(e) is correct because regulatory agencies set industry standards to ensure both the quality of products and the safety of industrial workers and to oversee industries, agencies often send inspectors to determine whether specific companies are complying with industry standards.

Page reference: 493, AP Topic: Bureaucracy

44.   Members of Congress are most likely to endorse a president's proposal when

(a) is incorrect because party control in Congress is not as important as approval ratings.

(b) is incorrect because the end of the congressional session is not as important as approval ratings.

(c) is correct because public approval can be a powerful tool for the president due to the fact that if public opinion is high, Congress is more likely to endorse his proposals.

(d) is incorrect because issues not being well publicized is not as important as approval ratings.

(e) is incorrect because the issue of tax codes is not as important as approval ratings.

Page reference: 366, AP Topics: The Congress and The Presidency

45.   Which of the following is a basic weakness inherent in the presidency?

(a) is correct because presidents are not legislators so they may propose policies indirectly or try to influence the policy process but this means that they must rely heavily on the support of other people to help them pursue their political agenda.

(b) is incorrect because term limits are not a weakness inherent in the presidency.

(c) is incorrect because media attention is not a weakness inherent in the presidency.

(d) is incorrect because it is a false statement.

(e) is incorrect because the Electoral College is not a weakness inherent in the presidency.

Page reference: 419, AP Topic: The Presidency

46.   Despite their influence over the political agenda, interest groups may be seen as democratic institutions in that they

(a) is incorrect because it does not make interest groups more democratic.

(b) is incorrect because funding campaigns does make interest groups more democratic.

(c) is incorrect because running ads does not make interest groups more democratic.

(d) is incorrect because they do not promote equal representation of political beliefs.

(e) is correct because interest groups play a role in democratizing government by serving as linkage institutions between politicians and the public and thereby represent the needs of different groups of people to lawmakers, so these groups help the constituency to be heard.

Page reference: 513, AP Topic: Interest Groups

47.   The power of the president has expanded for which of the following reasons?

(a) is incorrect because II is only a partial answer to the question.

(b) is incorrect because the easing of tensions has not expanded the president's power.

(c) is correct because the new global economy and frequent military crises have increased the president's power and prominence as chief diplomat. The president has also become more powerful because he may act more independently than ever before. Television allows presidential candidates to reach the public directly without having to rely on political parties, and it also provides presidents with a means to address the public directly and to gain its support.

(d) is incorrect because III and IV have not increased the powers of the president.

(e) is incorrect because III has not increased the powers of the president.

Page reference: 419, AP Topic: The President

48.   Which of the following is true of federal systems of government?

(a) is incorrect because the central government does not completely regulate the states in a federal system.

(b) is incorrect because citizens vote for state government officials, as well.

(c) is correct because federalism imposes a tiered structure on government where more than one level shares authority over the people.

(d) is incorrect because most governments are unitary.

(e) is incorrect because federal systems do not tend to have just two political parties.

Page reference: 77, AP Topic: Federalism

49.   The House of Representatives differs from the Senate in all of the following ways EXCEPT

(a) is incorrect because it is a correct description of representation in the two houses.

(b) is incorrect because it is a correct description of debate in the two houses.

(c) is correct because senators actually act more independently of their party due to the fact that they have longer terms than representatives do and party affiliations and party leadership are also much stronger in the House, so representatives tend to vote along party lines.

(d) is incorrect because it is a correct description of how power is distributed in the two houses.

(e) is incorrect because it is a correct description of filibuster rules for the two houses.

Page reference: 366, AP Topic: The Congress

50.   An American citizen's approval of the president depends most heavily on

(a) is incorrect because the president's ability to stand up to Congress is not what approval depends on most heavily.

(b) is correct because party identification plays a large role in the public's perception of the president and An American citizen is more likely to approve of a president who is of the same party.

(c) is incorrect because the president's focus on foreign or domestic policy is not what approval depends on most heavily.

(d) is incorrect because the president's accessibility if not what approval depends on most heavily.

(e) is incorrect because media bias is not what approval depends on most heavily.

Page reference: 419, AP Topic: The Presidency

51.   One way the executive branch may attempt to influence the outcome of a Supreme Court case is by

(a) is correct because once justices have been appointed to the bench, there is little that the government can do to directly influence their decisions; however, through the solicitor general, it may submit briefs stating the official position of the federal government on the issue at hand.

(b) is incorrect because the government cannot select the justices to hear the case.

(c) is incorrect because the solicitor general cannot preside over the justices.

(d) is incorrect because it would be inappropriate for the president to meet with the president concerning a case.

(e) is incorrect because the government cannot issue an opinion on the case.

Page reference: 419, AP Topics: The Presidency and the Federal Courts

52. The president may exercise authority over the federal bureaucracy in all of the following ways EXCEPT by

    (a) is incorrect because the president can advise cabinet members and agency heads.

    (b) is incorrect because the president can propose budgets.

    (c) is incorrect because the president can appoint department secretaries.

    (d) is incorrect because the president can create or dismantle agencies.

    (e) is correct because Congress, not the president, is responsible for conducting oversight of federal agencies.

Page reference: 419, AP Topics: The Presidency and the Bureaucracy

53. In some states, citizens can participate directly in lawmaking by

    (a) is incorrect because citizens do not appoint legislators to committees.

    (b) is incorrect because citizens do not propose budgets in state legislatures.

    (c) is correct because some states allow citizens to participate directly in policymaking at the state level by placing a bill on the ballot, and voters can either choose to approve or kill it.

    (d) is incorrect because writing letters to the governor is not a form of direct participation in lawmaking.

    (e) is incorrect because citizens cannot set the requirements for who can run for office.

Page reference: 314, AP Topic: Policymaking

54. Which of the following is a true statement about the Voting Rights Act of 1965?

    (a) is incorrect because the Voting Rights Act did not address women voters.

    (b) is incorrect because the Voting Rights Act abolished literacy tests.

    (c) is incorrect because it did not give the states more control over federal elections.

    (d) is incorrect because it did not pass without opposition.

    (e) is correct because the Voting Rights Act of 1965, a law designed to help end formal and informal barriers to African American suffrage, resulted in dramatic gains in African American voter registration, voting, and engagement in politics more generally.

Page reference: 163, AP Topics: Civil Rights and Political Participation

55. In a state that has six electoral votes, the Republican candidate wins the popular vote, earning 54 percent to the Democratic candidate's 46 percent. The electoral votes would most likely be allocated in which of the following ways?

(a) is incorrect because electoral votes are not split.

(b) is incorrect because electoral votes are not split.

(c) is incorrect because electoral votes are not split.

(d) is correct because generally, the winner of a state's popular election receives all of that state's electoral votes and in this case, the Republican would receive all six of the electoral votes.

(e) is incorrect because electoral votes are not split.

Page reference: 419, AP Topic: Elections

56. Senators are often more willing to allow a filibuster than they are to vote for cloture because

(a) is incorrect because voting for cloture does not have a negative impact on a senator's records.

(b) is correct because senators like to reserve the power of filibustering, so they are unlikely to do anything to encourage their colleagues from trying to prevent them from using it.

(c) is incorrect because voting for cloture does stop a filibuster.

(d) is incorrect because senators do not fear losing public support.

(e) is incorrect because filibusters block the implementation of policies.

Page reference: 366, AP Topic: The Congress

57. The president exercises the most influence over policymaking by

(a) is correct because the veto is one of the president's strongest legislative tools and most of the time it allows him the final say on every piece of legislation.

(b) is incorrect because the president does not set the congressional agenda.

(c) is incorrect because the president does not introduce legislation for debate.

(d) is incorrect because the president does not participate in committee hearings.

(e) is incorrect because the president does not appoint party leaders in Congress.

Page reference: 419, AP Topics: The Presidency and The Congress

58.   Which of the following sets of states has the most Electoral College votes?

(a) is correct because since the number of representatives each state has is based on the size of its population, more populous states have more Electoral College votes. California, New York, and Texas are the top three most populous states in the U.S.

(b) is incorrect because Iowa, New Hampshire, and South Carolina are not the most populous states.

(c) is incorrect because Florida, New Jersey and Ohio are not the most populous states.

(d) is incorrect because Maine, Massachusetts, and Vermont are not the most populous states.

(e) is incorrect because North Carolina, Oregon, and Pennsylvania are not the most populous states.

Page reference: 419, AP Topic: Elections

59.   If one sees candidates from more than one political party on a ballot, one may be voting in

(a) is incorrect because open primaries have candidates from only one party on the ballot.

(b) is incorrect because I is an incorrect answer.

(c) is incorrect because I is an incorrect answer.

(d) is correct because blanket primaries list candidates from all parties, and voters are free to participate in the nomination of candidates from different parties and the general election generally features the nominees of the different parties.

(e) is incorrect because a general election is only part of the correct answer

Page reference: 292, AP Topic: Elections

60.   Which of the following is the presiding officer of the U.S. Senate?

(a) is incorrect because the Speaker is the presiding officer of the House.

(b) is incorrect because the majority leader is not the presiding officer of the Senate.

(c) is incorrect because the majority whip is not the presiding officer of the Senate.

(d) is incorrect because the chief clerk is not the presiding officer of the Senate.

(e) is correct because the Constitution makes the vice president of the United States the president of the Senate.

Free-Response Questions

This rubric provides examples of many, but not all of the possible correct responses to the free-response questions.

1. The writers of the Constitution favored the ideals of democracy, yet they feared putting too much power in the hands of the people.

    a. Identify TWO changes from the original Constitution that increased the democratic nature of government.

        -   Seventeenth Amendment.

        -   Nineteenth Amendment.

        -   Twenty-Third Amendment.

    b. Explain how each of the two factors identified in part *a*, above, has resulted in a more democratic nation.

        -   **Seventeenth Amendment.** Under the original Constitution, U.S. senators were selected by state legislators. The Seventeenth Amendment, ratified in 1913, provides for the direct election of senators by the people.

        -   **Nineteenth Amendment.** Women were disenfranchised in the original Constitution. The Nineteenth Amendment, ratified in 1920, gave women the right to vote.

        -   **Twenty-Third Amendment.** The Twenty-Third Amendment, ratified in 1961, provided the District of Columbia with Electoral College votes in presidential elections. This gave the citizens of the District of Columbia a voice and influence in presidential politics.

2. Incumbent members of Congress have a tremendous advantage over challengers in elections. But the many advantages notwithstanding, incumbents do sometimes lose elections.

    a. Identify three possible sources of incumbency advantage.

        -   advertising

        -   credit claiming

        -   position taking

- weak opponents
- campaign spending

b. Describe how each of the items you identified in part *a*, above, works to an incumbent's advantage.

- **Advertising.** Incumbents gain visibility and name recognition from communicating with their constituents. Members of Congress have franking privileges, which allow them to use congressional funds to send newsletters, memos, and emails to voters and potential voters in their district. The name recognition that is gained from this gives incumbents an advantage on Election Day.

- **Credit claiming.** Members of Congress engage in credit claiming, which involves enhancing their standing with constituents through service to individuals or the district. Casework and so-called pork barrel projects are two common ways representatives service their constituency.

- **Position taking.** Members of Congress often take policy stances that enhance their public image and might affect the outcome of an election. Because of the office they hold, they generally receive media coverage for such actions.

- **Weak opponents.** Another advantage for incumbents is they are likely to face weak opponents.

- **Campaign spending.** Incumbents tend to have a tremendous advantage in campaign fundraising. In House races, typical incumbents usually outspend challengers by a ratio of 15 to 1. Among other things, money buys name recognition.

c. Identify and explain two reasons why incumbents tend to lose elections.

- **Corruption/Scandal.** An incumbent tarnished by scandal or corruption is almost instantly vulnerable.

- **Redistricting.** Incumbent House members may be redistricted out of their district as a result of the reapportionment and redistricting processes that take place after each census.

3. The above graph details how the composition of the American population has changed over the last 40 years. Using the data above and your knowledge of U.S. government and politics, identify and explain THREE ways that these shifting populations will have an impact on government and politics.

- Changes in the demographics of the nation place new demands on the government. As the percentage of Latino/as in the population increases, for example, the prevalence of the Spanish language increases. This necessitates more English-as-a-second-language (ESL) programs and increases the cost to government to print materials in multiple languages. Other issues, such as immigration, may also become more salient in light of these changes.

- The increasing percentage of minority groups in the population makes changing the representativeness of Congress increasingly important. Right now, minority groups are significantly underrepresented in our nation's legislatures.

- Changes in the composition of society may change the partisan composition of the country. African Americans and most Hispanics (except Cubans) are more likely to identify as Democrats than Republicans. This has an effect on electoral politics in localities, states, and the nation at large.

4. During the budgetary process, Congress weighs revenues and expenditures to determine how to allocate money within the federal government. Social spending has become a major component of the federal budget in recent decades, but in some cases Congress is not able to adjust spending for it.

   a. Identify TWO items in the budget that cannot usually be amended during the budgetary process.

   - Social Security
   - Medicare

   b. For each one, explain why spending is not cut.

   - **Social Security** pays benefits to senior citizens who have paid into the system during their careers because they no longer work to earn an income. The government must pay benefits to those entitled. Not only are Social Security recipients more likely to vote than other citizens, there are also a number of well-organized interest groups that oppose reductions in spending for Social Security. This makes it difficult for members of Congress to go on record supporting cuts in this program.

   - **Medicare:** Medicare is an entitlement program that helps pay for medical care for the elderly. The number of recipients has grown steadily. Congress, again, finds it difficult, if not impossible, to amend Medicare funding during the budgetary process. Senior citizens are very protective of their claim to health care benefits, which places members of Congress under significant pressure to not cut Medicare services.

Government and Politics: United States AP Exam Practice Test 3

☐ Government and Politics: United States

Section I
Time: 45 minutes
60 Questions

Directions: Each of the questions or incomplete statements below is followed by five suggested answers or completions. Select the one that is best in each case and then fill in the corresponding oval on the answer sheet.

1. The Constitutional requirement that the Senate advise and consent on presidential appointments to the Supreme Court is an example of
    a. full faith and credit.
    b. federalism.
    c. selective incorporation.
    d. checks and balances.
    e. an attempt to limit the power of political parties.

2. All of the following are protected by the right to free speech EXCEPT
    a. the right to express unpopular political opinions.
    b. the right to engage in symbolic speech.
    c. the right to disagree with elected officials.
    d. obscene speech.
    e. disobedience of laws an individual feels are unjust.

Percent Registering and Voting by Race and Hispanic Origin: Congressional Elections

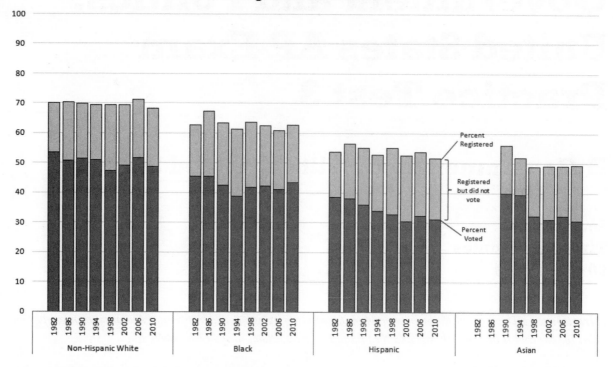

Note: Percent of the citizen civilian noninstitutionalized population, age 18 and over.
Source: Current Population Survey, Voting and Registration Supplements, historical table A-4.
Available: http://www.census.gov/hhes/www/socdemo/voting/index.html

United States Census Bureau

3. Which of the following generalizations is supported by the information in the graph above?
   a. The proportion of the registered electorate has declined sharply across all racial/ethnic groups.
   b. The number of Asians voting in Congressional elections has consistently exceeded the number of Hispanics.
   c. Voter registration consistently yields political success.
   d. As Hispanics have become the largest ethnic minority in the United States, their political clout has exceeded that of Blacks.
   e. Despite growing minority populations, non-Hispanic Whites maintain political supremacy in most Congressional elections.

4. In a primary election, voters
   a. nominate a candidate for the party in whose primary they are voting.
   b. elect a candidate to office.
   c. nominate candidates for both major political parties.
   d. are only expressing a preference. The outcome has no effect on political parties.
   e. can vote for multiple candidates.

5. Political Action Committees (PACs)
   a. support challengers more than incumbents.
   b. are a means of legally buying votes.
   c. are organized by candidates.
   d. advise the President on policy matters.
   e. raise money to support campaigns of candidates they would like to see win.

6. In both the original Constitution and today, voters directly elect
   a. the President.
   b. the Vice-President.
   c. Federal Judges.
   d. U.S. Senators.
   e. U.S. Representatives.

7. Supreme Court Justices can leave the Court in all of the following ways EXCEPT
   a. death.
   b. retirement.
   c. impeachment.
   d. being fired by the President.
   e. resignation.

8. To produce identical bills to send to the President for his consideration, the House and Senate use
   a. the Rules Committee.
   b. the Ways and Means Committee.
   c. a Conference Committee.
   d. a Joint Committee.
   e. a standing committee.

9. Most of the work in Congress is done
   a. on the floor of the two chambers.
   b. in committees or subcommittees.
   c. by the majority party.
   d. by conference committees.
   e. by the Rules Committees in the two chambers.

10. All of the following make it more likely that the Supreme Court will hear a case EXCEPT
    a. four Justices think it should be heard.
    b. different U.S. Courts of Appeals have reached different interpretations of the Constitution.
    c. Congress fails to certify a case for review.
    d. multiple interest groups file *amicus curiae* briefs.
    e. the Solicitor General weighs in on the case.

11. Presidents may not be successful in getting a judiciary that agrees with them because
    a. federal judges are often swayed by the media or public.
    b. Congress may pass laws overriding the Supreme Court's constitutional decisions.
    c. federal judges serve for life during good behavior.
    d. federal judges change when the party in the White House changes.
    e. they nominate Supreme Court Justices, but Senators appoint district court judges.

12. The innovative system of distributing power adopted in the Constitution is
    a. a unitary form of government.
    b. federalism.
    c. a confederation.
    d. libertarianism.
    e. a democracy.

13. States have an impact on national government by
    a. ratifying proposed constitutional amendments.
    b. selecting U.S. Senators.
    c. regulating political campaign spending.
    d. paying taxes based on population.
    e. deciding whether national laws apply.

14. Different public policies are followed in different states because of
    a. the full faith and credit clause.
    b. the supremacy clause.
    c. federalism.
    d. different representation in the House of Representatives.
    e. separation of powers.

15. Protection against self-incrimination was applied to the states in
    a. *Miranda v. Arizona.*
    b. *Mapp v. Ohio.*
    c. *Gideon v. Wainwright.*
    d. *Gitlow v. New York.*
    e. *Loving v. Virginia.*

16. Establishing an educational system is
    a. specifically listed in the Tenth Amendment.
    b. a concurrent power of the national and state governments.
    c. a reserved power.
    d. an implied power granted to the states.
    e. implied in the First Amendment freedom of association.

17. Turnout in presidential elections
    a. is highest among young voters.
    b. is at the same levels across all age groups.
    c. is highest among independents.
    d. is highest among older voters.
    e. is the same across all education levels.

18. Mass media coverage of election campaigns often focuses on
    a. who is ahead in the polls.
    b. the parties' conventions.
    c. the parties' platforms.
    d. the full range of candidates running under the parties' banners.
    e. likely voter turnout.

19. Political parties in the United States
    a. are strongly organized from the national through the local levels.
    b. control who runs under their party label.
    c. have strict membership requirements.
    d. welcome competition from "third" parties.
    e. are focused on winning elections.

20. The national government's power has been greatly expanded by its expressed power to
    a. establish post offices and post roads.
    b. establish a national educational system.
    c. establish Social Security.
    d. regulate occupations.
    e. regulate interstate commerce.

OUTLAYS BY MAJOR SPENDING CATEGORY, 1970–2002
(in billions of dollars)

Year	Discretionary Spending	Entitlements and Other Mandatory Spending	Net Interest	Total Outlays
1970	120.3	72.5	14.4	195.6
1975	158.0	169.4	23.2	332.3
1980	276.3	291.2	52.5	590.9
1985	415.8	448.2	129.5	946.4
1990	500.6	626.9	184.3	1,253.2
1995	544.9	818.5	232.1	1,515.8
2000	614.8	1,029.8	223.0	1,788.8

Source: Congressional Budget Office.

21. Which of the following can be drawn from the table above?
    a. For the time period covered, it would require congressional action not to spend a majority of federal outlays.
    b. States significantly affect the national budget.
    c. Interest is an insignificant part of the national budget.
    d. The national deficit is a significant public policy problem.
    e. The national debt is a significant public policy problem.

22. The group of advisors closest to the president is
    a. the Cabinet.
    b. the Executive Office of the President.
    c. the Speaker of the House and the President pro tem of the Senate.
    d. the Vice President and his staff.
    e. the President's party caucus.

23. Bureaucratic power arises from
    a. federalism.
    b. generally positive public opinion.
    c. discretion to implement vague Congressional mandates.
    d. PAC funds.
    e. separation of powers.

24. Clarence Gideon argued that he had the right to
    a. place Bibles in motel rooms.
    b. counsel.
    c. privacy.
    d. speech.
    e. bear arms.

25. The right to privacy is based on
    a. implied powers.
    b. enumerated powers.
    c. Supreme Court decisions.
    d. Executive Orders.
    e. bureaucratic rules.

26. Protecting property rights
    a. is undemocratic was, therefore, rejected by the Framers of the Constitution.
    b. is reflected in the expressed powers in the Constitution.
    c. is left to state governments in the Constitution.
    d. is solely a function of the courts.
    e. is a function of bureaucratic agencies.

27. The "Rule of Four"
    a. sets the minimum number of electoral votes each state has.
    b. sets a precedent in Supreme Court cases.
    c. sets the maximum number of terms a president may serve.
    d. generally is sufficient for the Supreme Court to hear a case.
    e. is the maximum number of candidates to which an individual can contribute money in a year.

28. For which federal office would the average AP student be constitutionally qualified?
    a. Representative
    b. Senator
    c. President
    d. Vice-President
    e. Judge

29. If your right against unreasonable search and seizure is violated, the remedy is
    a. the exclusionary rule.
    b. the plea bargaining.
    c. an *ex post facto* law.
    d. *habeas corpus.*
    e. a bill of attainder.

30. Cloture
    a. removes a President or Justice who has been impeached.
    b. is a Constitutional provision to protect minority rights.
    c. is used only in the Senate.
    d. is used only in the House.
    e. limits the amount of time each side can argue a case before the Supreme Court.

31. The number of interest groups has grown because
    a. "organization begets counterorganization."
    b. political parties charge more to join.
    c. interest groups get good media coverage..
    d. interest groups are subsidized by the government.
    e. interest groups are specifically mentioned in the Constitution.

32. The group most closely associated with voting for the Democratic Party is
    a. Black Americans.
    b. Asian Americans.
    c. Hispanic Americans.
    d. Southerners after 1964.
    e. regular church attendees.

33. State and local party organizations have less control over who their candidates are than in the past. This is because of the growth in the use of
    a. public campaign financing.
    b. partisanship.
    c. ideology.
    d. mass media.
    e. primaries.

34. The fact that members of Congress serve on committees that allow them to contribute to their constituencies contributes to
    a. the party in the electorate.
    b. the incumbency effect.
    c. the committee effect.
    d. corruption.
    e. Turnover among committees.

35. The Equal Employment Opportunity Commission is organized into 15 districts located throughout the United States, the Virgin Islands and Puerto Rico. This organization model illustrates
    a. the impact of federalism on public policy.
    b. that the law enforced by the Equal Employment Opportunity Commission differs across the country.
    c. that the Equal Employment Opportunity Commission is independent of partisan politics.
    d. that the implementation of public policy can be decentralized.
    e. that most equal employment opportunity issues arise in cities.

36. Budget preparation by the Office of Management and Budget is a function of the
    a. legislative branch of government.
    b. executive branch of government.
    c. judicial branch of government .
    d. independent regulatory commissions.
    e. quasi-governmental corporations.

37. The most common act of political participation is
    a. lobbying.
    b. campaigning.
    c. contributing money.
    d. voting.
    e. running for office.

38. Most protections in the "Bill of Rights" have been extended to the states through a process known as
    a. cooperative federalism.
    b. selective incorporation.
    c. the legislative veto.
    d. dual federalism.
    e. presidential power.

39. The fact that states can be "laboratories of democracy" is an advantage of
    a. checks and balances.
    b. federalism.
    c. separation of powers.
    d. primary elections.
    e. political parties.

40. Congress affects the power of the courts by all of the following EXCEPT
    a. establishing new federal courts.
    b. creating new federal judgeships.
    c. determining the jurisdiction of federal courts.
    d. determining the number of Supreme Court Justices.
    e. reduce the pay of sitting federal judges..

41. The winner-take-all electoral system in the U.S. is a primary reason for
    a. only two major political parties.
    b. the high costs of electoral campaigns.
    c. the way states allocate Electoral College votes.
    d. "third" parties that routinely win elections.
    e. clear differences between liberals and conservatives in political parties.

42. All of the following are reasons an interest group would have a great deal of influence in the policy area in which they are interested EXCEPT
    a. a monopoly on relevant information.
    b. a large membership.
    c. cohesion.
    d. high levels of Congressional expertise and commitment in the area.
    e. significant financial resources and legal expertise.

43. If you were trying to predict the outcome of an upcoming congressional election, the most valuable information you could have is
    a. a candidate's incumbency status.
    b. the amount of money each candidate has to spend.
    c. how the President performed in the district in the last election.
    d. the number of voters who voted in the last election.
    e. the state in which the candidate lives.

44. Voting turnout in the United States
    a. increases every time we increase suffrage.
    b. is lower than in most other Western democracies.
    c. is lower than in most other countries, because most other countries require voting.
    d. does not vary across type of election—presidential or local.
    e. is highest among college students, who understand the political system well.

45. Primary election voters
    a. are likely to be independents.
    b. are likely to be moderates.
    c. must be registered with their political party.
    d. are a large proportion of the electorate.
    e. are "activists" in politics.

46. In striking down discrimination in public accommodations, e.g. hotels and restaurants, Congress, upheld by the Supreme Court, relied on
    a. the interstate commerce clause.
    b. the First Amendment's right to freedom of assembly.
    c. the Equal Protection Clause.
    d. the expressed powers of Congress.
    e. judicial activism.

47. The First Amendment protection for free speech is most limited when the Supreme Court applies the
    a. Clear and Present Danger Test.
    b. Dangerous Tendency Test.
    c. Child Benefit Theory.
    d. Symbolic Speech Doctrine.
    e. "Rule of Four."

48. The Framers of the Constitution, compared to the Articles of Confederation,
    a. gave more power to the states.
    b. gave more power to the people.
    c. did not change the relationship between the national government and the states.
    d. gave more power to the national government.
    e. made it more difficult to amend the basic governing document..

49. Pluralist theory emphasizes the role of
    a. individuals.
    b. competition among groups.
    c. wealth.
    d. the limited number of access points to government.
    e. the three branches of government.

50. If one wanted to insulate decisions from partisan political influence, one might house the policy responsibility in
    a. a cabinet department.
    b. state governments.
    c. the bureaucracy.
    d. an interest group.
    e. an independent regulatory commission.

51. The committee that sets the guidelines for floor debate in the House of Representatives, but not in the Senate is
    a. the Administration Committee.
    b. the Ways and Means Committee.
    c. the Procedure Committee.
    d. the Ethics Committee.
    e. the Rules Committee.

52. Congressional staffers
    a. are often also members of the media.
    b. are part of the executive bureaucracy.
    c. communicate between members of Congress and constituents.
    d. are insulated from contact with interest groups.
    e. spend much of their time in congressional offices fund-raising.

53. The right to privacy
    a. is an enumerated right.
    b. is based on federal statute.
    c. was first articulated in *Roe v. Wade.*
    d. was first articulated in *Griswold v. Connecticut.*
    e. is enforced by "iron triangles."

54. The power to decide the constitutionality of a law was assumed by the Supreme Court in
    a. *Marbury v. Madison*
    b. *McCullouch v. Maryland*
    c. *Plessy v. Ferguson*
    d. *Barron v. Baltimore*
    e. *Brown v. Board of Education*

55. Taxing and spending are examples of
    a. monetary policy.
    b. executive powers.
    c. judicial powers.
    d. fiscal policy.
    e. independent regulatory authority.

56. The Office of Management and Budget has primary responsibility for
    a. auditing agencies.
    b. levying and collecting taxes.
    c. preparing executive spending proposals.
    d. preparing congressional spending proposals.
    e. making sure "pork barrel" legislation is not passed by Congress.

57. In the 2012 election, which of the following would be most likely to vote for the Democratic presidential candidate
    a. a black teacher from Los Angeles.
    b. a white doctor from Atlanta.
    c. a fundamentalist Protestant minister from Virginia.
    d. a voter with no partisan affiliation.
    e. an anti-abortion activist.

58. "Judicial activism" means that
    a. the Supreme Court hears more case each succeeding year.
    b. judges actively seek cases to hear.
    c. judges lobby Congress for more funding.
    d. liberal judges make public policy, unlike conservative judges.
    e. judges interpret the Constitution according to their own attitudes.

59. Interest groups attempt to influence public policy by
    a. running candidates for office.
    b. filing *amicus curiae* briefs.
    c. holding conventions.
    d. holding primaries.
    e. holding caucuses to nominate candidates.

60. The relationship between Congress and public opinion is that
    a. members of Congress always vote the way their constituents want them to vote.
    b. members of Congress always vote the way the majority of citizens want them to vote.
    c. the public does not trust members of Congress, as evidenced by how often they vote them out of office.
    d. the public has a low opinion of Congress as a whole, but a high opinion of their own member of Congress.
    e. members of Congress do not pay much attention to public opinion.

END OF SECTION I.

IF YOU FINISH BEFORE TIME IS CALLED, YOU MAY CHECK YOUR WORK ON THIS SECTION.

DO NOT GO ON TO SECTION II UNTIL YOU ARE TOLD TO DO SO.

☐ Government and Politics: United States

Section II
Time: 100 minutes

Directions: *You have 100 minutes to answer all four of the following questions. It is suggested that you take a few minutes to plan and outline each answer. Spend approximately one-fourth of your time (25 minutes) on each question. Illustrate your essay with substantive examples where appropriate. Make certain to number each of your answers as the question is numbered below.*

1. In 2010 the Supreme Court ruled in *McDonald v. Chicago* that the Second Amendment applied to the states.

   a. Identify the term that is used to describe the application of one of the amendments in "Bill of Rights" to the states.

   b. Explain why it is necessary for the Supreme Court to render such a decision if the Second Amendment is to be applied to the states..

   c. Identify two (2) other Supreme Court cases that applied one of the amendments in the "Bill of Rights" to the states and describe which right was extended by the case.

2. Representation is central to the functioning of United States government and politics.

   a. Explain two ways the national executive branch contributes to representation.

   b. Explain two ways the national legislative branch contributes to representation.

   c. Explain one way the national judicial branch contributes to representation.

Percent Voting by Educational Attainment

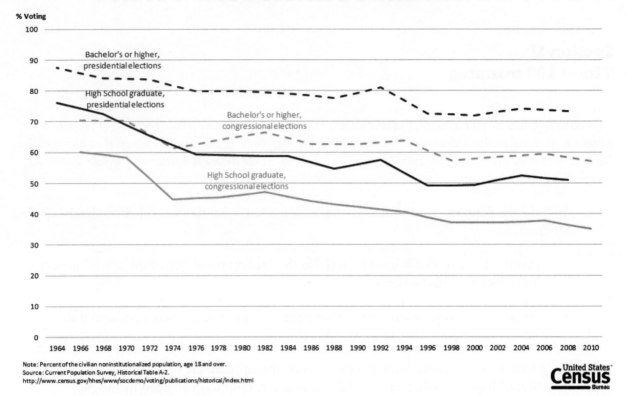

% Voting

Bachelor's or higher, presidential elections

High School graduate, presidential elections

Bachelor's or higher, congressional elections

High School graduate, congressional elections

1964 1966 1968 1970 1972 1974 1976 1978 1980 1982 1984 1986 1988 1990 1992 1994 1996 1998 2000 2002 2004 2006 2008 2010

Note: Percent of the civilian noninstitutionalized population, age 18 and over.
Source: Current Population Survey, Historical Table A-2.
http://www.census.gov/hhes/www/socdemo/voting/publications/historical/index.html

United States Census Bureau

3. The above graph shows the proportion of the civilian, noninstitutionalized population, age 18 and over voting in various elections. Using this information and your knowledge of U.S. politics:

   a. Briefly describe two trends depicted in this graph.

   b. Identify two factors that may have produced the trends you describe.

   c. Explain why there are differences between the levels of voting for presidential and congressional elections.

   d. Explain why there are differences based on educational attainment.

4. The Framers of the Constitution were concerned that power would be too concentrated in government. Some citizens today complain that government cannot get anything done.

   a. Identify three mechanisms that the Framers adopted to make sure power was not too concentrated in government.

   b. Explain how each of these mechanisms were meant to make sure power was not too concentrated in government.

   c. Identify one mechanism used today to try to make sure government accomplishes something.

d. Explain how this mechanism used today is meant to make sure government accomplishes something.

END OF EXAMINATION

□ Answers and Explanations

Practice Test 3
Section I

1. The Constitutional requirement that the Senate advise and consent on presidential appointments to the Supreme Court is an example of

    (a) is incorrect because full faith and credit deals with relations among the states and not checks and balances.

    (b) is incorrect because federalism deals with relations between the national and state governments and not checks and balances.

    (c) is incorrect because selective incorporation deals with federalism and not checks and balances.

    (d) is correct because the Constitution creates a system of checks and balances and advise and consent is an example of that.

    (e) is incorrect because limiting the power of political parties does not relate to checks and balances.

    Page reference: 52, AP Topic: Checks and Balances

2. All of the following are protected by the right to free speech EXCEPT

    (a) is incorrect because expressing unpopular opinions is protected by the 1st Amendment.

    (b) is incorrect because symbolic speech is protected by the 1st Amendment.

    (c) is incorrect because the right to disagree with elected officials is protected by the 1st Amendment.

    (d) is correct because obscene speech is not of form of speech protected by the 1st Amendment.

    (e) is incorrect because civil disobedience is protected by the 1st Amendment.

    Page reference: 119, AP Topic: Civil Rights and Civil Liberties

3. Which of the following generalizations is supported by the information in the graph above?

    (a) is incorrect because the graph indicates an increase of registered voters across all ethnic groups.

(b) is incorrect because the graph indicates that the number of Asian voters overall is less than the number of Hispanic voters.

(c) is incorrect because the graph does not provide information on political success.

(d) is incorrect because the graph does not provide information on political clout.

(e) is correct because the graph indicates that non-Hispanic whites are more politically active than minority populations, regardless of the population growth in the minority populations.

Page reference: 311, AP Topic: Voting/Elections

4.   In a primary election, voters

(a) is correct because a primary election allows voters to nominate a candidate for the party conducting the primary.

(b) is incorrect because primary elections do not elect candidates to office.

(c) is incorrect because primary elections only nominate candidates for a specific political party.

(d) is incorrect because primary elections do have an effect on the political party's selection of a candidate.

(e) is incorrect because primary elections only allow voters to vote for one candidate.

Page reference: 267, AP Topic: Political Parties and Elections

5.   Political Action Committees (PACs)

(a) is incorrect because PACs support like-minded candidates regardless of incumbency.

(b) is incorrect because PACs do not buy votes.

(c) is incorrect because PACs are organized by interest groups.

(d) is incorrect because PACs do not advise the president.

(e) is correct because the purpose of a PAC is to raise money and distribute the funds to candidates the group supports.

Page reference: 302, AP Topic: Characteristics and Roles of PACs

6.   In both the original Constitution and today, voters directly elect

(a) is incorrect because the President is elected by the Electoral College and not directly elected by the people.

(b) is incorrect because the Vice-President is also elected by the Electoral College.

(c) is incorrect because federal judges are appointed by the president.

(d) is incorrect because Senators were originally elected by state legislatures and not directly elected by the people.

(e) is correct because members of the House of Representatives were originally and are still directly elected by the people, as established by the Constitution.

Page reference: 364, AP Topics: The Constitution and Institutions of the National Government

7. Supreme Court Justices can leave the Court in all of the following ways EXCEPT

    (a) is incorrect because Supreme Court Justices can leave office upon their deaths.

    (b) is incorrect because Supreme Court Justices can leave office by retiring.

    (c) is incorrect because Supreme Court Justices can be removed from office through impeachment.

    (d) is correct because Supreme Court Justices are appointed by the President, but cannot be fired by the President.

    (e) is incorrect because Supreme Court Justices can leave office by resigning.

Page reference: 515, AP Topics: The Federal Courts

8. To produce identical bills to send to the President for his consideration, the House and Senate use

    (a) is incorrect because the Rules Committee reviews bills in the House before sending them to the floor.

    (b) is incorrect because the Ways and Means Committee writes the tax codes.

    (c) is correct because a Conference Committee is created by party leadership from both houses to iron out the differences and bring back a single bill.

    (d) is incorrect because a Joint Committee is made up of members of both houses to address a specific topic.

    (e) is incorrect because a standing committee is a subject matter committee in each house dealing with bills in specific policy areas.

Page reference: 374, AP Topic: The Congress

9. Most of the work in Congress is done

(a) is incorrect because bills must make it through committee before ever reaching the floor of the two chambers.

(b) is correct because the majority of the work in both houses of Congress is done in committees and subcommittees.

(c) is incorrect because committees are made up of members from both parties.

(d) is incorrect because a conference committee is only created to work out the differences in the House and Senate versions of a bill.

(e) is incorrect because the Rules Committee acts as a gatekeeper for bills but does not complete the work on the bill.

Page reference: 374, AP Topic: The Congress and The major formal and informal arrangements of power

10.   All of the following make it more likely that the Supreme Court will hear a case EXCEPT

(a) is incorrect because if at least four justices vote to hear a case, it will be heard by the Court.

(b) is incorrect because if U.S. Courts of Appeal have different interpretations of the Constitution, it is likely the Supreme Court will hear the case to settle the dispute.

(c) is correct because Congress does not have to certify a case in order for the Supreme Court to hear it.

(d) is incorrect because if the Court receives several *amicus curiae* briefs it is apparent the issue is of importance to a large group of people and they may be more likely to hear the case.

(e) is incorrect because the Solicitor general represents the U.S. but does not weigh in on whether or not the Court should hear the appeal.

Page reference: 525, AP Topics: The Federal Courts; The major formal and informal arrangement of power

11.   Presidents may not be successful in getting a judiciary that agrees with them because

(a) is incorrect because, due to their life appointments, federal judges are insulated from public opinion.

(b) is incorrect because Congress cannot override Supreme Court decisions through the legislative process.

(c) is correct because federal judges serve for life and a president may not have the opportunity to make appointments to the federal courts during his term of office.

(d) is incorrect because federal judges are appointed for life and do not change with administrations.

(e) is incorrect because the President appoints all federal judges, not the Senate.

Page reference: 518, AP Topics: The Federal Courts; Relationships among institutions and varying balances of power

12. The innovative system of distributing power adopted in the Constitution is

    (a) is incorrect because a unitary government has all power residing in a central government.

    (b) is correct because the Constitution divides power between a national and state governments, thus creating a federal government.

    (c) is incorrect because a confederation has the power residing at the local level in an alliance of independent states,

    (d) is incorrect because libertarianism is not an organization of government, but a political philosophy.

    (e) is incorrect because a democracy is not an organization of government, but a political philosophy.

Page reference: 75, AP Topic: Federalism

13. States have an impact on national government by

    (a) is correct because states must ratify constitutional amendments before they become part of the Constitution which allows the states to have an impact on the national government.

    (b) is incorrect because U.S. Senators are chosen by the people, not the states.

    (c) is incorrect because campaign spending is regulated by federal law.

    (d) is incorrect because the income tax replaced taxes being paid based on population.

    (e) is incorrect because states cannot nullify national laws.

Page reference: 84, AP Topic: Federalism

14. Different public policies are followed in different states because of

    (a) is incorrect because full faith and credit requires each state to cooperate in certain areas, but does not require the policies to be the same.

    (b) is incorrect because the supremacy clause makes national law supreme over state laws, but does not require state policies to be the same.

    (c) is correct because federalism divides the government into national and state governments, which allows the individual states to adopt different public policies.

    (d) is incorrect because different representation in the House does not relate to the policies which are established at the state level.

(e) is incorrect because separation of powers relate to the power relationships among the branches of the national government and does not apply to the relations among the states.

Page reference: 94, AP Topic: Federalism

15. Protection against self-incrimination was applied to the states in

    (a) is correct because the *Miranda* case set guidelines for police questioning to protect accused persons against self-incrimination.

    (b) is incorrect because the *Mapp* case dealt with searches and seizures.

    (c) is incorrect because the *Gideon* case dealt with the right to an attorney.

    (d) is incorrect because the *Gitlow* case dealt with freedoms of press and speech.

    (e) is incorrect because the *Loving* case dealt with laws prohibiting interracial marriage.

    Page reference: 134, AP Topic: Civil Liberties

16. Establishing an educational system is

    (a) is incorrect because reserved powers are not specifically listed in the 10th Amendment.

    (b) is incorrect because the national government cannot establish a national educational system; therefore it is not a concurrent power.

    (c) is correct because the 10th Amendment reserved powers for the states and establishing an educational system is one of those reserved powers.

    (d) is incorrect because implied powers belong to the national government, not the states.

    (e) is incorrect because reserved powers are found in the 10th Amendment, not the 1st.

    Page reference: 98, AP Topics: Policymaking and Federalism

17. Turnout in presidential elections

    (a) is incorrect because younger voters have the lowest voter turnout in presidential elections.

    (b) is incorrect because voter turnout is very different among age groups.

    (c) is incorrect because being "independent" is a political philosophy and not a demographic area.

    (d) is correct because the group with the highest voter turnout in presidential elections is the 65 and older group.

(e) is incorrect because there are differences among education levels as it relates to voter turnout with the more highly educated having the highest voter turnout.

Page reference: 216, AP Topic: Factors that influence citizens to differ from one another in terms of political behaviors

18. Mass media coverage of election campaigns often focuses on

(a) is correct because mass media focuses on the front runners to the almost exclusion of other candidates.

(b) is incorrect because convention coverage is a small part of campaign coverage.

(c) is incorrect because the party platforms receive very little coverage.

(d) is incorrect because the mass media focuses on the candidates who are leading in the polls and others receive little to no coverage.

(e) is incorrect because media coverage of an election devotes little to no time to the issue of voter turnout.

Page reference: 227, AP Topic: The Mass Media

19. Political parties in the United States

(a) is incorrect because political parties vary in organization through the country and the different levels of government.

(b) is incorrect because political parties do not always have control of who runs under their party label.

(c) is incorrect because anyone can become a member of a political party.

(d) is incorrect because the two main political parties do not like competition from third parties that might draw voters away from them.

(e) is correct because a political party's main goal is to control the governing institutions by getting their candidates elected to office.

Page reference: 279, AP Topic: Political Party Functions

20. The national government's power has been greatly expanded by its expressed power to

(a) is incorrect because establishing post offices and post roads has not expanded the power of the national government.

(b) is incorrect because the national government does not have the power to establish a national educational system.

(c) is incorrect because establishing Social Security has not greatly increased the powers of the national government.

(d) is incorrect because the national government cannot regulate occupations.

(e) is correct because commerce clause, and all the implied powers related to it, have greatly increased the power of the national government.

Page reference: 82, AP Topic: Constitutional Underpinnings of the U.S. Government

21.   Which of the following can be drawn from the table above?

(a) is correct because entitlements and other mandatory spending has increased since 1970 and not spending that money would require action from Congress.

(b) is incorrect because the budget is set by Congress and the states do not play a significant role in the process.

(c) is incorrect because interest is, as indicated by the chart, a significant part of the national budget.

(d) is incorrect because the national deficit is not addressed by the chart.

(e) is incorrect because the national debt is not addressed by the chart.

Page reference: 460, AP Topic: Public Policy

22.   The group of advisors closest to the president is

(a) is incorrect because the Executive Office of the President includes staff agencies which help the president carry out his/her duties, but does not closely advise the president.

(b) is correct because the Cabinet, which is selected by the president, is the group of advisors who work closest to the president.

(c) is incorrect because the Speaker of the House and President pro tem of the Senate provide the leadership for Congress and do not closely advise the president.

(d) is incorrect because the Vice President and his staff do not serve in an advisory role to the president.

(e) is incorrect because the President's party caucus does not serve in an advisory role to the president.

Page reference: 410, AP Topics: The Presidency; The major formal and informal arrangements of power

23.   Bureaucratic power arises from

(a) is incorrect because federalism is geographic arrangement of power and does not relate to the creation of the bureaucracy.

(b) is incorrect because the public generally has a negative opinion of the bureaucracy.

(c) is correct because the bureaucracy was created to implement the mandates of the government and as the size and power of the government grew, so did the size and power of the bureaucracy.

(d) is incorrect because the bureaucracy does not receive funds from PACs.

(e) is incorrect because separation of powers related to the power arrangement among the branches of the national government and does not relate to the power of the bureaucracy.

Page reference: 475, AP Topics: The Bureaucracy and Major formal and informal arrangements of power

24.   Clarence Gideon argued that he had the right to

(a) is incorrect because Clarence Gideon did not want to place Bibles in hotel rooms.

(b) is correct because Clarence Gideon appealed his conviction on the basis of his constitutional right to an attorney.

(c) is incorrect because Gideon's right to an attorney was violated, not his right to privacy.

(d) is incorrect because Gideon's right to free speech was not violated.

(e) is incorrect because Gideon's right to bear arms was not violated.

Page reference: 136, AP Topic: Civil Liberties

25.   The right to privacy is based on

(a) is incorrect because the right to privacy is not part of the implied powers of Congress.

(b) is incorrect because the right to privacy is not one of the enumerated powers of Congress.

(c) is correct because the right to privacy is not specifically stated in the Constitution but is based on Supreme Court decisions.

(d) is incorrect because the right to privacy was not established with an executive order.

(e) is incorrect because the right to privacy was not establish be bureaucratic rules.

Page reference: 143, AP Topic: Civil Liberties

26.   Protecting property rights

(a) is incorrect because the Constitution makes it clear that the founding fathers were very concerned about property rights.

(b) is correct because the basis for protecting property rights is found in Article I of the Constitution, such as the guidelines for taxing property.

(c) is incorrect because Congress is given power to protect property rights.

(d) is incorrect because Congress is given power to protect property rights.

(e) is incorrect because Congress is given power to protect property rights.

Page reference: 38, AP Topic: Constitutional Underpinnings of the United States Government

27.   The "Rule of Four"

(a) is incorrect because the "rule of four" does not deal with electoral votes.

(b) is incorrect because the "rule of four" is not a Supreme Court precedent.

(c) is incorrect because the "rule of four" does not relate to the executive branch.

(d) is correct because it takes only four Supreme Court justices to agree to hear a case and this is known as the "rule of four."

(e) is incorrect because the "rule of four" does not relate to campaign laws.

Page reference: 525, AP Topic: The Federal Courts

28.   For which federal office would the average AP student be constitutionally qualified?

(a) is incorrect because the age requirement for a Representative is 25 years old.

(b) is incorrect because the age requirement for a Senator is 30 years old.

(c) is incorrect because the age requirement for the President is 35 years old.

(d) is incorrect because the age requirement for the Vice-President is the same as for the President.

(e) is correct because the Constitution sets no specific requirements for becoming a federal judge.

Page reference: 50, AP Topics: The Federal Courts and The major formal and informal arrangements of power

29.   If your right against unreasonable search and seizure is violated, the remedy is

(a) is correct because the exclusionary rule says that evidence that is not constitutionally obtained cannot be introduced as evidence in court.

(b) is incorrect because plea bargaining is a form a guilty plea and does not involve the exclusion of evidence.

(c) is incorrect because an *ex post facto* is a retroactive criminal law and is prohibited by the Constitution.

(d) is incorrect because *habeas corpus* is a writ requiring an arrested person to be brought to court and does not involve the exclusion of evidence.

(e) is incorrect because a bill of attainder punishes without a trial and is prohibited by the Constitution.

Page reference: 132, AP Topic: Civil Liberties

30.   Cloture

(a) is incorrect because cloture relates to debate and not impeachment.

(b) is incorrect because cloture relates to debate and not minority rights.

(c) is correct because cloture, a procedure for terminating debate, can only be used in the Senate to stop a filibuster.

(d) is incorrect because cloture can only be used in the Senate, not the House.

(e) is incorrect because cloture limits debate in the Senate, not the Supreme Court.

Page reference: 371, AP Topics: The Congress and The major formal and informal arrangements of power

31.   The number of interest groups has grown because

(a) is correct because for each interest group that is created, an opposite interest group will be created in response, causing the number of interest groups to grow dramatically.

(b) is incorrect because political parties charges to join is not related to the growth of interest groups.

(c) is incorrect because media coverage of interest groups is not necessarily related to the growth of interest groups.

(d) is incorrect because the possibility of subsidies has not caused the number of interest groups to grow.

(e) is incorrect because interest groups are not specifically mentioned in the Constitution.

Page reference: 331, AP Topic: Interest Groups

32.   The group most closely associated with voting for the Democratic Party is

(a) is correct because Black Americans tend to vote for Democrats more than the other groups listed.

(b) is incorrect because Asian Americans are not as closely associated with voting for Democrats as are Black Americans.

(c) is incorrect because Hispanic Americans are not as closely associated with voting for Democrats as are Black Americans.

(d) is incorrect because Southerners after 1964 are not as closely associated with voting for Democrats as are Black Americans.

(e) is incorrect because regular church attendees are not as closely associated with voting for Democrats as are Black Americans.

Page reference: 311, AP Topic: Factors that influence citizens to differ from one another in terms of political behaviors

33. State and local party organizations have less control over who their candidates are than in the past. This is because of the growth in the use of

(a) is incorrect because public campaign financing has not impacted the control of candidates.

(b) is incorrect because partisanship has not impacted the control of candidates.

(c) is incorrect because ideology has not impacted the control of candidates.

(d) is incorrect because mass media has not impacted the control of candidates.

(e) is correct because primaries have moved the control of party candidates more to the national party organization away from the state and local organizations.

Page reference: 291, AP Topic: Political Parties

34. The fact that members of Congress serve on committees that allow them to contribute to their constituencies contributes to

(a) is incorrect because committee service is not directly related to the party in the electorate.

(b) is correct because the serving on committees gives members of Congress the opportunity to help constituents; the constituents tend to return them to Congress in order to retain that help.

(c) is incorrect because this is not a valid option.

(d) is incorrect because serving on committees does not necessarily lead to corruption.

(e) is incorrect because committee service to constituents does not lead to turnover on committees.

Page reference: 364, AP Topic: The Congress

35. The Equal Employment Opportunity Commission is organized into 15 districts located throughout the United States, the Virgin Islands and Puerto Rico. This organization model illustrates

(a) is incorrect because federalism would involve state involvement, not federal districts.

(b) is incorrect because the EEOC law does not differ across the country.

(c) is incorrect because the organization does not relate to partisan politics.

(d) is correct because the organization of the locations of the EEOC districts, indicates that this area of public policy has been decentralized.

(e) is incorrect because the organization does not contain information about the location of equal employment opportunities.

Page reference: 484, AP Topic: Public Policy

36. Budget preparation by the Office of Management and Budget is a function of the

(a) is incorrect because the OMB is not part of the legislative branch.

(b) is correct because the OMB is a part of the executive branch making budget preparation a function of the executive branch.

(c) is incorrect because the OMB is not part of the judicial branch.

(d) is incorrect because the OMB is not an independent regulatory commissions.

(e) is incorrect because the OMB is not a quasi-governmental corporation.

Page reference: 462, AP Topic: Public Policy

37. The most common act of political participation is

(a) is incorrect because lobbying is a form of participation, but it is not as common as voting.

(b) is incorrect because campaigning is a form of participation, but it is not as common as voting.

(c) is incorrect because contributing money is a form of participation, but it is not as common as voting.

(d) is correct because most people participate in politics by voting.

(e) is incorrect because running for office is a form of participation, but it is not as common as voting.

Page reference: 311, AP Topic: Political Beliefs and Behaviors

38.   Most protections in the "Bill of Rights" have been extended to the states through a process known as

(a) is incorrect because cooperative federalism describes how policy and power assignments are shared between the national government and the states.

(b) is correct because the process by which the Supreme Court used the 14th Amendment to make the provisions of the Bill of Rights applicable to the states is known as selective incorporation.

(c) is incorrect because the legislative veto is the process of Congress overriding a presidential decision and does not relate to the Bill of Rights.

(d) is incorrect because dual federalism deals with spheres of powers and not specifically to the application of the Bill of Rights to the states.

(e) is incorrect because presidential power does not relate to applying the Bill of Rights to the states.

Page reference: 110, AP Topic: Civil Liberties

39.   The fact that states can be "laboratories of democracy" is an advantage of

(a) is incorrect because checks and balances does not relate to state governments.

(b) is correct because federalism provides for a national and state governments with separate spheres of power which allows states to experiment with different applications of democratic principles.

(c) is incorrect because separation of powers does not relate to state governments.

(d) is incorrect because primary elections do not relate directly to the power of state governments.

(e) is incorrect because political parties do not specifically relate to the topic of the question.

Page reference: 94, AP Topic: Federalism

40.   Congress affects the power of the courts by all of the following EXCEPT

(a) is incorrect because Congress can affect the power of the courts by establishing new federal courts.

(b) is incorrect because Congress can affect the power of the courts by creating new federal judgeships.

(c) is incorrect because Congress can affect the power of the courts by determining the jurisdiction of federal courts.

(d) is incorrect because Congress can affect the power of the courts by determining the number of Supreme Court Justices.

(e) is correct because Congress is prohibited from reducing the pay of sitting judges.

Page reference: 511, AP Topic: Relationships among institutions and varying balances of power

41.   The winner-take-all electoral system in the U.S. is a primary reason for

(a) is correct because the winner-take-all electoral system is the primary reason for only two major political parties because additional parties dilute the vote and make declaring a winner difficult.

(b) is incorrect because the high cost of campaigns does not impact the number of political parties.

(c) is incorrect because the way states allocate Electoral College votes does not impact the number of political parties.

(d) is incorrect because third parties rarely win elections.

(e) is incorrect because there are not clear differences between liberals and conservatives in political parties.

Page reference: 278, AP Topic: Electoral Laws and Systems

42.   All of the following are reasons an interest group would have a great deal of influence in the policy area in which they are interested EXCEPT

(a) is incorrect because if an interest group has a monopoly on relevant information, they will have a great deal of influence.

(b) is incorrect because if an interest group has a large membership, Congress will be more likely to be influenced by the group.

(c) is incorrect because if an interest group has cohesion it will carry more influence.

(d) is correct because if there is a high level of Congressional expertise and commitment in a particular area, an interest group would be an unnecessary source of information.

(e) is incorrect because if an interest group has significant financial resources and legal expertise it will carry more influence.

Page reference: 336, AP Topic: Interest Groups

43.   If you were trying to predict the outcome of an upcoming congressional election, the most valuable information you could have is

(a) is correct because incumbency is the greatest predictor of the outcome of an election.

(b) is incorrect because money is not as important as incumbency in an election.

(c) is incorrect because the President's performance in the last election is not as important as incumbency in an election.

(d) is incorrect because the number of voters who voted in the last election is not as important as incumbency in an election.

(e) is incorrect because the state in which the candidate lives is not as important as incumbency in an election.

Page reference: 364, AP Topics: The Congress and The major formal and informal arrangements of power

44.   Voting turnout in the United States

(a) is incorrect because voter turnout is not increasing.

(b) is correct because, as compared to other Western democracies, voter turnout in the United States is among the lowest.

(c) is incorrect because most other countries do not require voting.

(d) is incorrect because voter turnout is lower in a non-presidential election year.

(e) is incorrect because voter turnout is highest among older Americans.

Page reference: 7, AP Topic: Political Beliefs and Behaviors

45.   Primary election voters

(a) is incorrect because primary election voters are of all party affiliations.

(b) is incorrect because primary election voters are of all party philosophies.

(c) is incorrect because primary election voters do not necessarily have to be registered with a particular political party.

(d) is incorrect because primary election voters are not a large proportion of the electorate.

(e) is correct because citizens who vote in primaries are considered to be "activists" in politics because they are actively participating in shaping the ticket.

Page reference: 311, AP Topic: Political Beliefs and Behaviors

46.   In striking down discrimination in public accommodations, e.g. hotels and restaurants, Congress, upheld by the Supreme Court, relied on

(a) is correct because the interstate commerce clause provided the interstate jurisdiction which allowed to Supreme Court to strike down discrimination in public accommodations in all states.

(b) is incorrect because the 1st Amendment's freedom of assembly provision does not apply to public accommodations.

(c) is incorrect because the Equal Protection Clause does not relate to interstate commerce.

(d) is incorrect because the expressed powers of Congress do not apply to this case.

(e) is incorrect because judicial activism does not relate to jurisdiction.

Page reference: 90, AP Topic: Civil Rights

47. The First Amendment protection for free speech is most limited when the Supreme Court applies the

(a) is incorrect because the Clear and Present Danger test is not as restrictive as the Dangerous Tendency Test and require the speech to create an imminent danger.

(b) is correct because the Dangerous Tendency Test permits legislature to forbid speech that tends to encourage people to engage in illegal activities.

(c) is incorrect because the Child Benefit Theory does not relate to speech.

(d) is incorrect because the Symbolic Speech Doctrine does not deal with dangerous or illegal activities.

(e) is incorrect because the "rule of four" relates to the Supreme Court's process of accepting cases.

Page reference: 116, AP Topic: Civil Liberties

48. The Framers of the Constitution, compared to the Articles of Confederation,

(a) is incorrect because the Constitution took powers away from the states.

(b) is incorrect because the Constitution did not give the people more power relative to the Articles of Confederation.

(c) is incorrect because the relationship between the national government and the states was radically changed by the Constitution.

(d) is correct because the Constitution created a central government with significantly more power compared to the Articles of Confederation.

(e) is incorrect because the Constitution made it easier to amend the basic governing document.

Page reference: 40, AP Topic: The Constitution and Federalism

49.   Pluralist theory emphasizes the role of

(a) is incorrect because the role of individuals is minimized in pluralism.

(b) is correct because the pluralist theory states that the policymaking process is very open to the participation of groups with shared interests, with no single group usually dominating.

(c) is incorrect because wealth is not a component of pluralism.

(d) is incorrect because pluralism has proposes virtually unlimited access points.

(e) is incorrect because pluralism emphasizes participation from interest groups.

Page reference: 16, AP Topic: Theories of Democratic Government

50.   If one wanted to insulate decisions from partisan political influence, one might house the policy responsibility in

(a) is incorrect because a cabinet department is headed by a secretary who is a partisan appointment.

(b) is incorrect because state governments are partisan bodies.

(c) is incorrect because the bureaucracy is a partisan body.

(d) is incorrect because interest groups are partisan bodies.

(e) is correct because the independent regulatory commission is by definition, independent from influence, and that independence is protected by Congress.

Page reference: 481, AP Topic: The Bureaucracy

51.   The committee that sets the guidelines for floor debate in the House of Representatives, but not in the Senate is

(a) is incorrect because the Administration Committee is the Senate counterpart of the House Rules Committee.

(b) is incorrect because the Ways and Means Committee is the chief tax writing committee.

(c) is incorrect because the Procedure Committee is a committee in the House of Commons.

(d) is incorrect because the Ethics Committee sets standards of official conduct.

(e) is correct because the Rules Committee has more power in the House than it does in the Senate and can set guidelines for debate in the House, but not in the Senate.

Page reference: 371, AP Topic: The Congress

52.   Congressional staffers

(a) is incorrect because congressional staffers are not members of the media.

(b) is incorrect because staffers are a part of the legislative branch and not the executive branch.

(c) is correct because congressional staffers perform the function of communication between the members of Congress and constituents.

(d) is incorrect because staffers interact with interest groups.

(e) is incorrect because their time is spent interacting with constituents.

Page reference: 379, AP Topic: Linkages between Congress and voters

53.   The right to privacy

(a) is incorrect because the right to privacy is not specifically stated in the Constitution.

(b) is incorrect because the right to privacy is established by a Supreme Court case.

(c) is incorrect because the right to privacy was addressed for the second time in the *Roe* case.

(d) is correct because the right to privacy was first established in the *Griswold* case by overturning a Connecticut law which denied access to birth control.

(e) is incorrect because iron triangles in unrelated to this issue.

Page reference: 143, AP Topic: Civil Liberties

54.   The power to decide the constitutionality of a law was assumed by the Supreme Court in

(a) is correct because *Marbury v. Madison* established the Supreme Court's right to declare the acts of Congress unconstitutional.

(b) is incorrect because the *McCullouch* case upheld implied powers.

(c) is incorrect because the *Plessy* case established the separate but equal doctrine.

(d) is incorrect because the *Barron* case said the Bill of Rights restrained only the national government.

(e) is incorrect because the *Brown* case declared segregation in public school unconstitutional.

Page reference: 52, AP Topic: Federal Courts

55. Taxing and spending are examples of

(a) is incorrect because monetary policy is the manipulation of the money supply to influence the economy.

(b) is incorrect because executive powers do not include taxing and spending.

(c) is incorrect because judicial powers do not include taxing and spending.

(d) is correct because fiscal policy is using taxing, spending, and borrowing to influence the economy.

(e) is incorrect because independent regulatory authority does not include taxing and spending.

Page reference: 555, AP Topic: Public Policy

56. The Office of Management and Budget has primary responsibility for

(a) is incorrect because the OMB does not engage in auditing activities.

(b) is incorrect because levying and collecting taxes is a delegated power of Congress.

(c) is correct because the OMB is the office that prepares the president's budget.

(d) is incorrect because the OMB is part of the executive branch.

(e) is incorrect because the OMB does not have a role in the legislative process.

Page reference: 411, AP Topic: Public Policy

57. In the 2012 election, which of the following would be most likely to vote for the Democratic presidential candidate

(a) is correct because Black Americans tend to vote for democratic candidates more than any other demographic group.

(b) is incorrect because white Americans do not necessarily vote for the democratic candidate.

(c) is incorrect because fundamentalists tend to vote republican.

(d) is incorrect because a voter with no partisan affiliation may vote for any candidate.

(e) is incorrect because an anti-abortion activist would tend to vote republican.

Page reference: 311, AP Topic: Political Beliefs and Behaviors

58. "Judicial activism" means that

(a) is incorrect because judicial activism does not relate to caseload.

(b) is incorrect because judicial activism does not cause justices to seek out cases.

(c) is incorrect because judges do not lobby Congress.

(d) is incorrect because both conservative and liberal judges will make policy.

(e) is correct because judicial activism is an approach to decision making where judges sometimes make bold policy decisions.

Page reference: 538, AP Topic: The Federal Courts

59.   Interest groups attempt to influence public policy by

(a) is incorrect because running candidates for office has no influence on the Court.

(b) is correct because filing *amicus curiae* briefs interest groups can raise additional points of view and present information not contained in briefs in order to influence the Court.

(c) is incorrect because holding conventions has no influence on the Court.

(d) is incorrect because holding primaries has no influence on the Court.

(e) is incorrect because holding caucuses has no influence on the Court.

Page reference: 511, AP Topic: Interest Groups

60.   The relationship between Congress and public opinion is that

(a) is incorrect because Congress does not always vote the wishes of their constituents.

(b) is incorrect because Congress does not always vote the way the majority of citizens want them to vote.

(c) is incorrect because incumbency is still the best predictor of who will win an election.

(d) is correct because research shows that even though constituents have a low opinion of Congress in general, when asked about their own representatives; their opinions tend to be high.

(e) is incorrect because members of Congress are very aware of public opinion.

Page reference: 358, AP Topic: Congress and public opinion

Free-Response Questions

This rubric provides examples of many, but not all of the possible correct responses to the free-response questions.

1. In 2010 the Supreme Court ruled in *McDonald v. Chicago* that the Second Amendment applied to the states.

    a. Identify the term that is used to describe the application of one of the amendments in "Bill of Rights" to the states.

        - "Selective incorporation" is the preferred term. Anything that communicates that the Supreme Court has never ruled that all of the Bill of Rights applies to the states merits credit. A description that indicates that this is process is done on a case-by-case basis communicates this. "Nationalization of the Bill of Rights" also merits credit.

    b. Explain why it is necessary for the Supreme Court to render such a decision if the Second Amendment is to be applied to the states.

        - The original interpretation of whether the Bill of Rights limited states came in *Barron v. Baltimore* (1833), in which the Supreme Court limited only what the national government, not states' governments, could do. The ratification of the Fourteenth Amendment, with its due process clause, offered hope for overturning this decision, but it took multiple cases to reach this point. Finally, in 1925, in the case of *Gitlow v. New York*, the Supreme Court ruled that the First Amendment rights of freedom speech and press limited the states. Since then, other parts, but not all, of the Bill of Rights have been applied to the states.

    c. Identify two (2) other Supreme Court cases that applied one of the amendments in the "Bill of Rights" to the states and describe which right was extended by the case.

        - Any two cases can be listed and the provision described.

Provision	Case	Year
1st Amendment		
Freedom of Speech & Press	*Gitlow v. New York*	1925
Freedom of Assembly	*DeJonge v. Oregon*	1937
Freedom of Petition	*Hague v. CIO*	1939
Free Exercise of Religion	*Cantwell v. Connecticut*	1940
Establishment of Religion	*Everson v. Board of Education*	1947
4th Amendment		
Unreasonable Search & Seizure	*Wolf v. Colorado*	1949
Exclusionary Rule	*Mapp v. Ohio*	1961
5th Amendment		
Payment of Compensation for Taking of Private Property	*Chicago, Burlington & Quincy Railway Co. v. Chicago*	1897
Self-Incrimination	*Malloy v. Hogan*	1964
Double Jeopardy	*Benton v. Maryland*	1969
When Jeopardy Attaches	*Crist v. Bretz*	1978
6th Amendment		
Public Trial	*In re Oliver*	1948
Due Notice	*Cole v. Arkansas*	1948
Right to Counsel (Felonies)	*Gideon v. Wainwright*	1963
Confrontation & Cross-Examination of Adverse Witnesses	*Pointer v. Texas*	1965
Speedy Trial	*Klopfer v. North Carolina*	1967
Compulsory Process to Obtain Witnesses	*Washington v. Texas*	1967
Jury Trial	*Duncan v. Louisiana*	1968
Right to Counsel (Misdemeanor when Jail is Possible)	*Argersinger v. Hamlin*	1972
8th Amendment		
Cruel & Unusual Punishment	*Louisiana ex rel. Francis v. Resweber*	1947
9th Amendment		
Privacy (Not Specifically Mentioned)	*Griswold v. Connecticut*	1965

2.   Representation is central to the functioning of United States government and politics.

   a. Explain two ways the national executive branch contributes to representation.

- The President is generally the elected official who has garnered the most votes of any elected official and, therefore, can lay claim to representing the whole nation better than anyone else. Secondly, the President is the Chief Executive Officer, presiding over the federal bureaucracy. The federal bureaucracy, although unelected, descriptively represents the general population better than any other governmental body.

b. Explain two ways the national legislative branch contributes to representation.

- Members of the House of Representatives are most closely tied to the people, both by the size of their districts and the frequency of their election. Senators, while generally having larger constituencies and longer terms than Representatives, still can be thought of as more representative than members of the executive or judicial branches. Both Representatives and Senators devote a lot of their time and effort to staying in touch with their home districts or states and constituency service, which contributes to representation.

c. Explain one way the national judicial branch contributes to representation.

- While the judicial branch is generally thought of as the most insulated of the branches of the nation government, the Framers still made sure that district courts had a local flavor. All federal district courts are totally contained with a state, and the politics of judicial appointments often means that federal district judges are products of their state's political system.

3. The above graph shows the proportion of the civilian, noninstitutionalized population, age 18 and over voting in various elections. Using this information and your knowledge of U.S. politics:

a. Briefly describe two trends depicted in this graph.

- And two of the trends on the graph can be described as moving slightly downward over time.

b. Identify two factors that may have produced the trends you describe.

- Identifying a decline in trust in government or a decline in partisan identification or an increase in the proportion of the electorate composed of racial/ethnic minorities who generally have lower turnout rates are creditable responses.

c. Explain why there are differences between the levels of voting for presidential and congressional elections.

- More people vote in presidential elections than in congressional elections because they are drawn out to vote for a higher level office for which there is a better financed, more high visibility campaign.

d. Explain why there are differences based on educational attainment.

- People with higher levels of education tend to vote at higher levels because they have higher levels of political knowledge and higher incomes, both of which are associated with greater political participation.

4. The Framers of the Constitution were concerned that power would be too concentrated in government. Some citizens today complain that government cannot get anything done.

a. Identify three mechanisms that the Framers adopted to make sure power was not too concentrated in government.

- Identification of any of the following would qualify for credit.
- Federalism
- Separation of Powers ("Separate Institutions Sharing Power")
- Bicameralism
- Differing Terms
- Differing Means of Selection, ergo Differing Constituencies
- Differing Formal Qualifications
- Checks & Balances
- The Formal Amendment Process

b. Explain how each of these mechanisms were meant to make sure power was not too concentrated in government.

- For the chosen mechanisms, the student needs to communicate that this mechanism deconcentrates power "BY …."

c. Identify one mechanism used today to try to make sure government accomplishes something.

- Political parties

d. Explain how this mechanism used today is meant to make sure government accomplishes something.

- Political parties are meant to organize political interests to achieve policy goals.